THE DAWN OF A NEW DAY IN HUMAN RELATIONS

Why Men Wage War on Each Other and How to Prevent It

Address By
DR. WALTER RUSSELL
At Portsmouth, Va.
Armed Forces Day Celebration
May 19, 1951

The University of Science and Philosophy
Swannanoa
Waynesboro, Virginia 22980

The Dawn of a New Day
In Human Relations
By
Walter Russell
(1871-1963)

Printed in the United States of America

ISBN 1-879605-32-5

Emilia Lee Lombardi
Editor

Lance King
Cover Design

Mid Valley Press
Printers

PREFACE

On his eightieth birthday, May 19, 1951, Dr. Walter Russell addressed an Armed Forces Day celebration on the causes of war. As usual, he simplified what others had taken volumes to explain.

Man makes war, he concluded, because man has not learned to love his fellow man. War is perhaps the most gruesome example of man's failure to understand that what he does to others inexorably comes back to him in kind.

As the twentieth century ends, there are still wars raging in many parts of the world. Yet there is hope. Enlightened people on every continent are bringing greater understanding of the universal lesson that no man can hurt another without equally hurting himself and the whole of humanity.

Dr. Russell anticipated the events of today and understood that loving people leading balanced lives could ultimately erode the bedrock cause of war.

J. B. Yount III
Member of the Board of Directors
University of Science and Philosophy

November 1991

The world is our stage and every man plays his role in the great cosmic drama. Each player is of vital and equal importance in the whole Play of Creation.

Life, itself, is our great teacher. Through trial and error, we learn what to do and what not to do. ***That is why the seemingly hard experiences teach us more than the happy, easy ones.***

When we learn to face ourselves and analyze our weak points, then we begin to make real progress.

THE DAWN OF A NEW DAY IN HUMAN RELATIONS

Why Men Wage War on Each Other and How to Prevent It

On such a great day as this when the Armed Forces which protect us from our enemies get together to remind each other that we still have enemies who are eager to kill us, it is appropriate to ask ourselves why do we still have enemies who wish to kill us?

Why is it that these splendid men of the Armed Forces of the United States have to go out into the world and be killed or horribly maimed for life by those who hate us? Why the agonies of wars, the terrors of wholesale killings, the grief of kindly mothers? WHY? WHY? What is the matter with our human relations which keeps us from living together in brotherly good will, friendly neighborliness and happiness? Why do we have enemies?

We cannot understand the faults of the whole human race by looking at only one generation of it, so let us go back to the beginnings of man and look at the whole human race squarely in the face. By doing so, we will find the CAUSE of all wars.

First Great Lesson

For millions of years, man lived the life of the wild animal of the jungle. During those long ages he had but one law — the law of self-survival which he enforced with the brute power of might. He did not know right from wrong. He had no Conscience or Consciousness. He did not even think.

He took what he wanted to satisfy his own greed. He killed without compunction or regret when he wanted anything. He made every man fear him and he feared every man. During that period he began to learn his first great lesson, *that whatsoever he gave to other men he got back in kind.* That is the way man began. He made every man his enemy because he was every man's enemy.

Gradually men grouped into herds, and herds into nations for each other's protection. For long ages tribes attacked other tribes, killing those whom they could not use and making slaves and concubines of the others.

Then came the Dawn of Conscience in man. *He began to think.*

That was only a few thousand years ago. Think of it — millions of years of killing and bloodshed in the jungle and only about ten thousand years out of it. Those millions of years of bloodlust could not be forgotten and put aside. Nature does not work that way. Nature unfolds slowly. The age of idolatry comes with the first suspicion of a Supreme Being.

Blood sacrifices were made to appease their god of wrath. Thousands upon thousands of bullocks and sheep were slain upon the very altars of their temples even until after the time of Christ. They also sacrificed their own children to appease their gods!

Bloodlust and cruelty persisted for many centuries. Gladiators killed each other by the hundreds for the pleasure of the people of Rome, and mothers took their children to the arenas to see lions tear human beings apart, just as we take our children to the circus today.

Every thought and deed delivers an unseen chisel blow toward the sculpturing of man's destiny.

The Beginning of Empire Building

Now let us leap ahead and see how the world looked in the year 1910 — only forty years ago. The world was then divided into empires which had all been built by the jungle methods of might-over-right. All were built up through bloodshed and conquest, just as the ancient empires were built.

Great Britain was a great and powerful empire in 1910. She ruled the seas and many great nations like India, Australia, New Zealand, South Africa, Canada, and had other strongholds in countries which she had exploited, such as China. She was rich and prosperous beyond measure. Her titled class owned great estates and her power was seemingly invulnerable. Today England is on rations, her empire breaking up — her best blood being killed — her titled class becoming impoverished and their great estates disappearing. India and Egypt have revolted and England's splendid morale so lowered that her power is at a low ebb.

All of this within forty years. WHY? Because her enemies all rose up against her and smote her. Why did England have enemies smite her? Because England was the enemy of other countries.

The United States was also rich and powerful. Its culture was at a high standard. It had built a great empire which had reached from coast to coast. It had no income tax and no youth worried about conscription—and mothers had no worries about such a possibility.

Today the United States is in debt for hundreds of billions, incomes are taxed to almost confiscation point and hundreds of thousands of our best blood have been killed. Its young men are being called to war and mothers who have before known war's agonies are again preparing to face them.

All of this in forty years. WHY? Because her enemies rose up against her to smite her. Why did the United States have enemies to smite her? Because she made enemies by being the enemy of other men.

Consider France, the world center of art with its great African and Indo-Chinese empire — Austria, the world music center — Holland, with its East Indies — Belgium, with its Congo wealth — Germany, Italy, Czarist Russia and other countries which were powerful forty years ago.

Where are these mighty empires today? Impoverished, all of them. Millions of their best blood have been killed — millions more maimed and crippled — morale almost gone — all of them infiltrated with traitors, spies and fifth column saboteurs — all of them — the world over.

All of this agony in forty years. WHY? Because their enemies rose up and smote them. Why did all of these countries have enemies to smite them? Because they were the enemies of all other men.

Let Us Return To The Beginning

Now we will return to the beginning of civilization again. Tribes grew into nations and empires by the inherited jungle methods of killing, robbing and enslaving. Read your history of early man. Read how Babylon, Byzantium, Macedonia, Sparta, Greece, and Rome rose and fell through cruelty and slaughter. Read in your Bible how tribes slaughtered tribes, robbed them of their treasures and made slaves and concubines of their women. Then read how these conquering tribes were in turn conquered and slaughtered by the enemies they had themselves made.

Let us look at our own nation face to face. How did we build our empire from the handful of pioneers who landed here about five hundred years ago? We gradually killed the entire race of Indians which we found here and kidnapped thousands of Africans to enslave, just as our savage ancestors did ages ago. We fought over one hundred wars and killed hundreds of thousands of people whom we made our enemies by being their enemies.

That is the way we built our empire. We lived by the sword and now seem very much astonished that we are threatened with death by the sword. We made every man our enemy and now wonder why we should have enemies. We violated God's law by robbing and killing to gain happiness and prosperity for ourselves — but taking away the happiness and prosperity of others.

All empires were built that way — all in strict violation of God's Law of Love. All of them took what they wanted by the power of might-over-right just as our ancestors of the jungle did. And all of them prayed fervently to God for conquest over their enemies as the early tribes of Bible history prayed to God for power to smite their enemies.

God's law always works. Whatever seed you sow, you harvest in kind multiplied by a hundred.

Every nation made enemies by being enemies. We fear man today because we made man fear us yesterday.

We made Hitler, Mussolini and Stalin that way. Yes, it was we who made these monsters by creating the conditions which bred them. Hitler tried to build an empire by the sword and died by that same sword. Mussolini tried it and committed his people to untold suffering. Stalin is trying to enslave not only the rest of the world but his own people. Stalin is reaching farther toward the unnatural than any tribe or nation in history, for they enslaved others for their own tribe's benefit while Stalin is attempting to enslave the whole world for his own benefit. God's law will not allow him to do that. He will die by his own sword as Hitler and Mussolini died.

Second Great Lesson

Slowly civilizing man was at the beginning of learning his second great lesson which is that no man can prosper and find peace through destroying the peace and happiness of others. Man had not yet begun to learn another great lesson of life — *which is that no man can hurt another without hurting himself and the whole world.*

Early man thus built a world of fear and hatred. He drew boundary lines around his tribes which slowly grew to be nations. Every man and nation feared every other man and nation. That is the kind of world early man built as his remembrance of the jungle, and that is the kind of world we are inheriting today from our primate ancestors. We are still building a world of hate and fear for we are still barbarians and will be so long as we kill our fellow men.

Today, as yesterday, every man fears

every other man, and every nation fears every other nation. Every man locks his doors at night for fear of his neighbor. We police our streets for fear of other men, and nations carry heavy armaments to slaughter their neighbors or to resist being slaughtered by them.

Is it any wonder that there is WAR — WAR — and still more WAR?

Every empire on earth has tried to build peace and prosperity for itself by taking away the peace and prosperity of others — and one class of people has tried to find security and peace for itself by destroying the security and peace of the other class.

Nations have lived by the sword and have died by the sword — and as long as they persist in killing their neighbors they will be killed by their neighbors. There is not one innocent nation on earth. All of them have been the enemies of all the others. All have been aggressors and exploiters of others. All have lived for self and for greed and all have practiced the power of might-over-right to build their empires.

Why do we have such human monsters as Hitler, Mussolini and Stalin? We have them because we have made them. We could not help having them. I will tell you how it happened.

The Greatest War in History

Human beings, the world over, divided themselves into two opposite classes and went to war with each other within their own countries. These two enemies were THE UPPER CLASS and THE LOWER CLASS. The upper class exploited the lower class to get all it could for itself and give as little as possible to the lower class.

The two classes were kings and subjects — nobility and serfs — capital and labor — rich and poor — owner and laborer. The upper class gained riches and security for itself by destroying the riches and security of the lower class. **Gradually this division of man became the greatest war in all history,** for fear was multiplied by this war of man against man — this war of exploitation of man by man.

The worker-half of the world feared security for his family — while the exploiting-half had everything. He had the money. He was the owner. The laborer could be hired and fired at will. He was lucky to have a job at starvation wages. Gradually the pendulum began to swing the other way. The enemies the upper class had made began to rise up against them to smite them. **And that is the war we are fighting today.** It is not a war of nations for each other's lands. It is a world war of the under-privileged, long-suffering lower class against the upper class. That is what world communism is. The slave of the land owner now wishes to destroy the land owner and take his lands for himself.

Here in America a better form of communism came into being through the vision and wisdom of great and free Americans who began to realize the mutual interdependence of capital and labor. Industry realized that labor could be the best customer of its products if the laborer were given more money to buy those products and more leisure to spend it.

Wages were drastically raised and hours were shortened to make the poor man rich enough to buy the products of the upper class, for there were not enough of the rich to buy their own products.

The tide began to turn. The standard of living of the lower class began to leap higher and higher. Every farmer and laborer had a car, a washing machine and power machines to lighten the labor of both men and women. Harmony was on the way. The rising standard of living in the United States made the American workman poor food for the arguments of communist dictators whose millions of followers were responding to the call of the land serf to destroy the landlord and take his lands away from him.

Harmony was on the way in this country *but not in the rest of the big starving world of the very rich and the very poor.* It touched too little of the world. While every laborer in this country owned a car, dread squalor existed in other parts of the world. The movement was too slow, too little and too late for the yeast of prosperity of the workman of this country to leaven the whole loaf.

Lack of security, hunger, and fear for tomorrow bred the seeds of fascism, naziism and communism in millions upon millions of the under-privileged who were made to hate the upper class because of fear for their daily bread. In this condition lies the power of dictators who make promises which they never intend to fulfill as bait for the starved ones. The workers find that they have but exchanged ten thousand masters for one. They find themselves still enslaved, still poor and still afraid.

When they at last find that out, they turn like wolves and rend their new master to pieces.

Stalin's destroyer is behind the iron curtain. We should reach out our hands to him and let him know that we are coming to liberate him.

The Only Remedy For Wars

The only remedy for stopping wars is to entirely reverse the old selfish and greedy basis upon which human relations of the past have been built and substitute the *Golden Rule* basis of equal interchange in all transactions between men.

Hate and fear have dominated human relations. Brotherly love and the unity of man must replace our primate practices. Mankind has a great new lesson to learn — which is that *Nature never takes anything. Nature only gives for regiving. That is the secret of Nature's continuance. When man learns the love prin-*

ciple upon which God founded His universe, the growth of man toward prosperity, peace and happiness will be as continuous as the continuity of solar systems.

The earth gives all it has of forests, crops and vapors to the heavens and the heavens give them all back again to earth for regiving, over and over forever.

Man has tried to perpetuate himself by taking instead of giving and has destroyed his civilizations over and over again for ages — and is on the way to again destroying his world.

You cannot take happiness away from another for yourself. You can only give happiness to find it for yourself. Likewise, you cannot take love — you can only GIVE love.

That is the next great lesson which mankind must eventually learn. That is the lesson of the brotherhood-of-man which the spiritual Messengers of the last three thousand years have given to their people. Laotzu and Confucius gave it to the Chinese — Buddha told it to the Hindus — Mohammed told it to the Arabians — the unknown mystic who wrote *The Bhagavad Gita* told it to the Persians — and God's beloved Son, Jesus, the greatest of all the illumined, gave it to the world.

Jesus said, *"Love ye one another,"* and *"Do ye unto one another as ye would have them do unto you,"* but few since that day have known what He meant, or have practiced it in their daily lives.

The people of the world have never understood that the *Golden Rule* was Law which must be obeyed as much as the law of gravity must be obeyed, else it would break one as surely as though one threw himself over a cliff in defiance of the law of gravity.

People considered it just an ideal for

practice in close family and social relations, but not for business dealings. *No one had discovered that the law of equal interchange between all pairs of opposites in human relations demanded the same equality as those in Nature.* Just as the piston stroke of compression must equal the expansion stroke in an engine, or in one's heartbeat, so must that which every man receives from another man, or from Nature, be equalled by what he gives.

If you desire love and friendship, you must first give love and friendship. When you do thus give love, the Law gives it back to you in equal measure as surely as the giving of vapors to the heavens is regiven as rain to the earth. The underlying principle of the whole universe is balanced mutual service — service given for service received. When the whole world practices the **giving** of service FIRST instead of **taking** first, wars will be impossible between nations or between any pair of opposites like capital and labor, buyer and seller, husband and wife, or Government and people.

If, for example, a manufacturer desires prosperity, he must first give prosperity by going out into his factories and seeing to it that those who are working for his enrichment are themselves made prosperous. That is the way the law of equal interchange works — *and the Golden Rule is that Law.*

It has not been practiced that way, however, for the manufacturer has considered that his prosperity came from his customers, so he hired labor as cheaply as possible and gave to the workman as little as possible. That policy has been the most expensive policy in history.

Out of the suppression of man by man grew the ideologies about which we are now fighting. We are not fighting to expand national boundaries primarily as in the past. We are fighting fanatical hate generated for ages by the suppression of one-half of mankind by the other half.

In other words, we are fighting because

of the old selfishness and greed which began in the jungle and still is destroying us. People still want what they want and go after it no matter how it hurts themselves or their neighbors.

Witness, for example, the self-made war which is taking place between our own people, within our own borders, which is the result of selfishness and greed. Think of the hundreds of thousands of Americans who want to get rich quickly and gamble in the hope of getting rich quickly. This breed of selfishness and greed has developed within our borders a powerful gangster enemy which reaches its talons into every department of our lives and hurts every man, woman and child in America. Selfishness and greed of the gambling public is undermining our very government and will eventually destroy us if we do not check it. Billions of dollars have bought protection for gangsters by bribing millions of public service officials from petty sheriffs and policemen to mayors — and even Governors.

Then there is another war which many more Americans have bred within their borders because of selfishness and greed. THE BLACK MARKET IS WAR. It is a war of the people who want what they want and go after it no matter how it hurts themselves and every other person in the country.

INFLATION IS WAR started by the hoarding of people who are afraid they cannot get what they want when they want it, and are going to make sure of theirs NOW no matter how it hurts the whole nation.

That is what I mean when I say that God's Law of Balanced Interchange always works. If you work with the Law, it will work with you to fulfill your desire, but if you work against that Law it will as surely break you as that fire will burn you.

We made our own wars in past ages because of selfishness and greed. We are still making our own wars because of selfishness and greed, and the whole world of men is still suffering, bleeding and dying because of selfishness and greed.

How Can We Stop Wars?

Wars can stop only when we stop making them — and we shall stop making them only when we learn the great lesson of the unity of man — and the fact that other men are not only brothers but are actually ourselves.

When we learn that lesson, we will know that we cannot hurt any other man without hurting ourselves in the same measure.

You, as an individual, can stop all wars by stopping them in your home, your town and your whole sphere of influence. Unity begins in the home, then reaches out to your neighborhood. If every man in the world who desires prosperity, happiness and peace gives love out from himself to his home and his neighborhood, there would be no more wars, for war is the harvest of hate and fear while happiness and peace are the fruits of love.

The world is now due for the greatest transformation of man in all history. It may be that we still need the great punishment of another world war to chasten us into greater understanding of our relationship to our fellow man, but if another war is the cost of that knowledge of the unity of man, and causes him at long last to *practice the Golden Rule in every thought and action,* it will be worth it.

Man must some day learn to serve his fellow man with full knowledge that in so doing he is serving all men. When that day comes, the world of men will then know the real prosperity, happiness and peace which love alone will give to men.

EPILOGUE

Wrong concepts of what constitutes wealth and power have not only wrecked civilizations, nations and individuals, but are continuing to wreck them. As long as man's concept of wealth and power is a material one, based upon requirements and desires of the body, just so long will man make the gratification of his senses of paramount importance in the building of an environment for his body rather than for the enrichment of his soul. This coming new age will alter man's concepts of values and a new civilization will arise from that change.

Science and religion are the two most important elements of man's civilization. The two are opposite phases of the same thing, but have pulled apart for centuries. To bring them together in a marriage of complete mutual cooperation and understanding would vastly uplift the whole human race. To accomplish this purpose a *scientific* foundation is needed for religion and a *spiritual* foundation is needed for science.

THE MOST IMPORTANT AND NOBLE
ATTRIBUTE OF MAN
IS
CHARACTER

Thought For The Day

No earthly possessions can make you feel as rich and contented as spiritual knowledge, for earthly possessions give transitory joy while spiritual knowledge gives *eternal joy.*

Just as a tree obtains its strength from its invisible roots, so does man obtain his strength from his invisible spiritual Self.

There will be times when you may feel that you have even lost contact with God because many experiences come that try man's Soul. God's greatest messengers have known such moments. At the hour of Christ's crucifixion He, too, felt that as He cried: *"My God, my God, why hast thou forsaken Me?"*

No man ahead of his day has had an easy road and crucifixion has been the lot of many cosmic messengers. Laotzu slipped away from the world of man when he could no longer stand the "crowd's" indifference. That is how *you* will sometimes feel. It takes great courage and fortitude to continue to give God's Message in the face of indifference of the "crowds." However, the desire to slip away is only fleeting for with the dawn of a new day, inspiration is born.

It is not easy to keep strong when one sees such destruction taking place in the world of man as we have seen these past years. When you know that all this could change if man would only awaken to the CAUSE of his "sickness," it is hard not to feel frustration because of man's blindness. Do as we do when you feel that man is completely blind, go *within yourself* and commune with God. This is the one and only "place" where a renewal of strength can be found. Only in the sensed world of man are you a voice crying in the wilderness. In God-awareness, there is an ever-flowing source of courage and idea for action.

–Walter and Lao Russell

WALTER RUSSELL
Author of

The Secret of Light
The Message of the Divine Iliad - Vol. I
The Message of the Divine Iliad - Vol. II
A New Concept of the Universe
The Quest of the Grail
The Electric Nature of the Universe
The Sculptor Searches for Mark Twain's Immortality

WALTER and LAO RUSSELL
Co-Authors of

Home Study Course in *Universal Law, Natural Science and Living Philosophy*
Scientific Answer to Human Relations
Atomic Suicide?
The World Crisis —Its Explanation and Solution
A Vision Fulfilled!

LAO RUSSELL
Author of

God Will Work With You But Not For you.
Love—A Scientific & Living Philosophy of Love and Sex
Why You Cannot Die!—Reincarnation Explained

For catalog on additional books and teachings by Walter and Lao Russell, please write or phone:

The University of Science and Philosophy
Swannanoa, Waynesboro, Virginia 22980
(703) 942-5161
(800) 882-LOVE (5683) Book orders

3 as a percentage of 20.

divide 3 by 20 (3/20) then multiply by 100. = 15

156/365 x 100 = 42.7%

209/365 x 100 = 57.260273

infinity = bis ins Unendliche

mentor Grundwissen

Mathematik

bis zur 10. Klasse

Alle wichtigen Themen

Theo Waibel
Julia Inthorn
Dr. Rosemarie Benke-Bursian
Regine Hegedüs
Waltraud Mager
Andreas Faber
Irmgard Mayer

mentor
Eine Klasse besser.

Redaktion: Twin Books, München
Layout: Peter Pleischl, München
Vignetten: Ulf Marckwort, Kassel

Umwelthinweis: Gedruckt auf chlorfrei gebleichtem Papier.

mentor Grundwissen Band 13

Printed in Germany
ISBN 3-580-64013-5
www.mentor.de

3 4 5 6 08 07 06 05

Inhaltsverzeichnis

Einleitung: Was ist Mathematik?

Mathematische Probleme tauchen im Alltag eines jeden auf. Das beginnt bei der Rechnung im Café und geht über Flächenberechnungen hin bis zum Einschätzen der Gewinnchancen beim Lottospielen.

Mathematik bewegt sich nicht im völlig Abstrakten. In den Naturwissenschaften gibt es weite Anwendungsgebiete der Mathematik. Viele physikalische Theorien sind nur mit Hilfe von mathematischen Formeln ausdrückbar, die Relativitätstheorie zum Beispiel benötigt jede Menge auch komplizierter mathematischer Sätze. In der Biologie werden Populationsentwicklungen mit Hilfe mathematischer Formeln beschrieben, und Sachverhalte in der Gesellschaft werden mit Mitteln der Statistik erst anschaulich. In diesen Fällen ist die Mathematik eine Hilfswissenschaft, die anderen Wissenschaften Methoden an die Hand gibt, um ihre eigenen Theorien zu formulieren und zu formalisieren.

Auf der anderen Seite ist Mathematik eine Geisteswissenschaft, sie beruht auf einem Axiomensystem logischer Aussagen und auf Regeln, wie aus diesen Axiomen logische Schlüsse gezogen werden dürfen. Beide, die Axiome und die Regeln zum logischen Schließen lassen sich nicht mit Hilfe von Versuchen überprüfen. Durch diese Regeln ist das Vorgehen in der Mathematik streng eingeschränkt. Vermutlich ist das einer der Gründe, warum Mathematiker von der Klarheit und damit auch der Schönheit der Mathematik sprechen. Logische Schlüsse sind zwar zum Teil nur nach längerem Nachdenken nachvollziehbar, aber sie sind immer eindeutig wahr oder falsch. In wie weit mathematische Aussagen etwas mit der Wirklichkeit unserer Gedanken und dem logischen Aufbau der Welt zu tun haben, obwohl man Zahlen weder anfassen noch messen kann, ist eine philosophische Frage. Schon die Frage danach, was eine Zahl ist und ob sie weiter existiert, wenn wir aufhören an sie zu denken, ist ein altes philosophisches Problem.

Mathematik lässt sich also in vielen verschiedenen Formen anwenden, in einfachen und sehr komplizierten.

$\cup$ = vereinigt mit

$A \cup C$ = A ist v. mit C (S. 11)

Mathematische Zeichen und Symbole

Mengen

$\mathbb{N}$ Menge der natürlichen Zahlen
$\mathbb{Z}$ Menge der ganzen Zahlen
$\mathbb{Q}$ Menge der rationalen Zahlen
$\mathbb{R}$ Menge der reellen Zahlen
$\mathbb{L}$ Lösungsmenge
$\{\ \}$ leere Menge

$M \cap N$ Schnittmenge der Mengen M und N
$M \cup N$ Vereinigungsmenge der Mengen M und N
$M \subseteq N$ M Teilmenge von N
$m \in M$ m Element von M

logische Zeichen

$A \Rightarrow B$ aus A folgt B, wenn A dann B
$A \Leftrightarrow B$ A und B sind äquivalent, A genau dann wenn B

Verknüpfung von Zahlen

$a < b$ a (echt) kleiner als b
$a > b$ a echt größer als b
$a \leq b$ a kleiner oder gleich b
$a \geq b$ a größer oder gleich b
$a = b$ a gleich b
$a \neq b$ a ungleich b
$a \approx b$ a ungefähr gleich *b* (z. B. gerundet)

geometrische Symbole

$g \perp h$ g steht senkrecht auf h
$g \parallel h$ g und h sind parallel
$\perp$ rechter Winkel
$\vec{v}$ Vektor *v*

$\sum_{i=1}^{n} a_i = a_1 + a_2 + \ldots + a_n$ Summensymbol

1 Arithmetik

Die Grundlage für die mathematische Tätigkeit des Zählens bilden die natürlichen Zahlen. Diese sind ebenso Thema des folgenden Kapitels wie die vier Grundrechenarten, nämlich Addition, Subtraktion, Multiplikation und Division. Darauf folgt die Beschäftigung mit Potenzen als einer Sonderform der Multiplikation. Handelte es sich bisher um das Rechnen mit ganzen Zahlen, so geht es im Anschluss um die rationalen Zahlen bzw. die Bruchrechnung und ihre Regeln. Abschließend wird anhand von Beispielen, z. B. Gewichts- oder Größenumrechnungen, gezeigt, welche wichtige Funktion die Arithmetik im Alltag haben kann.

1 Mengen

Eine **Menge** ist eine Zusammenfassung von verschiedenen Objekten (Personen, Gegenstände, Zahlen, Buchstaben ...) zu einer Einheit. Wir reden z. B. von der Menge der Schüler einer Schule, von der Menge der Lehrer, von der Menge der Buchstaben des Alphabets, von der Menge der Edelsteine oder von der Menge der Fahrzeuge. Mengen in der Mathematik werden mit Großbuchstaben bezeichnet, z. B. Menge A.

Die einzelnen Bestandteile einer Menge nennt man **Elemente**. Sie werden in geschwungene Klammern eingeschlossen, z. B. $V = \{a, e, i, o, u\}$.
$a \in V$ heißt »a ist Element von V« oder »a liegt in V«.
$b \notin V$ heißt »a ist nicht Element von V« oder »a liegt nicht in V«.

Mengen kann man angeben in beschreibender Form oder in aufzählender Form.
Beschreibend: M = Menge der ersten fünf Buchstaben des Alphabets.
Aufzählend: $M = \{a, b, c, d, e\}$.

Zwischen Mengen können verschiedene Beziehungen bestehen.

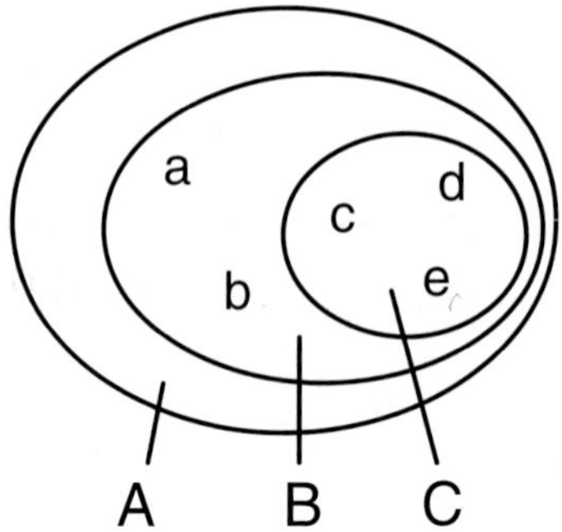

$B \subseteq A$ heißt »B ist **Teilmenge** (Untermenge) von A«. Alle Elemente von B sind auch in A. Das kann auch, wie in diesem Beispiel, bedeuten: $B = A$.
$C \subset B$ heißt »C ist echte Teilmenge von B (und auch von A)«. Das bedeutet: $C \subseteq B$, aber nicht $C = B$.

Man kann die Zeichen auch umdrehen ($\supseteq$, $\supset$) und bekommt dann die Begriffe Obermenge und echte Obermenge mit analogen Bedeutungen: $B \supset C$, $A \supseteq B$.

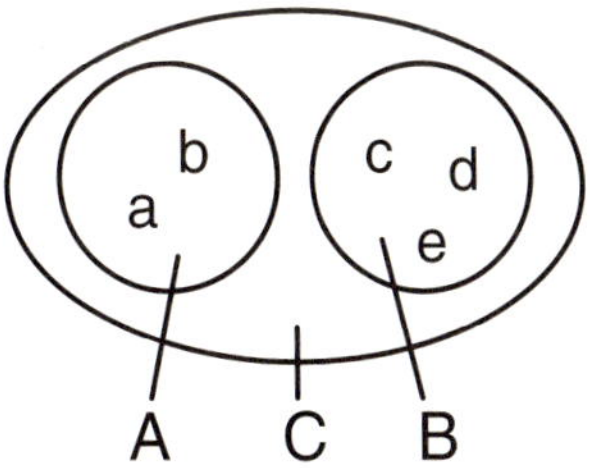

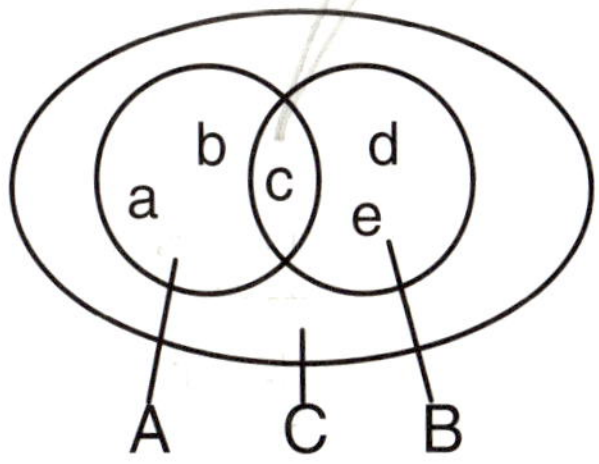

C ist die Vereinigungsmenge von *A* und *B*. Hier sagt man: $A \cup B = C$.
»*A* vereinigt mit *B* ist *C*.«

Die Vereinigungsmenge ist die Menge aller Elemente, die entweder in *A* oder in *B* oder in beiden Mengen enthalten sind.

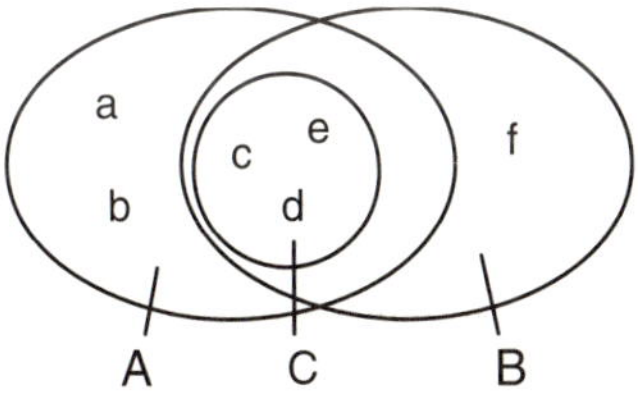

C ist die Schnittmenge der Mengen *A* und *B*. $C = A \cap B$. »*C* ist *A* geschnitten mit *B*.«

Die Schnittmenge zweier Mengen *A* und *B* ist die Menge aller Elemente, die sowohl in *A* als auch in *B* enthalten sind.

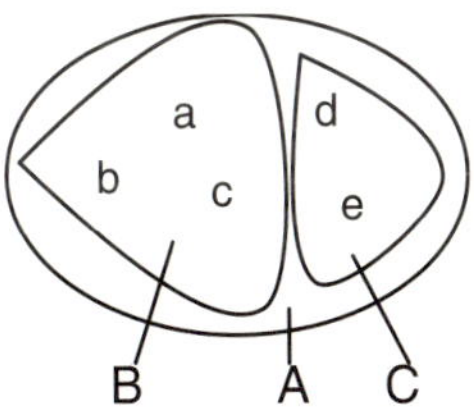

Eine **Restmenge** bleibt, wenn man die Elemente einer Menge aus einer anderen Menge entfernt.

$C = A \setminus B$. »*C* ist *A* ohne *B*.«

2 Natürliche Zahlen

Anzahl

Bei den verschiedenen Anwendungen der Mathematik werden unterschiedliche Zahlenarten verwendet. Die einfachste und ursprünglichste Art sind die natürlichen Zahlen. Man erhält sie, wenn man die **Anzahl** der Elemente einer Menge feststellt, z. B. die Anzahl der Schafe in einer Schafherde. Diese Anzahl unterschiedlicher Elemente wird auch als Mächtigkeit einer Menge bezeichnet.

Menge				
Zahl	1	2	3	4

Durch das schrittweise Hinzufügen von jeweils einem Element erhält man die **Menge der natürlichen Zahlen** $\mathbb{N} = \{1, 2, 3, 4 \ldots\}$. Da sich dieses Verfahren unendlich oft wiederholen lässt, gibt es auch unendlich viele natürliche Zahlen.

Zwei Mengen sind **gleich mächtig**, wenn sich ihre Elemente paarweise einander zuordnen lassen, ohne dass ein Rest bleibt.

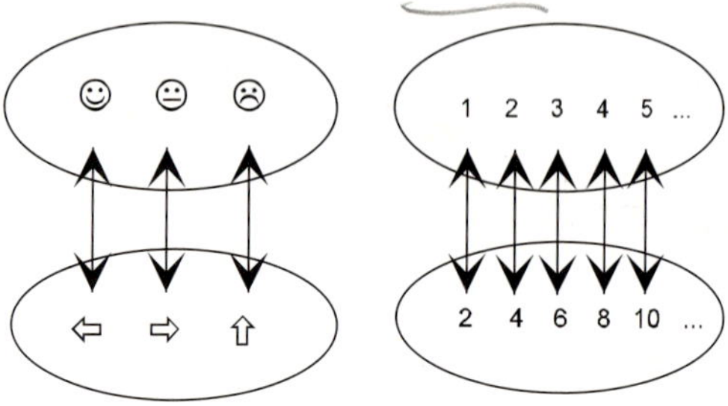

Anordnung

Jede natürliche Zahl hat einen unmittelbaren Nachfolger und, mit Ausnahme der Zahl 1, einen unmittelbaren Vorgänger. Diesen mangelnden Vorgänger der Zahl 1 kann man hinzufügen, indem man beispielsweise

aus der Menge $\{a\}$ das einzige Element *a* entfernt und damit die **leere Menge** $\{\ \}$ (anderes Symbol: $\emptyset$) erhält. Die Mächtigkeit dieser Menge ist 0 und durch die Erweiterung der Menge $\mathbb{N}$ um diese Zahl 0 kommt man zur Menge $\mathbb{N}_0$.
Für den Buchstaben a in der hier verwendeten Menge kann man beliebige Symbole, Gegenstände oder Zahlen einsetzen, z.B. die Zahl 4, das Zeichen »∇«, eine Münze oder ein Schaf. Eine solche Größe, die als Stellvertreter für Zahlen, Zeichen oder Gegenstände steht, nennt man **Variable.** (Das lateinische Wort »variabilis« bedeutet veränderlich.) In einem Teilgebiet der Mathematik, der **Algebra**, wird ausgiebig Gebrauch gemacht von solchen Variablen, um Aussagen zu formulieren und zu beweisen, die für alle Elemente einer Menge gelten.

In der Menge $\mathbb{N}_0$ lässt sich zum Beispiel folgende Aussage über die **Anordnung** der natürlichen Zahlen formulieren:

$\mathbb{N}_0$ ist (auf natürliche Weise) geordnet, das heißt, für je zwei Elemente *a* und *b* aus $\mathbb{N}_0$ gilt: *a* ist kleiner als *b* ($a < b$), *a* ist gleich groß wie *b* ($a = b$) oder *a* ist größer als *b* ($a > b$).

In mathematischer Formelschreibweise sieht das so aus:

$a \in \mathbb{N}_0 \wedge b \in \mathbb{N}_0 \Rightarrow a < b \vee a = b \vee a > b$

Der Pfeil $\Rightarrow$ ist das Zeichen für eine **Implikation** und bedeutet: »daraus folgt«.
Man sagt auch kurz in Worten: Für $a, b \in \mathbb{N}_0$ ist entweder $a < b$ oder $a = b$ oder $a > b$.
Der Ausdruck $a < b$ bedeutet gleichzeitig auch $b > a$.

Ein mathematischer Ausdruck der Art »$a < b$« oder »$a > b$« ist eine Zuordnung und wird als **Ungleichung** bezeichnet, die Zuordnung »$a = b$« stellt eine **Gleichung** dar. »Zuordnen« heißt einfach die Herstellung eines Zusammenhangs. Für solche Zuordnungen zwischen den Elementen einer Menge oder zwischen den Elementen verschiedener Mengen wird später der Begriff »Relation« verwendet.

Tauchen in einer Gleichung oder Ungleichung Variablen auf, so wird diese Gleichung oder Ungleichung als **Aussageform** bezeichnet. Wenn in einer Aussageform alle Variablen durch konkrete Werte ersetzt werden, z.B. $2 < 5$ oder $4 < 3$, entsteht dadurch eine **Aussage**. Einer Aussage kann der (Wahrheits-)Wert **»wahr«** (w) oder **»falsch«** (f) zugeordnet werden.

Auch Zuordnungen aus dem Alltag können als Aussageformen oder als Aussagen formuliert werden:

Aussageform	*x ist länger als* der Rhein. ($x \in$ Menge der Flüsse) *s liegt südlich von* München. ($s \in$ Menge der Städte)
Aussage	Die Donau ist länger als der Rhein. (w) Die Isar ist länger als der Rhein. (f) Hamburg liegt südlich von München. (f) Rom liegt südlich von München. (w)

An diesen Beispielen wird deutlich, dass nur für Aussagen die Werte »wahr« und »falsch« einen Sinn ergeben.

Die Aussageform $a \leq 5$ (in Worten: »a ist kleiner oder gleich 5«) ist eine Kurzform für die zusammengesetzte Aussageform $a < 5$ oder $a = 5$ ($a < 5 \vee a = 5$). $a \geq 5$ (»a ist größer oder gleich 5«) bedeutet entsprechend $a > 5 \vee a = 5$. $a \neq 5$ (»a ungleich 5« oder »a nicht gleich 5«) heißt $a < 5 \vee a > 5$.
$a < x < b$ steht für $x > a$ und zugleich ($\wedge$) $x < b$, oder mit anderen Worten: »x liegt zwischen a und b.«

Die Menge $\mathbb{N}_0$ kann anschaulich durch einen Zahlenstrahl dargestellt werden. Zahlen werden darauf als Bildpunkte oder als Pfeile abgebildet.

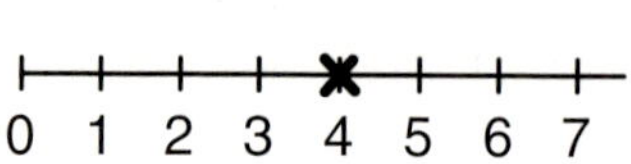

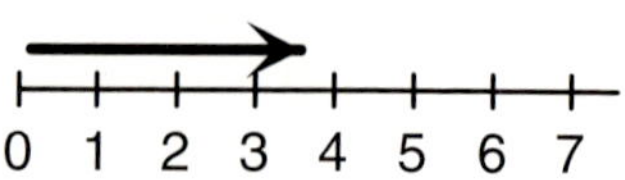

Auch Gleichungen und Ungleichungen lassen sich so darstellen.

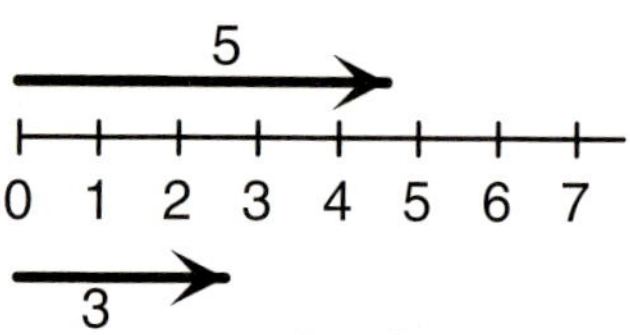

$5 > 3$

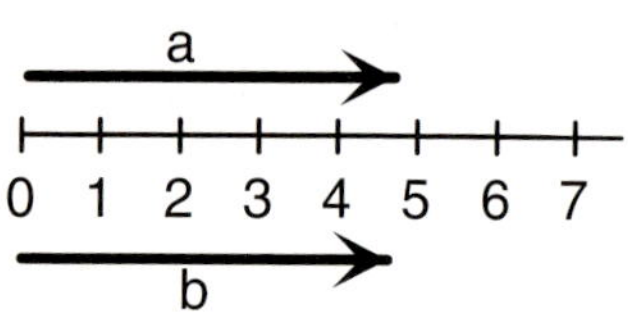

$a = b$

2.1 Die Grundrechenarten

Addition

Bekanntlich entsteht aus einer Menge von drei Äpfeln durch Hinzufügen von zwei weiteren Äpfeln eine Menge von fünf Äpfeln. Auf die Menge $\mathbb{N}_0$ übertragen wird das Hinzufügen als »**Addition**«, die Tätigkeit als »**addieren**« (»+«) bezeichnet.
Für die Addition gelten folgende Rechengesetze:

(I) $a + b = b + a$ (Vertauschungsgesetz oder **Kommutativgesetz**)

(II) $(a + b) + c = a + (b + c)$ (Verbindungsgesetz oder **Assoziativgesetz**)

Die Zahl 0 hat eine besondere Eigenschaft: $a + 0 = 0 + a = a$, also auch $0 + 0 = 0$.
Ein Element mit dieser Eigenschaft wird als **neutrales Element** der Addition bezeichnet.
In der Gleichung $a + b = c$ nennt man a und b **Summanden**, $a + b$ **Summe** und c den **Wert der Summe**, der meistens auch kurz Summe genannt wird.

Bei der Addition von beliebigen natürlichen Zahlen erhält man immer wieder eine natürliche Zahl. Diese Eigenschaft von $\mathbb{N}_0$ nennt man **Abgeschlossenheit** bezüglich der Addition.

Wenn bei mehr als zwei Summanden keine Klammern gesetzt werden, so ist damit die Addition in der angegebenen Reihenfolge gemeint, also $a + b + c = (a + b) + c$.
Die Gleichungen (I) und (II) führen für jede beliebige Einsetzung von a, b und c aus $\mathbb{N}_0$ zu wahren Aussagen, sie sind **allgemein gültig**.

Die Addition bedeutet auf dem Zahlenstrahl das Hintereinandersetzen von Pfeilen.

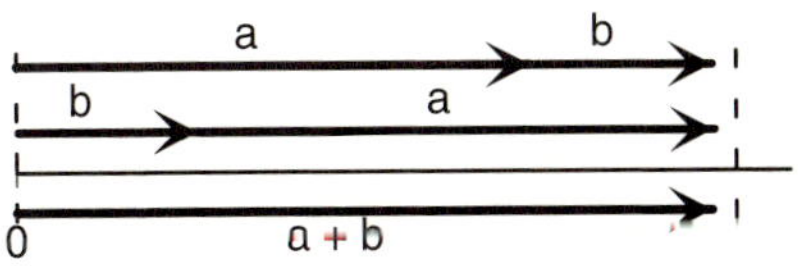

Wenn man die für Zahlen formulierten Gesetze (I) und (II) für Mengen formuliert, muss man andere Begriffe verwenden. Aus »$a + b = c$« wird $A \cup B = C$, in Worten: Menge A, vereinigt mit Menge B, ergibt die **Vereinigungsmenge** C.
Entsprechend gelten hier das Kommutativgesetz und das Assoziativgesetz:

(Ia) $A \cup B = B \cup A$
(IIa) $(A \cup B) \cup C = A \cup (B \cup C)$

Das neutrale Element ist die leere Menge, denn $A \cup \emptyset = \emptyset \cup A = A$.

Terme

Bei der Addition kommen Zeichen vor wie 3, 3 + 2, a, b, $a + b$, $a + (b + c)$, $a + 3$. Solche Gebilde nennt man Terme, das bedeutet Ausdrücke. Später kommen dazu auch Gebilde wie $a - 5$, $2 \cdot x$, $-\frac{1}{3}y$, $2a + 3$, $b : 3$, $(a + 2) \cdot (a - 2)$ ... Zahlen und Variablen sind also einfache Terme und aus einem Term entsteht durch Hinzufügen eines Rechenzeichens und eines Terms ein neuer Term. Durch dieses einfache Prinzip können beliebig komplexe Terme aufgebaut werden.
Terme, die keine Variablen enthalten, bedeuten Zahlen; Terme mit Variablen gehen in Zahlen über, wenn für die Variablen Zahlen eingesetzt werden. Wenn man z.B. in dem Term $3 + x$ nacheinander die Zahlen 2, 3 und 4 einsetzt, erhält man die Zahlen 5, 6 und 7.
Die Menge, aus denen man die Werte für die Variablen auswählen kann, nennt man **Grundmenge**. Vorläufig betrachten wir als Grundmenge meistens $\mathbb{N}$ oder $\mathbb{N}_0$.

Subtraktion

Das Hinzufügen von Elementen zu einer Menge hatten wir, übertragen auf $\mathbb{N}_0$, als Addition interpretiert. Nun betrachten wir das Wegnehmen von Elementen. Wenn man von fünf Äpfeln drei wegnimmt, bleiben nur noch zwei übrig. In $\mathbb{N}_0$ bedeutet das eine **Subtraktion**. Wir subtrahieren drei von fünf und erhalten als **Wert der Differenz** zwei: $5 - 3 = 2$.
Da wir nicht mehr Äpfel wegnehmen können als ursprünglich vorhanden waren, ergibt das Vertauschen $3 - 5$ in $\mathbb{N}_0$ keinen Sinn. Im Gegensatz zu den Summanden bei der Addition müssen also bei der Subtraktion die beiden Glieder der Differenz $a - b$ unterschieden werden: Das erste Glied a heißt **Minuend**, das zweite Glied b heißt **Subtrahend**.

Da bei der Differenz $a - b$ die Glieder a und b nicht beliebig gewählt werden können, sondern die Bedingung $a \geq b$ gestellt werden muss, ist $\mathbb{N}_0$ bezüglich der Subtraktion nicht abgeschlossen.

Es besteht ein enger Zusammenhang zwischen Addition und Subtraktion: Betrachtet man die Gleichungen $x + 5 = 8$ und $x = 8 - 5$, so stellt man fest, dass in beiden dieselben Zahlen und Variablen auftreten. Die Subtraktion ist die **Umkehrung** der Addition. Mit ihrer Hilfe lassen sich Additionssuchaufgaben wie die obige lösen, bei denen ein Summand unbekannt ist: »Zu welcher Zahl muss ich 5 addieren, um 8 zu erhalten?«

Allgemein kann folgender Satz formuliert werden:

Für $a, b \in \mathbb{N}_0$ mit $a \leq b$ haben die Gleichungen $a + x = b$ und $x + a = b$ genau eine Lösung in $\mathbb{N}$, nämlich $(b - a)$. Man schreibt $x = b - a$ und $\mathbb{L} = \{b - a\}$.
Das Zeichen $\mathbb{L}$ bedeutet **Lösungsmenge**. Die Lösungsmenge ist die Menge aller Werte, die in eine Aussageform eingesetzt werden können, sodass daraus eine wahre Aussage wird. Bei der Gleichung $2 + x = 5$ enthält die Lösungsmenge genau ein Element, nämlich $\mathbb{L} = \{3\}$. Die Gleichung $5 + x = 3$ hat keine Lösung, also $\mathbb{L} = \emptyset$. Die Lösungsmenge von Ungleichungen kann mehrere Elemente enthalten: $2 + x < 7$ hat $\mathbb{L} = \{0, 1, 2, 3, 4\}$.

Die Subtraktion auf dem Zahlenstrahl: $a - x = b$. Der Subtrahend wird in umgekehrtem Richtungssinn gezeichnet.

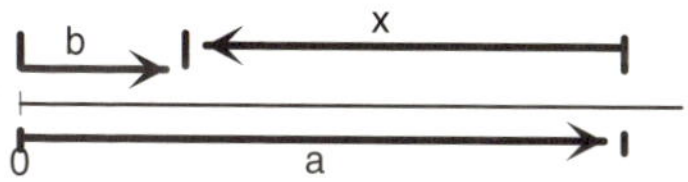

Multiplikation

Wenn wir uns vier Früchteteller mit je zehn Äpfeln vorstellen, so können wir die Gesamtzahl der Äpfel durch Addition ermitteln: $10 + 10 + 10 + 10$. Da die Summanden dieser Summe alle gleich sind, kann diese Berechnung verkürzt dargestellt werden als **Produkt**, indem man den gleich bleibenden Summanden und die Anzahl angibt: $10 \cdot 4$.

In der Produktgleichung $a \cdot b = c$ sind a und b **Faktoren**, c ist der **Wert des Produkts**. Manchmal werden die Faktoren unterschieden, der erste Faktor heißt dann **Multiplikand**, der zweite **Multiplikator**.

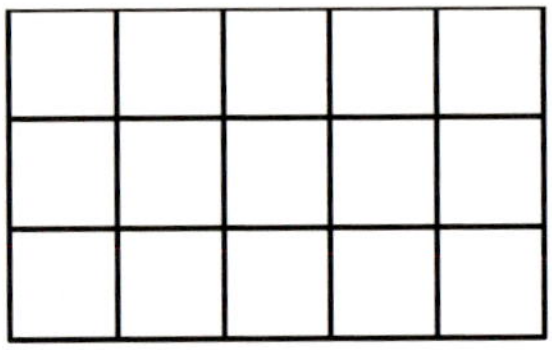

Das Rechteck besteht aus 3 Reihen zu je 5 Quadraten oder aus 5 Spalten zu je 3 Quadraten. Die Anzahl $3 \cdot 5$ ist also gleich $5 \cdot 3$.

Allgemein gelten für die Multiplikation das Kommutativgesetz und das Assoziativgesetz:

(I) $a \cdot b = b \cdot a$

(II) $(a \cdot b) \cdot c = a \cdot (b \cdot c)$

Für die Zahl 1 gilt: $1 \cdot a = a \cdot 1 = a$. Daher ist die Zahl 1 das neutrale Element der Multiplikation. Da für beliebige Zahlen aus $\mathbb{N}_0$ das Produkt dieser Zahlen wieder in $\mathbb{N}_0$ liegt, ist $\mathbb{N}_0$ auch gegenüber der Multiplikation abgeschlossen.

Ein wichtiger Sonderfall ist die Multiplikation mit der Zahl 0:

$0 \cdot a = a \cdot 0 = 0$, daher natürlich auch $0 \cdot 0 = 0$.

Daraus lässt sich ein sehr nützlicher Satz ableiten:

Ein Produkt ist dann 0, wenn mindestens ein Faktor 0 ist.

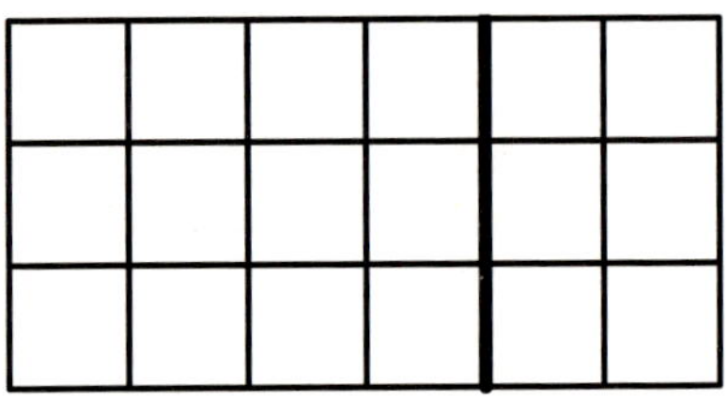

Dieses Rechteck besteht aus $3 \cdot (4 + 2)$ Quadraten, was offensichtlich das Gleiche ist wie $3 \cdot 4 + 3 \cdot 2$.

Allgemein gilt für die Verbindung von Addition und Multiplikation das Verteilungsgesetz oder **Distributivgesetz:**

$a \cdot (b + c) = a \cdot b + a \cdot c$

Ebenso gilt:

$a \cdot (b - c) = a \cdot b - a \cdot c$

Für die Schreibweise von Produkten gilt folgende Vereinbarung:
Der Multiplikationspunkt kann weggelassen werden, wenn der zweite Faktor eine Variable oder eine Klammer ist. Er bleibt aber erhalten zwischen zwei gleichen Variablen und wenn eine Klammer vor einer Variablen steht. Statt $3 \cdot a$, $a \cdot x$ und $a \cdot (x + y)$ schreibt man gewöhnlich $3a$, ax und $a(x + y)$. Es heißt aber $a \cdot 3$, $a \cdot a$ und $(a + 2) \cdot x$. Statt $1 \cdot a = 1a$ schreibt man a. Die Zahl 1 wird als Faktor also normalerweise weggelassen, umgekehrt kann man aber auch bei Bedarf jede Variable als Produkt mit 1 schreiben:

$y = 1y = 1 \cdot y = y \cdot 1$

In Termen wie $2a$ oder $5x$ nennt man die Zahlen 2 und 5 Beizahlen oder **Koeffizienten.** Terme mit gleichen Variablen werden addiert, indem man die Koeffizienten addiert und die Variablen beibehält.

$5a + 3a + 7a = (5 + 3 + 7) \cdot a = 15a$

Division
Wir stellen uns nun folgende Aufgabe: Eine Menge von 6 Äpfeln soll gleichmäßig auf 3 Kinder aufgeteilt werden. Diese Aufgabe lässt sich einfach lösen, indem man der Reihe nach jedem Kind einen Apfel gibt und diesen Vorgang so lange wiederholt, bis alle Äpfel verbraucht sind. Jedes Kind hat dann 2 Äpfel.
Mathematisch formuliert man diese Aufgabe als Gleichung:

$6 : 3 = 2$

Das ist eine **Division,** 6 wird durch 3 **dividiert.**
Allgemein schreiben wir wieder $a : b = c$. a nennt man **Dividend,** b **Divisor,** $a : b$ wird als **Quotient** bezeichnet und c ist der **Wert des Quotienten.** Häufig bezeichnet man c kurz als Quotient.

Bekanntlich lassen sich nicht alle Zahlen ohne Rest teilen. Solange wir nur Zahlen aus $\mathbb{N}_0$ betrachten, müssen wir an den Dividenden eine Bedingung stellen: a muss durch b teilbar sein oder anders ausgedrückt,

b muss Teiler von a sein. $\mathbb{N}_0$ ist also gegenüber der Division nicht abgeschlossen.
Es gilt das Distributivgesetz:

$(a + b) : c = a : c + b : c$

Das Ergebnis der Aufgabe $(6 + 9) : 3$ kann man also auf zwei Arten finden:

$(6 + 9) : 3 = 15 : 3 = 5$ oder
$(6 + 9) : 3 = 6 : 3 + 9 : 3 = 2 + 3 = 5$

So wie die Subtraktion die Umkehrung der Addition ist, ist die Division die Umkehrung der Multiplikation. $3 \cdot 5 = 15$ führt zu $3 = 15 : 5$. Die Multiplikation kann also als Probe für die Division verwendet werden.
Wegen $1 \cdot a = a$ ist $a : 1 = a$.

Die Division durch 0 ist verboten.

Denn wenn für eine Zahl $a \neq 0$ der Quotient $a : 0$ den Wert b hätte, dann müsste $a = b \cdot 0 = 0$ sein. Das ist aber ein Widerspruch zur Annahme $a \neq 0$.
Allgemein gilt der Satz:

Ist $a \in \mathbb{N}$, $b \in \mathbb{N}_0$ und b durch a teilbar, so haben die Gleichungen $a \cdot x = b$ und $x \cdot a = b$ genau eine Lösung, nämlich $(b : a) \in \mathbb{N}_0$. Wir schreiben dann:

Wenn $a \cdot x = b$ ist, dann ist $x = b : a$.

Wenn in Aufgaben die Rechenarten gemischt vorkommen, haben Multiplikation und Division Vorrang vor Addition und Subtraktion. Soll diese Vereinbarung nicht gelten, müssen Klammern gesetzt werden. Man kann sich diese Regel in einem kleinen Spruch merken:

Punkt geht vor Strich!
Klammern sagen: Erst komm ich!

Potenzen

Ebenso wie eine Addition mit mehreren gleichen Summanden abgekürzt werden kann durch eine Multiplikation, kann auch eine Multiplikation mit mehreren gleichen Faktoren abgekürzt werden durch eine Potenz.

$2 \cdot 2 \cdot 2 \cdot 2 = 2^4$

Allgemein bedeutet a^n, dass die Zahl a n-mal als Faktor geschrieben wird. a bezeichnet man als Grundzahl oder **Basis**, n als Hochzahl oder **Exponent**.
Das **Potenzieren** ist keine Grundrechenart. Es hat Vorrang vor den übrigen Rechenarten. Aber auch hier gehen Klammern wieder vor.
Beispiele:

a) $5 \cdot 2^3 + 7 = 5 \cdot (2 \cdot 2 \cdot 2) + 7 = 5 \cdot 8 + 7 = 47$
b) $10 - 3^2 = 10 - (3 \cdot 3) = 10 - 9 = 1$
c) $4 + (2 + 3)^2 = 4 + 5^2 = 4 + 25 = 29$

In den Beispielen a und b wären die Klammern nicht notwendig, sie dienen nur zur Verdeutlichung; im Beispiel c dagegen bedeuten sie, dass die Addition vor dem Potenzieren kommt.

Zwei Sonderfälle, die man auswendig lernen muss, sind Potenzen mit den Exponenten 1 und 0:

$a^1 = a$ und $a^0 = 1$ für $a \in \mathbb{N}_0$

Speziell gilt auch $0^0 = 1$. Warum man diese auf den ersten Blick nicht ganz einleuchtende Vereinbarung getroffen hat, wird an einer späteren Stelle geklärt.

Potenzen mit gleicher Basis werden multipliziert, indem man die Exponenten addiert und die Basis beibehält.

Diese Regel wird sofort an einem Beispiel klar:

$3^3 \cdot 3^2 = (3 \cdot 3 \cdot 3) \cdot (3 \cdot 3) = 3^{(3+2)} = 3^5$

2.2 Zahlensysteme

Die Zahlen, mit denen wir im Alltag umgehen, sind alle nach einem bestimmten System aufgebaut. Die Zahl 1523 zum Beispiel können wir zerlegen in 1 Tausender, 5 Hunderter, 2 Zehner und 3 Einer. Wir können sie so schreiben:

$$1523 = 1 \cdot 1000 + 5 \cdot 100 + 2 \cdot 10 + 3 \cdot 1 = 1 \cdot 10 \cdot 10 \cdot 10 + 5 \cdot 10 \cdot 10 + 2 \cdot 10 + 3 \cdot 1 = 1 \cdot 10^3 + 5 \cdot 10^2 + 2 \cdot 10^1 + 3 \cdot 10^0$$

Wir sehen also, dass das Grundgerüst dieses Systems aus Zehnerpotenzen besteht. Von rechts beginnend mit der Hochzahl 0 wird die Hochzahl für die jeweils nächste Stelle links davon immer um 1 erhöht. Deshalb wird es auch Zehnersystem oder Dezimalsystem genannt. Es benötigt die zehn verschiedenen Ziffern von 0 bis 9, um alle Zahlen aus $\mathbb{N}_0$ darzustellen. Aufgeschrieben wird immer nur die jeweils benötigte Anzahl der entsprechenden Potenz.

Statt der Zahl 10 können wir auch jede andere Zahl als Grundzahl nehmen. Besondere Bedeutung hat das System mit der Basis 2, auch Dualsystem oder Binärsystem genannt, das mit den zwei Ziffern 0 und 1 auskommt. Die gesamte Digitaltechnik und Computertechnik baut darauf auf, denn diese arbeiten vereinfacht gesehen mit zwei Zuständen: Strom oder nicht Strom bzw. Magnetisierung oder nicht Magnetisierung an einer bestimmten Stelle eines Magnetbandes oder einer Magnetplatte. Diese beiden Zustände werden mit den beiden Ziffern des Zweiersystems identifiziert.

Nun wollen wir eine Zahl aus dem Dezimalsystem in das Dualsystem übersetzen. Als Beispiel nehmen wir 154.
Zuerst stellen wir das benötigte Gerüst aus Zweierpotenzen zusammen:

$2^0 = \mathbf{1}$, $2^1 = \mathbf{2}$, $2^2 = \mathbf{4}$, $2^3 = \mathbf{8}$, $2^4 = \mathbf{16}$, $2^5 = \mathbf{32}$, $2^6 = \mathbf{64}$, $2^7 = \mathbf{128}$, $2^8 = \mathbf{256}$.

Hier können wir abbrechen, denn 256 ist schon größer als 154.

Nun folgt eine Reihe von Divisionen mit oder ohne Rest. Wir beginnen mit dem Wert der höchsten Potenz, der kleiner ist als die umzuwandelnde Zahl:

154 : 128 = **1** Rest 26
26 : 64 = **0** Rest 26
26 : 32 = **0** Rest 26
26 : 16 = **1** Rest 10
10 : 8 = **1** Rest 2
2 : 4 = **0** Rest 2
2 : 2 = **1** Rest 0
0 : 1 = **0**

Die Zahl 154 können wir also schreiben als

$154 = \mathbf{1} \cdot 2^7 + \mathbf{0} \cdot 2^6 + \mathbf{0} \cdot 2^5 + \mathbf{1} \cdot 2^4 + \mathbf{1} \cdot 2^3 + \mathbf{0} \cdot 2^2 + \mathbf{1} \cdot 2^1 + \mathbf{0} \cdot 2^0$.

Damit lautet sie im Dualsystem 10011010.

Die Umwandlung vom Dualsystem in das Dezimalsystem ist einfacher. Unser Beispiel ist hier die Dualzahl 1101001.
Wir benötigen wieder das obige Gerüst der Zweierpotenzen. Nun zerlegen wir die Zahl von rechts nach links:

$1101001 = 1 \cdot 2^0 + 0 \cdot 2^1 + 0 \cdot 2^2 + 1 \cdot 2^3 + 0 \cdot 2^4 + 1 \cdot 2^5 + 1 \cdot 2^6 =$
$1 + 0 + 0 + 8 + 0 + 32 + 64 = 105$

Ein anderes, ebenfalls in Computern verwendetes System ist das Sechzehnersystem oder Hexadezimalsystem. Hier hat man die Schwierigkeit, dass dieses System 16 Ziffern benötigt, also mehr, als im Dezimalsystem zur Verfügung stehen. Man behilft sich dadurch, dass man für die noch fehlenden Ziffern 10 bis 15 die Buchstaben A bis F verwendet. Die Dezimalzahl 12 ist also hexadezimal »C«. Im Hexadezimalsystem können mit den ein- und zweistelligen Zahlen »00« bis »FF« ($= 15 \cdot 16^0 + 15 \cdot 16^1 = 255$) die Dezimalzahlen von 0 bis 255 ausgedrückt werden. Die Hersteller von Computern und anderen Geräten wie z.B. Druckern haben sich auf eine einheitliche Tabelle geeinigt, den so genannten (erweiterten) ASCII-Code, in der Zeichen wie »%«, »5« und »z« von 0 bis 255 durchnummeriert sind. Diese Nummern werden im Rechner intern als Hexadezimalzahlen von »00« bis »FF« verwendet. Der Akzentbuchstabe »é« hat beispielsweise die Nummer 233.

2.3 Lösen von Gleichungen und Ungleichungen

Wir kehren nun zu den Gleichungen zurück, die ja in Form von Aussagen oder Aussageformen vorliegen können.

Interessant sind für uns hier nur die Aussageformen. Als Beispiel nehmen wir die Gleichung $x - 3 = 4$. Eine Gleichung lösen heißt, ihre Lösungsmenge finden. Die Lösungsmenge ist aber bekanntlich die Menge der Werte, die ich für die Variable einsetzen kann, sodass eine wahre Aussage entsteht. Dazu formt man die Gleichung in eine einfachere, äquivalente Gleichung um.

Äquivalente Gleichungen sind Gleichungen, die dieselbe Lösungsmenge haben. Um die Äquivalenz auszudrücken, schreibt man das Zeichen «$\Leftrightarrow$» (Äquivalenzpfeil) zwischen die Gleichungen.

Solche Umformungen haben wir schon kennen gelernt.
$x - 3 = 4 \Leftrightarrow x - 3 + 3 = 4 + 3 \Leftrightarrow x = 7$. Das ist die einfachste Form einer Gleichung und aus ihr lässt sich unmittelbar ablesen: $\mathbb{L} = \{7\}$.
Andere Beispiele:

$x + 3 = 8 \Leftrightarrow x + 3 - 3 = 8 - 3 \Leftrightarrow x = 5 \quad \mathbb{L} = \{5\}$

$2 \cdot x = 8 \Leftrightarrow 2 : 2 \cdot x = 8 : 2 \Leftrightarrow x = 4 \quad \mathbb{L} = \{4\}$

$x : 2 = 4 \Leftrightarrow x : 2 \cdot 2 = 4 \cdot 2 \Leftrightarrow x = 8 \quad \mathbb{L} = \{8\}$

Alle hier gezeigten Umformungen sind Äquivalenzumformungen, wie eine Probe durch Einsetzen der Lösung in die ursprüngliche Gleichung zeigt. (In Beispiel 2 und 3 wurden die Operationen in der Reihenfolge von links nach rechts ausgeführt.)

Gleichungen können vereinfacht werden durch Addition oder Subtraktion einer natürlichen Zahl oder durch Multiplikation oder Division mit einer natürlichen Zahl auf beiden Seiten des Gleichheitszeichens.

Die Multiplikation mit 0 ist nicht erlaubt, da sonst z. B. Folgendes möglich wäre:

$3x = 6 \quad 3 \cdot x \cdot 0 = 6 \cdot 0 \Leftrightarrow 0 = 0 \Leftrightarrow \mathbb{L} = \mathbb{N}_0$

(Hier ist absichtlich kein Äquivalenzpfeil zwischen die ersten beiden Gleichungen gesetzt.)

Eine Gleichung, die sich zu einer Gleichung der Form $a = a$ $(a \in \mathbb{N}_0)$ vereinfachen lässt, hat als Lösungsmenge die gesamte Grundmenge.

Diese Lösung ist hier aber falsch, wie man beispielsweise durch Einsetzen der Zahl 1 in die ursprüngliche Gleichung zeigen kann.
Die Umformungen in den obigen Beispielen sind zur Verdeutlichung sehr ausführlich aufgeschrieben. Normalerweise ist die Notation kürzer, etwa wie im folgenden Beispiel:

$2x + 4 = 10 \Leftrightarrow 2x = 6 \Leftrightarrow x = 3 \quad \mathbb{L} = \{3\}$

Oft schreibt man auch die Gleichungen untereinander, mit oder ohne Äquivalenzpfeile. Hinter der jeweiligen Gleichung kann man durch einen senkrechten Strich abgetrennt die nächstfolgende Umformung angeben:

$5x - 3 = 2x + 6 \quad | - 2x$
$3x - 3 = 6 \quad | + 3$
$3x = 9 \quad | : 3$
$x = 3 \quad \mathbb{L} = \{3\}$

Das letzte Beispiel zeigt, dass man die Lösungsmethode folgendermaßen umformulieren kann:

Eine Gleichung wird vereinfacht, indem man mit geeigneten Termen die Umkehrrechnung auf der anderen Seite des Gleichheitszeichens durchführt.

Ziel ist es, die gesuchte Variable auf einer Seite zu isolieren. Wegen der Regel »Punkt vor Strich« sind Terme durch die Punktrechnungen enger zusammengekettet als durch Strichrechnungen, d. h., zuerst müssen Additionen und Subtraktionen ausgeführt werden und erst ganz zum Schluss Multiplikationen und Divisionen.

Auf dieselbe Weise lösen wir Ungleichungen.

$3x - 4 < x + 8 \quad | + 4 - x$ (zwei Schritte auf einmal)
$2x < 12 \quad | : 2$
$x < 6 \quad \mathbb{L} = \{0, 1, 2, 3, 4, 5\}$

$8x + 5 \geq 4x + 13 \quad | - 4x - 5$
$4x \geq 8 \quad | : 2$
$x \geq 2 \quad \mathbb{L} = \{2, 3, 4, 5 \ldots\}$

Statt in aufzählender Form können wir die Lösungsmenge auch in beschreibender Form angeben: $\mathbb{L} = \{x \in \mathbb{N}_0 \mid x \geq 2\}$. In Worten: »Die Menge aller x aus $\mathbb{N}_0$, für die gilt: x ist größer oder gleich 2.«

Es folgen nun einige Textaufgaben, die auf Gleichungen führen.
1) In welchem Rechteck mit Umfang 40 cm ist eine Seite dreimal so lang wie die andere?

Lösung:
Nennen wir die kürzere Seite x, dann ist die längere Seite $3x$. Der Umfang ist die doppelte Summe von beiden Seiten, also:

$2 \cdot (x + 3x) = 40$ cm
$2 \cdot 4x = 40$ cm
$8x = 40$ cm
$x = 5$ cm

Die Seiten des Rechtecks sind 5 cm und 15 cm.

2) Auf einem Parkplatz stehen Autos und Motorräder, 15 Fahrzeuge mit insgesamt 54 Rädern. Wie viele Autos und wie viele Motorräder sind es?
Lösung: Wenn es x Autos sind, dann müssen es $(15 - x)$ Motorräder sein. Also gilt für die Anzahl der Räder:

$4x + 2 \cdot (15 - x) = 54$
$4x + 30 - 2x = 54$
$2x = 24$
$x = 12$

Es sind 12 Autos und 3 Motorräder.

3) Eine Mutter ist heute siebenmal so alt wie ihre Tochter. In vier Jahren wird sie nur noch viermal so alt sein wie die Tochter. Wie alt sind beide heute?

Lösung: Hier hilft uns eine Tabelle!

	Tochter	Mutter
heute	x	$7x$
in 4 Jahren	$x + 4$	$7x + 4$

Es muss also gelten:

$7x + 4 = 4 \cdot (x + 4)$

$7x + 4 = 4x + 16$

$3x = 12$

$x = 4$

Die Mutter ist heute 28, die Tochter vier Jahre alt.

Gliedern von Termen

Durch die Vorrangstellung der Punktrechnungen gegenüber den Strichrechnungen gliedern sich zusammengesetzte Terme von selbst.

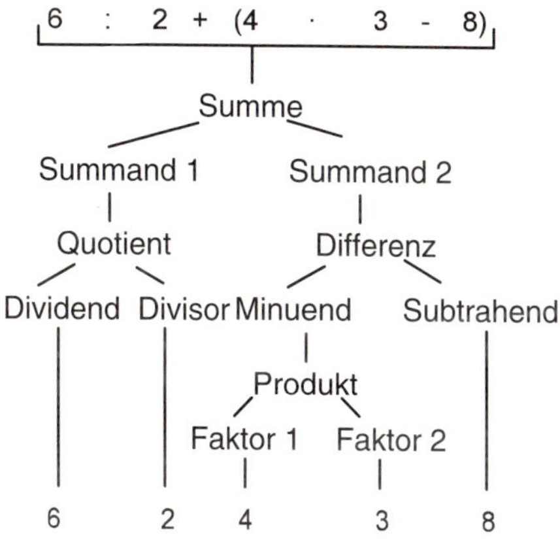

$2 \cdot 5 + 4 \cdot 3 + 2a - 8$

In diesem Term ist die Reihenfolge der Strichrechnungen von links nach rechts. Wir können Klammern einfügen und erhalten dann:

$[(2 \cdot 5 + 4 \cdot 3) + 2a] - 8$

Nun sehen wir, dass auf der obersten Stufe eine Differenz vorliegt, deren Minuend eine Summe ist usw.

Wenn in einem Term ohne Klammern Strichrechnungen vorkommen, handelt es sich immer um eine Summe oder Differenz.

2.4 Runden von Zahlen, Abschätzen von Größenordnungen

Bei vielen Dingen im Alltag ist es unmöglich oder nicht sinnvoll, eine genaue Anzahl anzugeben. Die Einwohnerzahl eines Landes oder einer Stadt ändert sich mit jeder Sekunde durch Geburten und Todesfälle. Deshalb ist es sinnlos zu sagen, das Land *XY* hat 83 296 127 Einwohner. Hier wird man die Zahl 83 000 000 nennen. In diesem Fall haben wir auf Millionen gerundet.

Bei einer Schule mit 582 Schülern können wir nach Bedarf auf 580 oder auf 600 runden. Im ersten Fall haben wir auf Zehner gerundet, im zweiten Fall auf Hunderter.

Wenn einmal festgelegt ist, auf welche Stelle gerundet werden soll, z. B. 582 auf Hunderter, sieht man sich die nächste Stelle rechts davon an, hier also die Zehner. Gewöhnlich gilt die Regel für alle Rundungsvorgänge:

> Ab 5 wird aufgerundet, sonst abgerundet.

Wir haben 8 Zehner, also wird auf die nächsthöhere Hunderterzahl gerundet. Wenn wir auf Zehner runden, landen wir wegen der 2 Einer bei 580.

Ein weiteres Beispiel: 7564
auf Zehner: 7560
auf Hunderter: 7600
auf Tausender: 8000

Die Genauigkeit, mit der Zahlen angegeben werden, kann sich nach dem Bedarf oder nach dem Interesse richten. Es ist interessant zu wissen, ob eine Stadt »etwa 20 000« oder »etwa 30 000« Einwohner hat, aber es ist nicht mehr so interessant zu unterscheiden, ob »etwa 920 000« oder »etwa 930 000«. Hier genügt uns die Angabe »etwa 900 000«.

2.5 Teiler einer Zahl

Wie wir schon weiter oben festgestellt haben, ist die Menge $\mathbb{N}_0$ nicht abgeschlossen gegenüber der Division, d.h., nicht alle Divisionsaufgaben haben eine Lösung in $\mathbb{N}_0$.

Wenn eine Zahl *z* durch eine Zahl *t* ohne Rest teilbar ist, dann ist *t* ein **Teiler** von *z*, $t \mid z$. Die Menge aller Teiler von *z* ist die **Teilermenge** von *z*.

$T_z = \{t \in \mathbb{N} \mid z : t \in \mathbb{N}_0\}$

Zum Beispiel:

$T_{12} = \{1, 2, 3, 4, 6, 12\}$
$T_{25} = \{1, 5, 25\}$
$T_{31} = \{1, 31\}$

Eine Zahl heißt **gerade**, wenn gilt: $2 \mid z$. Alle anderen (natürlichen) Zahlen sind **ungerade**.

Teilbarkeit
Für viele Aufgaben, zum Beispiel aus dem Kapitel Bruchrechnung, ist es wichtig, die Teiler einer Zahl zu kennen. Deshalb ist es sinnvoll, einige Regeln zu lernen, mit deren Hilfe man schnell entscheiden kann, ob eine Zahl, die man nicht beim Einmaleins gelernt hat, durch eine bestimmte andere Zahl teilbar ist.

Es gelten folgende Teilbarkeitsregeln:

Teilbarkeit durch 2: Eine Zahl ist durch 2 teilbar, wenn ihre letzte Ziffer 0, 2, 4, 6 oder 8 ist, d.h. alle geraden Zahlen.
524 ist durch 2 teilbar, 891 nicht.

Teilbarkeit durch 3: Eine Zahl ist durch 3 teilbar, wenn ihre Quersumme durch 3 teilbar ist. Die Quersumme ist die Summe der Ziffern, aus denen die Zahl zusammengesetzt ist, z.B. Quersumme von 29: 2 + 9 + 1 = 12.
291 ist also durch 3 teilbar.
Die Quersumme von 72164 ist 7 + 2 + 1 + 6 + 4 = 20, folglich ist 72164 nicht durch 3 teilbar.

Teilbarkeit durch 4: Eine Zahl ist durch 4 teilbar, wenn die aus den zwei letzten Ziffern gebildete Zahl durch 4 teilbar ist.
Infrage kommen nur gerade Zahlen, eine Zahl wie 2521 brauchen wir also gar nicht prüfen. 85**46** ist nicht durch 4 teilbar, weil 46 keine Viererzahl ist, 18**24** dagegen ist durch 4 teilbar.

Teilbarkeit durch 5: Eine Zahl ist durch 5 teilbar, wenn ihre letzte Ziffer 0 oder 5 ist.
613**5** ist durch 5 teilbar, 913**2** nicht.

Teilbarkeit durch 6: Eine Zahl ist durch 6 teilbar, wenn sie durch 2 und durch 3 teilbar ist.
Auch hier prüfen wir nur gerade Zahlen.
3984 ist durch 6 teilbar, denn 3 + 9 + 8 + 4 = 24, eine Dreierzahl.

Teilbarkeit durch 8: Eine Zahl ist durch 8 teilbar, wenn die aus den drei letzten Ziffern gebildete Zahl durch 8 teilbar ist.
Nur gerade Zahlen haben den Teiler 8.
25**368** ist durch 8 teilbar, 10**140** nicht.

Teilbarkeit durch 9: Eine Zahl ist durch 9 teilbar, wenn ihre Quersumme durch 9 teilbar ist.
3186 ist durch 9 teilbar, denn 3 + 1 + 8 + 6 = 18.

Die bisherigen Regeln helfen auch, die Teilbarkeit durch 12, 15, 18 und 36 festzustellen: Eine Zahl ist durch 12 teilbar, wenn sie durch 3 und durch 4, durch 15, wenn sie durch 3 und 5, durch 18, wenn sie durch 2 und 9, durch 36, wenn sie durch 4 und 9 teilbar ist.

Teilbarkeit durch 25: Eine Zahl ist durch 25 teilbar, wenn die aus den letzten zwei Stellen gebildete Zahl durch 25 teilbar ist.
Ein Produkt ist durch eine Zahl teilbar, wenn zumindest ein Faktor durch die Zahl teilbar ist.
$13 \cdot 14$ ist durch 7 teilbar, weil $14 = 2 \cdot 7$.
Eine Summe ist durch eine Zahl teilbar, wenn alle Summanden durch die Zahl teilbar sind. Das folgt aus dem Distributivgesetz:
$15 + 21 = 3 \cdot 5 + 3 \cdot 7 = 3 \cdot (5 + 7)$, also ist die Summe durch 3 teilbar.

Im Gegensatz zu den bisherigen Regeln aber gilt: Die Nichtteilbarkeit der Summanden bedeutet nicht die Nichtteilbarkeit der Summe.
Beispiel: 5 + 3 ist teilbar durch 2.

Primzahlen

Alle Zahlen, die genau zwei verschiedene Teiler haben, nennt man **Primzahlen.**

Diese Teiler sind dann die Zahl 1 und die Zahl selbst.
5 ist Primzahl, denn $T_5 = \{1, 5\}$; $T_4 = \{1, 2, 4\}$, daher ist 4 keine Primzahl.
Die Zahl 1 ist keine Primzahl, weil sie nur einen einzigen Teiler hat.

Es gibt unendlich viele Primzahlen.
Um die Primzahlen zu finden, kann man das so genannte »Sieb des Eratosthenes« anwenden:
Man streicht der Reihe nach die Vielfachen der Primzahlen p = 2, 3, 5 ..., jeweils beginnend mit dem Produkt $p \cdot p$. [Das bedeutet: $p \cdot p$, $p \cdot (p + 1)$, $p \cdot (p + 2)$ usw. oder $2 \cdot 2$, $2 \cdot 3$, $2 \cdot 4$ ..., $3 \cdot 3$, $3 \cdot 4$, ...] Die erste nicht gestrichene Zahl ist dann jeweils die nächste Primzahl.
Wenn man das Verfahren bis zu einer Zahl *p* durchgeführt hat, hat man alle Primzahlen bis p^2 gefunden. Das bedeutet, um beispielsweise alle Primzahlen bis 121 zu finden, genügt es, die Vielfachen der Primzahlen von 2 bis 11 zu streichen, denn $11^2 = 11 \cdot 11 = 121$.
Man sieht sofort, dass alle Primzahlen außer 2 ungerade sind:

	2	3	~~4~~	5	~~6~~	7	~~8~~	~~9~~	~~10~~
11	~~12~~	13	~~14~~	~~15~~	~~16~~	17	~~18~~	19	~~20~~
~~21~~	~~22~~	23	~~24~~	~~25~~	~~26~~	~~27~~	~~28~~	29	~~30~~
31	~~32~~	~~33~~	~~34~~	~~35~~	~~36~~	37	~~38~~	~~39~~	~~40~~
41	~~42~~	43	~~44~~	~~45~~	~~46~~	47	~~48~~	~~49~~	~~50~~
~~51~~	~~52~~	53	~~54~~	~~55~~	~~56~~	~~57~~	~~58~~	59	~~60~~

Zusammengesetzte Zahlen

Alle Zahlen, die mehr als zwei Teiler haben, heißen **zusammengesetzte Zahlen.**

15 ist eine zusammengesetzte Zahl, denn $T_{15} = \{1, 3, 5, 15\}$.
Zusammengesetzte Zahlen lassen sich als Produkt ohne den Faktor 1 schreiben.

$15 = 3 \cdot 5$

Die Zahl 1 ist die einzige Zahl, die nicht zusammengesetzt ist und auch keine Primzahl ist.

Wenn eine Primzahl Faktor in einem Produkt ist, nennt man sie auch Primfaktor.
Jede zusammengesetzte Zahl lässt sich in Primfaktoren zerlegen. Das ist für viele Rechnungen sehr zweckmäßig, z.B. wenn man die Teiler einer Zahl benötigt. Diese Zerlegung erfolgt für kleinere Zahlen durch Kopfrechnen, sonst schriftlich.
Als Beispiele zerlegen wir die Zahlen 80 und 90.

$80 : 2 = 40$
$40 : 2 = 20$
$20 : 2 = 10$
$10 : 2 = 5$
5 ist Primzahl. Also ist $80 = 2 \cdot 2 \cdot 2 \cdot 2 \cdot 5$.

$90 = 9 \cdot 10$
$9 = 3 \cdot 3$, $10 = 2 \cdot 5$
Also ist $90 = 2 \cdot 3 \cdot 3 \cdot 5$.

Gemeinsame Teiler, ggT
Die Primfaktoren sind Teiler einer Zahl. Die übrigen Teiler der Zahl findet man, indem man ihre Primfaktoren zu allen möglichen Produkten kombiniert und dann noch die Zahl 1 dazunimmt.

Für die Zahl 80 ergeben sich als mögliche Produkte:
$2 \cdot 2 = 4$
$2 \cdot 2 \cdot 2 = 8$
$2 \cdot 2 \cdot 2 \cdot 2 = 16$
$2 \cdot 2 \cdot 2 \cdot 2 \cdot 5 = 80$
$2 \cdot 5 = 10$
$2 \cdot 2 \cdot 5 = 20$
$2 \cdot 2 \cdot 2 \cdot 5 = 40$
$T_{80} = \{1, 2, 4, 5, 8, 10, 16, 20, 40, 80\}$

Wenn man die Teilermengen von 80 und 90 vergleicht, stellt man fest, dass die Zahlen 1, 2 und 10 in beiden vorkommen. $T_{80} \cap T_{90} = \{1, 2, 5, 10\}$.
Zahlen, die in den Teilermengen mehrerer Zahlen auftauchen, nennt man **gemeinsame Teiler**.

Als eine Anwendung betrachten wir folgendes Problem:

An einer Sportveranstaltung nehmen 80 Mädchen und 90 Jungen teil. Für einen Wettbewerb sollen gleichmäßig besetzte, gemischte Gruppen gebildet werden. Wie viele Möglichkeiten, solche Gruppen zu bilden, gibt es?

Antwort: Da die Zahlen 80 und 90 genau vier gemeinsame Teiler haben, gibt es auch vier Möglichkeiten für die gewünschte Gruppenbildung:

1. Eine einzige Gruppe, die aus allen Teilnehmern besteht. Diese Aufteilung ist hier sicher nicht sehr sinnvoll.
2. Zwei Gruppen mit je 80 : 2 = 40 Mädchen und 90 : 2 = 45 Jungen.
3. Fünf Gruppen mit je 80 : 5 = 16 Mädchen und 90 : 5 = 18 Jungen.
4. Zehn Gruppen mit je 80 : 10 = 8 Mädchen und 90 : 10 = 9 Jungen.

Zahlen, die außer der Zahl 1 keine gemeinsamen Teiler haben, nennt man **teilerfremd**.

Die Zahlen 9 und 10 sind teilerfremd, denn $T_9 = \{1, 3, 9\}$, $T_{10} = \{1, 2, 5, 10\}$.

Unter den gemeinsamen Teilern der Zahlen 80 und 90 ist 10 die größte Zahl. Deshalb nennen wir 10 den **größten gemeinsamen Teiler** der Zahlen 80 und 90, abgekürzt **ggT (80, 90)**.

Wenn wir den ggT von zwei Zahlen suchen, z. B. 60 und 140, können wir folgendermaßen vorgehen:

Wir machen eine Primfaktorenzerlegung und schreiben jeweils gleiche Faktoren untereinander:

$$\begin{array}{r} 60 = 2 \cdot 2 \cdot 3 \cdot 5 \\ 140 = 2 \cdot 2 \cdot 5 \cdot 7 \\ \hline 2 \cdot 2 \cdot 5 \end{array}$$

Unter dem Strich schreiben wir gemeinsame Faktoren noch einmal auf. Das Produkt aus diesen gemeinsamen Faktoren ist dann der größte gemeinsame Teiler, hier also ggT (60, 140) = $2 \cdot 2 \cdot 5 = 20$.

Vielfache einer Zahl, kgV

Nach den Teilern einer Zahl betrachten wir nun die **Vielfachen** einer Zahl. Das sind alle die Werte, die wir erhalten, wenn wir die Zahl nacheinander mit 1, 2, 3 usw. multiplizieren.

Die Vielfachen von 3 sind also 1 · 3 = **3**, 2 · 3 = **6**, 3 · 3 = **9** usw. Das ist gerade die Dreierreihe im Einmaleins. Die Menge aller Vielfachen einer Zahl ist die **Vielfachenmenge**. Zum Beispiel die Vielfachenmenge von 3 $V_3 = \{3, 6, 9, 12 \ldots\}$. Diese Aufzählung könnte man beliebig fortsetzen, sie bildet also eine unendliche Menge.
Vergleichen wir nun die Vielfachenmengen von 4 und 6.

$V_4 = \{4, 8, 12, 16, 20, 24, 28, 32, 36, 40, 44, 48 \ldots\}$
$V_6 = \{6, 12, 18, 24, 30, 36, 42, 48 \ldots\}$.

Wie bei den gemeinsamen Teilern von Zahlen stellen wir fest, dass es auch gemeinsame Vielfache von Zahlen gibt. $V_4 \cap V_6 = \{12, 24, 36, 48 \ldots\}$. Auch das ist eine unendliche Menge.
Unter diesen gemeinsamen Vielfachen gibt es also keine größte Zahl, aber es gibt eine kleinste, **das kleinste gemeinsame Vielfache** oder kurz **kgV**.

kgV (4, 6) = 12

Alle übrigen gemeinsamen Vielfachen der beiden Zahlen sind Vielfache des kgV.
Auch hier gibt es ein Verfahren, nach dem man das kgV von mehreren Zahlen aus ihren Primfaktoren berechnen kann.

$$\begin{array}{l} 4 = 2 \cdot 2 \\ \underline{6 = 2 \quad\cdot\ 3} \\ \quad\ 2 \cdot 2 \cdot 3 \end{array}$$

Im Unterschied zur Berechnung des ggT werden hier unter dem Strich die Faktoren aus jeder Spalte übertragen. Die Verfahren der Berechnung von ggT und kgV lassen sich auch auf mehr als zwei Zahlen anwenden. Berechnen wir z.B. kgV (6, 7, 8):

$$\begin{array}{l} 6 = \quad 2 \quad\cdot\quad 3 \\ 7 = 1 \qquad\cdot\qquad 7 \\ \underline{8 = \quad 2 \cdot 2 \cdot 2 \qquad} \\ \qquad 2 \cdot 2 \cdot 2 \cdot 3 \cdot 7 = 168 \end{array}$$

kgV (6, 7, 8) = 168.

Das kgV von Primzahlen und von teilerfremden Zahlen ist gerade das Produkt dieser Zahlen. Allgemein gilt: kgV $(a, b) \leq a \cdot b$. Im obigen Beispiel ist das Produkt von 6, 7 und 8 336.

3 Bruchzahlen

Wir haben uns bisher mit natürlichen Zahlen beschäftigt. Dabei ging es immer um ganze Dinge: ein ganzer Apfel, ein ganzes Schaf, eine ganze Torte usw. Im Alltag haben wir es aber sehr oft mit Teilen eines Ganzen zu tun: Ein Tortenstück ist ein Teil einer Torte, ein halber Apfel ist ein Teil eines Apfels.

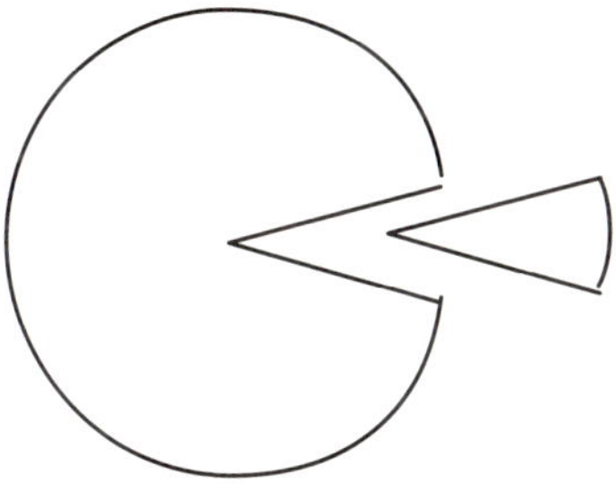

Diese Aufteilung eines Ganzen lässt sich mithilfe der Rechenarten Division und Multiplikation mathematisch beschreiben.

Wenn wir einen Apfel auf vier Personen verteilen, erhält jeder ein Viertel:

$$1 : 4 = \frac{1}{4},$$

Wenn wir eine Torte in 16 gleiche Stücke schneiden, dann ist ein Stück ein Sechzehntel der ganzen Torte. Man sagt auch »ein Stück von 16« und schreibt

$$1 : 16 = \frac{1}{16}.$$

Drei Stücke dieser Torte sind natürlich drei Sechzehntel,

$$3 \cdot \frac{1}{16} = \frac{3}{16}.$$

> $\frac{1}{4}$, $\frac{1}{16}$ und $\frac{3}{16}$ sind Bruchzahlen oder kurz Brüche.
> Ein Bruch entsteht durch Zerlegen eines Ganzen in gleiche Teile.

Den Strich nennt man **Bruchstrich**. Über dem Bruchstrich steht der **Zähler**, darunter steht der **Nenner**.

Der Zähler gibt die Anzahl der gleich großen Teile an, der Nenner den Anteil eines Stücks am Ganzen.
Je größer der Nenner, desto kleiner wird das einzelne Stück.

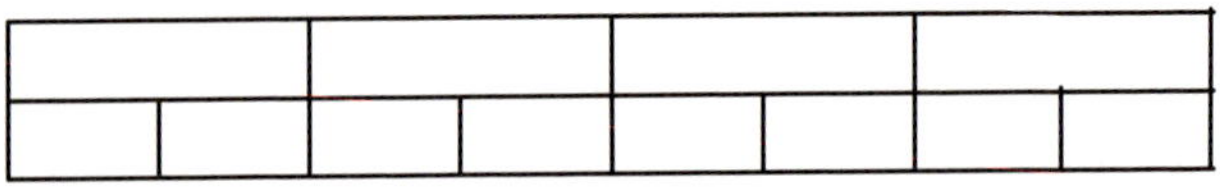

Zum Aussprechen dieser Bruchzahlen wird an die Zahl im Nenner die Endung -tel oder -stel angehängt, z.B. Vier**tel**, Zehn**tel**, Zwanzig**stel**, Hundert**stel**. Ausnahmen sind Halbe, Drittel, Siebtel und Achtel.

3.1 Brüche auf dem Zahlenstrahl

Wie die natürlichen Zahlen lassen sich auch die Brüche auf dem Zahlenstrahl darstellen. Zur Darstellung des Bruches $\frac{1}{4}$ teilt man die Strecke zwischen den Punkten 0 und 1 in vier gleiche Teile. Wir nehmen die Länge der Strecke zwischen dem Punkt 0 und dem Punkt der jeweiligen Bruchzahl als Maß für den Wert des Bruches.

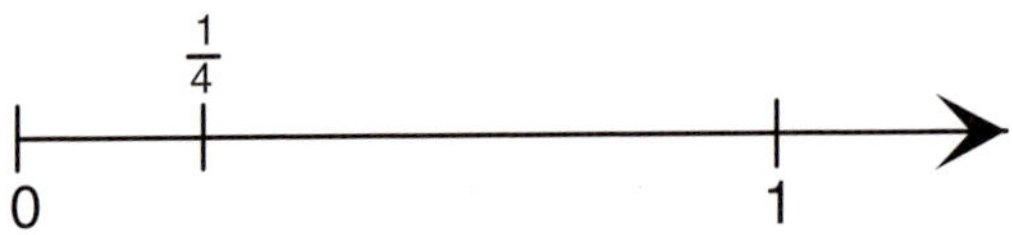

Wir bilden nun eine Folge von Brüchen, bei denen der Nenner immer größer wird:

$\frac{1}{2}, \frac{1}{4}, \frac{1}{5}, \frac{1}{10}$.

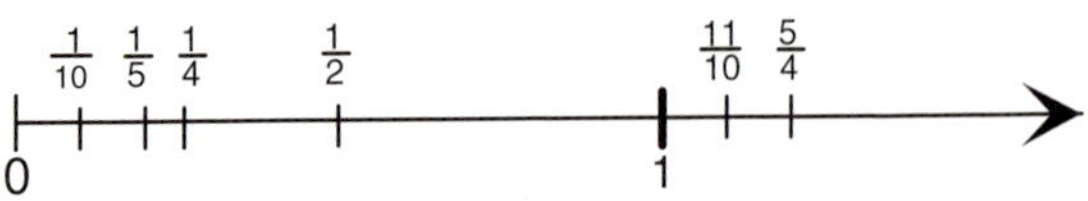

Wir stellen fest, dass bei größer werdendem Nenner die Teile immer kleiner werden und damit auch der Wert des Bruchs kleiner wird. Die entsprechenden Bildpunkte der Bruchzahlen rücken näher an einen bestimmten Punkt heran, ohne ihn aber je zu erreichen. Sie häufen sich bei diesem Punkt. In diesem Fall ist es die Zahl 0.

Bei den natürlichen Zahlen gab es für jede Zahl einen festen Nachfolger und mit Ausnahme der 1 einen Vorgänger. Diese Eigenschaft haben wir bei den Brüchen nicht. Es ist gleichgültig, wie nahe ein Bruch zu einer bestimmten Zahl liegt, wir können immer einen anderen Bruch finden, der noch näher liegt. Wenn wir uns z. B. der Zahl 0 auf $\frac{1}{100}$ genähert haben, dann liegt $\frac{1}{1000}$ noch näher. Zwischen 0 und $\frac{1}{1000}$ liegt $\frac{1}{10\,000}$, $\frac{1}{100\,000}$ usw. Zwischen $\frac{1}{2}$ und $\frac{1}{3}$ liegen z. B. $\frac{2}{5}$, $\frac{9}{20}$, $\frac{49}{100}$ usw.
Jede Bruchzahl kann Häufungspunkt sein.

Es gibt also bei den Bruchzahlen keinen bestimmten Vorgänger oder Nachfolger. Zwischen je zwei Brüchen können wir immer noch unendlich viele andere Brüche finden. Man sagt dazu, die Bruchzahlen liegen dicht.

3.2 Stammbrüche, echte und unechte Brüche, Scheinbrüche

Einen Bruch mit dem Zähler 1 nennt man **Stammbruch.**

$\frac{1}{2}$, $\frac{1}{3}$, $\frac{1}{4}$, $\frac{1}{10}$, $\frac{1}{529}$ usw. sind also Stammbrüche, $\frac{3}{4}$, $\frac{5}{8}$, $\frac{321}{323}$ usw. nicht.
Brüche, deren Zähler kleiner ist als der Nenner, heißen **echte Brüche.** Sie ergeben kein Ganzes.
$\frac{1}{4}$, $\frac{3}{4}$, $\frac{4}{12}$, $\frac{721}{843}$ usw. sind echte Brüche. Natürlich sind alle Stammbrüche auch echte Brüche.

Brüche, deren Zähler nicht kleiner ist als der Nenner, d. h. alle Brüche, die keine echten Brüche sind, heißen **unechte Brüche.**

$\frac{4}{3}, \frac{15}{2}, \frac{60}{60}$ und $\frac{793}{220}$ z. B. sind unechte Brüche.

Brüche, deren Zähler ein Vielfaches des Nenners ist, heißen **Scheinbrüche** oder **scheinbare Brüche**. Sie ergeben ganze Zahlen.

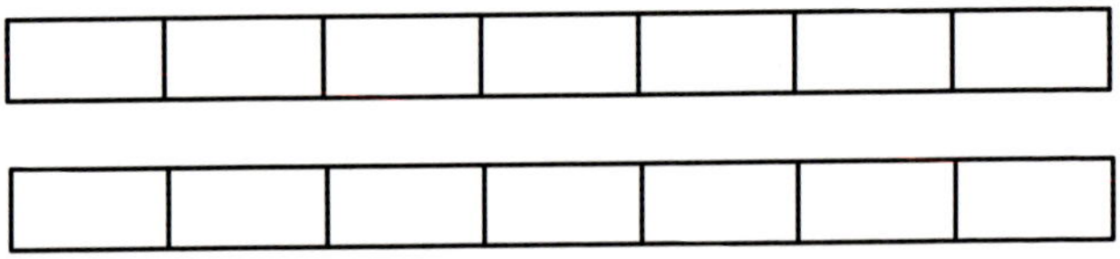

$$\frac{14}{7} = 2$$

$\frac{4}{4}, \frac{8}{4}, \frac{16}{8}$ und $\frac{240}{80}$ sind Scheinbrüche. Speziell sind auch alle Brüche mit dem Nenner 1 wie z. B. $\frac{5}{1}$ Scheinbrüche. Die Umwandlung in ganze Zahlen ist sehr einfach: $\frac{4}{4} = 4 : 4 = 1$, $\frac{8}{4} = 8 : 4 = 2$, $\frac{16}{8} = 16 : 8 = 2$, $\frac{240}{80} = 240 : 80 = 3$, $\frac{25}{1} = 25 : 1 = 25$.

Alle Scheinbrüche sind unechte Brüche.

Durch die Begriffe echter und unechter Bruch wird der Zahlenstrahl aufgeteilt in die beiden Bereiche von 0 bis 1 und von 1 bis Unendlich: Links von der 1 befinden sich die echten Brüche, bei der 1 und rechts davon die unechten.

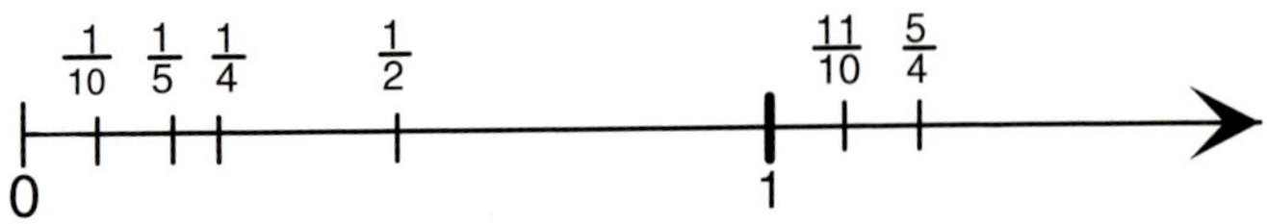

3.3 Erweitern und Kürzen

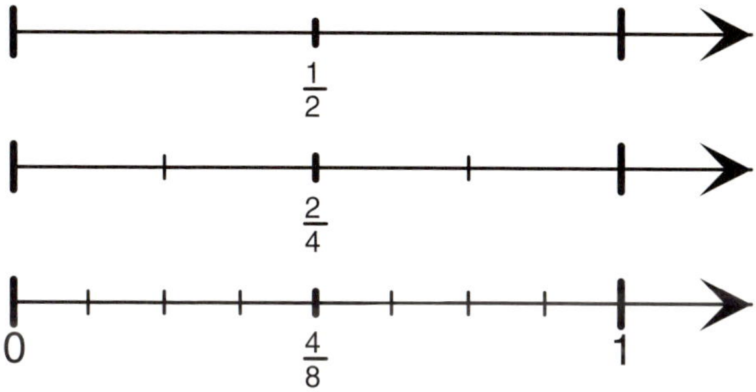

Es ist anschaulich klar, dass man den Wert eines Bruchs wie z. B. $\frac{1}{2}$ auch durch andere Brüche darstellen kann: $\frac{2}{4}, \frac{4}{8}, \frac{8}{16}$ usw. Durch schrittweises Halbieren der Teile erhält man bei jedem Schritt die doppelte Anzahl. Wenn man im ersten Schritt durch drei teilt, erhält man $\frac{3}{6}, \frac{6}{12}, \frac{12}{24}$ usw. Wenn man auch im zweiten Schritt durch drei teilt, ergibt das $\frac{9}{18}$. Fünf Teile im ersten Schritt ergibt $\frac{5}{10}, \frac{10}{20}$ usw.

Durch Variation dieses Verfahrens erhält man die Brüche
$\frac{1}{2}, \frac{2}{4}, \frac{3}{6}, \frac{4}{8}, \frac{5}{10}, \frac{6}{12} \ldots$ Diese lassen sich auch schreiben als
$\frac{1 \cdot 1}{1 \cdot 2}, \frac{2 \cdot 1}{2 \cdot 2}, \frac{3 \cdot 1}{3 \cdot 2}, \frac{4 \cdot 1}{4 \cdot 2}, \frac{5 \cdot 1}{5 \cdot 2}$ usw., also $\frac{1}{2} = \frac{k \cdot 1}{k \cdot 2}$ mit $k \in \mathbb{N}$.

Allgemein kann man schreiben: $\frac{a}{b} = \frac{k \cdot a}{k \cdot b}$ mit $a \in \mathbb{N}_0$; $b, k \in \mathbb{N}$.
Der Bruch $\frac{a}{b}$ wurde mit k erweitert.

> Ein Bruch wird erweitert, indem man Zähler und Nenner mit der gleichen Zahl multipliziert. Der Wert des Bruchs bleibt dabei erhalten.

Diese Zahl darf natürlich nicht Null sein, da sonst der gesamte Nenner Null wäre und die Division durch Null ist bekanntlich nicht erlaubt.

Als Beispiel erweitern wir den Bruch $\frac{2}{3}$ mit 5:

$$\frac{2}{3} = \frac{5 \cdot 2}{5 \cdot 3} = \frac{10}{15}$$

Die Umkehrung des Erweiterns nennt man **Kürzen**. Wenn Zähler und Nenner eines Bruchs nicht teilerfremd sind, sondern einen gemeinsamen Faktor $k \neq 1$ haben, können wir den Bruch schreiben als $\frac{k \cdot a}{k \cdot b}$ mit $a \in \mathbb{N}_0$; $b, k \in \mathbb{N}$.

Dieser Bruch hat aber den gleichen Wert wie der Bruch $\frac{a}{b}$.

> Ein Bruch wird gekürzt, indem man Zähler und Nenner durch die gleiche Zahl dividiert. Der Wert des Bruchs ändert sich dabei nicht.

Diese Zahl darf natürlich wieder nicht Null sein. Bei Division durch Eins würde sich zudem keine Veränderung bei Zähler und Nenner ergeben, also ist auch die Division durch Eins nicht sinnvoll.

Beispiele:

a) $\frac{6}{18} = \frac{3 \cdot 2}{3 \cdot 6} = \frac{2}{6}$

b) $\frac{6}{18} = \frac{6 \cdot 1}{6 \cdot 3} = \frac{1}{3}$

c) $\frac{6}{21} = \frac{3 \cdot 2}{3 \cdot 7} = \frac{2}{7}$

Die Beispiele a) und b) zeigen, dass man beim gleichen Bruch durch Kürzen zu unterschiedlichen Ergebnissen kommen kann. Allerdings lässt sich das Ergebnis von a) noch einmal kürzen mit 2, sodass man am Ende ebenfalls $\frac{2 \cdot 1}{2 \cdot 3} = \frac{1}{3}$ erhält. Die Ergebnisse von b) und c) können nicht weiter gekürzt werden.

> Ein Bruch, der sich nicht weiter kürzen lässt, bei dem also Zähler und Nenner teilerfremd sind, heißt vollständig gekürzt. Das ist die **Grundform** des Bruchs.

Aus einem Bruch $\frac{a}{b}$ erhält man sofort die Grundform, wenn man mit dem ggT (a, b) kürzt, wie in Beispiel b) und c).

> Brüche, die den gleichen vollständig gekürzten Bruch ergeben, haben den gleichen Wert.

So haben z.B. $\frac{6}{9}$, $\frac{10}{15}$ und $\frac{50}{75}$ den gleichen Wert, denn alle lassen sich kürzen zu $\frac{2}{3}$.

Weiter oben haben wir Scheinbrüche in ganze Zahlen umgewandelt. Dieses Verfahren funktioniert auch umgekehrt. Wir können eine ganze Zahl in einen Bruch mit einem bestimmten Nenner umwandeln. Anschaulich schreiben wir die Zahl zuerst als Bruch mit dem Nenner 1, dann erweitern wir den Bruch so, dass wir den gewünschten Nenner erhalten. Wollen wir z.B. die Zahl 20 als Bruch mit dem Nenner 4, so schreiben wir:

$$20 = \frac{20}{1} = \frac{4 \cdot 20}{4 \cdot 1} = \frac{80}{4}$$

Das gleiche Ergebnis erhalten wir, wenn wir einfach die Zahl mit dem gewünschten Nenner multiplizieren und diesen Nenner unter das Produkt setzen.

3.4 Gleichnamige Brüche

> Brüche, die den gleichen Nenner besitzen, heißen gleichnamig.

Die Brüche $\frac{3}{20}$, $\frac{7}{20}$, $\frac{20}{20}$ und $\frac{35}{20}$ sind gleichnamig, da sie alle den Nenner 20 haben.

Brüche, die nicht gleichnamig sind, heißen **ungleichnamig**.

Wenn bei zwei Brüchen der eine Nenner ein Vielfaches des anderen Nenners ist, so kann man die beiden Brüche durch Erweitern oder Kürzen eines der Brüche gleichnamig machen.

Bei $\frac{12}{9}$ und $\frac{2}{3}$ kann man den ersten Bruch kürzen zu $\frac{4}{3}$,
bei $\frac{7}{4}$ und $\frac{3}{2}$ können wir den zweiten Bruch mit 2 erweitern zu $\frac{6}{4}$.

Funktioniert das Gleichnamigmachen durch Kürzen oder Erweitern auf diese Art nicht, dann suchen wir den so genannten **Hauptnenner**.

Der Hauptnenner von mehreren Brüchen ist das kleinste gemeinsame Vielfache (kgV) der einzelnen Nenner.

Nehmen wir als Beispiel die Brüche $\frac{2}{3}$, $\frac{5}{6}$ und $\frac{4}{9}$. Die Brüche 1 und 2 bzw. 1 und 3 wären leicht gleichnamig zu machen durch Erweitern, aber für alle drei zusammen ergibt sich ein Problem. Wir suchen also das kleinste gemeinsame Vielfache aller drei Nenner:

kgV(3, 6, 9) = 18

Nun erweitern wir den ersten Bruch mit 18 : 3 = 6, den zweiten mit 18 : 6 = 3 und den letzten mit 18 : 9 = 2. Wir erhalten dann:

$$\frac{6 \cdot 2}{6 \cdot 3} = \frac{12}{18}, \frac{3 \cdot 5}{3 \cdot 6} = \frac{15}{18} \text{ und } \frac{2 \cdot 4}{2 \cdot 9} = \frac{8}{18}$$

3.5 Größenvergleich von Brüchen

Weiter oben haben wir schon festgestellt, dass zwei Brüche den gleichen Wert haben, wenn sie denselben vollständig gekürzten Bruch ergeben, d.h., wenn ihre Grundform gleich ist, z.B. $\frac{2}{3}$ und $\frac{4}{6}$.

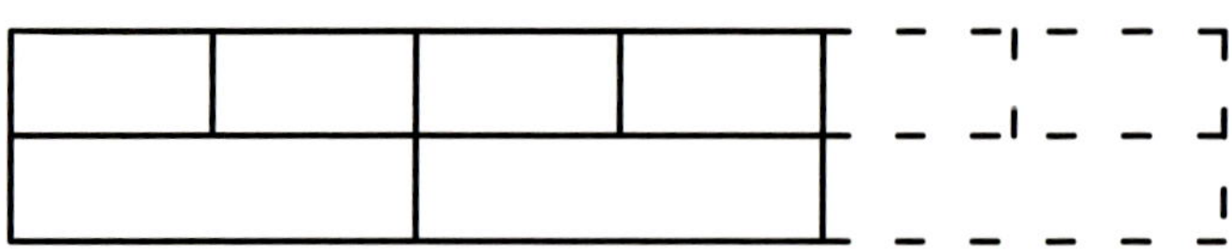

Wenn das nicht der Fall ist, können wir nachschauen, ob die Zähler gleich sind. Es ist anschaulich klar, dass bei gleicher Anzahl die Größe des Einzelstücks, also die Größe des Nenners entscheidend ist. So ergeben z.B. drei große Stücke zusammen mehr als drei kleine.

Bei gleichem Zähler hat der Bruch mit dem kleineren Nenner den größeren Wert: $\frac{3}{3} > \frac{3}{6}$.

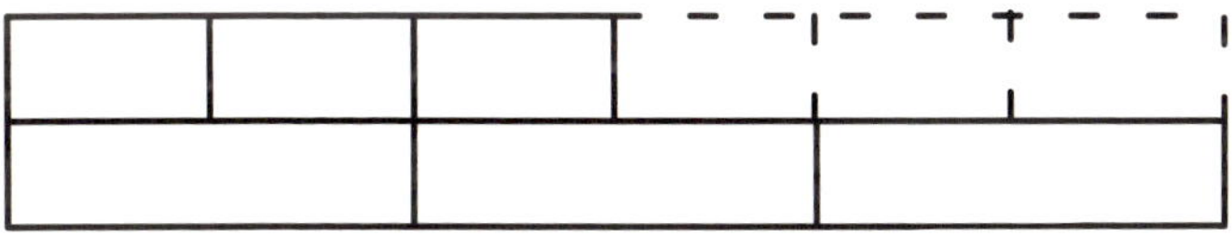

Sind die Zähler unterschiedlich, müssen wir die Brüche gleichnamig machen, falls sie noch nicht denselben Nenner haben. Es ist wieder einleuchtend, dass bei gleicher Größe der Stücke die Anzahl, also der Zähler entscheidet.

Bei gleichnamigen Brüchen hat der mit dem größeren Zähler den größeren Wert.

$\frac{3}{5} > \frac{2}{5}$

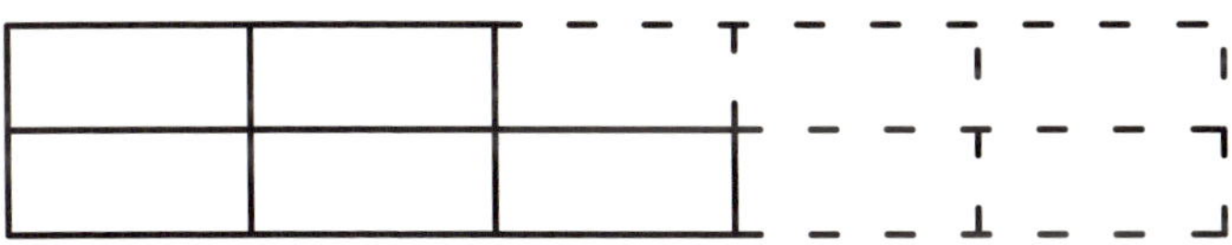

3.6 Rechnen mit Brüchen

Addition von Brüchen und gemischten Zahlen

Zuerst sehen wir uns die Addition eines Bruchs zu einer ganzen Zahl an, z.B. $3 + \frac{1}{4}$. Das ist besonders einfach, denn in diesem Fall kann man den Bruch hinter die Zahl schreiben und das Pluszeichen weglassen, hier ist das $3\,\frac{1}{4}$.

> Ein solches Gebilde, das aus einer ganzen Zahl und einem Bruch besteht, nennt man gemischte Zahl.

Es besteht ein enger Zusammenhang zwischen unechten Brüchen, gemischten Zahlen und der Division mit Rest:

Wir können jeden unechten Bruch in eine gemischte Zahl umwandeln, indem wir die zum Bruch gehörende Rechenoperation als Division mit Rest durchführen und den Rest als Bruchteil eines Ganzen schreiben.

Beispiele:

$\frac{29}{5} = 29 : 5 = 5$ Rest 4. Das ist $5 + \frac{4}{5}$, also $5\frac{4}{5}$

$\frac{7}{4} = 7 : 4 = 1\frac{3}{4}$

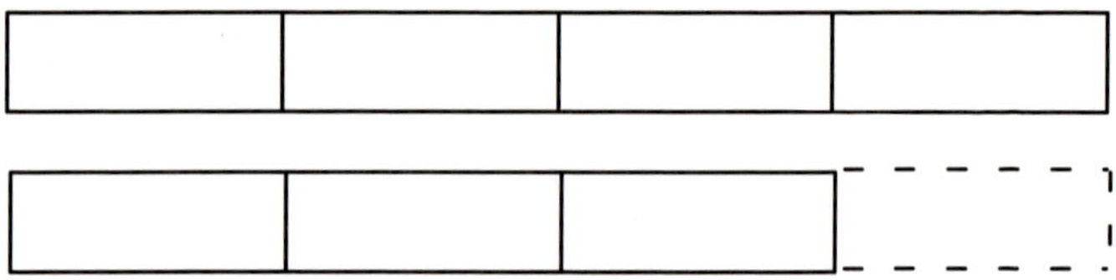

$\frac{7}{4} = 1\frac{3}{4}$

Da die Rechenart Addition auch bei Brüchen kommutativ ist, dürfen wir für den Fall, dass der Bruch der erste Summand ist, einfach die Summanden vertauschen und können so auch z. B. die Aufgabe $\frac{3}{7} + 2$ rechnen:

$\frac{3}{7} + 2 = 2 + \frac{3}{7} = 2\frac{3}{7}$

Nun kommen wir zu dem Fall, dass beide Summanden Brüche sind. Hier müssen wir beachten, dass man nur gleichartige Dinge zusammenzählen kann. Gleichartig bedeutet bei Brüchen gleichnamig. Die obige Abbildung macht auch plausibel, dass dann z. B. gilt: $\frac{4}{4} + \frac{3}{4} = \frac{7}{4}$.

Allgemein gilt für die Addition von Brüchen:

Gleichnamige Brüche werden addiert, indem man die Zähler addiert und den Nenner beibehält.

Sind zwei Brüche nicht gleichnamig, so bestimmen wir ihren Hauptnenner und erweitern entsprechend. Das Ergebnis der Summe kann dann eventuell wieder gekürzt werden.

Beispiele:

a) $\frac{1}{2} + \frac{1}{3}$. Hauptnenner ist kgV(2, 3) = 6.

Erweitern der beiden Brüche ergibt: $\frac{3}{6} + \frac{2}{6} = \frac{5}{6}$

b) $\frac{3}{7} + \frac{8}{10}$. Um mit möglichst kleinen Zahlen arbeiten zu können, ist es hier sinnvoll, den zweiten Summanden zuerst in die Grundform zu bringen: $\frac{8}{10} = \frac{4}{5}$

Nun ist der Hauptnenner 35: $\frac{15}{35} + \frac{28}{35} = \frac{43}{35} = 1\frac{8}{35}$

Mithilfe der Addition von Brüchen können wir nun auch gemischte Zahlen in unechte Brüche umwandeln. Dazu wandeln wir die ganze Zahl in einen Scheinbruch mit dem passenden Nenner um und addieren dazu den Bruch.

Beispiele:

a) $2\frac{3}{5} = \frac{10}{5} + \frac{3}{5} = \frac{13}{5}$

b) $5\frac{13}{15} = \frac{75}{15} + \frac{13}{15} = \frac{88}{15}$

Für die Addition von zwei gemischten Zahlen gibt es zwei Möglichkeiten:

1) Umwandlung beider Zahlen in unechte Brüche, Gleichnamigmachen und Addition, anschließend Rückumwandlung in eine gemischte Zahl.

2) Gleichnamigmachen der Brüche und Addition, Umwandlung in eine gemischte Zahl. Zum ganzzahligen Teil addieren wir die ursprünglichen ganzen Zahlen.

Als Beispiel für beide Wege nehmen wir die Zahlen $5\frac{2}{3}$ und $2\frac{3}{5}$.

1) $5\frac{2}{3} = \frac{17}{3}$, $2\frac{3}{5} = \frac{13}{5}$. Hauptnenner ist 15. Somit haben wir:

$$\frac{85}{15} + \frac{39}{15} = \frac{124}{15} = 8\,\frac{4}{15}$$

2) Hauptnenner von $\frac{2}{3}$ und $\frac{3}{5}$ ist 15, also $\frac{10}{15} + \frac{9}{15} = \frac{19}{15} = 1\,\frac{4}{15}$.

$$1\,\frac{4}{15} + 5 + 2 = 8\,\frac{4}{15}$$

Der zweite Weg ist oft angenehmer, da man mit kleineren Bruchzahlen rechnen kann.

Die Addition einer ganzen Zahl zu einer gemischten Zahl bedarf keiner Erklärung. Um einen Bruch zu einer gemischten Zahl zu addieren, fassen wir den Bruch als gemischte Zahl mit dem ganzzahligen Teil 0, also z.B. $\frac{5}{6} = 0\,\frac{5}{6}$.

Subtraktion von Brüchen und gemischten Zahlen
Ebenso wie bei den natürlichen Zahlen müssen wir vorläufig darauf achten, dass der Minuend größer ist als der Subtrahend. Da die Subtraktion die Umkehrung der Addition ist, müssen auch hier Minuend und Subtrahend gleichnamig sein.
Dann gilt:

Ein Bruch wird von einem gleichnamigen anderen Bruch subtrahiert, indem man den Zähler des Subtrahenden vom Zähler des Minuenden subtrahiert und den Nenner beibehält.

Beispiel:

$$\frac{5}{7} - \frac{3}{7} = \frac{(5-3)}{7} = \frac{2}{7}$$

Um einen Bruch von einer gemischten Zahl zu subtrahieren, wenn der Subtrahend größer ist als der Bruch des Minuenden, haben wir zwei Möglichkeiten:

1) Den kompletten Minuenden in einen unechten Bruch umwandeln, gleichnamig machen, subtrahieren und bei Bedarf das Ergebnis wieder umwandeln.

2) Wir machen den Bruch des Minuenden mit dem Subtrahenden gleichnamig und wandeln nur einen Teil der ganzen Zahl des Minuenden in einen Bruch um, und zwar so viel, dass dieser größer ist als der Bruch des Subtrahenden. Danach können wir die ganzen Zahlen und die Brüche getrennt subtrahieren.

Beispiel:

1) $5\frac{3}{8} - 2\frac{4}{5} = \frac{43}{8} - \frac{14}{5} = \frac{215}{40} - \frac{112}{40} = \frac{103}{40} = 2\frac{23}{40}$

2) $5\frac{3}{8} - 2\frac{4}{5} = 5\frac{15}{40} - 2\frac{32}{40} = 4\frac{55}{40} - 2\frac{32}{40} = 2\frac{23}{40}$

Die Subtraktion eines Bruches von einer natürlichen Zahl funktioniert auch wieder durch Umwandlung der ganzen Zahl entweder in einen Scheinbruch oder in eine gemischte Zahl mit jeweils passendem Nenner.

Beispiel:

1) $4 - \frac{2}{3} = \frac{12}{3} - \frac{2}{3} = \frac{10}{3} = 3\frac{1}{3}$

2) $4 - \frac{2}{3} = 3\frac{3}{3} - \frac{2}{3} = 3\frac{1}{3}$

Entsprechend verfahren wir im umgekehrten Fall: Bruch minus natürliche Zahl.

Beispiel:

$$\frac{35}{8} - 2 = \frac{35}{8} - \frac{16}{8} = \frac{19}{8} = 2\frac{3}{8}$$

Multiplikation

Die Multiplikation von Brüchen ist die einfachste Rechenart, da wir dazu nichts beachten müssen.

Zwei Brüche werden multipliziert, indem man Zähler mit Zähler und Nenner mit Nenner multipliziert.

Normalerweise empfiehlt es sich, Zähler und Nenner als Produkte mit einem einzigen Bruchstrich zu schreiben. Bevor wir nun die Multiplikationen ausführen, kürzen wir nach Möglichkeit die Faktoren.

Beispiel:

$$\frac{4}{5} \cdot \frac{3}{8} = \frac{4 \cdot 3}{5 \cdot 8} = \frac{\overset{1}{\cancel{4}} \cdot 3}{5 \cdot \underset{2}{\cancel{8}}} = \frac{1 \cdot 3}{5 \cdot 2} = \frac{3}{10}$$

Was hier sehr ausführlich aufgeschrieben ist, lässt sich normalerweise viel kürzer darstellen:

$$\frac{8}{9} \cdot \frac{3}{4} = \frac{\overset{2}{\cancel{8}} \cdot \overset{1}{\cancel{3}}}{\underset{3}{\cancel{9}} \cdot \underset{1}{\cancel{4}}} = \frac{2}{3}$$

Auf diese Art kann man natürlich nicht nur zwei, sondern beliebig viele Brüche miteinander multiplizieren.

Wenn die Zahlen in Zähler und Nenner größer sind, empfiehlt es sich, sie in ihrer Primfaktorenzerlegung aufzuschreiben, da man dann ganz leicht sehen kann, welche Faktoren gekürzt werden können.

Beispiel:

$$\frac{3150 \cdot 7}{17325 \cdot 13} = \frac{2 \cdot \cancel{3} \cdot \cancel{3} \cdot \cancel{5} \cdot \cancel{5} \cdot \cancel{7} \cdot 7}{\cancel{3} \cdot \cancel{3} \cdot \cancel{5} \cdot \cancel{5} \cdot \cancel{7} \cdot 11 \cdot 13} = \frac{2 \cdot 7}{11 \cdot 13} = \frac{14}{143}$$

Eine ganze Zahl wird mit einem Bruch multipliziert, indem man sie mit dem Zähler multipliziert und den Nenner beibehält.

$\frac{a}{b} \cdot c = \frac{ac}{b}$ für $a, c \in \mathbb{N}_0$; $b \in \mathbb{N}$.

Beispiel:

$$5 \cdot \frac{2}{3} = \frac{5 \cdot 2}{3} = \frac{10}{3} = 3\,\frac{1}{3}$$

Man formuliert in diesem Fall auch »$\frac{2}{3}$ von 5«. Dieses »von« erfordert also eine Multiplikation, wenn es nicht im Zusammenhang mit dem Wort »subtrahieren« als »subtrahieren von …« gebraucht wird.

Gemischte Zahlen können vor einer Multiplikation in Brüche umgewandelt werden.

Beispiele:

a) $2\,\frac{3}{4} \cdot \frac{4}{5} = \frac{11}{4} \cdot \frac{4}{5} = \frac{11 \cdot 4}{4 \cdot 5} = \frac{11}{5} = 2\,\frac{1}{5}$

b) $4\frac{2}{3} \cdot 2\frac{3}{8} = \frac{14}{3} \cdot \frac{19}{8} = \frac{7\,\cancel{14} \cdot 19}{3 \cdot \cancel{8}\,4} = \frac{133}{12} = 11\,\frac{1}{12}$

Division

Den Kehrbruch oder Kehrwert eines Bruchs erhalten wir, wenn wir Zähler und Nenner des Bruchs vertauschen. Der Kehrwert von $\frac{2}{3}$ ist $\frac{3}{2}$.

Ein Fremdwort für Kehrwert ist »reziproker Wert«.

Durch einen Bruch wird dividiert, indem man mit seinem Kehrwert (Kehrbruch) multipliziert.

Beispiele:

a) $\frac{2}{3} : \frac{4}{5} = \frac{2}{3} \cdot \frac{5}{4} = \frac{2 \cdot 5}{3 \cdot 4} = \frac{1 \cdot 5}{3 \cdot 2} = \frac{5}{6}$

b) $\frac{10}{13} : \frac{10}{7} = \frac{10}{13} \cdot \frac{7}{10} = \frac{7}{13}$

Wenn an der Division gemischte Zahlen beteiligt sind, müssen wir sie wieder in Brüche umwandeln.

Einen Bruch können wir durch eine ganze Zahl dividieren, indem wir diese Zahl in einen Bruch mit dem Nenner 1 umwandeln und dann die bekannte Regel anwenden.

Beispiel:

$$\frac{7}{10} : 2 = \frac{7}{10} : \frac{2}{1} = \frac{7}{10} \cdot \frac{1}{2} = \frac{7}{20}$$

Dieses Ergebnis, nämlich dass die Zahl am Ende mit dem Nenner multipliziert wird, können wir als Regel formulieren:

> Ein Bruch wird durch eine ganze Zahl dividiert, indem man die Zahl mit dem Nenner multipliziert.
>
> $\frac{a}{b} : c = \frac{a}{bc}$ für $a \in \mathbb{N}_0$; $b, c \in \mathbb{N}$.

3.7 Doppelbrüche

Im Zähler und Nenner eines Bruchs können wieder Brüche stehen. Einen solchen Bruch bezeichnet man als **Doppelbruch** oder **Etagenbruch**.

Beispiele:

a) $\dfrac{\frac{1}{6}}{\frac{2}{9}}$

b) $\dfrac{3 - \frac{1}{2}}{\frac{4}{5} - \frac{2}{3}}$

c) $\dfrac{4\frac{2}{3} - \frac{2}{9}}{12}$

Diese Etagenbrüche können wir auch in Form von Klammerausdrücken schreiben und vereinfachen oder auflösen:

a) $\frac{1}{6} : \frac{2}{9} = \frac{1 \cdot 9}{6 \cdot 2} = \frac{3}{2 \cdot 2} = \frac{3}{4}$

b) $\left(3 - \frac{1}{2}\right) : \left(\frac{4}{5} - \frac{2}{3}\right) = 2\frac{1}{2} : \left(\frac{12}{15} - \frac{10}{15}\right) = \frac{5}{2} \cdot \frac{15}{2} = \frac{75}{4} = 18\frac{3}{4}$

c) $\left(4\frac{2}{3} - \frac{2}{9}\right) : 12 = \left(4\frac{6}{9} - \frac{2}{9}\right) : 12 = \frac{40}{9} : 12 = \frac{40}{9 \cdot 12} = \frac{2 \cdot 2 \cdot 2 \cdot 5}{2 \cdot 2 \cdot 3 \cdot 3 \cdot 3}$

$= \frac{10}{27}$

3.8 Einfache Terme und Gleichungen

Jetzt folgen einige Textaufgaben, die auf Terme und Gleichungen mit Bruchzahlen führen.

a) Multipliziere die Summe der Zahlen $3\frac{1}{3}$ und $\frac{2}{5}$ mit dem Quotienten aus 25 und $\frac{1}{2}$.

Auch beim Rechnen mit Brüchen gilt die Regel: Punktrechnung geht vor Strichrechnung, daher müssen in diesem Rechenausdruck Klammern gesetzt werden.

$\left(3\frac{1}{3} + \frac{2}{5}\right) \cdot \left(25 : \frac{1}{2}\right) = \left(3\frac{5}{15} + \frac{6}{15}\right) \cdot \left(25 \cdot \frac{2}{1}\right) = \frac{56}{15} \cdot 50 = \frac{56 \cdot 50}{15} =$

$\frac{2800}{15} = 186\frac{10}{15} = 186\frac{2}{3}$

b) $\frac{1}{8}$ einer Schulklasse hat Grippe, das sind vier Schüler. Wie viele Schüler sind in der Klasse?

Für die unbekannte Anzahl setzen wir die Variable *x*. »$\frac{1}{8}$ von x« schreiben wir als Produkt $\frac{1}{8} \cdot x$. Dann gilt:

$\frac{1}{8} \cdot x = 4$

$x = 4 : \frac{1}{8}$

$x = 4 \cdot 8 = 32$

Antwort: In der Klasse sind 32 Schüler.

c) Eine Regentonne ist zu $\frac{3}{4}$ mit Wasser gefüllt. Nachdem jemand Wasser verbraucht hat, ist der Wasserspiegel um $\frac{2}{5}$ der Tonnenhöhe gesunken und beträgt jetzt noch 35 cm. Wie hoch ist die Tonne?

Auch hier bezeichnen wir die unbekannte Tonnenhöhe mit *x*. Damit erhalten wir die Gleichung:

$\frac{3}{4} \cdot x - \frac{2}{5} \cdot x = 35$ cm. Ausklammern von *x* ergibt $x\left(\frac{3}{4} - \frac{2}{5}\right) = 35$ cm.

$x\left(\frac{15}{20} - \frac{8}{20}\right) = 35 \text{ cm}$

$x \cdot \frac{7}{20} = 35 \text{ cm}$

$x = 35 : \frac{7}{20} \text{ cm} = \frac{35 \cdot 20}{7} \text{ cm} = 5 \cdot 20 \text{ cm}$

$x = 100 \text{ cm}$

Antwort: Die Tonne ist 1 m hoch.

d) Rolf bekommt monatlich 20 Euro Taschengeld. Im letzten Monat hat er mindestens $\frac{2}{5}$ davon für Süßigkeiten ausgegeben. Wie viele Euro hat er mindestens »versüßt«?

Hier könnten wir auch ohne Variable auskommen, aber es wird anschaulicher, wenn wir für den gesuchten Betrag die Variable *x* setzen:

$x \geq \frac{2}{5} \cdot 20$

$x \geq \frac{2 \cdot 20}{5} = 2 \cdot 4 = 8$

$x \geq 8$

Antwort: Rolf hat mindestens 8 Euro für Süßwaren ausgegeben.

4 Dezimalbrüche

Wie wir schon wissen, rechnen wir normalerweise im Zehnersystem und in diesem System sind die Stufenzahlen 1, 10, 100, 1000 usw. Der Wert einer Ziffer in einer Zahl wird bestimmt durch die Stelle, an der sie in einer Zahl steht. Der Aufbau geht von rechts nach links: An der ersten Stelle sind es Einer, an der zweiten Zehner, an der dritten Hunderter und so weiter.

Diese Stufenzahlen setzen wir nun als Nenner in Stammbrüchen ein: $\frac{1}{10}, \frac{1}{100}, \frac{1}{1000}$ usw. Wir setzen rechts neben der Einerstelle als Trennungszeichen ein Komma und sagen, dass die erste Stelle rechts von diesem Komma den Wert $\frac{1}{10}$ hat: $0{,}1 = \frac{1}{10}$.

Die nächste Stelle hat den Wert Hundertstel, also ist $0{,}01 = \frac{1}{100}$.

Diese Art von Zahlen nennen wir Dezimalzahlen oder Dezimalbrüche.

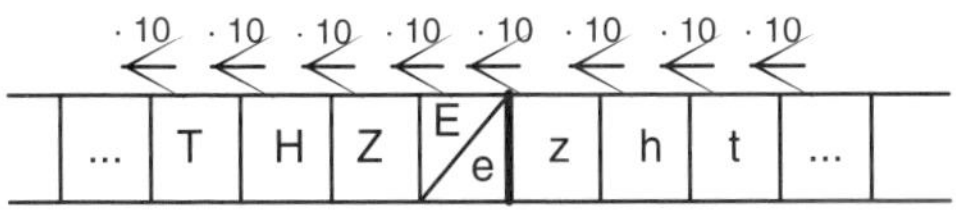

Wir haben also unser System aus Einern (E), Zehnern (Z), Hundertern (H), Tausendern (T) usw. erweitert um Zehntel (z), Hundertstel (h), Tausendstel (t) usw. Die Eintel (e), die ja keine echten Brüche darstellen und eigentlich Einer sind, bilden ein Verbindungsglied zwischen den ganzen Zahlen und den echten Brüchen.

Die Anzahl der Ziffern hinter dem Komma nennt man oft kurz Kommastellen.
Der Dezimalbruch 1,523 hat drei Kommastellen.

Aus dem Alltag ist bekannt, dass die Länge *ein Meter* aufgeteilt werden kann in 100 Zentimeter. Das bedeutet:

$1 \text{ cm} = \frac{1}{100} \text{ m} = 0{,}01 \text{ m}$

Entsprechend gilt:

$$5 \text{ cm} = \frac{5}{100} \text{ m} = 0{,}05 \text{ m}$$

$$70 \text{ cm} = \frac{70}{100} \text{ m} = \frac{7}{10} \text{ m} = 0{,}7 \text{ m}$$

$$1 \text{ m } 20 \text{ cm} = 1\frac{20}{100} \text{ m} = 1{,}2 \text{ m}$$

Da wir die Dezimalzahlen mit Brüchen identifizieren können, können wir sie auch erweitern und kürzen:

$$\frac{1}{10} = \frac{10}{100} = \frac{100}{1000}$$

Daher gilt auch:

$0{,}1 = 0{,}10 = 0{,}100$

Das Anhängen einer Null hinter der letzten Stelle nach dem Komma bedeutet eine Erweiterung der Dezimalzahl mit 10. Das Weglassen einer Null am Ende hinter dem Komma bedeutet Kürzen mit 10. Der Wert der Zahl wird dadurch nicht verändert.

Die Form, bei der hinter dem Komma am Ende keine Nullen stehen, entspricht der Grundform der Brüche.

Die Anzahl der Stellen hinter dem Komma entspricht der Anzahl der Nullen bei der entsprechenden Stufenzahl.

Beispiel: $0{,}001 = \frac{1}{1000}$

Natürliche Zahlen können durch Anhängen eines Kommas und einer Null hinter der Einerstelle in Dezimalzahlen umgewandelt werden.
Beispiel:

$15 = 15{,}0$

4.1 Addition und Subtraktion von Dezimalbrüchen

Zur Addition und Subtraktion von Dezimalbrüchen schreiben wir die Zahlen so, dass die Kommas untereinander stehen. Falls die Stellenzahl nach dem Komma nicht übereinstimmt, erweitern wir die kürzere Zahl so lange durch Anhängen von Nullen, bis überall gleich viele Nachkommastellen sind. Nun können wir mit ihnen genauso rechnen wie mit den natürlichen Zahlen.

Beispiele:

$$\begin{array}{r} 9{,}25 \\ +\,13{,}40 \\ \hline 22{,}65 \end{array} \qquad \begin{array}{r} 187{,}200 \\ -\;\;12{,}719 \\ \hline 174{,}481 \end{array}$$

Beim Subtrahieren darf der Minuend nicht kleiner sein als der Subtrahend.

4.2 Multiplikation von Dezimalbrüchen

Zuerst betrachten wir die Multiplikation einer Dezimalzahl mit einer Stufenzahl des Zehnersystems. Als Beispiel nehmen wir $0{,}01 \cdot 10$:

$$0{,}01 = \frac{1}{100}$$

$$\frac{1}{100} \cdot 10 = \frac{10}{100} = \frac{1}{10} = 0{,}1$$

> Die Multiplikation mit den Stufenzahlen 10, 100, 1000 usw. entspricht einer Verschiebung des Kommas nach rechts um so viele Stellen, wie die entsprechende Stufenzahl Nullen hat.

Beispiel:

$1{,}335 \cdot 100 = 133{,}5$

Die Multiplikation von zwei Dezimalbrüchen kann an einem Beispiel klargemacht werden:

$$0{,}5 \cdot 0{,}07 = \frac{5}{10} \cdot \frac{7}{100} = \frac{5 \cdot 7}{10 \cdot 100} = \frac{35}{1000} = 0{,}035$$

Das Produkt hat so viele Kommastellen wie die beiden Faktoren zusammen.

Ein weiteres Beispiel:

$0{,}05 \cdot 10{,}4$

Wir berechnen $5 \cdot 104 = 520$.
Das Produkt muss drei Kommastellen haben. Da aber eine Zahl nicht mit einem Komma beginnen kann, setzen wir vor das Komma eine Null, also $0{,}05 \cdot 10{,}4 = 0{,}520$.
Dieses Ergebnis kann gekürzt werden zu 0,52.

Die Multiplikation einer Dezimalzahl mit einer natürlichen Zahl funktioniert genau gleich, wie die folgende Rechnung zeigt:

$$1{,}25 \cdot 20 = \frac{125}{100} \cdot \frac{20}{1} = \frac{2500}{100} = 25{,}00$$

Das Produkt hat 2 + 0 Kommastellen.
Nullen hinter dem Komma am Ende einer Zahl können weggelassen werden, daher ist das Ergebnis die natürliche Zahl 25.

Ein Problem haben wir im folgenden Beispiel:

$0{,}3 \cdot 0{,}002$
$3 \cdot 2 = 6$

Wir müssten nun vier Kommastellen abzählen, haben aber nur eine Stelle zur Verfügung. In einem solchen Fall ergänzen wir vor der Zahl so viele Nullen, wie benötigt werden, damit wir das Komma setzen können und dass vor dem Komma noch eine Null steht: 0,0006

Insgesamt gilt für die Multiplikation von Dezimalbrüchen die Regel:

Wir multiplizieren zwei Dezimalzahlen miteinander, indem wir die Zahlen ohne Rücksicht auf die Kommas miteinander multiplizieren und dann das Komma so setzen, dass das Ergebnis so viele Kommastellen hat wie die beiden Ausgangszahlen zusammen. Wenn die Stellenzahl zum Setzen des Kommas nicht ausreicht, wird am Anfang der Zahl eine entsprechende Anzahl von Nullen ergänzt.
Für die Multiplikation einer Dezimalzahl mit einer natürlichen Zahl kann man die natürliche Zahl als Dezimalzahl ohne Kommastellen betrachten.

Die bisherigen Beispiele konnten alle im Kopf gerechnet werden. Nun folgt noch ein schriftliches Beispiel:

```
12,9 · 3,14
-----------
   38 7
    1 29
      516
   ------
   40,506
```

4.3 Division von Dezimalbrüchen

Zuerst betrachten wir wieder den einfachsten Fall, nämlich die Division einer Dezimalzahl durch eine Stufenzahl.

Beispiel:

$$0{,}3 : 10 = \frac{3}{10} \cdot \frac{1}{10} = \frac{3}{100} = 0{,}03$$

Wir verschieben also das Komma um eine Stelle nach links und ergänzen eine Null vor dem Komma.

> Die Division durch die Stufenzahlen 10, 100, 1000 usw. entspricht einer Verschiebung des Kommas nach links um so viele Stellen, wie die entsprechende Stufenzahl Nullen hat.

Für die Division einer Dezimalzahl durch eine natürliche Zahl betrachten wir folgendes Beispiel:

```
6,560 : 5 = 1,312
5
-
1 5
1 5
---
  06
   5
  --
   10
   10
   --
    0
```

Wir dividieren eine Dezimalzahl durch eine natürliche Zahl, indem wir eine ganz normale Divisionsrechnung durchführen. An der Stelle, bei der wir das Komma überschreiten, setzen wir auch beim Ergebnis ein Komma. Nach Bedarf können wir beim Dividenden nach dem Komma am Ende beliebig viele Nullen ergänzen.

Für die Division einer Zahl durch eine Dezimalzahl erweitern wir Dividend und Divisor durch Verschiebung der Kommas so, dass der Divisor zu einer ganzen Zahl wird. Danach können wir fortfahren wie oben.

Beispiel:

3,5 : 0,07 = 350 : 7 = 50

4.4 Verwandlung von Brüchen in Dezimalbrüche

Die Umwandlung von Brüchen mit den Nennern 10, 100, 1000 usw. wurde schon gezeigt.

Für Brüche mit anderen Nennern betrachten wir zuerst zwei Beispiele, $\frac{1}{2}$ und $\frac{1}{3}$, und lösen die zugehörigen Divisionsaufgaben 1 : 2 und 1 : 3:

```
1 : 2 = 0,5          1 : 3 = 0,333 ...
10                   10
--                     10
                         10
```

Wir sehen, dass im ersten Fall die Rechnung nach zwei Schritten abbricht, im zweiten Fall können wir unendlich weiterrechnen.

> Zahlen wie 0,5 bezeichnet man als endliche Dezimalbrüche oder endliche Dezimalzahlen, Zahlen wie 0,333 ... nennt man unendliche Dezimalbrüche oder unendliche Dezimalzahlen.

Den Bruch $\frac{1}{2}$ können wir auch so erweitern, dass im Nenner eine Stufenzahl steht:

$\frac{1}{2} = \frac{5}{10} = 0{,}5$

$\frac{1}{3}$ lässt sich nicht so erweitern, da 3 nicht Teiler einer Stufenzahl ist (deren Quersumme ist immer 1).

Einen Bruch wandelt man in einen Dezimalbruch um, indem man den Bruch so erweitert, dass im Nenner eine der Stufenzahlen steht, oder indem man die entsprechende Divisionsaufgabe löst.

Weitere Beispiele für Dezimalbrüche:

$$\frac{1}{4} = \frac{25}{100} = 0{,}25$$

$$\frac{1}{4} = 1{,}00 : 4 = 0{,}25$$

$$\frac{3}{5} = \frac{6}{10} = 0{,}6$$

$$\frac{3}{5} = 3{,}0 : 5 = 0{,}6$$

$$\frac{1}{11} = 0{,}090909\ \ldots$$

Bei gemischten Zahlen wird nur der Bruch umgewandelt:

$$2\frac{1}{2} = 2 + \frac{1}{2} = 2{,}0 + 0{,}5 = 2{,}5$$

$$5\frac{1}{11} = 5 + 0{,}090909\ \ldots = 5{,}090909\ \ldots$$

Eine solche Ziffer oder Ziffernfolge, die sich immer wiederholt wie z. B. 3 oder 09, nennt man Periode.
Eine Zahl wie 5,090909 ... nennt man auch periodische Zahl mit der Periode 09, periodische Dezimalzahl oder periodischer Dezimalbruch.

Eine Periode wird oft durch einen so genannten Periodenstrich gekennzeichnet; das ist ein Querstrich über die sich wiederholende Ziffernfolge.

$$\frac{1}{7} = 0{,}142857142857\ldots = 0{,}\overline{142857}$$

Manchmal beginnt die Periode nicht sofort hinter dem Komma wie z. B. bei der Zahl $2{,}134\overline{53}$. Hier spricht man von einer **Vorperiode**

4.5 Umwandlung von Dezimalbrüchen in Brüche

Im Falle der endlichen Dezimalbrüche ist die Umwandlung in einen Bruch einfach: Wir schreiben den Dezimalbruch als Bruch mit einer der Stufenzahlen 10, 100, 1000 usw. als Nenner. Anschließend kürzen wir diesen Bruch.

Beispiel:

$$0{,}64 = \frac{64}{100} = \frac{16}{25}$$

Bei den unendlichen periodischen Dezimalbrüchen (mit oder ohne Vorperiode) erhält man bei der Umwandlung einen (gemeinen) Bruch, dessen Zähler gleich ist der Differenz aus der Zahl, bestehend aus den nicht periodischen Stellen (Vorperiode) und der ersten Periode minus der Zahl, die aus den vorperiodischen Ziffern gebildet ist. Dessen Nenner ist eine Zahl, gebildet aus so vielen Neunen (9), wie die Periode Ziffern enthält, und so vielen rechtsfolgenden Nullen, wie die Vorperiode Ziffern hat.

Beispiel:

$$0{,}29333\ldots = \frac{293 - 29}{900} = \frac{264}{900} = \frac{22}{75}$$

Bei rein periodischen Dezimalbrüchen ist die Vorperiode 0.

4.6 Runden von Dezimalbrüchen

Wir haben den Begriff »Runden« schon bei den natürlichen Zahlen kennen gelernt.
Wenn wir eine natürliche Zahl auf Hunderter runden, heißt das, dass wir die Zehnerziffer betrachten: Ist sie größer oder gleich 5, so wird die Hunderterziffer um eins erhöht, sonst bleibt sie gleich. Dann werden alle Ziffern rechts von der Hunderterziffer auf Null gesetzt.

Bei den Dezimalbrüchen funktioniert es genau gleich mit den Zehnteln, Hundertsteln, Tausendsteln usw. Wenn wir die Zahl 3,14159 auf Hundertstel runden, schauen wir uns die Tausendstel an: Hier steht eine 1, also bleiben die vier Hundertstel erhalten und alle Ziffern rechts davon werden 0. Wir erhalten 3,14000. Hier können wir kürzen, sodass 3,14

übrig bleibt.
Die Aufgabe »Runde auf Hundertstel« kann auch formuliert werden als »Runde auf die zweite Stelle nach dem Komma« oder »Runde auf zwei Stellen nach dem Komma« oder kurz »Runde auf zwei Stellen«.

Eine Aufgabe kann lauten:
Berechne die Fläche eines Zimmers der Länge 4,65 m und Breite 3,58 m und runde das Ergebnis auf zwei Stellen.

Die Fläche eines Rechtecks ist Länge · Breite, also $4{,}65 \cdot 3{,}58 = 16{,}647\ m^2$.
Runden auf zwei Stellen heißt, dass wir uns die dritte Stelle nach dem Komma ansehen. Hier steht eine 7, also runden wir auf: Aus der 4 an der zweiten Stelle nach dem Komma wird eine 5 und alle weiteren Stellen – hier ist es nur eine – fallen weg.
Die Antwort lautet: Die Fläche des Zimmers beträgt $16{,}65\ m^2$.

Wenn wir beispielsweise die Zahl 4,996 auf zwei Stellen runden, erhalten wir 5,00. Hier lassen wir die zwei Nullen nach dem Komma stehen als Zeichen dafür, dass es sich nicht um die natürliche Zahl 5 handelt, sondern um eine gerundete Zahl. Für weitere Berechnungen macht es aber keinen Unterschied, ob wir mit 5,00 oder mit 5 rechnen.

5 Größen aus dem Alltag

5.1 Längenmaße

Wir haben schon Längenmaße in einigen Beispielen und Aufgaben verwendet.
Die Einheit der Länge ist 1 Meter, abgekürzt 1 m.
Die Länge 1 m ist die Länge eines Metallstabes, der in Paris aufbewahrt wird. Diese Länge wurde in internationalen Abkommen als Einheit festgelegt. Alle Längenmessungen beruhen auf einem Vergleich mit der Länge von Kopien dieses »Urmeterstabs«. (Dies ist eine längst überholte »geschichtliche« Definition des Meters, die aber für unsere Vorhaben genügt.)
Diese Einheit ist aber für viele Anwendungen zu unhandlich. Wenn man z. B. ausdrücken will, wie groß bzw. wie lang ein Marienkäfer ist, müsste man sagen, er ist $\frac{5}{1000}$ m oder 0,005 m. Mit solchen Angaben verbindet man kaum eine Vorstellung. Viel anschaulicher ist es da zu sagen, dass der Käfer einen halben Zentimeter oder 5 Millimeter lang ist.
Ebenso unpraktisch ist die Einheit Meter, wenn wir den Umfang der Erde angeben sollen. Da ist die Angabe 40 000 Kilometer viel praktischer als 40 000 000 Meter.

Wie die unterschiedlichen Einheiten ineinander umgerechnet werden, lässt sich aus folgender Aufstellung erkennen:

$\cdot 10 \leftarrow \quad \cdot 10 \leftarrow \quad \cdot 10 \leftarrow \quad \cdot 10 \leftarrow \quad \cdot 10 \leftarrow \quad \cdot 10 \leftarrow \quad \cdot 10 \leftarrow \quad \cdot 10 \leftarrow \quad \cdot 10 \leftarrow$

km			m	dm	cm	mm			µm

$\rightarrow :10 \quad \rightarrow :10 \quad \rightarrow :10 \quad \rightarrow :10 \quad \rightarrow :10 \quad \rightarrow :10 \quad \rightarrow :10 \quad \rightarrow :10 \quad \rightarrow :10$

1 km = 1000 m, 1 m = 1000 mm, 1 mm = 1000 µm (Mikrometer).
Umgekehrt gilt:

$$1\text{ mm} = \frac{1}{10}\text{ cm} = 0{,}1\text{ cm} = \frac{1}{100}\text{ dm} = 0{,}01\text{ dm} = \frac{1}{1000}\text{ m} = 0{,}001\text{ m},$$

$$1\text{ m} = \frac{1}{1000}\text{ km usw.}$$

Eine Längenangabe besteht immer aus den beiden Teilen »Maßzahl« und »Maßeinheit«.
Bei der Angabe 40,8 km haben wir die Maßzahl »40,8« und die Einheit »km«.

Wenn wir mit Längen rechnen, müssen wir darauf achten, dass sie die gleiche Maßeinheit besitzen.

Beispiel:

3,2 m + 115 cm + 80 mm

Es ist sinnvoll, alle Summanden in die Einheit umzurechnen, bei der man die wenigsten Kommazahlen oder die kürzesten Maßzahlen erhält. Wir wählen hier die Einheit Zentimeter.

320 cm + 115 cm + 8 cm = 443 cm = 4,43 m

Wenn wir die Einheit Meter gewählt hätten, würde die Rechnung so aussehen:

3,20 m + 1,15 m + 0,08 m = 4,43 m

Aufgabe:
Um ein rechteckiges Grundstück von 48 m Länge und 30 m Breite einzuzäunen, will der Besitzer Pfosten im Abstand von 120 cm setzen. Wie lang wird der Zaun und wie viele Pfosten benötigt er?

Lösung:
Der Umfang eines Rechtecks ist $U = 2 \cdot \text{Länge} + 2 \cdot \text{Breite}$. Hier ist also:

$U = 2 \cdot 48\ m + 2 \cdot 30\ m = 96\ m + 60\ m = 156\ m$
1560 dm : 12 dm = 130

Antwort: Der Zaun wird 156 m lang und man benötigt 130 Pfosten.

5.2 Flächenmaße

Auch die Flächenmessung beruht auf einem Vergleich: Man vergleicht jede zu messende Fläche mit der Einheit 1 Quadratmeter (1 m^2). Das ist die Fläche eines Quadrats mit der Seitenlänge 1 m.
Die Fläche bezeichnet man mit dem Buchstaben *A* (von lat. area = Fläche) oder auch F.

Beispiel:
Die Flächenformel für das Rechteck lautet $A = l \cdot b$.

Wie bei der Längenmessung kann auch hier diese Einheit unhandlich sein. Daher gibt es größere und kleinere Einheiten, die man ineinander umrechnen kann.

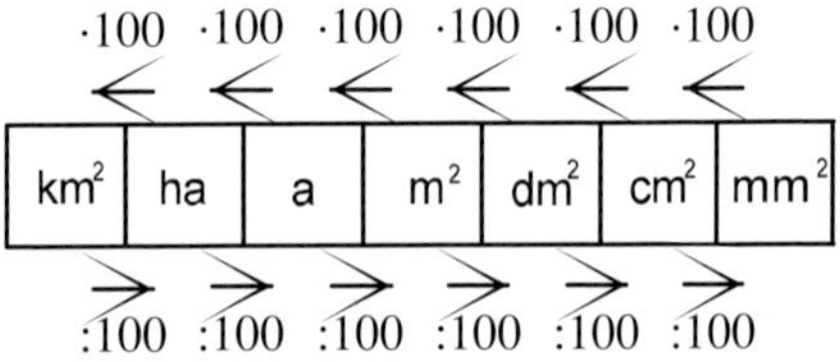

Im Vergleich mit den Längeneinheiten fällt auf, dass der Umrechnungsfaktor hier nicht 10, sondern 100 ist. Man kann sich das leicht merken, wenn man einen Zusammenhang mit der Hochzahl der Einheit herstellt: Hochzahl 2 $\Rightarrow$ der Umrechnungsfaktor hat zwei Nullen $\Rightarrow$ das Komma wird um jeweils zwei Stellen verschoben.

Beispiel: 0,0857 dm^2 = 8,57 cm^2

Außerdem fällt noch auf, dass zwischen den Einheiten Quadratmeter und Quadratkilometer noch zwei andere Einheiten liegen, nämlich 1 Ar (= 100 m^2) und 1 Hektar (= 100 a = 10000 m^2).

Als Beispiel berechnen wir die Fläche eines rechteckigen Grundstücks mit l = 500 m und b = 350 m.
A = 500 m · 350 m = 175000 m^2 = 1750 a = 17,5 ha

Aufgabe:
Wie viele quadratische Fliesen von 15 cm Seitenlänge werden mindestens benötigt, um eine 6 m lange Wand 14 dm hoch zu fliesen?

Wir berechnen zuerst die Wandfläche A_W, die gefliest werden soll. Dabei müssen wir wieder auf die Einheiten achten.

A_W = 6 m · 1,4 m = 8,4 m^2.
Die Fläche einer Fliese A_F = 15 cm · 15 cm = 225 cm^2.
Die Anzahl der Fliesen sei x. Dann gilt: $x \cdot 225\ \text{cm}^2 = 8{,}4\ \text{m}^2$.

$$x = 84\,000\ \text{cm}^2 : 225\ \text{cm}^2 = 373\frac{1}{3}.$$

Wir benötigen also mindestens 374 Fliesen.

5.3 Raummessung

Die Einheit des Raummaßes oder Volumens ist 1 Kubikmeter (m^3). Das ist der Inhalt eines Würfels mit der Kantenlänge 1 m. Ausgehend von dieser Größe gibt es wieder größere und kleinere Einheiten:

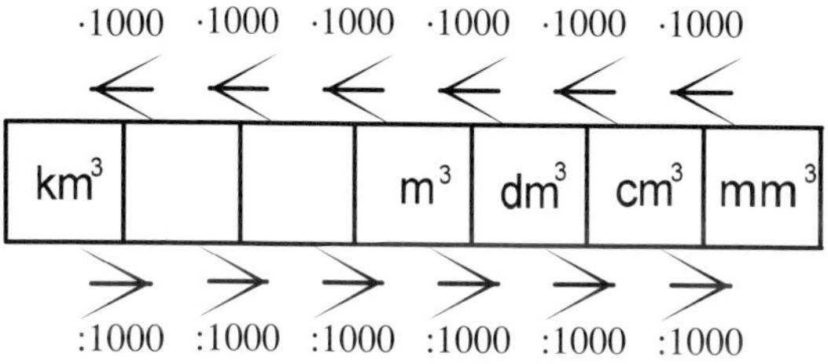

Die Hochzahl der Einheit ist 3 $\Rightarrow$ der Umrechnungsfaktor hat drei Nullen $\Rightarrow$ das Komma wird um jeweils drei Stellen verschoben.
Beispiel: 0,00253 m^3 = 2,53 dm^3.

Es besteht ein sehr großer Sprung zwischen den Einheiten m^3 und km^3:
1 km^3 = 1000000000 m^3

Auch die 1000er-Sprünge zwischen m^3, dm^3, cm^3 und mm^3 sind für viele Anwendungen im Alltag unpraktisch. Es gibt daher noch ein zweites System: Die Einheit 1 dm^3 erhält auch den Namen 1 Liter, 1 l.
Der Umrechnungsfaktor in diesem System ist 10.

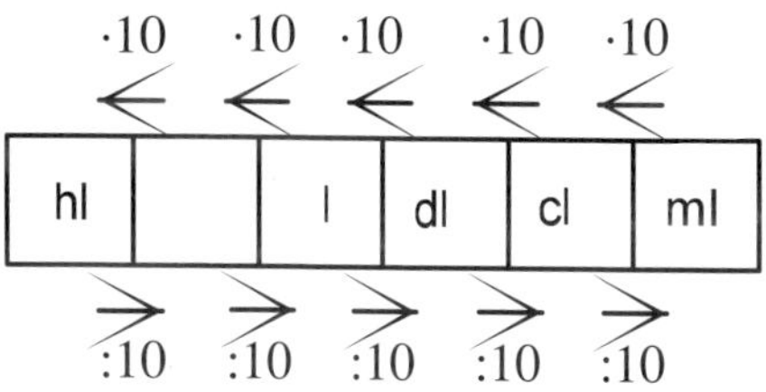

Wir sehen hier neben den bekannten Vorwörtern Dezi-, Zenti- und Milli- ein neues, das sonst bei wenigen physikalischen Einheiten verwendet wird: Hekto-.

1 Hektoliter (hl) sind 100 Liter (l).

Aufgabe:
6 hl Wein sollen aus einem Fass in 0,7-l-Flaschen abgefüllt werden. Wie viele Flaschen werden voll?

Lösung:
Wenn die Zahl der vollen Flaschen x ist, dann gilt:

$x \cdot 0{,}7\ \text{l} = 6\ \text{hl} = 600\ \text{l}$

$x = 600\ \text{l} : \frac{7}{10}\ \text{l} = 600 \cdot \frac{10}{7} = 857{,}1\ \ldots$

Antwort: Es gibt 857 volle Flaschen.

Aufgabe:
Für eine Stadt in Indien finden wir im Reiseführer für die durchschnittliche Niederschlagsmenge im Monat Juli die Angabe 350 mm. Wie viele Liter Regen fallen insgesamt im Monat Juli auf eine Fläche von 10 m^2? Wie hoch wäre der Flüssigkeitsstand in einem quaderförmigen Becken mit einer Grundfläche von 5 m^2, wenn man diese Wassermenge einfüllen würde?

Lösung:
Die Angabe der Niederschlagsmenge in mm bedeutet in unserem Fall, dass in einem gedachten Becken der Grundfläche 10 m^2 das Wasser 35 cm hoch steht. Die Formel für das Volumen eines Quaders ist $V = G \cdot h$ (Grundfläche · Höhe). Hier sind das also $V = 10\ m^2 \cdot 0{,}35\ m = 3{,}5\ m^3$.
Die Füllhöhe im Becken sei x m. Dann gilt:
$5\ m^2 \cdot x = 3{,}5\ m^3$
$x = 3{,}5\ m^3 : 5\ m^2 = 0{,}7\ m$
Antwort: Die Regenmenge ist 3,5 m^3 und die Füllhöhe im Becken ist 70 cm.

5.4 Masse

Man spricht oft vom Gewicht eines Körpers, obwohl man seine Masse meint. Der Unterschied zwischen dem Gewicht und der Masse eines Körpers ist der, dass die Masse überall gleich bleibt, das Gewicht bzw. die Gewichtskraft sich aber ändert mit dem Ort, an dem der Körper sich befindet. Ihre Einheit ist 1 Newton. Auf dem Mond z.B. wirkt auf die gleiche Masse nur etwa ein Sechstel der Gewichtskraft auf der Erde. Daher können Astronauten dort mühelos schwere Raumanzüge tragen.

Die Einheit der Masse ist ein Gramm, 1 g.

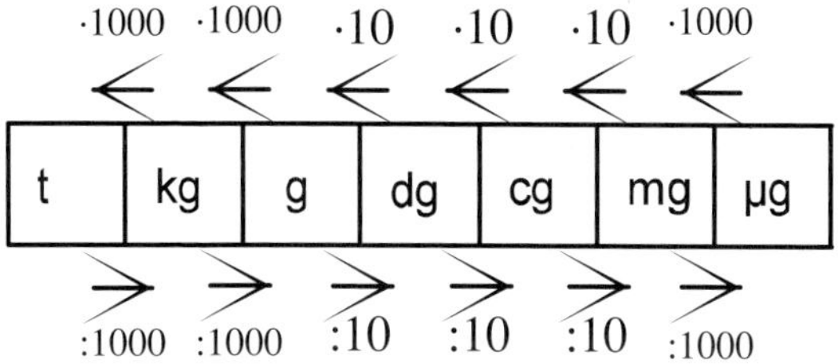

Der Umrechnungsfaktor ist 10, das Komma wird also jeweils um eine Stelle verschoben. Neben der größeren Einheit 1 kg gibt es noch die Tonne: 1 t = 1000 kg. Offiziell nicht mehr verwendete Einheiten sind 1 Pfund = 500 g, 1 Zentner = 50 kg und 1 Doppelzentner = 100 kg.

Beispiel:
Wir rechnen 0,00079 t in Gramm um.
Von t nach kg müssen wir das Komma um drei Stellen nach rechts verschieben, von kg nach g noch einmal um drei, insgesamt also um sechs Stellen. Die Zahl hat aber nur fünf Stellen nach dem Komma, deshalb müssen wir am Ende eine Null ergänzen.

0,00079 t = 0,79 kg = 790 g

Aufgabe:
Vater geht zum Einkaufen. Er kauft 2,5 kg Kartoffeln, 0,85 kg Gemüse, 150 g Wurst, 250 g Käse und 750 g Brot. Wie schwer ist der Inhalt der Einkaufstasche ohne Verpackung?

Lösung:
Wir müssen wieder beachten, dass wir nur Maßzahlen mit gleicher Einheit addieren können. Obwohl hier von Schwere geredet wird, ist bei solchen Aufgaben normalerweise die Masse in kg oder g gemeint.

2500 g + 850 g + 150 g + 250 g + 750 g = 4500 g = 4,5 kg

Antwort: Der Inhalt der Tasche wiegt 4,5 kg.

5.5 Zeitmessung

Die Umrechnung der Einheiten in der Zeitmessung beruht nicht wie die bisher betrachteten Systeme auf dem Dezimalsystem, sondern teilweise auf dem Sechzigersystem: Eine Stunde (1 h) hat 60 Minuten und eine Minute (1 min) hat 60 Sekunden (s). Ein Tag (1 d) hat 24 Stunden, ein Jahr (1 a) hat 365 Tage.
Für die Zeit benutzen wir den Buchstaben t (von lat. tempus = engl. time).
Wenn wir die dezimale Angabe 7,5 h umrechnen in Stunden und Minuten, gilt natürlich $0{,}5\ \text{h} = 0{,}5 \cdot 60\ \text{min} = 30\ \text{min}$.
Also $7{,}5\ \text{h} = 7\ \text{h}\ 30\ \text{min}$.

Die Angabe einer Uhrzeit, z.B. 9.25 Uhr, bedeutet, dass an diesem Tag 9 h 25 min vergangen sind. Wenn eine zu diesem Zeitpunkt angefangene Arbeit 2 h dauert, ist es beim Beenden der Arbeit 11.25 Uhr.

Aufgabe:
Carolin braucht für ihre Hausaufgaben in den einzelnen Fächern folgende Zeitdauern:

Mathematik 1,2 h, Deutsch 37 min, Englisch $\frac{1}{2}$ h, Pause 14 min.

Um wie viel Uhr ist sie fertig, wenn sie um 13.45 Uhr anfängt?

Lösung:

$0{,}2\ \text{h} = \frac{2}{10}\ \text{h} = 2 \cdot 6\ \text{min} = 12\ \text{min}$

$t = 1\ \text{h}\ 12\ \text{min} + 37\ \text{min} + 30\ \text{min} + 14\ \text{min} = 2\ \text{h}\ 33\ \text{min}$

$13\ \text{h}\ 45\ \text{min} + 2\ \text{h}\ 33\ \text{min} = 16\ \text{h}\ 18\ \text{min}$

Antwort: Carolin ist um 16.18 Uhr mit ihren Aufgaben fertig.

5.6 Geschwindigkeit

Bisher haben wir einfache Größen (Grundgrößen) betrachtet: Länge, Masse, Zeit und Produkte von solchen Größen: Fläche (= Länge · Länge), Volumen (= Länge · Länge · Länge).
Nun betrachten wir einen Quotienten aus zwei einfachen Größen, nämlich Weg (s) durch Zeit (t), anders ausgedrückt: Länge : Zeit.
Dieser Quotient erhält die Bezeichnung Geschwindigkeit (v). Ihre Formel lautet also $v = \frac{s}{t}$. Sie wird normalerweise in der Einheit Kilometer pro Stunde (km/h) oder Meter pro Sekunde (m/s) angegeben.

Beispiel:
Ein Radfahrer, der für eine Strecke von 3,5 km 7 min benötigt, fährt mit einer Durchschnittsgeschwindigkeit von $\frac{3{,}5\text{ km}}{7\text{ min}} = \frac{0{,}5\text{ km}}{1\text{ min}} =$
$= \frac{60 \cdot 0{,}5\text{ km}}{60 \cdot 1\text{ min}} = 30\text{ km/h}$.

Aufgabe:
Ein Autofahrer, der um 7.25 Uhr in München losfährt, fährt auf der 600 km langen Strecke nach Düsseldorf mit einer Durchschnittsgeschwindigkeit von 125 km/h. Er macht unterwegs eine halbe Stunde Pause. Um wie viel Uhr kommt er in Düsseldorf an?

Lösung:
$v = \frac{s}{t}$, dann ist $t = \frac{s}{v}$
$t_1 = 600\text{ km} : 125\text{ km/h} = 4{,}8\text{ h}$
$t_2 = 4{,}8\text{ h} + 0{,}5\text{ h} = 5{,}3\text{ h} = 5\text{ h }18\text{ min}$
$7\text{ h }25\text{ min} + 5\text{ h }18\text{ min} = 12\text{ h }43\text{ min}$

Antwort: Der Fahrer kommt um 12.43 Uhr in Düsseldorf an.

5.7 Währung

Unter Währung versteht man die Einheit des Geldes, das in einem bestimmten Land als Zahlungsmittel gilt. In vielen europäischen Ländern gilt die Währung »Euro« (€). 1 € = 100 Cent (C).

Aufgabe:
1 kg Käse kostet 11 € 20 C. Wie viel kosten 250 g?

Lösung:
Wir können so rechnen:
11,2 €/kg · 0,25 kg = 2,8 € = 2 € 80 C

6 Prozentrechnen und Proportionalität

6.1 Der Prozentbegriff

Mit Brüchen kann man Anteile von einem Ganzen berechnen. Ein Viertel von 2 kg Mehl sind zum Beispiel $\frac{1}{4} \cdot 2$ kg = 500 g und drei Achtel von 800 km sind 300 km. Im Alltag kommen Anteile, die sich auf ein Hundertstel beziehen, besonders häufig vor. Sie haben deshalb eine eigene Bezeichnung: »Prozent«.

Es ist definiert:

$$1\,\% = \frac{1}{100} \text{ und}$$

$$p\% = \frac{p}{100}$$

Prozente sind immer positiv und bezeichnen Anteile an einem Ganzen. Sie lassen sich auch als Bruch mit dem Nenner 100 schreiben. Prozente kann man in einen Bruch umwandeln, indem man sie als Hundertstel schreibt und entsprechend kürzt. Ein Bruch lässt sich in Prozent umwandeln, indem man ihn so erweitert, dass sein Nenner 100 wird. Es gilt z. B.:

$$100\,\% = \frac{100}{100} = 1 \qquad 50\,\% = \frac{50}{100} = \frac{1}{2}$$

$$62{,}5\,\% = \frac{62{,}5}{100} = \frac{625}{1000} = \frac{5}{8} \qquad \frac{2}{5} = \frac{40}{100} = 40\,\%$$

$$\frac{1}{3} = \frac{33\frac{1}{3}}{100} = 33\frac{1}{3}\,\%$$

Analog wie Prozent werden Promille als Tausendstel definiert. Es gilt:

$$1\,‰ = \frac{1}{1000} \text{ und } p\,‰ = \frac{p}{1000}$$

6.2 Prozentrechnung

Prozentangaben werden verwendet, um Anteile an einem Ganzen anzugeben. Das Ganze oder die Grundgröße, von der der Anteil berechnet wird, heißt Grundwert, der entsprechende Teil davon heißt Prozentwert. Die Prozentangabe, die den Anteil angibt, heißt Prozentsatz.

Man schreibt: Grundwert $\hat{=}$ 100 %
Prozentwert $\hat{=}$ Prozentsatz p %

Aus jeweils zwei gegebenen Größen lässt sich die dritte berechnen.

Es gilt: Grundwert · Prozentsatz % = Prozentwert

$$\frac{\text{Prozentwert}}{\text{Grundwert}} \cdot 100\,\% = \text{Prozentsatz}\,\%$$

$$\frac{\text{Prozentwert}}{\text{Prozentsatz}\,\%} = \text{Grundwert}.$$

Beispiele:
Es wurden 470 kg Kartoffeln geerntet, davon waren 5 % faul. Wie viel Kilogramm faule Kartoffeln wurden geerntet?
Gegeben sind der Grundwert mit 470 kg und der Prozentsatz mit 5 %. Berechnet wird der Prozentwert.

$$5\,\% \cdot 470\text{ kg} = \frac{5}{100} \cdot 470\text{ kg} = 23{,}5\text{ kg}$$

23,5 kg Kartoffeln sind faul.

In einem ausverkauften Kino mit 250 Plätzen sind 155 der Besucher männlich. Wie hoch ist der Anteil der männlichen Besucher in Prozent? Gegeben sind der Grundwert 250 und der Prozentwert 155, gesucht ist der Prozentsatz. Dazu berechnet man den Anteil der männlichen Kinobesucher unter allen Kinobesuchern als Bruch.

$$\frac{155}{250} = \frac{620}{1000} = \frac{62}{100} = 62\,\%$$

62 % der Besucher sind männlich.

Auf einer Keksschachtel steht, der Schokoladenanteil beträgt 16% oder 40 g. Wie schwer ist der gesamte Inhalt der Schachtel?
Gegeben ist der Prozentwert mit 40 g und der Prozentsatz mit 16%. Gesucht ist der Grundwert:

$$\frac{40\text{ g}}{16\%} = \frac{40\text{ g}}{\frac{16}{100}} = \frac{40\text{ g} \cdot 100}{16} = 250\text{ g}$$

In der Schachtel sind 250 g Kekse.

Mit Prozenten werden nicht nur Anteile berechnet, sondern häufig auch Gewinne und Verluste, auch: Zu- und Abnahmen bezeichnet. Dabei ist es wichtig, sich zuerst klarzumachen, welche der Zahlen der Grundwert bzw. Prozentwert sind und welche Zahlen daraus berechnet wurden. Der Grundwert ist die ursprüngliche Größe, daraus entsteht durch Zu- oder Abnahme eine neue Größe. Die Differenz zwischen beiden ist der Prozentwert und entspricht dem dazugehörigen Prozentsatz der Zu- oder Abnahme.

Beispiel:
Die Zahl der Verkehrsunfälle einer Region ist von 1400 auf 1470 gestiegen. Wie hoch ist die Steigerung in Prozenten?
Der Grundwert ist die ursprüngliche Zahl der Unfälle, 1400. Sie erhöht sich auf 1470. Das ist eine Steigerung um 1470 – 1400 = 70. Der Prozentwert ist 70. Daraus berechnet sich der Prozentsatz:

$$\frac{70}{1400} = \frac{5}{100} = 5\%$$

Es ist eine Steigerung um 5%.

Die Zahl der Übernachtungen in einem Hotel ist um 12% auf 2112 gesunken. Wie hoch ist die ursprüngliche Übernachtungszahl?
Die ursprüngliche Zahl der Übernachtungen ist der Grundwert und soll berechnet werden. Die neue Übernachtungszahl ist um 12% niedriger als die ursprüngliche. Sie beträgt also nur noch 100% – 12% = 88% der ursprünglichen Übernachtungen. 88% ist der Prozentsatz und entspricht dem Prozentwert 2112. Zu berechnen ist der Grundwert:

$$\frac{2112}{88\%} = \frac{2112 \cdot 100}{88} = 2400$$

Ursprünglich waren es 2400 Übernachtungen.

6.3 Zinsrechnung

Die Zinsrechnung ist ein spezielles Beispiel der Prozentrechnung. Der Zinsfuß ist dabei in Prozent angegeben und gibt an, wie viel Prozent des Grundkapitals als Zinsen pro Jahr zum Grundkapital dazukommen. Es sind folgende Bezeichnungen üblich:

K_0 Grundkapital
K_n Kapital nach n Jahren
$p\%$ Zinsfuß
I Zinsen nach einem Jahr

Ein Kapital K_0 bringt bei einer jährlichen Verzinsung von $p\%$ nach einem Jahr

$I = K_0 \cdot p\,\% = K_0 \cdot \frac{p}{100}$ Zinsen.

Damit gilt für das Kapital nach einem Jahr:

$$K_1 = K_0 + I = K_0 + K_0 \cdot \frac{p}{100} = K_0 \cdot \left(1 + \frac{p}{100}\right).$$

In jedem weiteren Jahr wird die Summe aus Grundkapital und bereits erhaltenen Zinsen neu verzinst, damit wächst das Kapital mit jedem Jahr um den Faktor $\left(1 + \frac{p}{100}\right)$. Es gilt also allgemein:

$$K_n = K_0 \cdot \left(1 + \frac{p}{100}\right)^n$$

Mit dieser Formel lassen sich einige Fragestellungen berechnen.

Beispiele:

Ein Kapital von 2000,– € wird jährlich mit 5% verzinst.
Wie hoch ist das Kapital nach acht Jahren?
$K_0 = 2000,\text{–}\ €$, $n = 8$, $p\% = 5\%$

$$K_8 = 2000,\text{–}\ € \cdot \left(1 + \frac{5}{100}\right)^8$$

$$= 2000,\text{–}\ € \cdot \left(1 + \frac{1}{20}\right)^8$$

$$= 2954{,}91\ €$$

Wie hoch muss das Grundkapital sein, damit es nach zwei Jahren auf 3307,50 € angewachsen ist?

$K_2 = 3307{,}50$ €, n = 2, $p\% = 5\%$

$$3307{,}50\text{ €} = K_0 \cdot \left(1 + \frac{5}{100}\right)^2$$

$$K_0 = 3307{,}50\text{ €} : \left(1 + \frac{1}{20}\right)^2$$

$$K_0 = 3307{,}50\text{ €} \cdot \left(\frac{20}{21}\right)^2 = 3000{,}\text{– €}$$

Wird das Kapital nicht ein ganzes Jahr verzinst, sondern nur *t* Tage, berechnen sich die Zinsen anteilig pro Tag; dabei wird vereinfachend mit 360 Tagen pro Jahr und 30 Tagen pro Monat gerechnet. Die Formel für die Zinsen lautet:

$$I_t = K_0 \cdot \frac{t}{360} \cdot \frac{p}{100}$$

Im Beispiel berechnet man die Zinsen bei $K_0 = 2000{,}$– € und $p\% = 5\%$ für drei Monate dann wie folgt:

$$t = 3 \cdot 30 = 90$$

$$I_{90} = 2000{,}\text{– €} \cdot \frac{90}{360} \cdot \frac{5}{100} = 25\text{ €}$$

Nach drei Monaten erhält man 25,– € Zinsen.

6.4 Direkte Proportionalität

Zwei Größen *a* und *b* heißen zueinander direkt proportional, wenn ihr Quotient konstant ist. Man schreibt $a \sim b$. Es gilt $\frac{a}{b}$ = Konstante oder a = Konstante $\cdot\, b$. Die Konstante heißt Proportionalitätsfaktor.
Ein Beispiel aus der Physik dafür sind Stromstärke und Spannung. Es ist $I \sim U$ und $\frac{U}{I} = R$. *R*, der elektrische Widerstand, ist konstant.

Die dazugehörigen Zahlenpaare der direkt proportionalen Größen *a* und *b* lassen sich in einer Tabelle darstellen.

Beispiele:

a	1	2	3	4	5	6
b	2	4	6	8	10	12

Für alle Zahlenpaare gilt: $a : b = 1 : 2 = 2 : 4 = 3 : 6 = 4 : 8 = 5 : 10 = 6 : 12.$
$\frac{a}{b} = \frac{1}{2}$, der Proportionalitätsfaktor ist $\frac{1}{2}$.

a	1	2	3	4	5	6
b	$\frac{1}{3}$	$\frac{2}{3}$	1	$\frac{4}{3}$	$\frac{5}{3}$	2

In diesem Fall ist $a : b = 1 : \frac{1}{3} = 3 : 1 = 3$, der Proportionalitätsfaktor ist 3.

Weiß man, dass zwei Größen direkt proportional sind, lassen sich weitere Zahlenpaare berechnen, z. B. für $a = 7$ und $\frac{a}{b} = 3 \Rightarrow b = \frac{1}{3} \cdot 7 = \frac{7}{3}$.

Allgemein gilt für alle Zahlenpaare von direkt proportionalen Größen: Je kleiner die eine Größe ist, desto kleiner ist auch die andere Größe und umgekehrt, je größer die eine, desto größer ist auch die andere. Entweder nehmen beide Größen zu oder beide Größen nehmen ab. Betrachtet man zwei Zahlenpaare, sagt man für den Fall $a_1 : b_1 = a_2 : b_2$ a_1 verhält sich zu b_1 wie a_2 zu b_2.
Aus der Tatsache, dass bei direkter Proportionalität alle Zahlenpaare den gleichen Quotienten besitzen, lassen sich einige hilfreiche Formeln ableiten.

Es gilt: $a : b = c : d$ oder $\frac{a}{b} = \frac{c}{d} \Leftrightarrow a \cdot d = b \cdot c$

Aus $\frac{a}{b} = \frac{c}{d}$ lässt sich durch entsprechende Addition bzw. Subtraktion herleiten:

$\frac{a}{b} + 1 = \frac{c}{d} + 1$ bzw. $\frac{a}{b} - 1 = \frac{c}{d} - 1 \Leftrightarrow$

$\frac{a+b}{b} = \frac{c+d}{d}$ bzw. $\frac{a-b}{b} = \frac{c-d}{d}$

Daraus folgt durch Division:

$$\frac{a+b}{a-b} = \frac{c+d}{c-d}$$

6.5 Indirekte Proportionalität

Zwei Größen a und b sind indirekt proportional zueinander, wenn ihr Produkt konstant ist, $a \cdot b =$ Konstante. Ein Beispiel aus der Physik ist das Gesetz von Boyle-Mariotte: In einem idealen eingeschlossenen Gas ist bei konstanter Temperatur das Produkt aus Druck und Volumen konstant, $p \cdot V =$ Konstante. Das heißt, je größer das Volumen wird, desto geringer wird der Druck des Gases und je höher der Druck, desto kleiner ist das Volumen des Gases.
Auch indirekt proportionale Größen lassen sich tabellarisch darstellen:

a	1	2	3	4	5	6
b	1	$\frac{1}{2}$	$\frac{1}{3}$	$\frac{1}{4}$	$\frac{1}{5}$	$\frac{1}{6}$

Es gilt: $a \cdot b = 1 \cdot 1 = 2 \cdot \frac{1}{2} = 3 \cdot \frac{1}{3} = 4 \cdot \frac{1}{4} = 5 \cdot \frac{1}{5} = 6 \cdot \frac{1}{6} = 1$

So lassen sich weitere Zahlenpaare berechnen.

$a = 12$ und $a \cdot b = 1 \Rightarrow b = \frac{1}{12}$

a	1	2	3	4	5	6
b	12	6	4	3	$2\frac{2}{5}$	2

Hier ist $a \cdot b = 1 \cdot 12 = 12$. Für $a = \frac{2}{5}$ folgt mit $a \cdot b = 12$

$\frac{2}{5} \cdot b = 12 \Rightarrow b = 12 \cdot \frac{5}{2} = 30.$

Für Größen, die indirekt proportional zueinander sind, gilt: Je größer die eine Größe wird, desto kleiner wird die andere und umgekehrt, je mehr eine Größe fällt, desto mehr steigt die andere Größe an.

6.6 Schlussrechnung - Dreisatz

Weiß man von Größen, dass sie direkt oder indirekt proportional zueinander sind, lassen sich, wie in den vorangegangenen Abschnitten gesehen, aus einem gegebenen Zahlenpaar weitere Zahlenpaare berechnen. Der Dreisatz oder die Schlussrechnung ist eine Berechnungsart dafür. Der Dreisatz ermöglicht dabei, direkt von einem Zahlenpaar auf ein anderes zu schließen, ohne den Proportionalitätsfaktor oder eine andere Konstante in einem Zwischenschritt berechnen zu müssen. Im Folgenden wird anhand von Beispielen das schrittweise Vorgehen beim Berechnen eines Dreisatzes vorgestellt.
Gegeben sei die folgende Problemstellung:

Ein Auto fährt mit konstanter Geschwindigkeit, nach 45 min ist es 69 km gefahren. Wie viel Zeit benötigt es bei gleicher Geschwindigkeit für 230 km?
Gegeben sind eine Zeitspanne, 45 min, und eine dazugehörige Strecke, 69 km. Man könnte nun die Geschwindigkeit des Autos und daraus die gesuchte Zeit berechnen. Hier wird die Aufgabe ohne diesen Zwischenschritt mithilfe eines Dreisatzes gelöst. Dazu muss man zunächst feststellen, welche Art von Proportionalität vorliegt. (Natürlich muss man bei einer völlig neuen Aufgabe auch feststellen, ob überhaupt Proportionalität vorliegt, bei Dreisatzaufgaben kann das aber vorausgesetzt werden.) Das geschieht am einfachsten durch »Je-desto«-Aussagen. »Je größer der eine Wert, desto größer der andere« bedeutet direkte Proportionalität, beide Größen wachsen gleichermaßen. »Je größer die eine, desto kleiner die andere« ist ein Zeichen für indirekte Proportionalität. Bei konstanter Geschwindigkeit legt ein Auto in gleichen Zeitabschnitten gleich lange Strecken zurück – je länger die Strecke, desto länger auch die Fahrzeit. Weg und Zeit sind also direkt proportional zueinander.
Nun kann der Dreisatz aufgestellt werden. Dazu schreibt man zusammengehörende Größen in eine Zeile und bezeichnet die gesuchte Größe mit x.

$69\text{ km} \mathrel{\hat{=}} 45\text{ min}$
$\underline{230\text{ km} \mathrel{\hat{=}} x}$

Nun lässt sich aus den vier Größen eine Gleichung entsprechend der direkten Proportionalität aufstellen.

$$\frac{45\text{ min}}{69\text{ km}} = \frac{x}{230\text{ km}}$$

Durch Umformen der Gleichung wird x berechnet.

$$x = \frac{45\text{ min}}{69\text{ km}} \cdot 230\text{ km} = 150\text{ min}$$

Das Auto benötigt für 230 km 150 min oder $2\frac{1}{2}$ Stunden.

Aus diesem Beispiel ergibt sich:

Schrittweises Vorgehen zum Lösen von Dreisatzaufgaben:

- Feststellen der Art der Proportionalität (direkt oder indirekt) durch »Je-desto«-Aussagen
- Aufstellen des Dreisatzes mit unbekannter Größe x

  zusammengehörige Größen in eine Zeile

  Größen mit gleichen Einheiten untereinander

  $a \mathrel{\hat{=}} b$

  $\underline{c \mathrel{\hat{=}} x}$
- Aufstellen der Gleichung, entsprechend der Proportionalität

  direkte Proportionalität: $\frac{a}{b} = \frac{c}{x}$

  indirekte Proportionalität: $a \cdot b = c \cdot x$
- Umformen der Gleichung und Berechnen von x.

Weitere Beispiele:

Fünf Arbeiter benötigen drei Stunden, um einen Graben auszuheben. Wie lange dauert die gleiche Arbeit, wenn zwei Arbeiter mehr mithelfen?

»Je mehr Arbeiter, desto kürzer ist die Dauer des Aushebens.« Es liegt indirekte Proportionalität vor.

$5 \mathrel{\hat{=}} 3\text{h}$

$\underline{5 + 2 \mathrel{\hat{=}} x}$

$5 \cdot 3\text{ h} = 7 \cdot x$

$$x = \frac{5 \cdot 3\text{ h}}{7} = \frac{15}{7}\text{ h} \approx 2\text{ h }9\text{ min}$$

Die Arbeit dauert dann 2 h 9 min.

In einer Wechselstube erhält man für 210,– € etwa 176000 Tansanische Schillinge (TSh). Wie viel Euro muss man für 1 Mio. TSh hinlegen?
Je mehr TSh, desto mehr €, es liegt direkte Proportionalität vor.

$210\text{ €} \mathrel{\hat{=}} 176\,000\text{ TSh}$

$\underline{\quad x \mathrel{\hat{=}} 1\,000\,000\text{ TSh}\quad}$

$$\frac{210\text{ €}}{176\,000\text{ TSh}} = \frac{x}{1\,000\,000\text{ TSh}}$$

$$x = \frac{210\text{ €}}{176\,000\text{ TSh}} \cdot 1\,000\,000\text{ TSh} = 1193{,}10\text{ €}$$

1 Mio. TSh kosten etwa 1193 €.

Auch Prozentaufgaben lassen sich mittels Dreisatzrechnung lösen:
Moritz hat in einer Klausur 135 Punkte, das sind 45% der erreichbaren Punkte. Seine Banknachbarin hat 210 Punkte erreicht. Wie viel Prozent sind das?
Je mehr Punkte man hat, desto mehr Prozent der erreichbaren Punkte hat man, es liegt direkte Proportionalität vor.

$135 \mathrel{\hat{=}} 45\,\%$

$\underline{210 \mathrel{\hat{=}} x\quad}$

$$\frac{45\,\%}{135} = \frac{x}{210}$$

$$x = \frac{45\,\%}{135} \cdot 210 = 70\,\%$$

Die Banknachbarin hat 70% der Punkte erreicht.

Auf einen Blick: Arithmetische Regeln und Sätze

Mengen

Mengen sind Zusammenfassungen von Dingen zu einer Einheit.
Es gibt eine aufzählende Form und eine beschreibende Form der Mengenangabe:

$G = \{0, 2, 4, 6, ...\}$ oder $G = \{a \in \mathbb{N}_0 \mid a \text{ ist gerade}\}$

Die Schnittmenge zweier Mengen A und B enthält die Elemente, die in A und in B liegen, die Vereinigungsmenge enthält die Elemente, die in A oder in B liegen.

Natürliche Zahlen

Die Menge der natürlichen Zahlen erhält man durch Abzählen der Elemente von Mengen.

Jede natürliche Zahl hat einen Nachfolger und mit Ausnahme der 1 auch einen Vorgänger.

$\mathbb{N}$ ist angeordnet: Für zwei Elemente a und b aus $\mathbb{N}$ gilt: $a < b$, $a = b$ oder $a > b$.

Eine Variable ist ein Platzhalter oder Stellvertreter.

Eine Aussageform enthält eine Variable, z.B. $x + 3 < 7$, eine Aussage nicht, z.B. $2 + 3 < 7$.

Eine Aussage kann wahr oder falsch sein.

Für die Rechenart Addition gelten Kommutativgesetz (Vertauschungsgesetz) und Assoziativgesetz (Verbindungsgesetz):

$a + b = b + a$
$(a + b) + c = a + (b + c)$

Terme sind Rechenausdrücke mit Zahlen oder Variablen.

Die Subtraktion ist die Umkehrung der Addition:

$2 + x = 5 \Rightarrow x = 5 - 2$

Die Lösungsmenge ist die Menge der Werte, die für eine Variable eingesetzt werden können, um aus einer Aussageform eine wahre Aussage zu machen.

$5 + x < 10 \quad \mathbb{L} = \{0, 1, 2, 3, 4\}$

Die Multiplikation ist eine abgekürzte Addition:

$a + a + a + a = a \cdot 4$

Für die Multiplikation gelten Kommutativgesetz und Assoziativgesetz:

$a \cdot b = b \cdot a$

$(a \cdot b) \cdot c = a \cdot (b \cdot c)$

Ein Produkt ist Null, wenn ein Faktor Null ist.

Die Division ist die Umkehrung der Multiplikation.

$a \cdot x = b \Rightarrow x = b : a$ falls $a \neq 0$

Eine Division durch Null ist verboten.

Bei den Grundrechenarten haben wir folgende Begriffe:

Addition	Summe Summand + Summand	=	Wert der Summe kurz: Summe
Subtraktion	Differenz Minuend - Subtrahend	=	Wert der Differenz kurz: Differenz
Multiplikation	Produkt Faktor · Faktor Multiplikand · Multiplikator	=	Wert des Produkts kurz: Produkt
Division	Quotient Dividend : Divisor	=	Wert des Quotienten kurz: Quotient

Für die Verbindung von Punkt- und Strichrechnung gilt das Distributivgesetz (im Falle der Division nur bezüglich Dividend):

$a \cdot (b + c) = ab + ac$

$a \cdot (b - c) = ab - ac$

$(a + b) : c = a : c + b : c$

$(a - b) : c = a : c - b : c$

Für die Verbindung von Punkt- und Strichrechnung gilt die Regel: Punktrechnung geht vor Strichrechnung, wenn nicht Klammern eine andere Reihenfolge vorschreiben.

Eine Potenz ist eine abgekürzte Multiplikation:

$a \cdot a \cdot a \cdot a = a^4$

Zahlensysteme

Das Zehnersystem oder Dezimalsystem beruht auf den Zehnerpotenzen 1, 10, 100, 1000 usw. Diese Zahlen werden auch als Stufenzahlen des Dezimalsystems bezeichnet.

Die Multiplikation und Division einer Zahl mit einer Stufenzahl erfolgt durch Anhängen bzw. Weglassen einer entsprechenden Anzahl von Nullen:

$3 \cdot 1000 = 3000$
$500 : 10 = 50$

Das Zweiersystem oder Dualsystem beruht auf den Zweierpotenzen 1, 2, 4, 8, 16 usw.

dual $1011 = 1 \cdot 8 + 0 \cdot 4 + 1 \cdot 2 + 1 \cdot 1 = 11$ (dezimal).

Gleichungen

Äquivalente Gleichungen sind Gleichungen, die die gleiche Lösungsmenge besitzen.

Eine Gleichung geht in eine äquivalente Gleichung über durch Addition oder Subtraktion des gleichen Terms auf beiden Seiten des Gleichheitszeichens und durch Division oder Multiplikation mit dem gleichen Term außer Null.

Um eine natürliche Zahl auf eine bestimmte Stelle zu runden, betrachtet man die folgende Ziffer: Ab 5 wird aufgerundet, d. h., die Ziffer an der betreffenden Stelle wird um 1 erhöht, sonst wird abgerundet, d. h., die Ziffer bleibt gleich. Alle folgenden Ziffern werden durch Nullen ersetzt:

13 187 auf Hunderter gerundet: 13 200
13 187 auf Tausender gerundet: 13 000

Die Teilermenge einer Zahl ist die Menge aller Zahlen, durch die diese Zahl ohne Rest teilbar ist.

$T_{12} = \{1, 2, 3, 4, 6, 12\}$

Primzahlen sind Zahlen, deren Teilermenge genau zwei Elemente enthält.

Zahlen, die mehr als zwei Teiler haben, heißen zusammengesetzte Zahlen.

Der größte gemeinsame Teiler (ggT) von mehreren Zahlen ist das größte Element der Schnittmenge der Teilermengen dieser Zahlen.

Die Vielfachenmenge einer Zahl enthält alle Vielfachen dieser Zahl.

Das kleinste gemeinsame Vielfache (kgV) von mehreren Zahlen ist das kleinste Element der Schnittmenge der Vielfachenmengen dieser Zahlen.

Bruchzahlen

Wenn man ein Ganzes in gleiche Teile aufteilt, wird der Anteil eines Stücks (oder mehrerer Stücke) am Ganzen als Bruch geschrieben: Ein Teil von 6 ist: $\frac{1}{6}$

Ein Bruch hat die Gestalt: $\frac{\text{Zähler}}{\text{Nenner}}$

Der Bruchstrich bedeutet eine Division: $\frac{3}{4} = 3 : 4$

Brüche mit dem Zähler 1 heißen Stammbrüche.

In der Grundform sind Zähler und Nenner teilerfremd.

Für echte Brüche gilt: Zähler < Nenner
Für unechte Brüche gilt: Zähler ≥ Nenner
Für Scheinbrüche gilt: Zähler = $k \cdot$ Nenner $(k \in \mathbb{N})$

Scheinbrüche stellen ganze Zahlen dar, insbesondere: $\frac{a}{a} = 1$

Eine gemischte Zahl ist ein Gebilde, das aus einem ganzzahligen Teil und einem Bruch besteht: $1\frac{2}{3} = 1 + \frac{2}{3}$

Ein unechter Bruch kann in eine gemischte Zahl umgewandelt werden und umgekehrt.

Einen Bruch erweitern heißt Zähler und Nenner mit der gleichen Zahl multiplizieren.

Einen Bruch kürzen heißt Zähler und Nenner durch die gleiche Zahl dividieren.

Brüche mit gleichem Nenner heißen gleichnamig.

Ungleichnamige Brüche werden gleichnamig gemacht, indem man den Hauptnenner sucht (das ist das kgV der einzelnen Nenner) und dann jeden Bruch entsprechend erweitert.

Nur gleichnamige Brüche können addiert oder subtrahiert werden. Brüche werden addiert (subtrahiert), indem man die Zähler addiert (subtrahiert) und den Nenner beibehält:

$$\frac{3}{6}+\frac{2}{6}=\frac{3+2}{6}=\frac{5}{6}$$

$$\frac{7}{9}-\frac{4}{9}=\frac{7-4}{9}=\frac{3}{9}=\frac{1}{3}$$

Brüche werden multipliziert, indem man Zähler mit Zähler und Nenner mit Nenner multipliziert:

$$\frac{2}{7}\cdot\frac{3}{5}=\frac{2\cdot 3}{7\cdot 5}=\frac{6}{35}$$

Den Kehrwert oder Kehrbruch eines Bruchs erhält man, indem man den Zähler mit dem Nenner des Bruchs vertauscht.

Kehrwert von $\frac{2}{3}$ ist $\frac{3}{2}$.

Durch einen Bruch wird dividiert, indem man mit dem Kehrwert des Bruchs multipliziert:

$$\frac{3}{5}:\frac{2}{3}=\frac{3}{5}\cdot\frac{3}{2}=\frac{9}{10}$$

Einen Bruch, in dessen Zähler und/oder Nenner wieder ein Bruch vorkommt, nennt man Doppelbruch oder Etagenbruch.

Doppelbrüche können mithilfe von Klammerausdrücken aufgelöst werden:

$$\frac{2\frac{3}{5}-\frac{2}{3}}{2\left(\frac{1}{4}+\frac{1}{3}\right)}=\left(2\frac{3}{5}-\frac{2}{3}\right):\left[2\left(\frac{1}{4}+\frac{1}{3}\right)\right]$$

Dezimalbrüche

Dezimalbrüche haben die Gestalt
... T H Z E, z h t ...
(Tausender, Hunderter, Zehner, Einer, Zehntel, Hundertstel, Tausendstel ...)

Einen Dezimalbruch erweitern heißt, am Ende Nullen anhängen, ihn kürzen heißt, Nullen am Ende weglassen:
1,3 = 1,30 = 1,300 ...

Dezimalbrüche werden addiert oder subtrahiert, indem man sie mit den Kommas untereinander schreibt, eventuell durch Ergänzen von Nullen am Ende auf die gleiche Stellenzahl bringt und dann die Rechnung ohne Rücksicht auf die Kommas durchführt. Das Ergebnis hat gleich viele Kommastellen wie die Ausgangszahlen.

Multiplikation und Division einer Dezimalzahl mit einer Stufenzahl (10, 100, 1000 ...) bedeutet eine Verschiebung des Kommas, bei Multiplikation nach rechts, bei Division nach links, um so viele Stellen, wie die Anzahl der Nullen angibt:

$2{,}359 \cdot 100 = 235{,}9$
$71{,}8 : 10 = 7{,}18$

Zwei Dezimalzahlen werden multipliziert, indem man sie ohne Beachtung der Kommas multipliziert und beim Ergebnis so viele Kommastellen abzählt, wie die Faktoren zusammen haben:

$2{,}8 \cdot 1{,}5 = 4{,}20 = 4{,}2$

Dezimalzahlen werden dividiert, indem man den Quotienten so erweitert, dass der Divisor eine ganze Zahl wird. Danach wird normal dividiert; beim Überschreiten der Kommastelle erhält auch das Ergebnis ein Komma; beim Dividenden können wir am Ende beliebig viele Nullen hinzugefügen.

Das Ergebnis einer Division kann ein endlicher oder unendlicher (periodischer) Dezimalbruch sein.

Brüche lassen sich in Dezimalbrüche umwandeln, indem man die entsprechende Division durchführt:

$\frac{1}{8} = 0{,}125$

$\frac{4}{9} = 0{,}444\ ...$

Viele Brüche kann man auch durch Erweitern in einen Bruch mit einer Stufenzahl im Nenner umwandeln.

$\frac{3}{4} = \frac{75}{100} = 0{,}75$

Endliche Dezimalbrüche lassen sich in Brüche umwandeln, indem man sie als Bruch mit einer Stufenzahl im Nenner schreibt und anschließend kürzt.

$0{,}8 = \frac{8}{10} = \frac{4}{5}$

Dezimalbrüche werden auf eine bestimmte Stelle gerundet, indem man die nächste Stelle beachtet: Ab der Ziffer 5 wird aufgerundet, sonst abgerundet.

3,587 auf eine Stelle gerundet ergibt 3,6.
20,5244 auf zwei Stellen gerundet ergibt 20,52.

Größen aus dem Alltag

Die Einheiten Meter (m), Gramm (g) und Liter (l) sind Einheiten für Länge (Weg), Masse und Volumen (= Rauminhalt).

Größere und kleinere Einheiten zu m, g und l werden durch Zusammensetzung mit Vorsätzen gebildet.

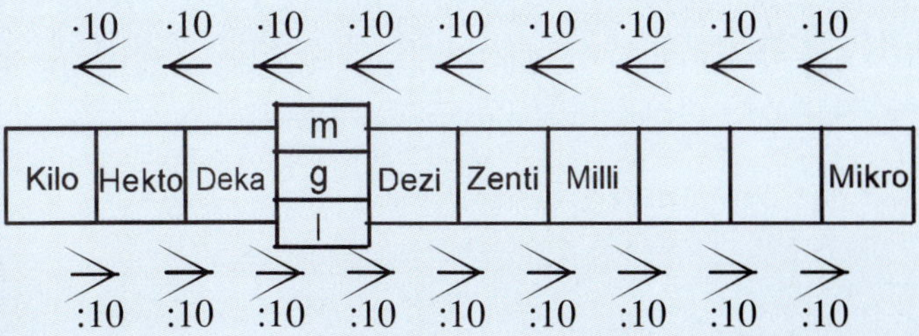

Deka- ist üblich nur bei Gramm, Hekto- nur bei Liter, Mikro- ist nicht üblich bei Liter.
Umrechnungsfaktor ist 10. Das Komma wird jeweils um eine Stelle verschoben.

Beispiel: 1 m = 10 dm

Eine Maßangabe besteht aus Maßzahl und Einheit, z. B. 100 mg.

Bei Flächen gilt der Umrechnungsfaktor 100 (Hochzahl der Einheit ist 2), das Komma wird um jeweils zwei Stellen verschoben.

Bei Volumen gilt der Umrechnungsfaktor 1000 (Hochzahl der Einheit ist 3), das Komma wird um jeweils drei Stellen verschoben.

Die Umrechnung der Zeiteinheiten ist unregelmäßig:
1 a = 365 d; 1 d = 24 h; 1 h = 60 min; 1 min = 60 s, 1 s = 1000 ms (Millisekunde).

Für die Währung Euro gilt: 1 € = 100 C (Cent)

2

Algebra

Um eine Gleichung zu lösen, eine Rechnung zu überprüfen oder den Graph einer Funktion zu zeichnen, benötigt man Rechenregeln. Mit genau diesen Regeln beschäftigt sich die Algebra. Im folgenden Kapitel werden sowohl die Regeln für das Bruchrechnen in $\mathbb{Q}$ dargestellt als auch der Umgang mit Potenzrechnungen und Logarithmen erläutert, alle wichtigen Regeln werden hergeleitet und erklärt. Und damit neben dem Verstehen die Anwendung nicht zu kurz kommt, wird an Hand von vielen Beispielen gezeigt, wie damit schrittweise Aufgaben gelöst werden, wie zum Beispiel lineare oder quadratische Gleichungen.

1 Die rationalen Zahlen $\mathbb{Q}$

1.1 Die Mengen $\mathbb{Z}$ und $\mathbb{Q}$

Erweiterung von $\mathbb{N}$ zu $\mathbb{Z}$

Innerhalb der Menge der natürlichen Zahlen $\mathbb{N}_0$ kann man zwar bereits viele Aufgaben und Aufgabentypen lösen, einigen Rechnungen lassen sich in $\mathbb{N}_0$ allerdings nicht ausführen. Die Aufgabe 5 – 10 ist ein Beispiel dafür, sie hat in $\mathbb{N}_0$ keine Lösung. Um auch diese Rechnung lösen zu können, muss die Menge der natürlichen Zahlen erweitert werden. Zu jeder natürlichen Zahl n wird ihr negatives Gegenstück, ihre Gegenzahl –n dazugenommen und eine neue Menge gebildet. So erhält man die Menge der ganzen Zahlen $\mathbb{Z}$. In aufzählender Schreibweise lautet die Menge der ganzen Zahlen

$$\mathbb{Z} = \{0, +1, -1, +2, -2, ...\} = \{... -3, -2, -1, 0, +1, +2, +3, ...\}$$

Offensichtlich gilt $\mathbb{N}_0 \subset \mathbb{Z}$.

Die Aufgabe von oben lässt sich jetzt lösen: $5 - 10 = -5$

Die negativen Zahlen sind uns im Alltag aus der Temperaturmessung oder auch von einem überzogenen Konto bekannt.

Erweiterung von $\mathbb{Z}$ zu $\mathbb{Q}$

Auch bei den Punktrechenarten gibt es Aufgaben, die in $\mathbb{Z}$, und damit auch in $\mathbb{N}_0$, nicht lösbar sind. Ein Beispiel hierfür ist die Aufgabe 5 : 3. Wie bereits gesehen, wird darum $\mathbb{N}_0$ bzw. $\mathbb{Z}$ um die Menge der Brüche erweitert. Zu jedem Zahlenpaar (a, b) mit $a \in \mathbb{Z}$ und $b \in \mathbb{N}$ $b \neq 0$ (!) wird die Zahl $\frac{a}{b}$ zu $\mathbb{Z}$ dazugefügt. So entsteht $\mathbb{Q}$. $\mathbb{Q}$ lässt sich schreiben als

$$\mathbb{Q} = \{x \mid \text{es gibt ein } a \in \mathbb{Z} \text{ und } b \in \mathbb{N} \text{ mit } x = \tfrac{a}{b}\}$$

Wie man leicht sieht (z.B. $b = 1$) ist $\mathbb{N} \subset \mathbb{Z} \subset \mathbb{Q}$.

Die Elemente von $\mathbb{Q}$ lassen sich als Dezimalbrüche wie 10,75 und –3,38 und als Bruchzahlen wie $7\frac{1}{2}$ und $-\frac{3}{8}$ schreiben.

Alle Zahlen in $\mathbb{Q}$ sind bestimmt durch ihr Vorzeichen und ihren Betrag. Das Vorzeichen + oder – zeigt an, ob die Zahl positiv oder negativ ist und damit, ob sie auf dem Zahlenstrahl rechts oder links von 0 liegt.

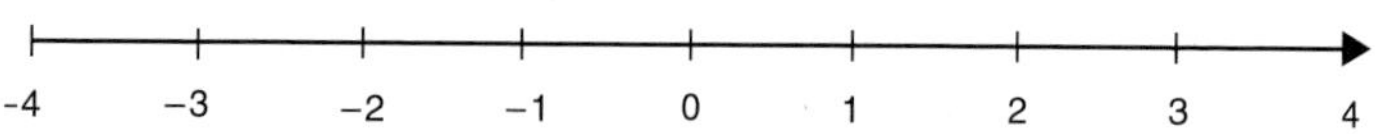

Der Betrag einer Zahl in $\mathbb{Q}$

Den Abstand einer Zahl vom Nullpunkt bezeichnet man als ihren Betrag. Schreibweise: $|-3{,}8|$ Der Betrag einer Zahl ist immer positiv oder Null.

Beispiele: $|-3| = 3$

$|0| = 0$

$\left|5\frac{2}{3}\right| = 5\frac{2}{3}$

Je größer der Abstand einer Zahl vom Nullpunkt ist, desto größer ist ihr Betrag. Wie man am Zahlenstrahl gut erkennt, ist −5 weiter vom Nullpunkt entfernt als −2, −3 ist weiter vom Nullpunkt entfernt als 1,3. Vergleicht man die Beträge von −5 und 2,5 formal, so erhält man:

$|-5| = 5$ und $|2{,}5| = 2{,}5$

$5 > 2{,}5$, also $|-5| > |2{,}5|$

Gleichzeitig gilt aber: $-5 < 2{,}5$

Denn für den Vergleich von Zahlen in $\mathbb{Q}$ gilt: Je weiter links eine Zahl auf dem Zahlenstrahl liegt, desto kleiner ist sie.

Zahlen werden geschrieben als ihr Betrag und ihr Vorzeichen. Ein + als Vorzeichen darf auch weggelassen werden: $+23 = 23$

Die Zahl mit dem gleichen Betrag, aber dem entgegengesetzten Vorzeichen heißt Gegenzahl zu einer Zahl. 5 ist die Gegenzahl von −5, $-\frac{1}{3}$ ist die Gegenzahl von $\frac{1}{3}$. Jede Zahl hat eine Gegenzahl in $\mathbb{Q}$. Die Gegenzahl von 0 ist 0.

Innerhalb einer Aufgabe können die Zeichen + und − also nicht nur als Zeichen für eine Rechenoperation, sondern auch als Vorzeichen auftauchen.

Beispiel: $-3 + (-7)$

Die beiden Minuszeichen dienen als Vorzeichen, das Pluszeichen kennzeichnet die Rechenoperation.

Damit klar erkennbar ist, welche Bedeutung ein Zeichen hat, ist es häufig sinnvoll, Klammern zu verwenden. Zwei Rechenzeichen dürfen in einer Rechnung nicht direkt nebeneinander stehen.

1.2 Die vier Grundrechenarten in $\mathbb{Q}$

Addition

Um zwei Zahlen in $\mathbb{Q}$ zusammenzuzählen oder zu addieren, muss man sowohl ihre Beträge als auch ihre Vorzeichen berücksichtigen. Es gelten die Regeln:

- Haben zwei Zahlen gleiches Vorzeichen, so werden ihre Beträge addiert und die Summe hat das gleiche Vorzeichen wie die beiden Zahlen.
- Haben zwei Zahlen verschiedene Vorzeichen, wird der kleinere Betrag vom größeren abgezogen und das Ergebnis erhält das Vorzeichen der Zahl, die den größeren Betrag hat.

Beim Zusammenzählen der Beträge von Brüchen darf man die Regeln für die Addition von Brüchen nicht vergessen: Zuerst muss man den gemeinsamen Hauptnenner bilden, beide Brüche passend erweitern und dann die Zähler addieren.

Beispiele für die Addition von Zahlen mit gleichem Vorzeichen:

$-5 + (-7) =$ | – als gemeinsames Vorzeichen, addieren der Beträge

$-(5 + 7) = -12$

$-\frac{1}{2} + \left(-\frac{1}{3}\right) =$ | – als gemeinsames Vorzeichen

$-\left(\frac{1}{2} + \frac{1}{3}\right) =$ | Hauptnenner bilden

$-\left(\frac{3}{6} + \frac{2}{6}\right) = -\frac{5}{6}$

$1\frac{1}{2} + \frac{7}{8} = \frac{3}{2} + \frac{7}{8} = \frac{12}{8} + \frac{7}{8} = \frac{19}{8} = 2\frac{3}{8}$

Beispiele für die Addition von Zahlen mit unterschiedlichen Vorzeichen:

$5 + (-10) =$ | 10 > 5, 10 gibt das Vorzeichen an

$-(10 - 5) = -5$

$-8 + \frac{25}{3} = -8 + 8\frac{1}{3} = +\left(8\frac{1}{3} - 8\right) = \frac{1}{3}$

Subtraktion

Eine Zahl in $\mathbb{Q}$ wird von einer anderen abgezogen oder subtrahiert, indem man ihre Gegenzahl addiert. Wenn man die Vorzeichen richtig ändert, können sich Addition und Subtraktion also gegenseitig ersetzen. Auch bei der Subtraktion darf man die Regeln für das Rechnen mit Brüchen nicht vergessen.

Beispiele:

$5 - (+7) =$ | Addition der Gegenzahl -7

$5 + (-7) =$ | Addition von Zahlen mit verschiedenen Vorzeichen, $7 > 5$

$-(7 - 5) = -2$

$-9 - \left(-\frac{3}{2}\right) =$ | Addition der Gegenzahl

$-9 + \left(+\frac{3}{2}\right) =$ | verschiedene Vorzeichen, $9 > \frac{3}{2}$

$-\left(9 - \frac{3}{2}\right) =$ | Hauptnenner bilden

$-\left(\frac{18}{2} - \frac{3}{2}\right) = -\frac{15}{2} = -7\frac{1}{2}$

$-1 - \frac{4}{9} = -1 + \left(-\frac{4}{9}\right) = -\left(1 + \frac{4}{9}\right) = -1\frac{4}{9}$

$28 - (-66) = 28 + 66 = 94$

Multiplikation

Zwei Zahlen in $\mathbb{Q}$ werden miteinander malgenommen oder multipliziert, indem man ihre Beträge multipliziert und das Produkt nach folgenden Regeln sein Vorzeichen erhält.

»+« · »+« = »+«

»–« · »+« = »–«

»+« · »–« = »–«

»–« · »–« = »+«

Sind die Beträge der Zahlen Brüche, müssen die Regeln für die Multiplikation von Brüchen angewendet werden, also »Zähler mal Zähler« und »Nenner mal Nenner«.

Beispiele: $3 \cdot 2\frac{2}{5} = 3 \cdot \frac{12}{5} = \frac{36}{5} = 7\frac{1}{5}$

$-\frac{1}{2} \cdot 2 =$ | »–« · »+« gibt »–«

$-\left(\frac{1}{2} \cdot 2\right) =$ | Kürzen

-1

$17 \cdot \left(-\frac{5}{3}\right) =$ | Vorzeichenregel

$-\left(17 \cdot \frac{5}{3}\right) = -\frac{85}{3} = -28\frac{1}{3}$

$-1 \cdot \left(-\frac{2}{7}\right) =$ | »–« · »–« gibt »+«

$\frac{2}{7}$

Division

Zwei Zahlen in $\mathbb{Q}$ werden durch einander geteilt oder dividiert, indem man ihre Beträge dividiert, der Quotient bekommt sein Vorzeichen entsprechend der folgenden Regeln:

»+« : »+« = »+«

»–« : »+« = »–«

»+« : »–« = »–«

»–« : »–« = »+«

Auch hier gelten weiterhin die Regeln zum Bruchrechnen: Durch einen Bruch wird dividiert, indem man mit dem Kehrbruch multipliziert.

Beispiele: $\frac{2}{7} : \frac{1}{14} =$ | mit Kehrbruch multiplizieren

$\frac{2}{7} \cdot \frac{14}{1} =$ | Kürzen

$\frac{4}{1} = 4$

$-\frac{3}{5} : (+9) =$ | Vorzeichenregel, Kehrbruch

$-\left(\frac{3}{5} \cdot \frac{1}{9}\right) =$ | Kürzen

$-\frac{1}{5 \cdot 3} = -\frac{1}{15}$

$4 : (-12) = -(4 : 12) = -\left(4 \cdot \frac{1}{12}\right) = -\frac{4}{12} = -\frac{1}{3}$

$(-3) : \left(-\frac{2}{3}\right) = +\left(3 : \frac{2}{3}\right) = +\left(3 \cdot \frac{3}{2}\right) = \frac{9}{2} = 4\frac{1}{2}$

Wendet man die Vorzeichenregeln auf einen Bruch an, sieht man, dass gilt: $\frac{-3}{5} = -\frac{3}{5} = \frac{3}{-5}$

1.3 Terme und Formeln

Als einen Term bezeichnet man jede sinnvolle Kombination aus Zahlen und Rechenzeichen. 5 + 3 ist ein Term ebenso wie $3 \cdot (\frac{-3}{5} + 0{,}275)$. Auch eine einzelne Zahl ist bereits ein Term.
Da die vier Grundrechenarten +, – , · und : besonders häufig vorkommen, haben die aus ihnen entstehenden Terme eigene Namen, ebenso die Terme, die in diesen Rechnungen vorkommen. Einige dieser Namen sind schon an früherer Stelle aufgetaucht, hier werden sie einmal alle gesammelt vorgestellt.

Addition: Summand + Summand = Summe
Subtraktion: Minuend – Subtrahend = Differenz
Multiplikation: Faktor · Faktor = Produkt
Division: Dividend : Divisor = Quotient oder $\frac{\text{Zähler}}{\text{Nenner}}$ = Quotient

Die Subtraktion $(-2 \cdot \frac{1}{8}) - 6$ beispielsweise setzt sich zusammen aus zwei Termen, dem Minuend $(-2 \cdot \frac{1}{8})$ und dem Subtrahend 6. Auch $(-2 \cdot \frac{1}{8}) - 6$ ist wieder ein Term, den man Differenz nennt. Der Minuend ist dabei ein Produkt aus den Faktoren –2 und $\frac{1}{8}$, jeder der Faktoren ist auch gleichzeitig ein Term. Man kann also aus verschiedenen Termen durch Verknüpfung mit Rechenoperationen wieder neue Terme entstehen lassen.
Terme lassen sich auch vergleichen. Das geschieht durch die Zeichen =, ≠, >, <, ≥ und ≤. Dadurch entstehen Aussagen. Aussagen sind wahr oder falsch. Ein Beispiel für eine Aussage ist

$5 + 3 > 7 - 2$

Hier wird eine Summe mit einer Differenz verglichen. In Worten lautet die Aussage: Die Summe aus 5 und 3 ist größer als die Differenz aus 7 und 2. Die Aussage ist wahr. Weitere Beispiele für wahre Aussagen:

$\frac{1}{2} - \frac{5}{2} = -2$

$18 : 3 \neq 5$

$\frac{7}{9} \leq 1$

Eine falsche Aussage erhält man zum Beispiel, wenn man sich verrechnet.

Viele Aussagen sind einander sehr ähnlich. Sie folgen dem gleichen Muster oder der gleichen Regel, wie die folgenden drei Gleichungen.

$5 + 3 = 3 + 5$

$8 + (-6) = (-6) + 8$

$\frac{1}{2} + \frac{1}{3} = \frac{1}{3} + \frac{1}{2}$

Bei genauem Hinsehen erkennt man, dass alle drei auf der gleichen Regel beruhen, nämlich: Bei der Addition darf man die Summanden vertauschen. Diese Regel nennt man das Kommutativgesetz oder Vertauschungsgesetz der Addition.

Um diese Regel nicht nur mit Hilfe verschiedener Beispiele darzustellen, sondern um sie allgemein angeben zu können, ist es sinnvoll, statt der Zahlen Buchstaben als Platzhalter in der Gleichung zu verwenden. Die Gleichung lautet dann:

$a + b = b + a \quad a, b \in \mathbb{Q}$

a und b heißen Platzhalter oder Variable. Für die Variablen a und b darf man in der Gleichung Zahlen aus $\mathbb{Q}$ einsetzen. $\mathbb{Q}$ ist die Definitionsmenge für a und b. Sie gibt an, aus welcher Menge man für die Variablen a und b Werte einsetzen darf. Die Definitionsmenge wird häufig mit $\mathbb{D}$ bezeichnet. Setzt man $a = 2$ und $b = 4$, erhält man die Gleichung $2 + 4 = 4 + 2$. Beim Einsetzen muss man darauf achten, dass man für gleiche Buchstaben auch immer gleiche Zahlen einsetzt. Kommt derselbe Buchstabe in einer Gleichung mehrmals vor, muss man für ihn immer dieselbe Zahl einsetzen.
Es gibt eine wichtige Einschränkung für die Definitionsmenge eines Terms. Die Definitionsmenge muss immer so gewählt sein, dass durch das Einsetzen keine ungültigen Terme entstehen. Der Term $\frac{5}{c}$ ist z.B. nur dann gültig, wenn $c \neq 0$ ist. Die Definitionsmenge darf also 0 nicht enthalten. Eine sinnvolle Definitionsmenge für c ist $\mathbb{D} = \mathbb{Q}\setminus\{0\}$, auch $\mathbb{N}$ wäre eine gültige Definitionsmenge für den Term.

Ist eine Aussage immer wahr, egal welche Zahlen man für ihre Variablen einsetzt, so nennt man sie allgemein gültig. Das Kommutativgesetz der Addition ist eine allgemein gültige Aussage.
$a + a = 2 \cdot a$ mit $a \in \mathbb{Q}$ ist eine weitere allgemein gültige Aussage. $\mathbb{Q}$ ist die Definitionsmenge für die Variable a, kurz $\mathbb{D} = \mathbb{Q}$. Setzt man für $a = 8$, so lautet die Gleichung: $8 + 8 = 2 \cdot 8$. Für a muss immer die gleiche Zahl eingesetzt werden.

Für zwei verschiedene Variablen a und b in einer Gleichung darf man auch gleiche Zahlen einsetzen.

Beispiel: $a + 1 < b + 3$ mit $a, b \in \mathbb{Q}$

Setzt man $a = 6$ und $b = 6$, erhält man die wahre Ungleichung $6 + 1 < 6 + 3$. Für $a = 3$ und $b = 0$ wird die Ungleichung falsch.

Eine kurze Anmerkung zur Schreibweise: Wenn der Sinn erhalten bleibt, kann der Mal-Punkt zwischen Termen oft auch weggelassen werden, man schreibt kurz: $2a$ für $2 \cdot a$ oder $7(ab - 5)$ für $7 \cdot (a \cdot b - 5)$.

1.4 Umformen und Rechnen mit Termen

Das Rechnen mit Buchstaben und Buchstabentermen folgt den gleichen Regeln wie das Rechnen mit Zahlen. Alle wichtigen Regeln werden hier nacheinander aufgeführt. Die erste Regel lautet:

Klammern haben Vorrang.

Beispiel: $a - (5 + 3) = a - 8$

$a - 5 + 3 = a - 2$

Im ersten Fall steht im Term eine Klammer. Die Klammer hat Vorrang und muss zuerst gerechnet werden, das Minuszeichen gilt dann für das Ergebnis der Klammer. Im zweiten Fall gehört das Minuszeichen nur zu 5.

Punkt vor Strich

Die Punktrechenarten »·« und »:«, also die Multiplikation und Division, müssen vor den Strichrechenarten »+« und »–«, also der Addition und Subtraktion durchgeführt werden. Auch der Bruchstrich gilt, da er eine Division anzeigt, als Punktrechenart. Durch die Regel »Punkt vor Strich« kann man sich an vielen Stellen Klammern sparen.

Beispiel: $5 \cdot 3 + 2 \cdot 4 = (5 \cdot 3) + (2 \cdot 4) = 15 + 8 = 23$

$2 \cdot a + 3 \cdot b = 2a + 3b$

Kommutativgesetz
- der Addition $a + b = b + a \quad a, b \in \mathbb{Q}$
- der Multiplikation $a \cdot b = b \cdot a \quad a, b \in \mathbb{Q}$

Die Kommutativgesetze oder Vertauschungsgesetze besagen, bei der Addition darf man die Reihenfolge der Summanden vertauschen, bei der Multiplikation darf man die Reihenfolge der Faktoren vertauschen.

Beispiele: $7 + \left(-\frac{1}{7}\right) = -\frac{1}{7} + 7$

$5 \cdot 3 = 3 \cdot 5$

$2 \cdot a + b \cdot 3 = 2 \cdot a + 3 \cdot b = 3 \cdot b + 2 \cdot a$

Im dritten Beispiel muss man die Regel »Punkt vor Strich« beachten. Es wurden nacheinander das Kommutativgesetz der Multiplikation und das Kommutativgesetz der Addition angewendet.

Assoziativgesetz
- der Addition $(a + b) + c = a + (b + c) = a + b + c \quad a, b, c \in \mathbb{Q}$
- der Multiplikation $(a \cdot b) \cdot c = a \cdot (b \cdot c) = a \cdot b \cdot c \quad a, b, c \in \mathbb{Q}$

Das Assoziativgesetz besagt, bei der Addition und der Multiplikation ist es egal, in welcher Reihenfolge man die Rechnung ausführt.

Beispiel: $(a + 6) + 3 = a + (6 + 3) = a + 9$

$3 \cdot (5 \cdot a) = (3 \cdot 5) \cdot a = 15 \cdot a = 15a$

Die obenstehenden Regeln lassen sich auch verbinden, wie die nächsten beiden Beispiele zeigen.

$(3 + a) + 7 =$ | Kommutativgesetz der Addition

$(a + 3) + 7 =$ | Assoziativgesetz der Addition

$a + (3 + 7) =$

$a + 10$

$(3 \cdot a) \cdot \frac{1}{3} =$ | Kommutativgesetz der Multiplikation

$\frac{1}{3} \cdot (3 \cdot a) =$ | Assoziativgesetz der Multiplikation

$\left(\frac{1}{3} \cdot 3\right) \cdot a =$

$1 \cdot a = a$

Die wichtigste Regel für die Verknüpfung von Punkt- und Strichrechenarten ist das Distributivgesetz.

Distributivgesetz
$a \cdot (b + c) = a \cdot b + a \cdot c \quad a, b, c \in \mathbb{Q}$

Mit Hilfe der Kommutativgesetze lässt sich das Distributivgesetz auch so schreiben: $(b + c) \cdot a = a \cdot b + a \cdot c$
Das Distributivgesetz gibt an, wie eine Klammer, die eine Summe enthält, ausmultipliziert wird. Der Faktor vor der Klammer wird mit jedem Summanden in der Klammer einzeln multipliziert. Dabei muss man die Vorzeichenregeln beachten.

Beispiele: $3 \cdot (b + 6) =$ | Distributivgesetz – Ausmultiplizieren
$3 \cdot b + 3 \cdot 6 =$
$3b + 18$

$-2 \cdot (1 - a) =$ | Distributivgesetz
$-2 \cdot 1 + (-2) \cdot (-a) =$ | Vorzeichenregeln
$-2 + 2a$

Wichtig ist, das Assoziativgesetz und das Distributivgesetz nicht zu verwechseln. Im ersten Fall sind <u>alle</u> Rechenoperationen Punktrechenarten (oder Strichrechenarten), im zweiten Fall kommen Punkt- <u>und</u> Strichrechenarten gemeinsam in einer Rechung vor.

Beispiel für das Assoziativgesetz: $6 \cdot (2 \cdot a) = (6 \cdot 2) \cdot a = 12 \cdot a = 12a$
Beispiel für das Distributivgesetz: $6 \cdot (2 + a) = 6 \cdot 2 + 6 \cdot a = 12 + 6a$

Liest man das Distributivgesetz von rechts nach links, erhält man eine Regel für das Ausklammern von Faktoren aus Summen. Haben alle Summanden einer Summe einen gemeinsamen Teiler, so darf man diesen Teiler ausklammern.

Beispiele: $a + 5ab = a\,(1 + 5b)$
$2a + 3a = a \cdot 2 + a \cdot 3 = a \cdot (2 + 3) = a \cdot 5 = 5a$

Wie das zweite Beispiel zeigt, erhält man durch das Distributivgesetz eine wichtige Regel für das Rechnen mit Buchstaben. Es ermöglicht zusammen mit dem Kommutativgesetz, Terme mit gleichen Buchstaben zusammenzufassen. Weitere Beispiele:

$4a + 3a + c - 6c =$ | Zusammenfassen von Termen mit gleichen Buchstaben

$7a - 5c$

$x - y + 3x - y =$ | Vertauschen der Summanden

$x + 3x - y - y =$ | Zusammenfassen der Summanden mit gleichen Buchstaben

$4x - 2y$

$4a^2bx - 3bxa^2 =$ | Vertauschen der Faktoren im zweiten Summanden

$4a^2bx - 3a^2bx =$ | Summanden haben die gleichen Buchstabenkombinationen - Ausklammern

$(4 - 3)a^2bx = a^2bx$

$3b - b^2 + 3b^2 - 4b + b - 3b =$ | Ausklammern von b

$b(3 - b + 3b - 4 + 1 - 3) =$ | Zusammenfassen in der Klammer

$b(2b - 3) =$ | Ausmultiplizieren

$2b^2 - 3b$

$6ab + 4a - 2ab - 8a = 6ab - 2ab + 4a - 8a = 4ab - 4a$

Um Rechnungen zu vereinfachen, fasst man Terme mit gleichen Buchstabenkombinationen so weit wie möglich zusammen. Dafür wendet man alle oben genannten Regeln an.

Beispiel:

$6ab + b \cdot (a - 3) + 2 \cdot (b \cdot 2) =$ | Distributivgesetz

$6ab + ba - b \cdot 3 + 2 \cdot (b \cdot 2) =$ | Kommutativgesetz der Multiplikation

$6ab + ab - 3b + 2\,(2b) =$ | Assoziativgesetz der Multiplikation

$6ab + ab - 3b + 4b =$ | Zusammenfassen

$7ab + b$

Selbstverständlich lassen sich nicht alle Terme zusammenfassen. Der Term $ab - 3a$ z.B. lässt sich nicht weiter vereinfachen. Man kann Terme nur zusammenfassen, wenn sie in ihrer Buchstabenkombination genau übereinstimmen.

Ausmultiplizieren von Klammern

Das Distributivgesetz besagt, wie man beim Ausmultiplizieren des Produkts $a \cdot (b + c)$ vorgehen muss. Auch bei Produkten der Form $(s + t) \cdot (u + v)$ kann man das Distributivgesetz anwenden. Das geschieht in zwei Schritten. Zunächst behandelt man die erste Klammer als einen Term – das »a« im Distributivgesetz $a(b + c) = ab + ac$ – und multipliziert diesen Term mit der nachfolgenden Klammer aus. Man setzt also in der Regel des Distributivgesetzes für a, b und c die folgenden Terme ein $a = (s + t)$, $b = u$ und $c = v$. Auf das Ergebnis wendet man das Distributivgesetz ein zweites Mal an.

$(s + t) \cdot (u + v) = (s + t)u + (s + t)v = su + tu + sv + tv$

So erhält man eine allgemein gültige Regel für das kreuzweise Ausmultiplizieren von Summen. Zwei Summen werden miteinander multipliziert, indem man jeden Summanden der ersten Summe mit jedem Summanden der zweiten Summe – unter Beachtung der Vorzeichen – multipliziert. Formal lautet die Regel:

$(a + b) \cdot (c + d) = ac + ad + bc + bd \quad a, b, c, d \in \mathbb{Q}$

Beispiel: $(5 - a)\,(3a + 1) =$
$5 \cdot 3a + 5 \cdot 1 + (-a) \cdot 3a + (-a) \cdot 1 =$
$15a + 5 - 3a^2 - a =$
$-3a^2 + 14a + 5$

So wie das Distributivgesetz zum Ausmultiplizieren mehrmals hintereinander angewendet werden kann, kann man es auch zum Faktorisieren von Summen in mehreren Schritten verwenden.

Beispiele:
$ab + b + 3a + 3 =$ | Einführen passender Klammern
$(ab + b) + (3a + 3) =$ | Ausklammern von b bzw. 3
$b(a + 1) + 3(a + 1) =$ | Ausklammern von $(a + 1)$ aus beiden Summanden
$(a + 1) \cdot (b + 3)$

$a^2 + 2a - 2 - a =$ | Einführen passender Klammern
$(a^2 + 2a) - 2 - a =$ | Ausklammern von a bzw -1
$a(a + 2) - 1(2 + a) =$ | Ausklammern von $(a + 2)$
$(a - 1)\,(a + 2)$

Die binomischen Formeln

Besonders häufig kommen in Rechnungen Produkte aus gleichen Summen vor, wie z. B. $(5 - a)\,(5 - a)$ kurz $(5 - a)^2$. Sie stellen einen Sonderfall des Ausmultiplizierens von Summen dar. Man unterscheidet an Hand der Vorzeichen drei Fälle, die die drei binomischen Formeln bilden.

I. $(a + b)^2 = (a + b)\,(a + b) = a^2 + ab + ab + b^2 = a^2 + 2ab + b^2$
II. $(a - b)^2 = (a - b)\,(a - b) = a^2 - ab - ab + (-b)^2 = a^2 - 2ab + b^2$
III. $(a + b)(a - b) = a^2 - ab + ab - b^2 = a^2 - b^2$

Für $a, b \in \mathbb{Q}$ gilt:
1. binomische Formel: $(a + b)^2 = a^2 + 2ab + b^2$
2. binomische Formel: $(a - b)^2 = a^2 - 2ab + b^2$
3. binomische Formel: $(a + b)\,(a - b) = a^2 - b^2$

Die Summanden $+2ab$ und $-2ab$ in der ersten und zweiten binomischen Formel heißen gemischte Glieder, a^2 und b^2 heißen quadratische Glieder der binomischen Formel. Mit Hilfe der binomischen Formeln kann man folgende Beispiele einfach berechnen:

$(3ax + 4c)^2 =$ | Anwenden der 1. binomischen Formel
$(3ax)^2 + 2 \cdot 3ax \cdot 4c + (4c)^2 =$ | Ausmultiplizieren
$9a^2x^2 + 24acx + 16c^2$

$(xy - 5)^2 =$ | Anwenden der 2. binomischen Formel
$(xy)^2 - 2 \cdot xy \cdot 5 + 5^2 =$ | Ausmultiplizieren
$x^2y^2 - 10xy + 25$

$(ab - 3cxy)\,(ab + 3cxy) =$ | Anwenden der 3. binomischen Formel
$(ab)^2 - (3cxy)^2 =$ | Ausmultiplizieren
$a^2b^2 - 9c^2x^2y^2$

Binomische Formeln lassen sich leicht erkennen. Dadurch erhält man eine weitere Möglichkeit, Summen in Produkte zu verwandeln.

Beispiele:
$25 - 10x + x^2 = 5^2 - 2 \cdot 5 \cdot x + x^2 = (5 - x)^2$ (2. binomische Formel)
$9x^2 - 81a^2 = (3x + 9a)\,(3x - 9a)$ (3. binomische Formel)
$9a^2 + 6a + 1 = (3a)^2 + 2 \cdot 3a \cdot 1 + 1^2 = (3a + 1)^2$ (1. binomische Formel)

Will man eine Summe faktorisieren, ist oft die binomische Formel nicht sofort erkennbar. Häufig muss man zuerst die Summanden umsortieren, d.h. mittels des Kommutativgesetzes vertauschen oder einen gemeinsamen Faktor ausklammern, also das Distributivgesetz anwenden. Dann erst kann man eine binomische Formel anwenden.

Beispiele: $-x^2 - a^2 - 2ax =$ | Kommutativgesetz der Addition
$-x^2 - 2ax - a^2 =$ | Ausklammern von -1
$-(x^2 + 2ax + a^2) =$ | 1. binomische Formel
$-(x + a)^2$

$18a^2 - 32x^2y^2 =$ | Ausklammern von 2
$2(9a^2 - 16x^2y^2) =$ | 3. binomische Formel
$2(3a + 4xy)(3a - 4xy)$

Bruchterme

Auch in Brüchen und Bruchtermen können Variable vorkommen. $\frac{3+x}{x-2}$ ist ein Beispiel für einen Bruchterm. Variable erfüllen in Bruchtermen die gleiche Platzhalterfunktion wie in Summen oder Produkten. Für die Variablen darf man aus der Definitionsmenge Zahlen einsetzen. Dabei haben Bruchterme, da sie eine Division darstellen, eine wichtige Besonderheit: Der Nenner darf nicht zu Null werden. Darum muss die Definitionsmenge der Variablen so gewählt sein oder so eingeschränkt werden, dass der Nenner nicht zu Null wird. Für den Term $\frac{3+x}{x-2}$ bedeutet das, es muss stets gelten $x - 2 \neq 0$. Aus dieser Bedingung lässt sich die Definitionsmenge bestimmen. Man berechnet, für welche Zahlen in $\mathbb{Q}$ der Nenner zu Null wird, und schließt diese Zahlen aus der Definitionsmenge aus.

$x - 2 = 0 \Leftrightarrow x = 2 \Rightarrow \mathbb{D} = \mathbb{Q}\backslash\{2\}$.

Kommen in einem Term oder einer Gleichung mehrere Bruchterme vor, muss die Definitionsmenge so eingeschränkt werden, dass keiner der vorkommenden Nenner zu Null wird.

Beispiel: $\frac{1}{x} - \frac{1}{\frac{x+2}{2x-1}}$

Es müssen folgende drei Bedingungen erfüllt sein:

I. $x \neq 0$;

II. $x + 2 \neq 0$;
$x + 2 = 0 \Leftrightarrow x = -2$
$\Rightarrow x \neq -2$

III. $2x - 1 \neq 0$
$2x - 1 = 0 \Leftrightarrow 2x = 1$
$\Leftrightarrow x = \frac{1}{2}$
$\Rightarrow x \neq \frac{1}{2}$

$\Rightarrow \mathbb{D} = \mathbb{Q}\backslash\left\{-2, 0, \frac{1}{2}\right\}$

Innerhalb der Definitionsmenge kann man wie gewohnt mit den Bruchtermen weiterrechnen. Man kann Bruchterme erweitern und kürzen und durch die vier Grundrechenarten miteinander verknüpfen. Durch den Bruchstrich sind Zähler und Nenner klar gekennzeichnet, es ist nicht notwendig, sie in Klammern zu setzen.

Erweitern von Bruchtermen

Erweitert man $\frac{x}{x-3}$ mit $\mathbb{D} = \mathbb{Q}\setminus\{3\}$ mit der Zahl 5, so erhält man

$$\frac{5 \cdot x}{5 \cdot (x-3)} = \frac{5x}{5x-15}$$

Wichtig ist beim Erweitern, den ganzen Zähler und den ganzen Nenner mit der gleichen Zahl zu multiplizieren. Dazu ist es in diesem Fall nötig, Klammern einzuführen.

Brüche dürfen auch mit Termen erweitert werden. Da ein Bruch nicht mit der Zahl Null erweitert werden darf, muss man zunächst sicherstellen, dass der Term mit dem man erweitert, ungleich Null ist. Als Beispiel soll der Bruchterm von oben mit dem Faktor $(x + 1)$ erweitert werden. $x + 1 = 0 \Leftrightarrow x = -1 \Rightarrow$ es muss gelten: $x \neq -1$. Für $x \neq -1$ darf man den Bruchterm erweitern. Man erhält

$$\frac{x}{x-3} = \frac{(x+1) \cdot x}{(x+1)(x-3)} = \frac{x^2 + x}{x^2 - 3x + x - 3} = \frac{x^2 + x}{x^2 - 2x - 3}$$

Kürzen von Bruchtermen

Entsprechend dem Erweitern kann man Bruchterme innerhalb der Definitionsmenge auch kürzen. Zum Beispiel kommt bei dem Bruch $\frac{(x+3)}{5(x+3)}$ mit $\mathbb{D} = \mathbb{Q}\setminus\{-3\}$ im Zähler und Nenner der Faktor $(x + 3)$ vor. Den gemeinsamen Faktor kann man im Zähler und Nenner herauskürzen. Der gekürzte Bruch lautet dann: $\frac{1}{5}$.

Weitere Beispiele für das Kürzen von Bruchtermen:

$$\frac{x}{x^2} = \frac{1}{x} \text{ mit } \mathbb{D} = \mathbb{Q}\setminus\{0\}$$

$$\frac{5x}{5(x+2)^2} = \frac{x}{(x+2)^2} \quad \text{mit } \mathbb{D} = \mathbb{Q}\setminus\{-2\}$$

Man darf nur kürzen, wenn im Zähler <u>und</u> im Nenner ein Produkt steht, das den gleichen Faktor enthält.

Viele Brüche lassen sich nicht auf Anhieb kürzen, weil der Zähler oder der Nenner nicht als Produkt dasteht. Durch Umformungen wie Ausklammern und Faktorisieren oder mit Hilfe der binomischen Formeln lassen sich viele Summen im Zähler oder Nenner in ein Produkt verwandeln. Anschließend kann man gleiche Faktoren dann kürzen.

Beispiele:

$\frac{x^2 + 3x}{x + 3} =$ | Ausklammern von x im Zähler

$\frac{x(x + 3)}{(x + 3)} =$ | Kürzen des Faktors $(x + 3)$

$x \qquad \mathbb{D} = \mathbb{Q}\backslash\{-3\}$

$\frac{x + 2}{x^2 - 4} =$ | 3. binomische Formel im Nenner

$\frac{x + 2}{(x + 2)(x - 2)} =$ | Kürzen des Faktors $(x + 2)$

$\frac{1}{x - 2} \qquad \mathbb{D} = \mathbb{Q}\backslash\{-2, +2\}$

$\frac{4x^2 + 12x + 9}{3y + 2xy} =$ | 1. binomische Formel im Zähler, Ausklammern von y im Nenner

$\frac{(2x + 3)^2}{y(2x + 3)} =$ | Kürzen des Faktors $(2x + 3)$

$\frac{2x + 3}{y} \qquad \mathbb{D}_x = \mathbb{Q}\backslash\left\{-\frac{3}{2}\right\}, \ \mathbb{D}_y = \mathbb{Q}\backslash\{0\}$

Beim Rechnen mit Brüchen und Bruchtermen gelten die gleichen Regeln wie in $\mathbb{Q}$ und beim Bruchrechnen. Zum Beispiel darf, wie schon gesehen, ein Minuszeichen vor einem Bruch wahlweise in den Zähler oder in den Nenner hineingenommen werden. Beispiel:

$$-\frac{x}{x - 2} = \frac{-x}{x - 2} = \frac{x}{-(x - 2)} = \frac{x}{-x + 2}$$

Addition und Subtraktion von Bruchtermen

Um die Zahlen $\frac{1}{2}$ und $\frac{2}{3}$ zu addieren, muss man erst beide Brüche erweitern. Dazu bildet man den gemeinsamen Hauptnenner, in diesem Fall 6, und erweitert dazu den ersten Bruch mit 3, den zweiten mit 2. Man erhält $\frac{3}{6}$ und $\frac{4}{6}$ und damit

$$\frac{1}{2}+\frac{2}{3}=\frac{3}{6}+\frac{4}{6}=\frac{7}{6}$$

als Ergebnis. Um zwei Bruchterme zu addieren oder zu subtrahieren, geht man genauso vor wie bei Bruchzahlen. Zuerst ermittelt man den gemeinsamen Hauptnenner und erweitert die Bruchterme entsprechend. Anschließend kann man die erweiterten Brüche dann addieren oder subtrahieren. Um den gemeinsamen Hauptnenner zu finden, ist es häufig sinnvoll, die Nenner so weit wie möglich zu faktorisieren, also in ein Produkt zu verwandeln. Dann sieht man, welche Faktoren in allen Nennern gemeinsam auftreten, und kann einen möglichst kleinen gemeinsamen Nenner bilden.

Beispiel für eine Addition:

$$\frac{1}{x+2}+\frac{-3}{1-x}= \qquad \mathbb{D}=\mathbb{Q}\setminus\{-2, 1\}$$

Hauptnenner: $(x+2)\,(1-x)$

Erweitern der Brüche

$$\frac{(1-x)}{(1-x)\,(x+2)}+\frac{(x+2)\,(-3)}{(1-x)\,(x+2)}=$$

Zusammenfassen auf einem Bruchstrich

$$\frac{(1-x)+(-3x-6)}{(1-x)\,(x+2)}=$$

$$\frac{-5-4x}{(1-x)\,(x+2)}$$

Beispiel für eine Subtraktion:

$$\frac{-2}{x}-\frac{8}{x-2}= \mid \text{Hauptnenner } x(x-2) \qquad \mathbb{D}=\mathbb{Q}\setminus\{0, 2\}$$

$$\frac{-2\,(x-2)}{x(x-2)}-\frac{8x}{x(x-2)}=$$

$$\frac{-2x+4-8x}{x(x-2)}=$$

$$\frac{-10x+4}{x(x-2)}$$

Häufig trifft man bei Additionen und Subtraktionen auf Terme, die nicht in Bruchform gegeben sind, also keinen Nenner haben. Sie sollen aber zu einem Bruchterm addiert werden. Um einen gemeinsamen Hauptnenner bilden zu können, müssen solche Terme ohne Nenner erst künstlich in einen Bruchterm umgewandelt werden. Das geschieht, indem man 1 als Nenner dieser Terme einführt. Danach kann die Addition wie gewohnt ausgeführt werden.

Beispiel: $x + \frac{x}{2} =$ | Ersetzen von x durch $\frac{x}{1}$

$\frac{x}{1} + \frac{x}{2} =$ | Hauptnenner 2

$\frac{2x}{2} + \frac{x}{2} =$

$\frac{3x}{2}$

Multiplikation von Bruchtermen

Zwei Bruchterme werden miteinander multipliziert, indem man ihre Zähler und ihre Nenner multipliziert. Es gilt also auch hier die gleiche Regel wie für Brüche aus $\mathbb{Q}$.

Beispiele:

$\frac{x}{3 - x} \cdot \frac{2}{x + 1} =$ $\quad$ $\mathbb{D} = \mathbb{Q}\backslash\{-1, 3\}$

$\frac{2x}{(3 - x)(x + 1)} = \frac{2x}{3x + 3 - x^2 - x} = \frac{2x}{-x^2 + 2x + 3}$

$-\frac{1}{x^2} \cdot \frac{x}{x - 1} =$ | Vorzeichenregel $\quad$ $\mathbb{D} = \mathbb{Q}\backslash\{0, 1\}$

$\frac{-1}{x^2} \cdot \frac{x}{x - 1} =$ | »Zähler mal Zähler und Nenner mal Nenner«

$\frac{-1 \cdot x}{x^2(x - 1)} =$ | Kürzen durch x

$\frac{-1}{x(x - 1)}$

Division von Bruchtermen und Doppelbrüche

Durch einen Bruch wird dividiert, indem man mit dem Kehrbruch multipliziert. Diese Regel gilt sowohl für Brüche in $\mathbb{Q}$ als auch für Bruchterme.

Beispiel: $\frac{1}{x} : \frac{1}{x^2} =$ | Multiplikation mit dem Kehrbruch $\quad$ $\mathbb{D} = \mathbb{Q}\backslash\{0\}$

$\frac{1}{x} \cdot \frac{x^2}{1} =$ | Zusammenfassen auf einen Bruchstrich

$$\frac{x^2}{x} = \mid \text{Kürzen von } x$$

$$x$$

Statt eines Divisionszeichens kann man in Rechnungen mit Brüchen auch wieder einen Bruchstrich einführen. Der Quotient aus obigen Beispiel wird dann geschrieben als

$$\frac{\frac{1}{x}}{\frac{1}{x^2}}$$

Es handelt sich nur um eine andere Schreibweise, der Wert des Terms ändert sich dadurch nicht.

Am einfachsten löst man einen Doppelbruch auf, indem man in einem Zwischenschritt das Divisionszeichen wieder einführt. Danach löst man die Divisionsaufgabe wie gewohnt, indem man mit dem Kehrbruch multipliziert. Hat man schon etwas mehr Routine im Umgang mit Doppelbrüchen, kann man den Zwischenschritt auch weglassen und gleich mit dem Kehrbruch des Nenners multiplizieren.

Beispiel: $\frac{\frac{1}{2x-1}}{\frac{x^2}{8}} = \mid$ Einführen des »:« $\quad \mathbb{D} = \mathbb{Q}\setminus\left\{0, \frac{1}{2}\right\}$

$$\frac{1}{2x-1} : \frac{x^2}{8} =$$

$$\frac{1}{2x-1} \cdot \frac{8}{x^2} =$$

$$\frac{8}{x^2(2x-1)}$$

2 Lineare Funktionen und ihre Graphen

2.1 Der Funktionsbegriff

Eine Funktion ist eine Abbildung von einer Menge $\mathbb{D}$ in eine andere Menge. $\mathbb{D}$ heißt die Definitionsmenge, die zweite Menge, z.B. $\mathbb{N}$, heißt die Zielmenge der Funktion. Man schreibt f: $\mathbb{D} \to \mathbb{N}$. Die Funktion ordnet jedem Element aus $\mathbb{D}$ genau ein Element aus $\mathbb{N}$ zu. Für jedes Element $a \in \mathbb{D}$ gibt es also ein Element $w_a \in \mathbb{N}$, auf das a abgebildet wird, und für das gilt $f(a) = w_a$. Die Definitionsmenge wird durch die Funktion vollständig ausgeschöpft, alle Elemente der Definitionsmenge werden abgebildet. Verschiedene Elemente a, $b \in \mathbb{D}$ können auf das gleiche Element in der Zielmenge abgebildet werden. Die Menge $\mathbb{W} = f(\mathbb{D}) = \{f(x) \mid x \in \mathbb{D}\}$ nennt man die Wertemenge der Funktion. Für jedes Element y der Wertemenge gibt es mindestens ein Element der Definitionsmenge $x \in \mathbb{D}$, für das gilt $y = f(x)$. Die Abbildungsvorschrift gibt an, wie die Zuordnung der Elemente geregelt ist. Funktionen und ihre Abbildungsvorschriften können auf verschiedene Arten dargestellt werden. Ist z.B. die Abbildungsvorschrift in Form einer Gleichung gegeben, lassen sich die Funktionswerte durch Einsetzen berechnen, dazu erstellt man eine Wertetabelle.

Beispiele für Funktionen:

$f_1: \mathbb{D} = \{1, 2, 5, 8\} \to \{0, 1, 2\}$ $f_1 = \{(1, 0), (2, 0), (5, 1), (8, 2)\}$

$f_2: \mathbb{Q} \to \mathbb{Q}$ $x \mapsto 1$

$$f_3: \mathbb{N} \to \{0, 1\} \quad x \mapsto \begin{cases} 0 \text{ falls } x \text{ gerade} \\ 1 \text{ falls } x \text{ ungerade} \end{cases}$$

Wertetabelle für f_3

x	1	2	3	4	5
$f(x)$	1	0	1	0	1

$f_4: \mathbb{Q} \to \mathbb{Q}$ $x \mapsto y = 2x - 1$

Wertetabelle für f_4

x	-2	-1	0	$\frac{1}{2}$	1	2
$f(x) = 2x - 1$	-5	-3	-1	0	1	3

f_2 ist eine konstante Funktion. f_4 ist ein Beispiel für eine lineare Funktion. f_2, f_3 und f_4 lassen sich auch graphisch in einem Koordinatensystem darstellen.

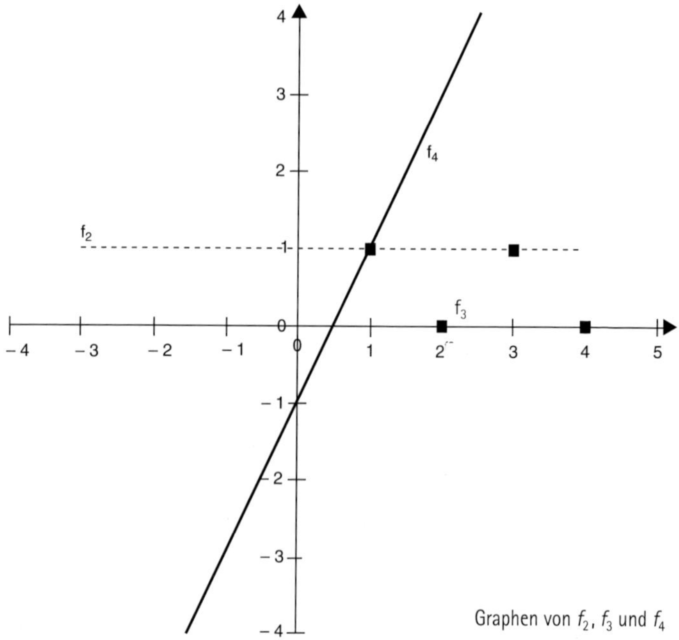

Graphen von f_2, f_3 und f_4

2.2 Lineare Funktionen in $\mathbb{Q}$

Eine Abbildung der Form $f\colon \mathbb{Q} \to \mathbb{Q}\ x \mapsto y = mx + t$ mit $m, t \in \mathbb{Q}$, $m \neq 0$ heißt lineare Funktion. Eine wichtige Besonderheit jeder linearen Funktion ist, dass in ihrer Abbildungsvorschrift x nur in der ersten Potenz vorkommt. Beispiele für lineare Funktionen sind:

$f_1: \mathbb{Q} \rightarrow \mathbb{Q} \; x \mapsto y = 3x - 1$

$f_2: \mathbb{Q} \rightarrow \mathbb{Q} \; x \mapsto y = -\frac{1}{3}x$

$f_3: \mathbb{Q} \rightarrow \mathbb{Q} \; x \mapsto y = -\frac{1}{3}x + 2$

Durch Ermitteln der Wertetabelle erhält man die Graphen der drei Funktionen.

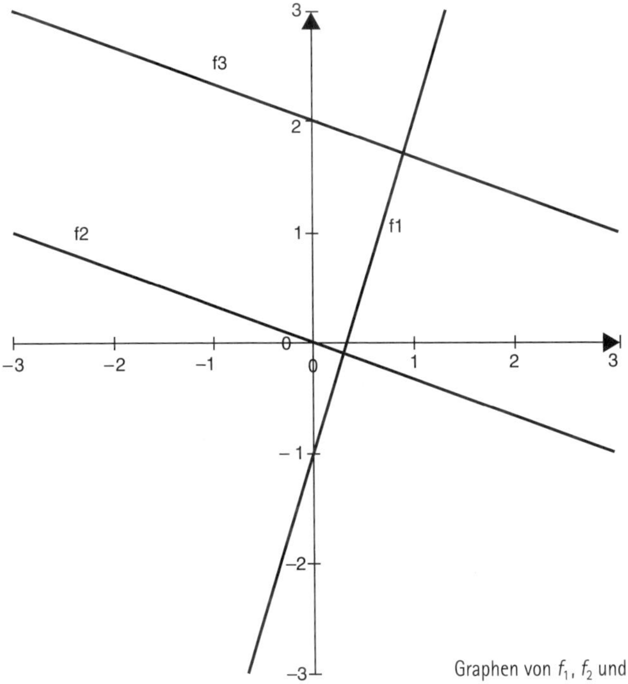

Graphen von f_1, f_2 und f_3

Die Graphen linearer Funktionen sind Geraden. Jede Funktion mit der Abbildungsvorschrift $x \mapsto y = mx + t$ ergibt in der graphischen Darstellung eine Gerade. $y = mx + t$ wird deshalb auch als Geradengleichung bezeichnet. m heißt dabei die Steigung der Gerade und t wird als Achsenabschnitt bezeichnet. Durch m und t ist die Gerade eindeutig festgelegt.

Schnittpunkt mit der y-Achse

Dort, wo der Graph einer Funktion die y-Achse schneidet, gilt $x = 0$. Ein Graph einer beliebigen linearen Funktion schneidet die y-Achse genau einmal. Für eine Gerade lässt sich der Schnittpunkt mit der y-Achse leicht ausrechnen. Es gilt $x = 0$

$\Rightarrow y = m \cdot 0 + t \Rightarrow y = t$

Eine Gerade als Graph einer linearen Funktion schneidet die y-Achse also im Punkt $(0, t)$. Daraus erklärt sich auch der Ausdruck Achsenabschnitt für t. Die Strecke auf der y-Achse zwischen Nullpunkt und Schnittpunkt mit der Geraden hat den gleichen Betrag wie t. Ist t positiv, schneidet die Gerade die y-Achse oberhalb des Nullpunkts, ist t negativ schneidet die Gerade sie unterhalb des Nullpunkts. Für den Fall, dass $t = 0$ ist, ist der Achsenabschnitt auch 0 und die Gerade geht durch den Koordinatenursprung. Geraden, die durch den Koordinatenursprung laufen, heißen Ursprungsgeraden. Die Zusammenhänge zwischen dem Vorzeichen von t und der Lage des Schnittpunkts (von Gerade und y-Achse) kann man sich auch an den Abbildungen verdeutlichen.

Das Steigungsdreieck

Eine Gerade hat an jeder Stelle die gleiche Steigung m. Kennt man bereits einen Punkt der Geraden, so genügt ein weiterer Punkt, um die Gerade eindeutig festzulegen. Durch die Steigung bzw. das Steigungsdreieck lässt sich von einem bekannten Punkt aus ein weiterer Punkt der Geraden bestimmen und so die Gerade zeichnen.

Man nimmt also einen bekannten Punkt der Geraden, z.B. den Punkt $(0, t)$, der durch den Achsenabschnitt gegeben ist. (Da die Steigung der Geraden überall gleich ist, kann man die Rechnung auch mit jedem beliebigen anderen Punkt (x_0, y_0) durchführen.) Die Frage ist, um wie viel der y-Wert steigt, wenn man den x-Wert um 1 erhöht. Im Bild des Steigungsdreiecks gesprochen ist die Frage, um wie viel man nach oben oder unten gehen muss, wenn man um 1 nach rechts geht. Rechnerische Lösung: (x_0, y_0) ist ein bekannter Punkt der Gerade, y_1 ist der gesuchte y-Wert zu $x_1 = x_0 + 1$. Dann gilt:

$\Leftrightarrow y_1 = m(x_0 + 1) + t$
$\Leftrightarrow y_1 = mx_0 + m + t$
$\Leftrightarrow y_1 = mx_0 + t + m$
$\Leftrightarrow y_1 = y_0 + m$

Die Gleichung zeigt: Erhöht man x um 1, erhöht sich y um m. Graphisch bedeutet das, geht man um 1 nach rechts, muss man um m nach oben oder unten gehen, um wieder einen Punkt auf der Geraden zu erhalten. Das Steigungsdreieck ist also ein rechtwinkliges Dreieck mit den Kathetenlängen 1 in x-Richtung und m in y-Richtung. Je nachdem, ob m positiv oder negativ ist, muss m nach oben (positiv) oder unten (negativ) abgetragen werden.

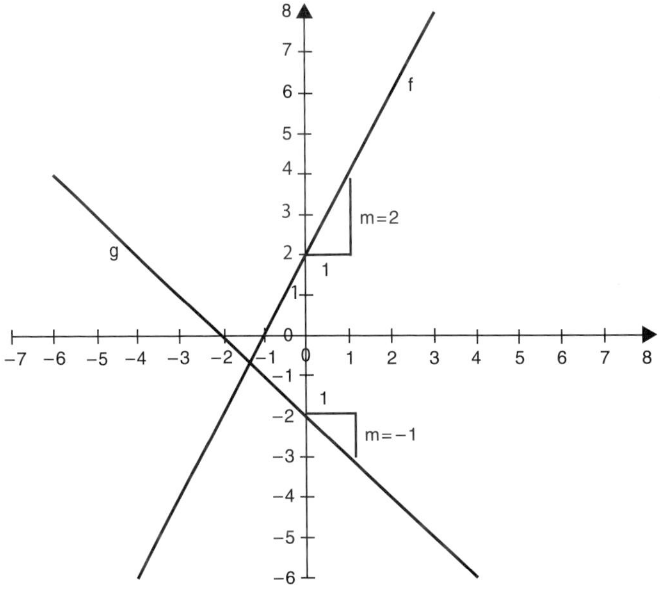

Steigungsdreieck für $f: x \mapsto 2x + 2$ und $g: x \mapsto -x - 2$

In der Abbildung ist die Funktion $f: \mathbb{Q} \to \mathbb{Q}\ x \mapsto 2x + 2$ dargestellt. Der Achsenabschnitt ist $t = 2$. Der Schnittpunkt der Gerade mit der y-Achse ist demnach der Punkt (0, 2). Das Steigungsdreieck zeichnet man, indem man vom Punkt (0, 2) um 1 nach rechts und um $m = 2$ nach oben geht.

Analog erhält man den Graphen von $g: \mathbb{Q} \to \mathbb{Q}\ x \mapsto -x - 2$. Der Achsenabschnitt ist $t = -2$, die Steigung ist $m = -1$. Daraus erhält man den Schnittpunkt mit der y-Achse (0, −2). Für das Steigungsdreieck geht man von diesem Punkt aus um 1 nach rechts und, weil $m = -1$, also negativ ist, um 1 nach unten.

Nullstelle einer Geraden

Eine Nullstelle einer Funktion ist ein x-Wert aus der Definitionsmenge, für den die Funktion gleich Null wird, kurz $f(x) = 0$ mit $x \in \mathbb{D}$. Der Graph einer Funktion schneidet die x-Achse genau an seinen Nullstellen.

Jede lineare Funktion hat genau eine Nullstelle in $\mathbb{Q}$. Das liegt daran, dass jede lineare Funktion als Graphen eine Gerade mit einer Steigung $m \neq 0$ hat. Der Graph ist damit nicht parallel zur x-Achse sondern schneidet sie in genau einem Punkt. Die Nullstelle der allgemeinen linearen Abbildung $f\colon \mathbb{Q} \to \mathbb{Q}\ x \mapsto y = mx + t$ lässt sich berechnen. Es gilt: $f(x) = 0$

$$\Leftrightarrow 0 = mx + t \,|\, -t$$

$$\Leftrightarrow -t = mx \,|\, \cdot \frac{1}{m}$$

$$\Leftrightarrow x = -\frac{t}{m}$$

Die Nullstelle einer linearen Abbildung liegt bei $x = -\frac{t}{m}$, der Schnittpunkt des Graphen mit der x-Achse ist der Punkt $(-\frac{t}{m}, 0)$.

Aufstellen von Geradengleichungen

Wie man aus der Geometrie weiß, ist eine Gerade durch zwei Punkte bereits genau festgelegt. Hat man nur zwei Punkte P und Q gegeben, stellt sich die Frage, wie man aus ihnen die Gleichung der dazugehörigen Gerade herleitet.

Als Beispiel seien die Punkte $P(3, 5)$ und $Q(-1, 1)$ gegeben. Gesucht ist die Gleichung der Geraden, die P und Q enthält. Da beide Punkte auf der Geraden liegen, müssen sie beide die Geradengleichung erfüllen. Es gilt also

I. $5 = m \cdot 3 + t$

II. $1 = m \cdot (-1) + t$ oder umgeformt

I* $5 = 3m + t$

II* $1 = -m + t \,|\, \cdot (-1)$

Man erhält ein Gleichungssystem aus zwei Gleichungen mit zwei Unbekannten. Im nachfolgenden Abschnitt werden verschiedene Lösungsmethoden für solche Gleichungssysteme dargestellt. An dieser Stelle wird die Lösung durch Subtraktion der beiden Gleichungen berechnet. D.h. man multipliziert II* mit –1, addiert anschließend die beiden Gleichungen und erhält:

$$\begin{aligned} \text{I}^* + (-1)\cdot \text{II}^* \quad 5 - 1 &= 3m + m + t - t \\ 4 &= 4m \\ m &= 1 \end{aligned}$$

Den errechneten Wert für m setzt man in eine der Ausgangsgleichungen ein.

m eingesetzt in I:
$$\begin{aligned} 5 &= 1 \cdot 3 + t \\ 5 &= 3 + t \;|\; -3 \\ t &= 2 \end{aligned}$$

Die Geradengleichung für die Gerade durch die Punkte P und Q lautet also:

$y = x + 2$.

Auch allgemein lässt sich die Steigung einer Geraden durch zwei gegebene Punkte berechnen. Für zwei gegebene Punkte $P_1(x_1, y_1)$ und $P_2(x_2, y_2)$ mit $x_1, y_1, x_2, y_2 \in \mathbb{Q}$ und $x_1 \neq x_2$ ergibt sich wieder ein Gleichungssystem aus zwei Gleichungen mit zwei Unbekannten, da die Koordinaten beider Punkte die selbe Geradengleichung erfüllen:

$$\begin{aligned} &I. \quad y_1 = mx_1 + t \;|\; - mx_1 \\ &II. \quad y_2 = mx_2 + t \;|\; - mx_2 \end{aligned}$$

Man löst zunächst beide Gleichungen nach t auf und setzt sie dann gleich. Dadurch verschwindet t aus dem Gleichungssystem und man erhält eine Gleichung mit der einen Unbekannten m, nach der man dann auflösen kann.

$$\begin{aligned} &\text{I}^* \quad y_1 - mx_1 = t \\ &\text{II}^* \quad y_2 - mx_2 = t \;|\; \text{Gleichsetzen von I}^* \text{ und II}^* \\ &y_1 - mx_1 = y_2 - mx_2 \;|\; + mx_1 - y_2 \\ &y_1 - y_2 = mx_1 - mx_2 \\ &y_1 - y_2 = m(x_1 - x_2) \;|\; :(x_1 - x_2) \\ &\frac{y_1 - y_2}{x_1 - x_2} = m \end{aligned}$$

Die Steigung einer Geraden durch zwei Punkte $P_1(x_1, y_1)$ und $P_2(x_2, y_2)$ mit $x_1 \neq x_2$ hat den Wert $m = \dfrac{y_1 - y_2}{x_1 - x_2}$

Durch Einsetzen von m in die Gleichung I oder II lässt sich t dann leicht berechnen.

Die Umkehrfunktion einer linearen Funktion

Umkehrbarkeit

Bei einer linearen Funktion $f\colon \mathbb{Q} \to \mathbb{Q}\ x \mapsto y = mx + t$ werden verschiedenen x-Werten auch verschiedene y-Werte zugeordnet. Zu jedem y-Wert in $\mathbb{Q}$ gibt es genau einen x-Wert, der darauf abgebildet wird und jeder y-Wert in $\mathbb{Q}$ wird genau einmal angenommen. Eine lineare Funktion ist also umkehrbar in $\mathbb{Q}$. Die Definitionsmenge und die Wertemenge der Umkehrfunktion sind wie die Definitionsmenge und Wertemenge der ursprünglichen Funktion gleich $\mathbb{Q}$.

Bestimmen der Umkehrfunktion f^{-1}

Die Umkehrfunktion lässt sich rechnerisch bestimmen, indem man in der Funktionsgleichung die Variablen x und y vertauscht und dann nach y auflöst.
Das soll zuerst an Hand der Beispielfunktion $h\colon \mathbb{Q} \to \mathbb{Q}\ x \mapsto y = 3x - 6$ gezeigt und parallel dazu für den allgemeinen Fall berechnet werden.

$h\colon \mathbb{Q} \to \mathbb{Q}\ x \mapsto y = 3x - 6$	$f\colon \mathbb{Q} \to \mathbb{Q}\ x \mapsto y = mx + t$
$y = 3x - 6 \mid$ Vertauschen der Variablen	$y = mx + t \mid$ Vertauschen der Variablen
$x = 3y - 6 \mid +6$	$x = my + t \mid -t$
$x + 6 = 3y \mid \cdot \frac{1}{3}$	$x - t = my \mid \cdot \frac{1}{m}$
$y = \frac{1}{3}x + 2$	$y = \frac{1}{m}x - \frac{t}{m}$

Die Umkehrfunktion h^{-1} zu h lautet: $h^{-1}\colon \mathbb{Q} \to \mathbb{Q}\ x \mapsto y = \frac{1}{3}x + 2$

> Die Umkehrfunktion zur linearen Funktion $f\colon \mathbb{Q} \to \mathbb{Q}\ x \mapsto y = mx + t$ mit $m, t \in \mathbb{Q}$, $m \neq 0$ ist die Funktion
> $f^{-1}\colon \mathbb{Q} \to \mathbb{Q}\ x \mapsto y = \frac{1}{m}x - \frac{t}{m}$

Graphisch erhält man die Umkehrfunktion zu einer Funktion, indem man die ursprüngliche Funktion an der Geraden $y = x$, der Winkelhalbierenden des I. und III. Quadranten spiegelt. Schneiden sich Funktion und Umkehrfunktion, liegt der Schnittpunkt auf der Winkelhalbierenden.

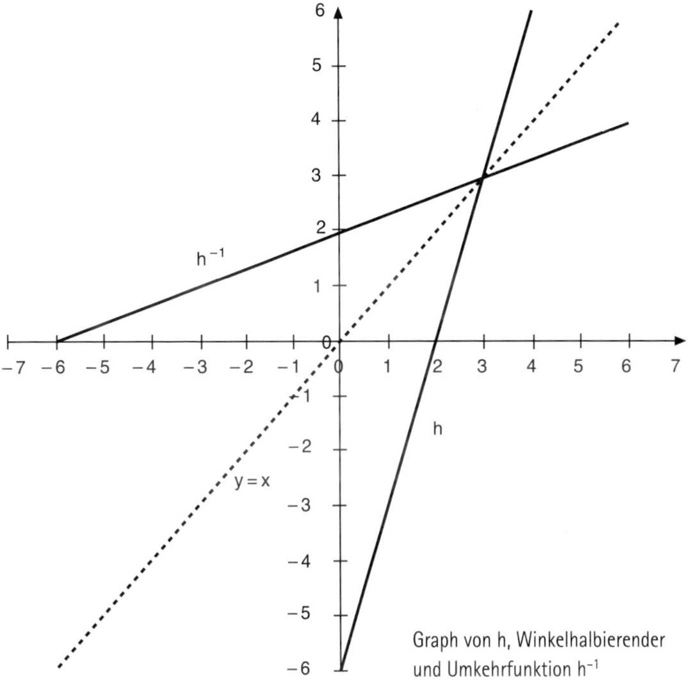

Graph von h, Winkelhalbierender und Umkehrfunktion h^{-1}

Die Lage von Geraden zueinander

Geraden in einer Ebene können zueinander parallel sein, sie können identisch sein oder sich in einem Punkt schneiden. Man hat verschiedene Möglichkeiten, um herauszufinden, wie zwei Geraden zueinander liegen. Man kann graphisch eine Lösung finden, indem man die Geraden zeichnet. Oder man geht rechnerisch an das Problem heran und setzt die Gleichungen der Geraden gleich. An Hand der Lösungsmenge kann man dann bestimmen, ob die Geraden sich schneiden oder nicht. Die Steigung *m* einer Geraden gibt bereits einen ersten Anhaltspunkt für die Lage dieser Geraden anderen gegenüber.

Parallele Geraden

Zwei Geraden sind parallel, wenn sie die gleiche Steigung *m* haben.

$f_1: \mathbb{Q} \to \mathbb{Q}\ x \mapsto y = m_1x + t_1$

$f_2: \mathbb{Q} \to \mathbb{Q}\ x \mapsto y = m_2x + t_2$

Die beiden Funktionen f_1 und f_2 sind genau dann parallel, wenn gilt $m_1 = m_2$.
Ein Beispiel für zwei parallele Geraden sind f_2 und f_3 in der Abbildung auf S. 111. Zwei Geraden mit gleicher Steigung sind zueinander parallel verschoben, ihre Gleichungen unterscheiden sich nur im Achsenabschnitt t. Sind die Achsenabschnitte auch gleich, sind die Geraden identisch, ihre Graphen überlagern sich.

Beispiel: f: $\mathbb{Q} \to \mathbb{Q}\ x \mapsto y = 2x - 4$
g: $\mathbb{Q} \to \mathbb{Q}\ x \mapsto y = 2x$
h: $\mathbb{Q} \to \mathbb{Q}\ x \mapsto y = 2(x - 2)$

Formt man die Abbildungsvorschrift von h etwas um, erhält man

h: $\mathbb{Q} \to \mathbb{Q}\ x \mapsto y = 2x - 4$

Die Steigung aller drei Geraden f, g und h ist $m = 2$. Die drei Geraden sind also parallel, kurz $f \| g \| h$. Die Achsenabschnitte von f und h sind ebenfalls gleich. f und h sind nicht nur parallel, sie sind sogar identisch, $f = h$.
Geraden, die nicht parallel oder identisch sind, schneiden sich in einem Punkt.

Aufeinander senkrecht stehende Geraden
Zwei Geraden f:
$\mathbb{Q} \to \mathbb{Q}\ x \mapsto y = m_1x + t_1$ und g: $\mathbb{Q} \to \mathbb{Q}\ x \mapsto y = m_2x + t_2$ stehen aufeinander senkrecht, wenn für das Produkt ihrer Steigungen gilt:

$m_1 \cdot m_2 = -1$

(Der Nachweis erfolgt über trigonometrische Funktionen oder den Höhensatz in rechtwinkligen Dreiecken und soll hier nicht erbracht werden.)
Ein Beispiel für aufeinander senkrecht stehende Geraden sind die Geraden f_1 und f_2 in der Abbildung auf S. 111.

3 Lineare Gleichungen und Ungleichungen

Lineare Gleichungen und Ungleichungen sind Aussagen, in denen genau eine Variable vorkommt. Für diese Variable wird eine Lösungsmenge gesucht. Dabei haben lineare Gleichungen und Ungleichungen eine wichtige Gemeinsamkeit. Die Variable, für die eine Lösungsmenge gesucht wird, kommt nur in der ersten Potenz vor. Sonst können diese Gleichungen und Ungleichungen sehr unterschiedlich sein. Mit Hilfe von Äquivalenzumformungen lassen sie sich aber (fast) alle lösen. Am Ende der Rechnung ist es wichtig, die Lösungsmenge $\mathbb{L}$ für die Variable anzugeben.
Wie im Abschnitt über lineare Funktionen gezeigt wurde, ist der Graph einer linearen Gleichung eine Gerade. Entsprechend kann man lineare Gleichungen darstellen und so eine graphische Lösung für die Variable finden.

3.1 Lineare Gleichungen mit einer Unbekannten

Gleichungen der Art $x + a = b$
Für die lineare Gleichung

$x + 2 = 6 \quad x \in \mathbb{Q}$

findet man in $\mathbb{N}$ oder in $\mathbb{Q}$ leicht eine Lösung. Mit Worten formuliert lautet die Frage, zu welcher Zahl muss ich 2 addieren, um 6 zu erhalten? Die Antwort ist 4. Rechnerisch erhält man das Ergebnis durch Äquivalenzumformungen.
Die Regel für Äquivalenzumformungen besagt: man darf auf beiden Seiten einer Gleichung die gleiche Zahl addieren (oder die gleiche Zahl subtrahieren) und ändert dadurch die Lösung der Gleichung nicht.
Im Fall des Beispiels addiert man auf beiden Seiten der Gleichung –2. Dadurch verschwindet auf der linken Seite der Gleichung die 2.

$x + 2 = 6 \mid + (-2)$
$x + 2 + (-2) = 6 + (-2)$
$x = 4 \qquad\qquad \mathbb{L} = \{4\}$

Salopp sagt man auch für die Äquivalenzumformung, »man bringt 2 auf die andere Seite der Gleichung«, dabei ändert sich ihr Vorzeichen. Allgemein bringt man einen Term von der einen Seite einer Gleichung auf die andere, indem man ihn auf beiden Seiten der Gleichung subtrahiert, bzw. (was nach den Regeln der Addition und Subtraktion in $\mathbb{Q}$ das Gleiche ist) auf beiden Seiten der Gleichung das negative Gegenstück addiert. Das gilt sowohl für Terme mit positivem Vorzeichen als auch für Terme mit negativem Vorzeichen, wie die nächsten Beispiele verdeutlichen.

$3 + x = 0 \mid -3$

$3 - 3 + x = 0 - 3$

$x = -3 \qquad \mathbb{L} = \{-3\}$

$x - \frac{1}{2} = -\frac{1}{2} \;\Big|\; +\frac{1}{2}$

$x - \frac{1}{2} + \frac{1}{2} = -\frac{1}{2} + \frac{1}{2}$

$x = 0 \qquad \mathbb{L} = \{0\}$

$a = x - 6 \mid +6$

$a + 6 = x - 6 + 6$

$x = a + 6 \qquad \mathbb{L} = \{a + 6\}$

$x - b = b \mid +b$

$x - b + b = b + b$

$x = 2b \qquad \mathbb{L} = \{2b\}$

> Die Regel für die Äquivalenzumformung der Gleichung
> $x + a = b \quad a, b, x \in \mathbb{Q}$ lässt sich allgemein herleiten:
>
> $x + a = b \mid -a$
>
> $x + a - a = b - a$
>
> $x = b - a \qquad \mathbb{L} = \{b - a\}$

Gleichungen der Art *ax* = *b*

Für die Gleichung $3x = 18$ mit $x \in \mathbb{Q}$ findet man durch Nachdenken oder Ausprobieren schnell eine Lösung. Mit welcher Zahl muss man 3 multiplizieren, damit man 18 erhält? Die richtige Lösung ist $x = 6$. Die Lösung erhält man formal auf dem Weg der Äquivalenzumformungen. Es gilt: Multipliziert (oder dividiert) man beide Seiten einer Gleichung mit demselben Term t ($t \neq 0$), verändert sich die Lösung der Gleichung dadurch nicht. Im Beispielsfall darf man beide Seiten der Gleichung mit $\frac{1}{3}$ multiplizieren (oder durch 3 dividieren) und ändert dadurch nichts an der Lösungsmenge für x.

$3x = 18 \mid \cdot \frac{1}{3}$

$\frac{1}{3} \cdot 3x = \frac{1}{3} \cdot 18 \mid$ Regeln für die Multiplikation von Brüchen

$x = \frac{18}{3} \mid$ Kürzen

$x = 6$ $\qquad\qquad\qquad\qquad \mathbb{L} = \{6\}$

Um am Ende der Äquivalenzumformung die Variable x allein auf einer Seite der Gleichung stehen zu haben, teilt man also beide Seiten der Gleichung durch den Faktor vor dem x oder einfacher, man multipliziert beide Seiten mit dem Kehrwert dieses Faktors. Dabei muss man das Vorzeichen dieses Faktors berücksichtigen.

Weitere Beispiele: Es gelte $x, a \in \mathbb{Q}$

$-x = 3 \mid \cdot (-1)$

$-1 \cdot (-x) = -1 \cdot 3$

$x = -3$ $\qquad\qquad\qquad\qquad \mathbb{L} = \{-3\}$

$\frac{x}{5} = -2 \mid \cdot 5$

$5 \cdot \frac{x}{5} = 5 \cdot (-2)$

$x = -10$ $\qquad\qquad\qquad\qquad \mathbb{L} = \{-10\}$

$-\frac{3}{2}x = a \mid \cdot \left(-\frac{2}{3}\right)$

$-\frac{2}{3} \cdot \left(-\frac{3}{2}x\right) = -\frac{2}{3}a$

$x = -\frac{2}{3}a$ $\qquad\qquad\qquad\qquad \mathbb{L} = \left\{-\frac{2}{3}a\right\}$

Einen besonderen Fall stellt die Gleichung $ax = 5a$ dar. Die Lösungsmenge muss an Hand einer Fallunterscheidung ermittelt werden.

$ax = 5a$ $\qquad\qquad\qquad\qquad a, x \in \mathbb{Q}$

1. Fall $a = 0$

$\Rightarrow 0 \cdot x = 0 \cdot 5$

$\Leftrightarrow 0 = 0$

Für den Fall $a = 0$ ist die Gleichung immer wahr, egal, welche Zahl man für x einsetzt. Für jedes x gilt $0 \cdot x = 0$. Im ersten Fall ist darum die Lösungsmenge gleich der gesamten Definitionsmenge, $\mathbb{L} = \mathbb{Q}$

2. Fall $a \neq 0$

$ax = 5a \mid \cdot \frac{1}{a}$ (erlaubt, da $a \neq 0$!)

$\frac{1}{a} \cdot ax = 5a \cdot \frac{1}{a} \mid$ Kürzen

$x = 5$ $\qquad\qquad$ $\mathbb{L} = \{5\}$

Für den Fall $a \neq 0$ hat die Lösungsmenge nur ein Element.

Allgemein gilt für die lineare Gleichung der Form

$ax = b \mid \cdot \frac{1}{a}$ mit $a, b, x \in \mathbb{Q}, a \neq 0$

$\frac{1}{a} \cdot ax = \frac{1}{a} \cdot b$

$x = \frac{b}{a}$ $\qquad\qquad$ $\mathbb{L} = \left\{\frac{b}{a}\right\}$

Allgemeine lineare Gleichungen

Die meisten linearen Gleichungen treten nicht in einer der beiden Reinformen, die eben besprochen wurden auf, sondern sind Mischformen aus beiden. Um z. B. die Gleichung $3x - 1 = -7$ mit $x \in \mathbb{Q}$ zu lösen, wendet man nacheinander die Regeln der Äquivalenzumformung aus den letzten beiden Abschnitten an. Zuerst bringt man -1 auf die andere Seite, dann können beide Gleichungsseiten mit $\frac{1}{3}$ multipliziert werden.

$3x - 1 = -7 \mid +1$

$3x = -7 + 1$

$3x = -6 \mid \cdot \frac{1}{3}$

$x = -6 \cdot \frac{1}{3}$

$x = -2$ $\qquad\qquad$ $\mathbb{L} = \{-2\}$

Bei Gleichungen, in denen auf beiden Seiten Summanden mit und ohne Variable stehen, empfiehlt sich folgendes Vorgehen:
- Alle Terme mit Variable auf die eine Seite der Gleichung bringen,
- dann alle Terme ohne Variable auf die andere Seite der Gleichung bringen und
- auf beiden Seiten zusammenfassen.
- Die Variable auf der entsprechenden Seite ausklammern und
- die gesamte Gleichung durch den Faktor vor der Variablen teilen.

Ein Vorgehen, wie es im Kasten beschrieben wird, kann man am nächsten Beispiel nachvollziehen: $x \in \mathbb{Q}$

$$-x - 8 = 2 - 3x \;\Big|\; + 3x$$
$$3x - x - 8 = 2 - 3x + 3x \;\Big|\; + 8$$
$$3x - x = 2 + 8$$
$$2x = 10 \;\Big|\; \cdot \frac{1}{2}$$
$$x = \frac{1}{2} \cdot 10$$
$$x = 5 \qquad\qquad \mathbb{L} = \{5\}$$

Mit den Äquivalenzumformungen lassen sich auch komplizierte Beispiele von linearen Gleichungen mit einer Unbekannten lösen.

$$x(a - 3) - 1 = \frac{1}{2}(-6x + 4a) + 2ax \qquad \text{mit } x, a \in \mathbb{Q}, a \neq 0$$

Auf den ersten Blick hat die Gleichung wenig mit einer linearen Gleichung gemeinsam. Nach Auflösen der Klammern sieht man aber, dass die gesuchte Variable x nur in der ersten Potenz vorkommt. Es handelt sich demnach um eine lineare Gleichung.

$$x(a - 3) - 1 = \frac{1}{2}(-6x + 4a) + 2ax$$
$$ax - 3x - 1 = -3x + 2a + 2ax \;\Big|\; + 3x - 2ax$$
$$ax - 2ax - 3x + 3x - 1 = 2a \;\Big|\; + 1$$
$$-ax = 2a + 1 \;\Big|\; \cdot -\frac{1}{a}$$
$$x = -\frac{2a + 1}{a} \qquad\qquad \mathbb{L} - \left\{-\frac{2a + 1}{a}\right\}$$

Es gibt auch Beispiele für lineare Gleichungen, die keine Lösung haben:

$x - 6 = x \mid - x$
$- 6 = 0$ Widerspruch

Egal, welchen Wert man für x einsetzt, die Gleichung wird immer falsch, die Lösungsmenge ist leer $\mathbb{L} = \{\ \}$

3.2 Lineare Ungleichungen mit einer Unbekannten

Auch bei linearen Ungleichungen ist die Frage, welche Elemente der Definitionsmenge ihr genügen oder, anders formuliert, wie die Lösungsmenge einer Ungleichung aussieht. Wie auch bei Gleichungen erhält man die Lösungsmenge einer linearen Ungleichung durch Äquivalenzumformungen.
Hier werden zwei Grundtypen von linearen Ungleichungen und die dazugehörigen Lösungswege dargestellt und anschließend für den allgemeinen Fall einer linearen Ungleichung zusammengesetzt. Für das Rechnen mit Ungleichungen ist es egal, welches Ungleichheitszeichen vorliegt, $>$, $\geq$, $<$ oder $\leq$. Die Regeln der Äquivalenzumformungen gelten für alle Zeichen in der gleichen Weise.

Lineare Ungleichungen der Form $x + a > b$
Gegeben ist die Ungleichung $x - 5 > 1$ mit $x \in \mathbb{Q}$. Um sie aufzulösen, muss 5 auf die andere Seite der Ungleichung gebracht werden. Dabei gilt für Ungleichungen im Bezug auf die Strichrechenarten die gleiche Regel wie für Gleichungen. Die Lösung einer Ungleichung wird nicht verändert, wenn man auf beiden Seiten der Ungleichung dieselbe Zahl addiert (oder subtrahiert). Im gegebenen Beispiel bedeutet das, man darf auf beiden Seiten 5 addieren und verändert dadurch die Lösungsmenge nicht.

$x - 5 > 1 \mid + 5$
$x - 5 + 5 > 1 + 5$
$x > 6$

Die Lösungsmenge für die Ungleichung $x - 5 > 1$ ist $\mathbb{L} = \{x \in \mathbb{Q} \mid x > 6\}$

Allgemein gilt für $a, b, x \in \mathbb{Q}$
$x + a < b \mid - a$
$x < b - a$ $\qquad \mathbb{L} = \{x \in \mathbb{Q} \mid x < b - a\}$

Ungleichungen der Form $ax > b$

Um diesen Fall einer Ungleichung allgemein lösen zu können, ist eine Vorüberlegung nötig. Es gilt folgender Zusammenhang zwischen Vorzeichen einer Variablen und Richtung der Ungleichung:

Für alle $x \in \mathbb{Q}$:

1. $x < 0 \Leftrightarrow -x > 0$
2. $x > 0 \Leftrightarrow -x < 0$

Durch Einsetzen kann man sich diesen Zusammenhang klarmachen, es gilt für

$x = -3$: $\quad -3 < 0 \Leftrightarrow -(-3) = 3 > 0$

$x = \frac{1}{2}$: $\quad \frac{1}{2} > 0 \Leftrightarrow -\frac{1}{2} < 0$

Man kann sich diesen Zusammenhang auch am Zahlenstrahl verdeutlichen.

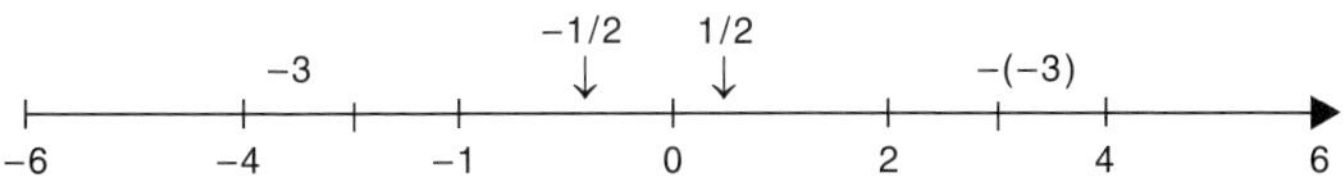

Zahlenstrahl-Ungleichungen

Liegt eine Zahl x links von Null, so liegt ihre Gegenzahl $-x$ rechts von Null. Es gilt also: Ist eine Zahl kleiner als null, so ist ihre Gegenzahl größer als null. Umgekehrt gilt: Liegt eine Zahl rechts von Null, so liegt ihre Gegenzahl links von Null und ist eine Zahl positiv, so ist ihre Gegenzahl negativ.

Für die Äquivalenzumformungen von Ungleichungen bedeutet dieser Zusammenhang: Multipliziert man eine Ungleichung auf beiden Seiten mit einer negativen Zahl, muss man das Ungleichheitszeichen umkehren, d.h. aus > wird < und umgekehrt und aus ≥ wird ≤ und umgekehrt. Nur dann bleibt die Lösungsmenge der Ungleichung erhalten.

Im Fall der Multiplikation mit positiven Zahlen muss man die Richtung des Ungleichheitszeichens nicht ändern. Multipliziert man beide Seiten einer Ungleichung mit der gleichen positiven Zahl, wird die Lösungsmenge der Ungleichung nicht verändert.

Beispiele für Äquivalenzumformungen nach dieser Regel:

$$-\frac{1}{2}x \leq 2 \;\Big|\cdot (-2)$$

$$(-2)\cdot\left(-\frac{1}{2}\right)x \geq 2\cdot(-2)$$

$$x \geq -4 \qquad\qquad \mathbb{L} = \{x \in \mathbb{Q} \mid x \geq -4\}$$

$$\frac{5}{3}x > 10 \;\Big|\cdot \frac{3}{5}$$

$$\frac{3}{5}\cdot\frac{5}{3}x > 10\cdot\frac{3}{5}$$

$$x > 6 \qquad\qquad \mathbb{L} = \{x \in \mathbb{Q} \mid x > 6\}$$

Im allgemeinen Fall $ax < b$ mit $a, b, x \in \mathbb{Q}$, $a \neq 0$ muss man eine Fallunterscheidung durchführen.

1. Fall $a > 0$

$$ax < b \;\Big|\cdot\frac{1}{a}\;\left(\frac{1}{a} > 0\right)$$

$$x < \frac{b}{a}$$

$$\mathbb{L} = \left\{x \in \mathbb{Q} \;\middle|\; x < \frac{b}{a}\right\}$$

2. Fall $a < 0$

$$ax < b \;\Big|\cdot\frac{1}{a}\;\left(\frac{1}{a} < 0\right)$$

$$x > \frac{b}{a}$$

$$\mathbb{L} = \left\{x \in \mathbb{Q} \;\middle|\; x > \frac{b}{a}\right\}$$

Allgemeine lineare Ungleichungen

Mit Hilfe der Regeln, die aus den beiden Spezialfällen hergeleitet wurden, lassen sich nun allgemeine lineare Ungleichungen mit einer Variablen x lösen. Wie beim Auflösen von Gleichungen ist es sinnvoll, die Reihenfolge der unten aufgeführten Schritte einzuhalten.

Reihenfolge für das Lösen linearer Ungleichungen:

1. Auflösen von Klammern und Ausmultiplizieren;
2. Sortieren der Summanden: Summanden mit x auf die eine Seite der Gleichung, Summanden ohne x auf die andere;
3. Zusammenfassen der Summanden;
4. Ausklammern von x;
5. Division beider Ungleichungsseiten durch den Faktor vor x (Vorzeichen beachten!) und gegebenenfalls Richung der Ungleichung ändern.

Es kann sein, dass einzelne Schritte beim Lösen der Ungleichung nicht nötig sind, man kann sie dann einfach überspringen.

Die nächsten Beispiele zeigen Anwendungen dieses Lösungsverfahrens für allgemeine lineare Ungleichungen:

$\frac{2}{3}(x+6) \leq -(4-x) \mid$ Klammern auflösen

$\frac{2}{3}x + 4 \leq -4 + x \mid -x$ (Terme sortieren)

$\frac{2}{3}x - x + 4 \leq -4 \mid -4$

$-\frac{1}{3}x \leq -4-4 \mid \cdot(-3)$

$x \geq (-8)\cdot(-3)$

$x \geq 24$ $\qquad\qquad \mathbb{L} = \{x \in \mathbb{Q} \mid x \geq 24\}$

Sei $a \neq 0$.

$ax - 1 > 3ax + a \mid -3ax$

$ax - 3ax - 1 > a \mid +1$

$-2ax > a + 1 \mid \cdot\left(-\frac{1}{2a}\right)$

Da a selbst eine Variable ist und nicht bekannt ist, ob a positiv oder negativ ist, muss eine Fallunterscheidung bezüglich des Vorzeichens von a durchgeführt werden.

1. Fall $-\frac{1}{2a} > 0 \Leftrightarrow \frac{1}{2a} < 0 \Leftrightarrow 2a < 0 \Leftrightarrow a < 0$

Dann gilt für die Ungleichung: $x > -\frac{a+1}{2a}$

2. Fall $-\frac{1}{2a} < 0 \Leftrightarrow \frac{1}{2a} > 0 \Leftrightarrow 2a > 0 \Leftrightarrow a > 0$

Dann gilt für die Ungleichung: $x < -\frac{a+1}{2a}$

Die Lösungsmenge hängt also davon ab, ob a positiv oder negativ ist,

für $a > 0$ ist $\mathbb{L} = \left\{x \in \mathbb{Q} \;\middle|\; x < -\frac{a+1}{2a}\right\}$

für $a < 0$ ist $\mathbb{L} = \left\{x \in \mathbb{Q} \;\middle|\; x > -\frac{a+1}{2a}\right\}$

3.3 Bruchgleichungen

Das Verfahren zur Lösung von linearen Gleichungen lässt sich auch bei Aufgaben anwenden, die auf den ersten Blick nicht viel mit linearen Gleichungen zu tun haben. Die Bruchgleichung der Form $\frac{ax+b}{cx+d} = e$ mit $a, b, c, d, e, x \in \mathbb{Q}$ und $cx + d \neq 0$ ist ein Beispiel dafür. Sie lässt sich in eine lineare Gleichung umformen und dann lösen. An Hand des nächsten Beispiels wird gezeigt, wie man den Lösungsweg einer solchen Bruchgleichung durch Äquivalenzumformungen ermittelt.

Beispiel: $\frac{3x-1}{8-2x} = -3 \mid \cdot (8-2x) \qquad \mathbb{D} = \mathbb{Q} \setminus \{4\}$

$$3x - 1 = -3\,(8 - 2x)$$
$$3x - 1 = -24 + 6x \mid -6x$$
$$3x - 6x - 1 = -24 \mid +1$$
$$-3x = -23 \;\Big|\; \cdot \left(-\frac{1}{3}\right)$$
$$x = \frac{23}{3} \qquad\qquad \mathbb{L} = \left\{\frac{23}{3}\right\}$$

Der wesentliche Schritt beim Auflösen der Bruchgleichung steht in diesem Beispiel in der ersten Zeile. Die Gleichung wird auf beiden Seiten mit dem Nenner des Bruchs multipliziert. Dadurch fällt der Nenner auf der linken Seite weg. Die entstehende lineare Gleichung löst man nach den bekannten Regeln.

Auch im nächsten Beispiel ist die lineare Gleichung, die sich dahinter verbirgt, nicht sofort zu erkennen, aber auch diese Gleichung aus zwei Brüchen lässt sich in eine lineare Gleichung umwandeln und so lösen.

Der erste Schritt dient dabei wieder dazu, die Nenner auf beiden Seiten aufzulösen. Dazu multipliziert man die Gleichung auf beiden Seiten mit dem Hauptnenner der beiden Brüche. So kürzen sich die Nenner heraus und man erhält eine lineare Gleichung.

Beispiel: $\mathbb{D} = \mathbb{Q} \setminus \left\{-1, \frac{1}{2}\right\}$

$$\frac{3}{x+1} = -\frac{5}{2x-1} \mid \cdot (x+1)\,(2x-1)$$
$$\frac{3\,(x+1)\,(2x-1)}{(x+1)} = -\frac{5\,(x+1)\,(2x-1)}{(2x-1)} \mid \text{Kürzen}$$

$3(2x - 1) = -5(x + 1) \mid \text{Ausmultiplizieren}$

$6x - 3 = -5x - 5 \mid +5x + 3$

$6x + 5x = -5 + 3$

$11x = -2 \left| \cdot \frac{1}{11} \right.$

$x = -\frac{2}{11} \qquad \mathbb{L} = \left\{-\frac{2}{11}\right\}$

3.4 Ungleichungen des Typs $(ax + b)(cx + d) > 0$

Eine Anmerkung zu Beginn: Alle Regeln in diesem Abschnitt gelten nicht nur für Ungleichungen mit einem > Zeichen sondern analog für Ungleichungen mit <, ≥ oder ≤ Zeichen. Die Ungleichheitszeichen lassen sich in den Regeln beliebig ersetzen.

In der Ungleichung $(ax + b)(cx + d) > 0$ mit $a, b, c, d, x \in \mathbb{Q}$ steht auf der linken Seite der Ungleichung ein Produkt. Nach den Vorzeichenregeln der Multiplikation gilt:

»+« · »+« = »+«

»–« · »+« = »–«

»+« · »–« = »–«

»–« · »–« = »+«

Das Produkt in der Ungleichung soll positiv sein. Dafür kommen nur die Fälle »+« · »+« = »+« und »-« · »-« = »+« in Frage. Das Produkt ist also genau dann positiv, wenn entweder $(ax + b)$ positiv und gleichzeitig $(cx + d)$ positiv ist oder wenn $(ax + b)$ negativ und gleichzeitig $(cx + d)$ negativ ist.

Formal schreibt man das in einer Fallunterscheidung:

1. Fall $(ax + b) > 0$ und $(cx + d) > 0$
2. Fall $(ax + b) < 0$ und $(cx + d) < 0$

Betrachtet man den ersten Fall der Fallunterscheidung, lässt sich gesondert für jede der beiden Ungleichungen eine Lösungsmenge bestimmen, die Lösungsmengen $\mathbb{L}_1$ und $\mathbb{L}_2$. Da beide Bedingungen gleichzeitig erfüllt sein müssen, ist die Lösungsmenge $\mathbb{L}_I$ für den gesamten ersten Fall die Schnittmenge aus $\mathbb{L}_1$ und $\mathbb{L}_2$, $\mathbb{L}_I = \mathbb{L}_1 \cap \mathbb{L}_2$.

Für den zweiten Fall ergibt sich analog die Lösungsmenge $\mathbb{L}_{II} = \mathbb{L}_3 \cap \mathbb{L}_4$. Die Lösungsmenge $\mathbb{L}$ der gesamten Ungleichung setzt sich aus den Lö-

sungsmengen der beiden Fälle zusammen, sie ist die Vereinigung der beiden, $\mathbb{L} = \mathbb{L}_I \cup \mathbb{L}_{II}$. Die Lösungsmenge der gegebenen Ungleichung setzt sich also aus vier einzelnen Lösungsmengen zusammen, die man durch eine Fallunterscheidung an Hand der Vorzeichen der Faktoren in der Ungleichung herleitet.
Das nächste Beispiel verdeutlicht, wie eine Ungleichung des gegebenen Typs gelöst werden kann.

$(x - 1)(3x + 9) > 0$

Da das Produkt positiv sein soll, ergeben sich die Fälle »+« · »+« = »+« und »–« · »–« = »+«.

1. Fall $(x - 1) > 0$ und $(3x + 9) > 0$

$\Leftrightarrow x > 1$ und $3x > -9 \;\Big|\; \cdot \frac{1}{3}$

$\Leftrightarrow x > 1$ und $x > -3$

$\mathbb{L}_1 = \{x \in \mathbb{Q} \mid x > 1\}$ und $\mathbb{L}_2 = \{x \in \mathbb{Q} \mid x > -3\}$

$\mathbb{L}_I = \mathbb{L}_1 \cap \mathbb{L}_2 = \{x \in \mathbb{Q} \mid x > 1\}$

2. Fall $x - 1 < 0$ und $3x + 9 < 0$

$\Leftrightarrow x < 1$ und $3x < -9$

$\Leftrightarrow x < 1$ und $x < -3$

$\mathbb{L}_3 = \{x \in \mathbb{Q} \mid x < 1\}$ und $\mathbb{L}_4 = \{x \in \mathbb{Q} \mid x < -3\}$

$\mathbb{L}_{II} = \mathbb{L}_3 \cap \mathbb{L}_4 = \{x \in \mathbb{Q} \mid x < -3\}$

$\mathbb{L} = \mathbb{L}_I \cup \mathbb{L}_{II} = \{x \in \mathbb{Q} \mid x < -3\} \cup \{x \in \mathbb{Q} \mid x > 1\}$

Da für die Division die gleichen Vorzeichenregeln gelten wie für die Multiplikation, lassen sich Bruchungleichungen des Typs $\frac{ax + b}{cx + d} > 0$ mit $cx + d \neq 0$ auf ähnliche Weise lösen. Auch hier wird je nach den Vorzeichen des Zählers und Nenners eine Fallunterscheidung vorgenommen. Dadurch lassen sich vier Teillösungsmengen bestimmen, aus denen man durch Schnitt und Vereinigung die Lösungsmenge der Bruchungleichung bildet.

Beispiel: $\frac{x}{x + 1} < 0$ $\qquad\qquad \mathbb{D} = \mathbb{Q}\setminus\{-1\}$

1. Fall »–« : »+« = »–«

$x < 0$ und $x + 1 > 0$

$\Leftrightarrow x < 0$ und $x > -1$

$\mathbb{L}_1 = \{x \in \mathbb{Q} \mid x < 0\}$ $\mathbb{L}_2 = \{x \in \mathbb{Q} \mid x > -1\}$

$\mathbb{L}_I = \mathbb{L}_1 \cap \mathbb{L}_2 = \{x \in \mathbb{Q} \mid -1 < x < 0\}$

2. Fall: »+« : »–« = »–«
$x > 0$ und $x + 1 < 0$
$\Leftrightarrow x > 0$ und $x < -1$
$\mathbb{L}_3 = \{x \in \mathbb{Q} \mid x > 0\}$ $\mathbb{L}_4 = \{x \in \mathbb{Q} \mid x < -1\}$

Da keine Zahl gleichzeitig größer als 0 und kleiner als – 1 sein kann, ist die Schnittmenge von $\mathbb{L}_3$ und $\mathbb{L}_4$ leer, der zweite Fall bringt keine zusätzlichen Lösungen. $\mathbb{L}_{II} = \mathbb{L}_3 \cap \mathbb{L}_4 = \{\ \}$
$\mathbb{L} = \mathbb{L}_I \cup \mathbb{L}_{II} = \{x \in \mathbb{Q} \mid -1 < x < 0\}$

3.5 Lineare Gleichungssysteme mit zwei Unbekannten

Im Rahmen von mathematischen Überlegungen, aber auch bei Aufgaben aus dem Alltag stellen sich nicht nur Fragen, die durch eine Gleichung mit einer Unbekannten zu lösen sind. Häufig ist ein Problem gegeben, in dem zwei lineare Gleichungen mit zwei Unbekannten vorkommen. Der Schnittpunkt von zwei Geraden oder das Aufstellen einer Geradengleichung durch zwei gegebene Punkte sind Beispiele dafür. Ein abstraktes Beispiel für ein Gleichungssystem aus zwei linearen Gleichungen mit zwei Unbekannten ($x, y \in \mathbb{Q}$) ist

I. $x + 2y = 3$
II. $-x - y = 1$

Es gibt verschiedene graphische und rechnerische Möglichkeiten, ein solches System von Gleichungen zu lösen. Wie man durch Umformen leicht sieht, stellen zwei lineare Gleichungen immer zwei Geraden dar. Geraden können zueinander parallel sein, identisch sein oder sich schneiden. Entsprechend diesen drei Fällen kann auch ein lineares Gleichungssystem mit zwei Unbekannten keine Lösung, unendlich viele Lösungen oder genau eine Lösung haben. Löst man im gegebenen Beispiel die Gleichungen nach y auf, erhält man die entsprechenden Geradengleichungen. Die Geraden kann man zeichnen und so graphisch ihre Lage zueinander und – falls sie sich schneiden – die Koordinaten x und y des Schnittpunkts ermitteln. Da graphische Lösungen aber nie ganz exakt sind, werden hier rechnerische Verfahren beschrieben, um lineare Gleichungssysteme zu lösen, das Verfahren durch Einsetzen bzw. Gleichsetzen und das Additionsverfahren.
Alle drei Verfahren haben in ihrem Vorgehen eine Gemeinsamkeit. Man versucht die gegebenen Gleichungen so zusammenzufassen, dass sie

auf eine lineare Gleichung mit einer Unbekannten zurückgeführt werden können.

Einsetzungsverfahren

Gegeben sei das Gleichungssystem von obigem Beispiel.

I. $x + 2y = 3$

II. $-x - y = 1$

Der Lösungsweg mittels des Einsetzungsverfahrens hat vier Schritte. Man löst zuerst eine der beiden Gleichungen nach einer der beiden Variablen auf. Im Beispiel wird Gleichung II nach x aufgelöst.

II. $-x - y = 1 \mid + x - 1$

$x = -y - 1$

Dann setzt man den erhaltenen Term in der anderen Gleichung für die entsprechende Variable ein. Im Beispiel wird in I für $x = -y - 1$ eingesetzt.

I* $(-y - 1) + 2y = 3$

Die erhaltene Gleichung ist eine lineare Gleichung mit einer Unbekannten. Sie wird mittels der bekannten Äquivalenzumformungen gelöst.

I* $-y - 1 + 2y = 3$

$y - 1 = 3 \mid + 1$

$y = 4$

Durch Einsetzen der erhaltenen Variablen in eine der Ausgangsgleichungen lässt sich die andere Variable berechnen.

$y = 4$ in I

$x + 2 \cdot 4 = 3$

$x + 8 = 3$

$x = -5$

Die Lösung des Gleichungssystems ist $x = -5$ und $y = 4$.
Das Einsetzungsverfahren liefert für jedes lösbare System eine Lösung. Allerdings hat es manchmal den Nachteil, dass die Rechnungen nach dem Einsetzen sehr unübersichtlich werden.

Lösung durch Gleichsetzen

Das Lösungsverfahren durch Gleichsetzen ist eine Variante des Einsetzungsverfahrens. Bei diesem Weg werden beide Gleichungen nach der selben Variablen aufgelöst und dann gleichgesetzt. So erhält man wieder eine lineare Gleichung mit einer Unbekannten, die sich mit Äquivalenzumformungen lösen lässt. Durch Einsetzen in eine der ursprünglichen Gleichungen ermittelt man im letzten Schritt die zweite gesuchte Variable. Das schrittweise Vorgehen in diesem Verfahren wird wieder an bekanntem obigen Beispiel gezeigt.

I. $x + 2y = 3$
II. $-x - y = 1$

Auflösen beider Gleichungen nach x:

I* $x = 3 - 2y$
II* $x = -y - 1$

Gleichsetzen I* = II*

$3 - 2y = -y - 1$

Auflösen nach y:

$3 - 2y = -y - 1 \mid +2y + 1$
$y = 4$

Einsetzen in I*

$x = 3 - 2 \cdot 4$ $\qquad$ $x = -5$

Auch dieses Verfahren führt immer zur Lösung, es bietet sich vor allem dann an, wenn man in beiden Gleichungen leicht nach einer Variablen auflösen kann.

Additionsverfahren

Auch beim Additionsverfahren ist das Ziel, die gegebenen zwei Gleichungen auf eine Gleichung mit einer Unbekannten zurückzuführen. Dazu werden die Gleichungen so umgeformt, dass bei der anschließenden Addition der Gleichungen eine der Variablen wegfällt. Die Gleichungen dazu werden so erweitert, dass der Koeffizient einer festgelegten Variablen in der ersten Gleichung die Gegenzahl seines Koeffizienten in der zweiten Gleichung ist. Durch die Addition der Gleichungen erhält man eine lineare Gleichung mit einer Unbekannten, die man wie gewohnt lösen kann.
Im oben gegebenen Beispiel ist das Additionsverfahren besonders einfach anzuwenden, da die Koeffizienten von x in I und II (1 und -1) bereits Gegenzahlen sind

I. $x + 2y = 3$
II. $-x - y = 1$
I + II: $x + 2y - x - y = 3 + 1$
$y = 4$

Durch Einsetzen in I erhält man wieder $x = -5$
Auch im folgenden Beispiel kann man das Additionsverfahren anwenden, allerdings müssen dazu erst alle Terme mit Variablen auf eine Gleichungsseite gebracht werden.

I. $x = -2 + y \mid -y$
II. $2x + 4 = -3y \mid +3y - 4$
I* $x - y = -2 \mid \cdot (-2)$
II* $2x + 3y = -4$

I* wird mit (– 2) erweitert, so dass die Koeffizienten von x in I* und II* Gegenzahlen sind

I** $-2x + 2y = 4$
II* $2x + 3y = -4$

Addition der Gleichungen

I** + II* $-2x + 2y + 2x + 3y = 4 - 4$
$5y = 0$
$y = 0$
Eingesetzt in I: $x = -2 + 0$ $\quad$ $x = -2$
Die Lösung des Gleichungssystems ist $x = -2$ und $y = 0$.

Das Additionsverfahren kommt vor allem bei komplizierteren Rechnungen, wie sie im nächsten Abschnitt besprochen werden, zum Einsatz.

4 Die Menge der reellen Zahlen $\mathbb{R}$

Wie in den vorangegangenen Abschnitten gesehen, lassen sich in der Menge der rationalen Zahlen eine Vielzahl verschiedener Aufgaben und Aufgabentypen lösen. Außerdem liegen die Zahlen in $\mathbb{Q}$ so dicht nebeneinander, dass man zu je zwei Zahlen in $\mathbb{Q}$ immer noch eine Zahl aus $\mathbb{Q}$ findet, die dazwischen liegt, egal, wie klein man den Abstand gewählt hat. Dennoch gibt es Gleichungen, die man in $\mathbb{Q}$ formulieren kann, die aber in $\mathbb{Q}$ keine Lösung haben. Ein Beispiel hierfür ist die Gleichung $x^2 = 2$.

Die Lösung dieser Gleichung lässt sich graphisch darstellen. Es ist nach dem Lehrsatz des Pythagoras die Länge der Diagonale in einem Quadrat mit der Kantenlänge 1.

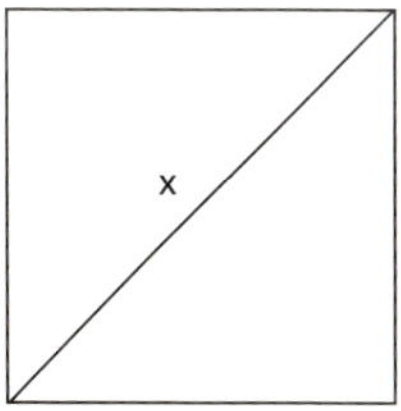

Da der Beweis, dass $x^2 = 2$ in $\mathbb{Q}$ keine Lösung hat, sehr einfach ist, wird er hier aufgeführt. Es ist ein Widerspruchsbeweis. D.h. man nimmt an, das Gegenteil dessen, was man beweisen will, ist wahr und führt diese Annahme auf einen Widerspruch. Damit ist die ursprüngliche Aussage bewiesen.

4.1 Beweis für die Unvollständigkeit von $\mathbb{Q}$

Annahme: Es gibt ein $q \in \mathbb{Q}$ mit $q^2 = 2$.

Jedes $q \in \mathbb{Q}$ lässt sich als Bruch aus Zahlen aus $\mathbb{N}$ bzw. $\mathbb{Z}$ darstellen. Da in diesem Fall das Vorzeichen von q durch das Quadrat wegfällt, genügt es hier, nur $\mathbb{N}$ zu betrachten. Es gibt also Zahlen a, $b \in \mathbb{N}$, für die gilt: $q = \frac{a}{b}$ und damit $(\frac{a}{b})^2 = 2$. a und b seien teilerfremd, d.h. $\frac{a}{b}$ ist ein so weit wie möglich gekürzter Bruch.

Aus $(\frac{a}{b})^2 = 2$ folgt: $a^2 = 2b^2$

Man unterscheidet nun zwei Fälle: 1. a ist gerade und 2. a ist ungerade. Für beide Fälle führt man die Annahme auf einen Widerspruch.

1. Fall a gerade
$\Rightarrow (a:2) \in \mathbb{N}$
$\Rightarrow (a:2) \cdot (a:2) \in \mathbb{N}$
$\Rightarrow a^2 : 4 \in \mathbb{N}$ und da $a^2 = 2b^2$
$2b^2 : 4 \in \mathbb{N}$. Durch Kürzen ergibt sich
$b^2 : 2 \in \mathbb{N}$
$\Rightarrow b^2$ ist durch 2 teilbar. Da $b \in \mathbb{N}$, ist damit auch b durch 2 teilbar.
Auch a ist, da a gerade ist, durch 2 teilbar.
Widerspruch zu a und b teilerfremd.

2. Fall a ungerade
$\Rightarrow a^2$ ist auch ungerade $\Rightarrow a^2 \neq 2b^2$ Widerspruch
Sowohl Fall 1 als auch Fall 2 führen auf einen Widerspruch.
Also ist die Annahme falsch. Die Gleichung $x^2 = 2$ hat in $\mathbb{Q}$ keine Lösung.

Für x mit $x^2 = 2$ schreibt man $x = \sqrt{2}$, $\sqrt{2}$ hat den ungefähren Wert $\sqrt{2} = 1{,}41421\ldots$, $\sqrt{2} \in \mathbb{R}$ und $\sqrt{2} \notin \mathbb{Q}$. Für andere Quadratwurzeln, z.B. $\sqrt{7}$ kann man einen analogen Beweis führen. Quadratwurzeln aus positiven Zahlen, die keine Quadratzahlen sind, sind alle Elemente von $\mathbb{R}$, nicht aber von $\mathbb{Q}$. Auch alle anderen Wurzeln, z.B. Kubikwurzeln wie $\sqrt[3]{2}$ als Lösung der Gleichung $x^3 = 2$, sind Elemente von $\mathbb{R}$.
Es gilt der

Eindeutigkeitssatz der n-ten Wurzel
Zu einem $a \in \mathbb{R}_0^+$ und $n \in \mathbb{N}$ gibt es höchstens eine n-te Wurzel, d.h. höchstens ein $x \in \mathbb{R}_0^+$, so dass $x^n = a$ ist. x heißt dann die n-te Wurzel von a.

Jede n-te Wurzel einer positiven Zahl ist also ein Element von $\mathbb{R}$.
Nicht nur Wurzeln, auch andere geometrisch erfassbare Größen lassen sich mit Zahlen aus $\mathbb{Q}$ nicht beschreiben. Die Länge einer Kreislinie eines Kreises mit Durchmesser 1 zum Beispiel ist kein Element von $\mathbb{Q}$. Die Länge eines solchen Kreisumfangs ist π (sprich: Pi) und hat den ungefähren Wert $\pi = 3{,}14159\ldots$ π ist ein unendlicher, nichtperiodischer Dezimalbruch. D.h. man kann die Stellen hinter dem Komma unendlich

weiterschreiben, ohne dass irgendwann eine Periode auftritt. Im Gegensatz dazu sind Dezimalbrüche in $\mathbb{Q}$ entweder endlich, z.B. 0,25, oder unendlich periodisch, z.B. $\frac{1}{11} = 0{,}09090909\ldots$ Unendliche nichtperiodische Dezimalbrüche nennt man irrational. Die Eulersche Zahl e, die im Gesetz des radioaktiven Zerfalls vorkommt, ist auch eine irrationale Zahl. Zahlen wie π oder e lassen sich weder durch Zahlen in $\mathbb{Q}$ noch als Wurzeln von Zahlen in $\mathbb{Q}$ darstellen.

$\mathbb{R}$, die Menge der reellen Zahlen, enthält also

- alle Elemente aus $\mathbb{Q}$ und damit auch aus $\mathbb{Z}$ und $\mathbb{N}$;
- alle n-ten Wurzeln aus positiven Zahlen aus $\mathbb{Q}$;
- irrationale Zahlen wie π oder e (transzendente Zahlen);

und mögliche Kombinationen aus solchen Elementen.

$\mathbb{R}$ lässt sich nicht mehr wie $\mathbb{Q}$ in aufzählender Weise darstellen oder aus (endlich oder abzählbar vielen) abzählbaren Mengen zusammensetzen. Dafür ist $\mathbb{R}$ zu groß. Man sagt, $\mathbb{R}$ ist eine überabzählbar unendliche Menge. $\mathbb{Q}$, $\mathbb{Z}$ und $\mathbb{N}$ dagegen sind abzählbare (unendliche) Mengen.

4.2 $\mathbb{Q}$ ist dicht in $\mathbb{R}$

Man betrachtet nun zwei beliebige Zahlen in $\mathbb{Q}$. Egal wie nah die beiden Zahlen in $\mathbb{Q}$ nebeneinander liegen, es liegt immer eine Zahl aus $\mathbb{R}$, die nicht Element von $\mathbb{Q}$ ist, dazwischen. Beispielsweise liegt zwischen 1,41422 und 1,41421 die Zahl $\sqrt{2}$. Man kann sich leicht auch andere unendliche nichtperiodische Dezimalzahlen vorstellen, die jeweils zwischen zwei solchen Zahlen liegen.
Andersherum gilt genauso: Egal, wie nah zwei Zahlen aus $\mathbb{R}$ nebeneinander liegen, man findet immer eine Zahl aus $\mathbb{Q}$, die zwischen den beiden liegt. Man kann also mit Zahlen aus $\mathbb{Q}$ beliebig dicht an Zahlen aus $\mathbb{R}$ herankommen, ohne sie jemals zu erreichen. Als Beispiel kann man sich endliche Dezimalbrüche vorstellen, zu denen man immer eine Stelle hinter dem Komma hinzunimmt. Die Zahlen 1,414 1,4142 1,41421 1,414213 ... nähern sich mit jedem Hinzunehmen einer neuen Dezimalstelle mehr an die Zahl $\sqrt{2}$ an. Jede der endlichen Dezimalbrüche ist dabei Element von $\mathbb{Q}$, während $\sqrt{2}$ nicht in $\mathbb{Q}$ liegt. Trotzdem kann man mit den endlichen Dezimalbrüchen unendlich nah an $\sqrt{2}$ herankommen. Wegen dieser Eigenschaft sagt man auch, $\mathbb{Q}$ ist dicht in $\mathbb{R}$.

Trotz dieser Eigenschaft liegen zwischen den dicht angeordneten Zahlen aus $\mathbb{Q}$ unendlich viele Zahlen aus $\mathbb{R}$, die nicht in $\mathbb{Q}$ sind. Graphisch kann man dieses Verhältnis von $\mathbb{R}$ zu $\mathbb{Q}$ nicht mehr darstellen.

Intervallschreibweise für Teilmengen von $\mathbb{R}$

Häufig will man Teilbereiche des Zahlenstrahls als Mengen angeben, z.B. die Lösungsmenge für $-3 < x \leq 29$. Für Intervalle in $\mathbb{R}$ hat man dazu eine Kurzschreibweise eingeführt.

Seien $a, b \in \mathbb{R}$ und $a < b$, dann schreibt man

$[a, b] = \{x \in \mathbb{R} \mid a \leq x \leq b\}$

$[a, b[= \{x \in \mathbb{R} \mid a \leq x < b\}$

$]a, b] = \{x \in \mathbb{R} \mid a < x \leq b\}$

$]a, b[= \{x \in \mathbb{R} \mid a < x < b\}$

Im ersten Intervall gehören die Intervallgrenzen a und b zum Intervall und damit zur Menge dazu. Beim zweiten Intervall gehört a dazu, b aber nicht, umgekehrt gehört b im dritten Fall zum Intervall dazu, a aber nicht. Im vierten Intervall gehören weder a noch b zum Intervall dazu. Die Schreibweise lässt sich so interpretieren: Deutet die Klammer des Intervalls nach außen, dann gehört die entsprechende Intervallgrenze nicht zum Intervall dazu, deutet sie nach innen, ist diese Intervallgrenze Element des Intervalls.

Das erste Intervall heißt dabei geschlossenes Intervall,
das zweite Intervall heißt links geschlossen, rechts offen,
das dritte Intervall ist links offen, rechts geschlossen und
das vierte Intervall heißt offenes Intervall.

Um anzuzeigen, dass die beschriebene Menge auf dem Zahlenstrahl eine Halbgerade ist, dass also das Intervall nur auf einer Seite beschränkt ist, verwendet man in der Intervallschreibweise das Zeichen ∞ oder $-\infty$ als Intervallgrenze. ∞ ist keine Zahl, also auch keine Zahl in $\mathbb{R}$. ∞, ebenso wie $-\infty$ kann darum nie zu einem Intervall in $\mathbb{R}$ gehören und muss immer ausgeschlossen werden. Auf der entsprechenden Seite muss das Intervall immer offen sein.

Man schreibt also für $a \in \mathbb{R}$

$[a, \infty[= \{x \in \mathbb{R} \mid x \geq a\}$

$]-\infty, a] = \{x \in \mathbb{R} \mid x \leq a\}$

Damit gilt $]-\infty, \infty[= \mathbb{R}$

Rechnen in $\mathbb{R}$

Alle Rechenregeln, die in $\mathbb{Q}$ gelten, gelten auch in $\mathbb{R}$. Sie werden hier noch einmal zusammenfassend dargestellt.

1. Klammern haben Vorrang
2. Punkt vor Strich
3. Kommutativgesetz
   der Addition $a + b = b + a$ $\quad a, b \in \mathbb{R}$
   der Multiplikation $a \cdot b = b \cdot a$ $\quad a, b \in \mathbb{R}$
4. Assoziativgesetz
   der Addition $(a + b) + c = a + (b + c) = a + b + c$ $\quad a, b, c \in \mathbb{R}$
   der Multiplikation $(a \cdot b) \cdot c = a \cdot (b \cdot c) = a \cdot b \cdot c$ $\quad a, b, c \in \mathbb{R}$
5. Distributivgesetz
   $a \cdot (b + c) = a \cdot b + a \cdot c$ $\quad a, b, c \in \mathbb{R}$

Auch die Regeln für Addition und Subtraktion und die Vorzeichenregeln bei der Multiplikation und Division bleiben bestehen. Aus den oben genannten Gesetzen lassen sich auf gleichem Weg wie in $\mathbb{Q}$ auch für die Elemente aus $\mathbb{R}$ Regeln wie das kreuzweise Ausmultiplizieren von Summen, die binomischen Formeln und das Lösen von Gleichungen und Ungleichungen durch Äquivalenzumformungen herleiten. Man kann also in $\mathbb{R}$ wie gewohnt rechnen.
Eine Besonderheit gilt für Terme mit Wurzeln. Da Wurzeln die positive Lösung einer Gleichung der Art $x^n = q$ mit $q \geq 0$ sind, gilt also $x = \sqrt[n]{q}$ und $\sqrt[n]{q^n} = \sqrt[n]{q}^{\,n} = x^n = q$

Beispiele:

$\sqrt{4} = \sqrt{2^2} = 2$
$\sqrt{2} + \sqrt{2} = 2\sqrt{2}$
$\sqrt{2}\,(2 - \sqrt{2}) = 2\sqrt{2} - \sqrt{2}\,\sqrt{2} = 2\sqrt{2} - 2$
$(3x - \sqrt{5})^2 = 9x^2 - 2 \cdot 3\sqrt{5}\,x + \sqrt{5} \cdot \sqrt{5} = 9x^2 - 6\sqrt{5}\,x + 5$

Rationalmachen des Nenners

Um die Größe eines Bruchs abschätzen zu können oder auch um einen einfacheren Hauptnenner zu erhalten, ist es oft hilfreich, im Nenner eines Bruchs keine Wurzel stehen zu haben. Indem man den Bruch geeignet erweitert, kann man bei jedem Bruch den Nenner rational machen. Die folgenden Beispiele erläutern dieses Vorgehen:

$$\frac{1}{\sqrt{2}} = \frac{\sqrt{2}}{\sqrt{2}} \cdot \frac{1}{\sqrt{2}} = \frac{\sqrt{2}}{\sqrt{2} \cdot \sqrt{2}} = \frac{\sqrt{2}}{2} = \frac{1}{2} \cdot \sqrt{2}$$

Im nächsten Beispiel steht im Nenner des Bruchs eine Summe aus einer Variablen und einer Wurzel. Erweitert man in diesem Fall den Bruch mit dem Nenner, wird, da dann im Nenner eine binomische Formel angewendet werden muss, die ein gemischtes Glied enthält, der Nenner nicht rational. Daher erweitert man den Bruch mit $(x - \sqrt{2})$. Im Nenner wird dann die dritte binomische Formel angewendet, die kein gemischtes Glied enthält.

$$\frac{1}{x + \sqrt{2}} = \frac{x - \sqrt{2}}{x - \sqrt{2}} \cdot \frac{1}{x + \sqrt{2}} = \frac{x - \sqrt{2}}{(x - \sqrt{2}) \cdot (x + \sqrt{2})} = \frac{x - \sqrt{2}}{x^2 - 2}$$

5 Quadratische Gleichungen und quadratische Funktionen

5.1 Quadratische Gleichungen

Darstellungsformen

Als quadratische Gleichung bezeichnet man eine Gleichung der Form

$ax^2 + bx + c = 0$ mit $a, b, c, x \in \mathbb{R}$, $a \neq 0$

Dabei heißt x Variable, a, b, c heißen Koeffizienten. Das entscheidende Merkmal für eine quadratische Gleichung ist, dass die Variable in der 2. Potenz steht.

Beispiele für quadratische Gleichungen sind:

$x^2 - 1 = 0$
$2x^2 + 5x - 17 = 0$
$x^2 - x - 1 = 0$
$3(x-2)^2 = 25$

Auch die letzte Gleichung ist eine quadratische Gleichung, wie sich durch äquivalente Umformungen leicht nachrechnen lässt.

	$3(x-2)^2 = 25$	| Auflösen der binomischen Formel
$\Leftrightarrow$	$3(x^2 - 4x + 4) = 25$	| Ausmultiplizieren
$\Leftrightarrow$	$3x^2 - 12x + 12 = 25$	| -25
$\Leftrightarrow$	$3x^2 - 12x - 13 = 0$	

Lösungsmethoden

Quadratische Gleichungen können in $\mathbb{R}$ 0, 1 oder 2 Lösungen besitzen.
Beispiele:

$x^2 = 0$		$\mathbb{L} = \{0\}$
$x^2 - x = 0$	$\Leftrightarrow x(x-1) = 0$	$\mathbb{L} = \{0, 1\}$
$x^2 + 1 = 0$	$\Leftrightarrow x^2 = -1$	$\mathbb{L} = \{\ \}$

Systematisch ergibt sich für den einfachsten allgemeinen Fall $x^2 = e$ die folgende Fallunterscheidung:

			Beispiele	
	$e < 0$:	$\mathbb{L} = \{\ \}$	$x^2 = -4$	$\mathbb{L} = \{\ \}$
$x^2 = e$ für	$e = 0$:	$\mathbb{L} = \{0\}$	$x^2 = 0$	$\mathbb{L} = \{0\}$
	$e > 0$:	$\mathbb{L} = \{\sqrt{e}, -\sqrt{e}\}$	$x^2 = 5$	$\mathbb{L} = \{\sqrt{5}, -\sqrt{5}\}$

Ist eine quadratische Gleichung in der Form einer binomischen Formel gegeben, so lässt sich die Lösungsmenge der quadratischen Gleichung durch Anwendung dieser Fallunterscheidung bestimmen.

Beispiel: $(x-3)^2 = 25$

Ersetzt man die Klammer durch die Variable u, erhält man:

$u := (x-3) \Rightarrow u^2 = (x-3)^2 \Rightarrow u^2 = 25$

Nun kann man die Fallunterscheidung anwenden. Sie ergibt:

$25 > 0$, also gibt es zwei Lösungen, nämlich $u_1 = 5$ und $u_2 = -5$.

Ersetzt man u wieder durch die Klammer $x - 3$, erhält man

$x_1 - 3 = 5$ und $x_2 - 3 = -5$
$x_1 = 8$ und $x_2 = -2$

Die Lösungsmenge lautet also $\mathbb{L} = \{8, -2\}$.

Quadratische Ergänzung

Die Lösungsmenge einer allgemeinen quadratischen Gleichung erhält man, indem man sie durch äquivalente Umformungen auf eine binomische Formel zurückführt. Auf diese binomische Formel wendet man dann die Fallunterscheidung an und bestimmt so die Lösungsmenge.
Eine quadratische Gleichung, die in Form einer binomischen Formel vorliegt, hat die Form

$(x + d)^2 = e$ (I) oder ausmultipliziert $x^2 + 2xd + d^2 = e$ (II)

Die allgemeine quadratische Gleichung $ax^2 + bx + c = 0$ wird schrittweise umgeformt, bis sie in der Form von (II) vorliegt. Dabei wird in jedem Schritt ein Koeffizient der quadratischen Gleichung mit dem entsprechenden Koeffizienten der binomischen Formel verglichen und so umgeformt, dass man am Ende die Gleichung in Faktorenschreibweise angeben kann.

Umformen der quadratischen Gleichung:

$ax^2 + bx + c = 0$ | $: a$

$\Leftrightarrow \quad x^2 + \frac{b}{a}x + \frac{c}{a} = 0$ | Umformen des gemischten Glieds entsprechend den Koeffizienten der binomischen Formel

$\Leftrightarrow \quad x^2 + 2x\frac{b}{2a} + \frac{c}{a} = 0$ | quadratische Ergänzung durch $\left(\frac{b}{2a}\right)^2 - \left(\frac{b}{2a}\right)^2$

$$\Leftrightarrow \quad x^2 + 2x\frac{b}{2a} + \left(\frac{b}{2a}\right)^2 - \left(\frac{b}{2a}\right)^2 + \frac{c}{a} = 0 \qquad \left| + \left(\frac{b}{2a}\right)^2 - \frac{c}{a}\right.$$

$$\Leftrightarrow \quad x^2 + 2x\,\frac{b}{2a} + \left(\frac{b}{2a}\right)^2 = \left(\frac{b}{2a}\right)^2 - \frac{c}{a}$$

| Zusammenfassen der linken Seite zur binomischen Formel

$$\Leftrightarrow \quad \left(x + \frac{b}{2a}\right)^2 = \left(\frac{b}{2a}\right)^2 - \frac{c}{a}$$

Nun kann die Fallunterscheidung angewendet werden, dafür ist das Vorzeichen der Differenz auf der rechten Gleichungsseite ausschlaggebend.

1. Fall:

Die Gleichung hat keine Lösung, falls $\left(\frac{b}{2a}\right)^2 - \frac{c}{a} < 0$.

2. Fall:

Die Gleichung hat eine Lösung, falls $\left(\frac{b}{2a}\right)^2 - \frac{c}{a} = 0$.

Die Lösung kann man folgendermaßen errechnen:

$$\left(x + \frac{b}{2a}\right)^2 = 0 \Rightarrow x + \frac{b}{2a} = 0 \Rightarrow x = -\frac{b}{2a}.$$

3. Fall:

Die Gleichung hat zwei Lösungen, falls $\left(\frac{b}{2a}\right)^2 - \frac{c}{a} > 0$.

Entsprechend der Fallunterscheidung erhält man für die Lösungen zwei Gleichungen:

$$\left(x_1 + \frac{b}{2a}\right) = \sqrt{\left(\frac{b}{2a}\right)^2 - \frac{c}{a}} \qquad \left(x_2 + \frac{b}{2a}\right) = -\sqrt{\left(\frac{b}{2a}\right)^2 - \frac{c}{a}}$$

$$\Leftrightarrow \quad x_1 + \frac{b}{2a} = \sqrt{\frac{b^2 - 4ac}{4a^2}} \qquad x_2 + \frac{b}{2a} = -\sqrt{\frac{b^2 - 4ac}{4a^2}}$$

$$\Leftrightarrow \quad x_1 = \sqrt{\frac{b^2 - 4ac}{4a^2}} - \frac{b}{2a} \qquad x_2 = -\sqrt{\frac{b^2 - 4ac}{4a^2}} - \frac{b}{2a}$$

$$\Leftrightarrow \quad x_1 = \frac{-b + \sqrt{b^2 - 4ac}}{2a} \qquad x_2 = \frac{-b - \sqrt{b^2 - 4ac}}{2a}$$

Mit der gefundenen Formel lässt sich leicht jede quadratische Gleichung lösen, indem man für die Koeffizienten entsprechend einsetzt.

Die quadratische Gleichung $ax^2 + bx + c = 0$ mit $a, b, c, x \in \mathbb{R}$ und $a \neq 0$ hat die Lösungen

$x_{1/2} = \frac{-b \pm \sqrt{b^2 - 4ac}}{2a}$ falls $b^2 - 4ac > 0$

die Lösung $x = -\frac{b}{2a}$ falls $b^2 - 4ac = 0$

und keine Lösung, falls $b^2 - 4ac < 0$.

5.2 Der Satz von Vieta

Eine quadratische Gleichung kann nicht nur in der allgemeinen sondern auch in faktorisierter Form vorliegen. Sie hat dann für $x, x_1, x_2, a \in \mathbb{R}$ mit $a \neq 0$ die Gestalt

$a(x - x_1)(x - x_2) = 0$

oder in Normalform $(x - x_1)(x - x_2) = 0$

Die Gleichung ist genau dann wahr, wenn einer der Faktoren gleich null ist, also genau dann, wenn $x - x_1 = 0$ oder wenn $x - x_2 = 0$. Das ist für $x = x_1$ oder für $x = x_2$ der Fall. Die Lösungsmenge der Gleichung lässt sich in diesem Fall ohne die Lösungsformel berechnen, sie ist $\mathbb{L} = \{x_1, x_2\}$. Multipliziert man die Gleichung in Normalform aus, erhält man sie in der Gestalt einer allgemeinen quadratischen Gleichung in Normalform.

$$(x - x_1)(x - x_2) = 0$$
$$x^2 - x_1x - x_2x + x_1x_2 = 0$$
$$x^2 - (x_1 + x_2)x + x_1x_2 = 0$$

Die allgemeine quadratische Gleichung in Normalform lautet:

$x^2 + px + q = 0.$

Beim Vergleich der Koeffizienten der beiden Gleichung erkennt man, dass gilt:

$x_1 + x_2 = -p$ und $x_1x_2 = q$.

Diesen Zusammenhang nennt man den

> Satz von Vieta:
> Sind x_1 und x_2 die Lösungen der quadratischen Gleichung
> $x^2 + px + q = 0$ mit $x_1, x_2, x, p, q \in \mathbb{R}$, dann gilt
> $x_1 + x_2 = -p$ und
> $x_1 x_2 = q$.

Die allgemeine quadratische Gleichung $ax^2 + bx + c = 0$ mit $a, b, c, x \in \mathbb{R}$ erhält man in Normalform, indem man sie durch a dividiert. Sie lautet dann $x^2 + \frac{b}{a}x + \frac{c}{a} = 0$. Auf die so umgeformte Gleichung lässt sich der Satz von Vieta anwenden:

Sind x_1 und x_2 die Lösungen der Gleichung $x^2 + \dfrac{b}{a}x + \dfrac{c}{a} = 0$, dann gilt $x_1 + x_2 = -\dfrac{b}{a}$ und $x_1 x_2 = \dfrac{c}{a}$.

5.3 Gleichungen, die sich auf quadratische Gleichungen zurückführen lassen

Gleichungen zweiten Grades können, wie gesehen, keine, eine oder zwei Lösungen haben. Wenn ihre Lösungsmenge nicht leer ist, lassen sich die Nullstellen mit der Lösungsformel, einige auch mit Hilfe der binomischen Formeln oder dem Satz von Vieta lösen. Gleichungen dritten oder sogar noch höheren Grades sind im allgemeinen Fall wesentlich komplizierter zu lösen. Einige lassen sich aber durch geeignete Umformungen auf quadratische Gleichungen zurückführen. Dazu folgen hier einige Beispiele.
Im ersten Beispiel wird durch Ausklammern der Variablen eine quadratische Gleichung erzeugt.

$-2x^3 + 4x^2 - 2x = 0 \mid$ Ausklammern von $-2x$
$-2x(x^2 - 2x + 1) = 0 \mid$ 2. binomische Formel
$-2x(x - 1)^2 = 0$

Das Produkt auf der linken Seite wird genau dann null, wenn einer der Faktoren gleich null ist. Man kann also schrittweise die Lösungen der Gleichung berechnen.

$-2x = 0 \Leftrightarrow x = 0$

$(x-1)^2 = 0 \Leftrightarrow x - 1 = 0 \Leftrightarrow x = 1$

Die Lösungsmenge ist $\mathbb{L} = \{0, 1\}$

Im zweiten Beispiel wird durch Anwenden einer binomischen Formel aus einer Gleichung vierten Grades eine quadratische Gleichung hergeleitet.

$4x^4 - 36x^2 + 81 = 0 \mid$ 2. binomische Formel

$(2x^2 - 9)^2 = 0 \mid$ Wurzelziehen

$2x^2 - 9 = 0 \mid +9$

$2x^2 = 9 \left| \cdot \frac{1}{2} \right.$

$x^2 = \frac{9}{2}$

$x_1 = +\sqrt{\frac{9}{2}}\,,\ x_2 = -\sqrt{\frac{9}{2}},\ \mathbb{L} = \left\{+\sqrt{\frac{9}{2}}, -\sqrt{\frac{9}{2}}\right\}$

Im dritten Beispiel liegt eine Bruchgleichung vor. Durch geeignetes Multiplizieren mit dem Hauptnenner fallen die Nenner auf der linken Seite weg und man erhält nach dem Umsortieren der Terme eine quadratische Gleichung.

Beispiel: Sei $x \in \mathbb{R}\backslash\{-2, 0\}$.

$\frac{x}{x+2} + \frac{3x-1}{x} = 3 \mid$ Multiplikation mit dem Hauptnenner $x(x+2)$

$x^2 + (3x-1)(x+2) = 3x(x+2) \mid$ Ausmultiplizieren

$x^2 + 3x^2 + 6x - x - 2 = 3x^2 + 6x \mid -3x^2 - 6x$

$x^2 - x - 2 = 0 \mid$ Lösungsformel

$x_{1/2} = \frac{1 \pm \sqrt{1 + 4 \cdot 2}}{2}$

$x_1 = \frac{1+3}{2} = 2$

$x_2 = \frac{1-3}{2} = -1$

Die Lösungsmenge der Bruchgleichung lautet $\mathbb{L} = \{-1, 2\}$.

5.4 Quadratische Funktionen und ihre Graphen

Eine Funktion $f\colon \mathbb{R} \to \mathbb{R}\ x \mapsto y = ax^2 + bx + c;\ a, b, c \in \mathbb{R},\ a \neq 0$ heißt quadratische Funktion. Das entscheidende Merkmal ist, dass die Variable x in der zweiten Potenz steht. Das einfachste Beispiel für eine quadratische Funktion ist

$f_1\colon \mathbb{R} \to \mathbb{R}\ x \mapsto y = x^2$

Weitere Beispiele für einfache quadratische Funktionen sind

$f_2\colon \mathbb{R} \to \mathbb{R}\ x \mapsto y = 2x^2$

$f_3\colon \mathbb{R} \to \mathbb{R}\ x \mapsto y = -x^2$

$f_4\colon \mathbb{R} \to \mathbb{R}\ x \mapsto y = -\frac{1}{2}x^2$

Durch Einsetzen lassen sich die y-Werte der Funktionen bestimmen und dadurch die Punkte, die die Funktion erfüllen. Sie bilden die Graphen der einzelnen Funktionen.

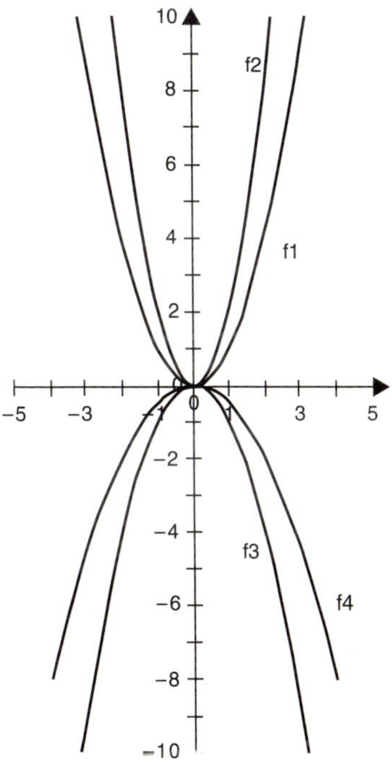

Die Graphen von quadratischen Funktionen heißen Parabeln. Den Graph der Funktion $f_1\colon \mathbb{R} \to \mathbb{R}\ x \mapsto y = x^2$ nennt man Normalparabel.
Bereits aus dem Graphen lassen sich Eigenschaften der Parabeln erkennen. Für Parabel mit Gleichungen $y = ax^2$ wie die oben dargestellten gilt, sie sind symmetrisch zur y-Achse. Offensichtlich hängt die Gestalt einer Parabel von dem Koeffizienten a des quadratischen Glieds ab. Er bestimmt, ob die Parabel nach oben oder unten geöffnet ist und wie steil sie ist. Da das Quadrat einer Zahl in $\mathbb{R}$ immer positiv ist, bestimmt das Vorzeichen von a auch das Vorzeichen von ax^2.

Für den Graphen der Funktion $f\colon \mathbb{R} \to \mathbb{R}\ x \mapsto y = ax^2$ gilt:
$a > 0 \Rightarrow$ die Parabel ist nach oben geöffnet
$a < 0 \Rightarrow$ die Parabel ist nach unten geöfnet
und
$a \in\ ]-1, 1[$ also $|a| < 1 \Rightarrow$ die Parabel ist flacher als die Normalparabel
$a < -1$ oder $a > 1$, d.h. $|a| > 1 \Rightarrow$ die Parabel ist steiler als die Normalparabel

Im nächsten Schritt wird eine allgemeine quadratische Funktion betrachtet. Als Beispiel sei
$f\colon \mathbb{R} \to \mathbb{R}\ x \mapsto y = \frac{1}{2}x^2 - 2x + \frac{3}{2}$ gegeben.

Es gilt $a = \frac{1}{2}$, die Parabel von f ist also flacher als die Normalparabel und nach oben geöffnet. Durch Einsetzen ermittelt man die Wertetabelle von f:

x	-1	0	1	2	3	4
$f(x)$	4	$\frac{3}{2}$	0	$-\frac{1}{2}$	0	$\frac{3}{2}$

Daraus lässt sich f zeichnen.

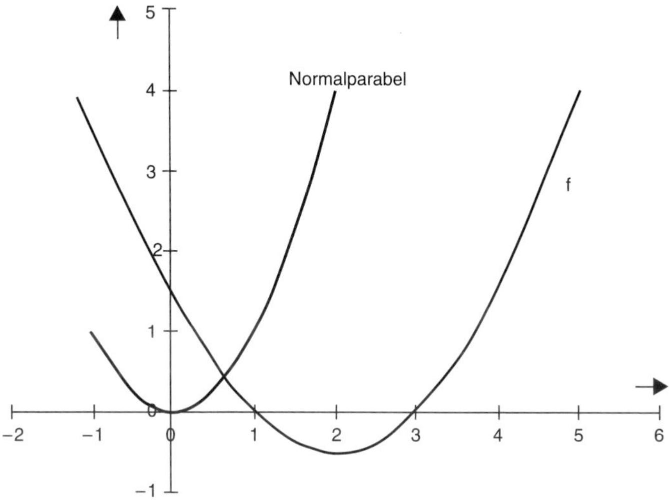

Der Graph von f ist gegenüber der Normalparabel im Koordinatensystem verschoben. Seine Symmetrieachse ist eine Parallele zur y-Achse und hat die Gleichung $x = 2$.

Achsenschnittpunkte von Parabeln

Schnitt mit der y-Achse

Für den Schnitt eines Graphen mit der y-Achse gilt: $x = 0$

Im Beispiel von f berechnet sich die y-Koordinate des Schnittpunktes als

$f(0) = \frac{3}{2}$

Allgemein ist der Schnitt der Parabel mit der Gleichung $y = ax^2 + bx + c$ mit der y-Achse bei $y = f(0) = c$. Der Schnittpunkt hat die Koordinaten $(0, c)$.

Schnitt mit der x-Achse – Nullstellen der Parabel

Jeder Schnittpunkt eines Graphen mit der x-Achse erfüllt folgende Bedingung: $f(x) = 0$

Für das gegebene Beispiel gilt $\frac{1}{2}x^2 - 2x + \frac{3}{2} = 0$

Mit der Lösungsformel erhält man die gesuchten Nullstellen der Funktion.

$$x_{1/2} = \frac{2 \pm \sqrt{4 - 4 \cdot \frac{1}{2} \cdot \frac{3}{2}}}{2 \cdot \frac{1}{2}}$$

$$x_{1/2} = \frac{2 \pm 1}{1} \qquad x_1 = 1 \;\; x_2 = 3$$

Allgemein sind die x-Koordinaten der Schnittpunkte einer Parabel mit der x-Achse die Lösungen der quadratischen Gleichung $ax^2 + bx + c = 0$. Wie bereits gesehen, kann eine solche quadratische Gleichung keine, eine oder zwei Lösungen haben. Für die Parabel bedeutet das, dass sie die x-Achse entweder gar nicht schneidet, in einem Punkt berührt oder in zwei Punkten schneidet. Die Normalparabel ist ein Beispiel für eine Parabel, die die x-Achse nur in einem Punkt berührt. Sie hat eine Nullstelle bei $x = 0$. Eine solche Nullstelle, bei der die Parabel die x-Achse nur berührt, heißt doppelte Nullstelle der Parabel. Die Beispielfunktion f hat zwei Nullstellen. Eine Parabel, die mit der x-Achse keinen Punkt gemeinsam hat, liegt je nach dem Vorzeichen des Koeffizienten a entweder vollständig oberhalb ($a > 0$) oder vollständig unterhalb ($a < 0$) der x-Achse.

Scheitelpunkt einer Parabel

Jede Parabel hat einen höchsten oder tiefsten Punkt, den man den Scheitelpunkt der Parabel nennt. Im Beispiel von f liegt der Scheitel bei $(2, -\frac{1}{2})$. Graphisch bedeutet das, dass man den Graphen von f erhält, wenn man die Parabel mit der Gleichung $y = \frac{1}{2}x^2$ um 2 nach rechts und um $\frac{1}{2}$ nach unten verschiebt. Legt man eine Gerade, die parallel zur y-Achse ist, durch den Scheitel einer Parabel, dann ist die Parabel bezüglich dieser Geraden als Spiegelungsachse symmetrisch. Im Beispiel hat die Gerade die Gleichung $x = 2$.

Die Scheitelform einer allgemeinen quadratischen Funktion f mit dem Scheitelpunkt $S\,(v, w)$ ist:

$f\colon \mathbb{R} \to \mathbb{R}\; x \mapsto y = u\,(x - v)^2 + w$

v ist die x-Koordinate des Scheitels und gibt an, um wie viel die Parabel gegenüber der Normalparabel nach rechts (bei negativem v nach links) verschoben ist.

w ist die y-Koordinate des Scheitels und gibt an, um wie viel die Parabel gegenüber der Normalparabel nach oben ($w > 0$) oder unten ($w < 0$) verschoben ist.
u ist der Streckungsfaktor der Parabel und gibt an, ob die Parabel nach oben oder unten geöffnet ist und ob sie steiler oder flacher als die Normalparabel ist.

Wie kommt man von einer allgemeinen quadratischen Funktion zu ihrer Scheitelform? Um diese Frage zu beantworten geht man ähnlich vor wie beim Herleiten der Lösungsformel. Der entscheidende Schritt ist eine quadratische Ergänzung.

$y = ax^2 + bx + c$ | Ausklammern von a

$$y = a\left(x^2 + \frac{b}{a}x + \frac{c}{a}\right) \quad \text{| quadratische Ergänzung} + \left(\frac{b}{2a}\right)^2 - \left(\frac{b}{2a}\right)^2$$

$$y = a\left(x^2 + \frac{b}{a}x + \left(\frac{b}{2a}\right)^2 - \left(\frac{b}{2a}\right)^2 + \frac{c}{a}\right)$$

$$y = a\left(x^2 + \frac{b}{a}x + \left(\frac{b}{2a}\right)^2\right) - \frac{b^2}{4a} + c \quad \text{| 1. binomische Formel}$$

$$y = a\left(x + \frac{b}{2a}\right)^2 - \frac{b^2}{4a} + c$$

Die letzte Zeile stellt die Scheitelform der allgemeinen quadratischen Funktion dar. Durch Koeffizientenvergleich sieht man, dass der Scheitel dieser Funktion bei $S\left(-\frac{b}{2a}, -\frac{b^2}{4a} + c\right)$ liegt.

5.5 Wurzelfunktion als Umkehrfunktion der quadratischen Funktion

Umkehrbarkeit der quadratischen Funktion

Man betrachtet zunächst den einfachsten Fall einer quadratischen Funktion, die Normalparabel mit

$f\colon \mathbb{R} \to \mathbb{R}\; x \mapsto y = x^2$

Die Wertemenge der Funktion ist $\mathbb{W} = f(\mathbb{D}) = \mathbb{R}_0^+$, die Funktion nimmt keine negativen Werte an. Jede Zahl in $\mathbb{R}_0^+$ ist das Bild von zwei x-Werten aus der Definitionsmenge $\mathbb{D} = \mathbb{R}$. Z. B. ist $(-2)^2 = 4 = 2^2$. 2 und -2 werden auf die selbe Zahl $y = 4$ abgebildet. f ist also in $\mathbb{R}$ nicht umkehrbar.

Verkleinert man die Definitionsmenge von f zu $\mathbb{D} = \mathbb{R}_0^+$, ist jeder y-Wert Bild von nur noch einem x-Wert, der eindeutig bestimmbar ist. Die Funktion ist innerhalb der eingeschränkten Definitionsmenge umkehrbar. Graphisch erhält man die Umkehrfunktion, indem man den Graphen von f (in $\mathbb{D} = \mathbb{R}_0^+$!) an der Geraden $y = x$ (der Winkelhalbierenden des I. und III. Quadranten des Koordinatensystems) spiegelt.

Zu einer rechnerischen Lösung kommt man, indem man die Variablen in der ursprünglichen Abbildungsvorschrift vertauscht und dann nach y auflöst. Es gilt: $x, y \in \mathbb{R}_0^+$

f: $y = x^2$ | Vertauschen der Variablen
$x = y^2$ | Wurzelziehen, $x, y \in \mathbb{R}_0^+$
$y = \sqrt{x}$

Die Funktion $f: \mathbb{R}_0^+ \to \mathbb{R}_0^+ \; x \mapsto y = x^2$ hat die Umkehrfunktion
$f^{-1}: \; \mathbb{R}_0^+ \to \mathbb{R}_0^+ \; x \mapsto y = \sqrt{x}$

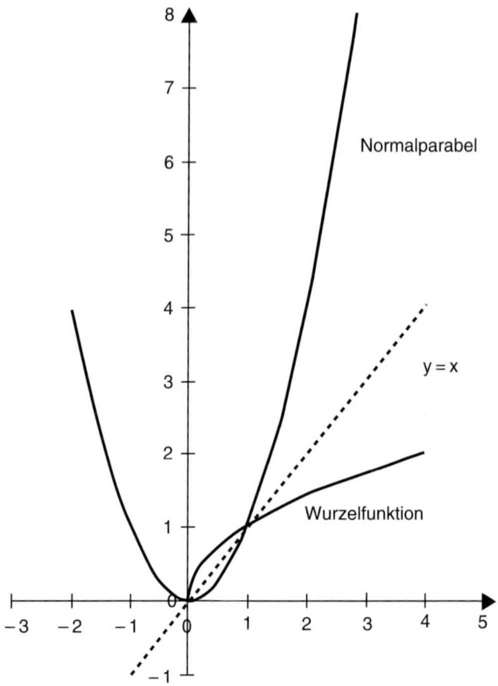

Zu jeder quadratischen Gleichung kann man nach geeigneter Einschränkung der Definitionsmenge die Umkehrfunktion bilden.
Für die Einschränkung der Definitionsmenge spielt der Scheitel bzw. die x-Koordinate des Scheitelpunkts einer Parabel eine wichtige Rolle. Aufgrund der Symmetrieeigenschaften der Parabel nimmt die quadratische Funktion in gleichen Abständen links und rechts vom Scheitel gleiche y-Werte an. Schränkt man die Definitionsmenge einer quadratischen Funktion so ein, dass sie nur noch den Teil rechts (oder links) des Scheitelpunkts enthält, ist die Funktion in diesem Bereich umkehrbar.

Das nächste Beispiel verdeutlicht das.

$f\colon \mathbb{R} \to \mathbb{R}\ x \mapsto y = x^2 + 2x$

Bestimmen des Scheitelpunkts

Durch quadratische Ergänzung erhält man die Scheitelform der Funktion

$y = x^2 + 2x + 1 - 1$
$y = (x + 1)^2 - 1$

Der Scheitelpunkt hat die Koordinaten $S\ (-1, -1)$. Die Parabel ist also achsensymmetrisch zur Geraden $x = -1$.

Einschränken der Definitionsmenge

Für $x \geq -1$ gehört zu jedem y-Wert genau ein x-Wert, der auf ihn abgebildet wird. Die eingeschränkte Definitionsmenge lautet $\mathbb{D} = [-1; \infty[$, in $\mathbb{D}$ ist die Funktion umkehrbar. Die Wertemenge dazu ist $\mathbb{W} = f(\mathbb{D}) = [-1; \infty[$.

Berechnen der Umkehrfunktion

Für den eingeschränkten Definitionsbereich lässt sich durch Vertauschen der Variablen die Umkehrfunktion bestimmen.

$y = x^2 + 2x \mid$ Vertauschen der Variablen
$x = y^2 + 2y \mid -x$
$y^2 + 2y - x = 0 \mid$ Anwenden der Lösungsformel, $x \geq -1 \Rightarrow 4 + 4x \geq 0$!

$$y_{1/2} = \frac{-2 \pm \sqrt{4 + 4x}}{2} \mid y \geq -1!$$

$y = \sqrt{x + 1} - 1$

Die Umkehrfunktion von f ist $f^{-1}\colon [-1; \infty[\to [-1; \infty[\ x \mapsto y = \sqrt{x + 1} - 1$

6 Potenzen und Potenzfunktionen

6.1 Potenzen mit Exponenten aus $\mathbb{N}$, $\mathbb{Z}$ und $\mathbb{Q}$

Definitionen:
Ein Term der Form
a^x heißt Potenz.
a ist die Basis und x der Exponent der Potenz.

Potenzen mit Exponenten in $\mathbb{N}$
Potenzen a^n mit natürlichem Exponenten $n \in \mathbb{N}$ sind bereits bekannt. Sie sind eine Kurzschreibweise für eine Multiplikation eines Terms mit sich selbst. Der Exponent n gibt an, wie oft der Term mit sich selbst malgenommen wird.

$a^2 = a \cdot a$
$a^3 = a \cdot a \cdot a$
$a^4 = a \cdot a \cdot a \cdot a$
$a^n = a \cdot a \cdot \ldots \cdot a$ (n Faktoren)
Speziell gilt $a^1 = a$

Durch Anwenden der Definition kann man bereits für $a \neq 0$ erste Rechnungen ausführen.

$a^2 \cdot a^3 = a \cdot a \cdot a \cdot a \cdot a = a^5$

$$\frac{a^5}{a^3} = \frac{a \cdot a \cdot a \cdot a \cdot a}{a \cdot a \cdot a} = a \cdot a = a^2$$

$(a \cdot b)^2 = a \cdot b \cdot a \cdot b = a \cdot a \cdot b \cdot b = a^2b^2$
$(a^2)^3 = a^2 \cdot a^2 \cdot a^2 = a \cdot a \cdot a \cdot a \cdot a \cdot a = a^6$

Der Potenzbegriff wird nun schrittweise erweitert. Zunächst werden Potenzen mit negativem Exponenten, dann solche mit positiven gebrochenrationalen und zuletzt die mit allgemeinem Exponenten aus $\mathbb{Q}$ definiert.

Potenzen mit Exponenten in $\mathbb{Z}$

Für $a \neq 0$ und $n \in \mathbb{Z}$ ist definiert:

$$a^0 = 1$$

$$a^{-1} = \frac{1}{a}$$

$$a^{-2} = \frac{1}{a^2}$$

$$a^{-3} = \frac{1}{a^3}$$

$$a^{-n} = \frac{1}{a^n} \text{ für } n \in \mathbb{N}$$

Statt eine Basis mit einem negativen Exponenten zu potenzieren, potenziert man den Kehrbruch der Basis mit der Gegenzahl des Exponenten.

Man berechnet damit:

$$\left(\frac{x+y}{x-y}\right)^{-2} = \left(\frac{x-y}{x+y}\right)^2$$

$$\frac{2b}{u^{-2}\,v^{1-m}} = 2b\,u^2\,v^{m-1}$$

In einem Bruchterm lassen sich die Potenzen also so umsortieren, dass alle Exponenten positiv werden.

$$\frac{21\,x^4 \cdot y^2 \cdot z^{-7}}{35x^5 \cdot y^{-2} \cdot z^{-1}} = \frac{21\,x^4 \cdot y^4 \cdot z}{35x^5 z^7} = \frac{3y^4}{5xz^6}$$

Potenzen mit Exponenten in $\mathbb{Q}$

Zunächst betrachtet man Exponenten der Form $\frac{1}{n}$ mit $n \in \mathbb{N}$, also $\frac{1}{n} \in \mathbb{Q}$. Ist $a \in \mathbb{R}_0^+$, dann soll $a^{\frac{1}{n}} \in \mathbb{R}_0^+$ so erklärt sein, dass

$(a^{\frac{1}{n}})^n = a$ ist.

Nach der Definition der Wurzelschreibweise ist $(a^{\frac{1}{n}})^n = (\sqrt[n]{a})^n = a$ und damit

$a^{\frac{1}{n}} = \sqrt[n]{a}$.

Es gilt der Eindeutigkeitssatz der n-ten Wurzel, der besagt:

Zu jedem $a \in \mathbb{R}_0^+$ gibt es höchstens eine n-te Wurzel, d. h. höchstens ein $x \in \mathbb{R}_0^+$, für das $x^n = a$ ist. Die oben angegebene Schreibweise für Exponenten der Form $\frac{1}{n}$ ist also eindeutig.

Eine Potenz, deren Exponent ein Bruch der Form $\frac{1}{n}$ ist, hat den Wert der n-ten Wurzel von a.

Man schreibt für $a \in \mathbb{R}_0^+$:

$a^{\frac{1}{2}} = \sqrt[2]{a}$

$a^{\frac{1}{3}} = \sqrt[3]{a}$

$a^{\frac{1}{6}} = \sqrt[6]{a}$

Beispiele:

$16^{\frac{1}{4}} = \sqrt[4]{16} = \sqrt[4]{2^4} = 2$

$27^{\frac{1}{3}} = \sqrt[3]{27} = \sqrt[3]{3^3} = 3$

$\left(\frac{1}{4}\right)^{\frac{1}{2}} = \sqrt[2]{\frac{1}{4}} = \sqrt[2]{\frac{1}{2} \cdot \frac{1}{2}} = \frac{1}{2}$

Man beachte:
1. Der Wert der n-ten Wurzel ist nur für $a \in \mathbb{R}_0^+$ erklärt. Aus negativen Zahlen darf man (in $\mathbb{R}$) keine Wurzeln ziehen!
2. Der Wert von $a^{\frac{1}{n}}$ ist entsprechend der Definition immer positiv. $x = a^{\frac{1}{n}} = \sqrt[n]{a}$ ist immer die positive Lösung der Gleichung $x^n = a$.

Nun kann man eine Definition für den allgemeinen Fall eines Exponenten $q \in \mathbb{Q}^+$ angeben.

Für alle $a \in \mathbb{R}^+$ und alle $m, n \in \mathbb{N}$ mit $q = \frac{n}{m}$ soll gelten:

$a^{\frac{n}{m}} = \sqrt[m]{a^n}$

Ist der Exponent einer Potenz eine positive gebrochenrationale Zahl, dann gibt der Zähler des Exponenten an, in welcher Potenz die Basis steht. Für die so entstehende Potenz bestimmt der Nenner des Exponenten den Grad der Wurzel.

Das bedeutet im einzelnen Beispiel:

$a^{\frac{2}{3}} = \sqrt[3]{a^2}$

$a^{\frac{3}{5}} = \sqrt[5]{a^3}$

$a^{\frac{2}{3}} = \sqrt[3]{a^2}$

$64^{\frac{2}{3}} = \sqrt[3]{64^2} = \sqrt[3]{(4^3)^2} = \sqrt[3]{(4^2)^3} = 16$

$100^{\frac{5}{2}} = \sqrt[2]{100^5} = \sqrt{(10^2)^5} = 100\,000$

Im hier angegebenen Fall von Exponenten aus $\mathbb{Q}^+$ gilt das Monotoniegesetz für Potenzen:

Für alle $a, b \in \mathbb{R}^+$ und alle $x \in \mathbb{Q}^+$ gilt

$a < b \Leftrightarrow a^x < b^x$

Das Monotoniegesetz lässt sich an Beispielen leicht nachvollziehen.

$2 < 5 \Leftrightarrow 2^4 < 5^4 \Leftrightarrow 16 < 625$

$27 < 64 \Leftrightarrow 27^{\frac{1}{3}} < 64^{\frac{1}{3}} \Leftrightarrow \sqrt[3]{3^3} < \sqrt[3]{4^3} \Leftrightarrow 3 < 4$

$4 < 7 \Leftrightarrow 4^{\frac{1}{2}} < 7^{\frac{1}{2}} \Leftrightarrow \sqrt{4} < \sqrt{7}$

$\frac{1}{2} < \frac{2}{3} \Leftrightarrow \left(\frac{1}{2}\right)^4 < \left(\frac{2}{3}\right)^4$

$\frac{4}{9} < 1 \Leftrightarrow \left(\frac{4}{9}\right)^{\frac{3}{2}} < 1^{\frac{3}{2}} \Leftrightarrow \sqrt[2]{\left(\frac{4}{9}\right)^3} < \sqrt[2]{1^3} \Leftrightarrow \frac{8}{27} < 1$

Im letzten Schritt betrachtet man Potenzen mit Exponenten mit beliebigem Vorzeichen $q \in \mathbb{Q}$. Dazu definiert man:
Für alle $a \in \mathbb{R}^+$ und $m, n \in \mathbb{N}$ soll gelten:

$$a^{-\frac{n}{m}} = \frac{1}{a^{\frac{n}{m}}} = \frac{1}{\sqrt[m]{a^n}}$$

Beispiele:

$$a^{-\frac{1}{3}} = \frac{1}{\sqrt[3]{a}}$$

$$a^{-\frac{4}{5}} = \frac{1}{\sqrt[5]{a^4}}$$

$$8^{-\frac{2}{3}} = \frac{1}{\sqrt[3]{8^2}} = \frac{1}{\sqrt[3]{64}} = \frac{1}{4}$$

$$(a^8)^{-\frac{3}{4}} = \frac{1}{\sqrt[4]{(a^8)^3}} = \frac{1}{\sqrt[4]{a^{24}}} = \frac{1}{a^6}$$

6.2 Potenzgesetze

Bereits durch schrittweises Anwenden der Definitionen lassen sich verschiedene Aufgaben mit Potenzen lösen. Für das Rechnen mit Potenzen gelten außerdem die

Potenzgesetze
Für $a, b \in \mathbb{R}^+$ und $x, z \in \mathbb{Q}$ gilt:

1. $a^x \cdot a^z = a^{x+z}$
2. $a^x : a^z = a^{x-z}$
3. $a^x \cdot b^x = (ab)^x$
4. $a^x : b^x = \left(\frac{a}{b}\right)^x$
5. $(a^x)^z = a^{x \cdot z}$

Für Werte von x und z aus $\mathbb{Z}$ lassen sich die Potenzgesetze einfach aus den Definitionen herleiten, wie man an den Beispielen im ersten Absatz nachvollziehen kann. Die Potenzgesetze gelten aber darüber hinaus für alle Exponenten aus $\mathbb{Q}$. Einige Beispiele zeigen die Anwendung der einzelnen Potenzgesetze und ihre Kombination in komplexeren Aufgaben.

$c^{\frac{2}{3}} \cdot c^{\frac{4}{3}} = c^{\frac{2}{3}+\frac{4}{3}} = c^{\frac{6}{3}} = c^2$

$u^{\frac{5}{2}} : u^{\frac{7}{4}} = u^{\frac{5}{2}-\frac{7}{4}} = u^{\frac{10}{4}-\frac{7}{4}} = u^{\frac{3}{4}}$

$2^{4x} \cdot 5^{4x} = (2 \cdot 5)^{4x} = 10^{4x}$

$896^{0,2} : 28^{0,2} = \left(\frac{896}{28}\right)^{0,2} = 32^{\frac{1}{5}} = 2$

$(x^{\frac{2}{1}})^{\frac{1}{4}} = x^{\frac{2}{1} \cdot \frac{1}{4}} = x^{\frac{1}{2}} = \sqrt{x}$

6.3 Potenzfunktionen

So wie die quadratische Funktion mit der Gleichung $y = x^2$ lassen sich auch Funktionen aus Potenzen mit anderen ganzzahligen Exponenten bilden. Sie gliedern sich in zwei Gruppen, je nach dem Vorzeichen der Exponenten. Zunächst werden Potenzfunktionen mit positivem Exponenten, anschließend die mit negativem Exponenten betrachtet.

Potenzfunktionen mit Exponenten aus $\mathbb{N}$

Eine Funktion, die durch die Zuordnung $f\colon \mathbb{R} \to \mathbb{R}\ x \mapsto y = x^n$ mit $n \in \mathbb{N}$ und $n \neq 0$ erzeugt wird, heißt Potenzfunktion.

Die Potenzfunktion hat die Definitionsmenge $\mathbb{D} = \mathbb{R}$. In der Abbildungsvorschrift ist der Exponent konstant, die Basis ist die Variable der Funktion. Ihr Graph heißt Parabel n-ter Ordnung.

Für die folgenden vier Funktionen wird durch Einsetzen eine Wertetabelle erstellt.

$f_1\colon \mathbb{R} \to \mathbb{R}\ x \mapsto y = x^2$

$f_2\colon \mathbb{R} \to \mathbb{R}\ x \mapsto y = x^3$

$f_3\colon \mathbb{R} \to \mathbb{R}\ x \mapsto y = x^4$

$f_4\colon \mathbb{R} \to \mathbb{R}\ x \mapsto y = x^5$

x	– 2	-1,5	– 1	– 0,5	0	0,5	1	1,5	2
$f_1(x)=x^2$	4	2,25	1	0,25	0	0,25	1	2,25	4
$f_2(x)=x^3$	– 8	– 3,375	– 1	– 0,125	0	0,125	1	3,375	8
$f_3(x)=x^4$	16	5,0625	1	0,0625	0	0,0625	1	5,0625	16
$f_4(x)=x^5$	– 32	– 7,59375	– 1	– 0,03125	0	0,03125	1	7,59375	32

Alle Potenzfunktionen gehen durch die Punkte (0, 0) und (1, 1). Die Wertetabelle zeigt bereits, dass sich die Funktionen sonst deutlich unterscheiden, je nachdem, ob der Exponent eine gerade oder ungerade Zahl ist. Darum werden diese beide Fälle getrennt betrachtet.

Potenzfunktionen mit geradem Exponenten

Graphische Darstellung siehe unten.

Aus dem Graphen werden bereits einige Eigenschaften der Funktionen klar, die sich auch rechnerisch für den allgemeinen Fall einer Potenzfunktion mit geradem Exponenten nachweisen lassen.

- Die Wertemenge der Potenzfunktionen mit geradem Exponenten ist $\mathbb{W} = \mathbb{R}_0^+$.
- Die Parabel ist zur y-Achse symmetrisch, denn es gilt: $(-x)^n = x^n$.
- Für alle $x \geq 0$ gilt nach dem Monotoniegesetz der Potenzen: $x_1 < x_2 \Leftrightarrow x_1^n < x_2^n$, man sagt dazu auch, die Funktion ist im Bereich $x \geq 0$ streng monoton steigend. Verschiedene x-Werte werden also immer auf verschiedene y-Werte abgebildet. Die Funktion ist im Bereich $x \geq 0$ umkehrbar.

  Für alle $x < 0$ gilt der umgekehrte Zusammenhang:
  $x_1 < x_2 \Leftrightarrow x_1^n > x_2^n$
  Die Funktion ist für $x < 0$ streng monoton fallend, sie ist in diesem Bereich umkehrbar.

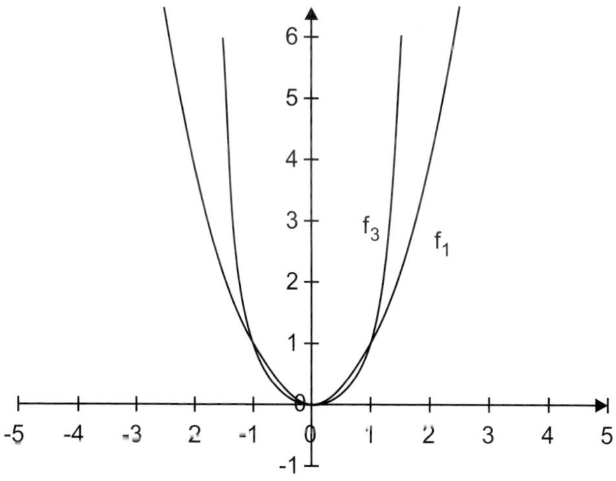

Für $x \in \mathbb{R}$ ist die Funktion nicht umkehrbar, da verschiedene x-Werte auf den selben y-Wert abgebildet werden.

Berechnung der Umkehrfunktion

Man betrachtet den eingeschränkten Definitionsbereich $\mathbb{D} = \mathbb{R}_0^+$. In diesem Bereich ist die Funktion umkehrbar. Die Wertemenge der Funktion ist ebenfalls $\mathbb{R}_0^+$. Durch Vertauschen der Variablen lässt sich die Umkehrfunktion bestimmen.

$f\colon \mathbb{R}_0^+ \to \mathbb{R}_0^+\ x \mapsto y = x^n$

$y^n = x$

$y = x^{\frac{1}{n}} = \sqrt[n]{x}$

Die Umkehrfunktion ist also eine Wurzelfunktion. Sie ist für $x \geq 0$ definiert und hat die Abbildungsvorschrift

$f^{-1}\colon \mathbb{R}_0^+ \to \mathbb{R}_0^+\ x \mapsto y = \sqrt[n]{x}$

Ihren Graphen erhält man durch Spiegelung des rechten Parabelasts an der Geraden $y = x$.

Potenzfunktionen mit ungeradem Exponenten

Graphische Darstellung siehe S. 161

Auch für Potenzfunktionen mit ungeradem Exponenten lassen sich verschiedene Eigenschaften nachweisen.

- Die Wertemenge der Potenzfunktionen mit ungeradem Exponenten ist $\mathbb{W} = \mathbb{R}$.
- Die Parabel ist punktsymmetrisch zum Ursprung (0, 0), denn es gilt: $(-x)^n = -x^n$.
- Es gilt für $x \in \mathbb{R}$: $x_1 < x_2 \Leftrightarrow x_1^n < x_2^n$. Die Funktion ist also im gesamten Definitionsbereich streng monoton steigend und damit auch in $\mathbb{R}$ umkehrbar.

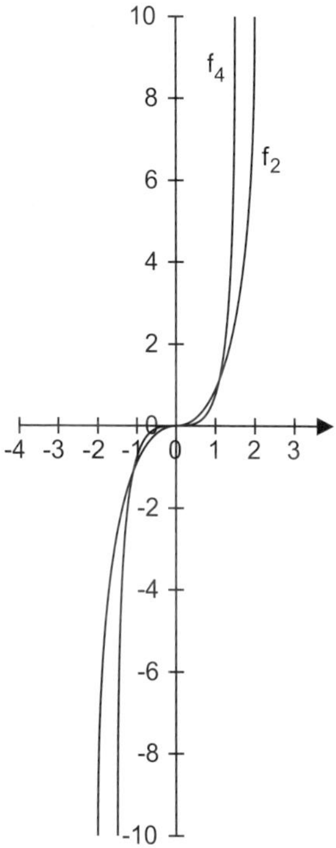

Berechnung der Umkehrfunktion

$f\colon \mathbb{R} \to \mathbb{R}\ x \mapsto y = x^n$

$y^n = x$

Da gebrochenrationale Exponenten nur für positive Zahlen definiert sind, muss man an dieser Stelle Betragsstriche und eine Fallunterscheidung an Hand des Vorzeichens von x einführen.

$$y = \begin{cases} x^{\frac{1}{n}} & \text{für } x \geq 0 \\ -|x|^{\frac{1}{n}} & \text{für } x < 0 \end{cases}$$

Die Umkehrfunktion ist auch hier wieder eine Wurzelfunktion. Sie ist für $x \in \mathbb{R}$ definiert und hat die Abbildungsvorschrift

$$f^{-1}\colon \mathbb{R} \to \mathbb{R}\ x \mapsto y = \begin{cases} x^{\frac{1}{n}} & \text{für } x \geq 0 \\ -|x|^{\frac{1}{n}} & \text{für } x < 0 \end{cases}$$

Ihren Graphen erhält man durch Spiegelung der Parabel an der Geraden $y = x$.
Hier ist f_2 mit $y = x^3$ und ihre Umkehrfunktion f_2^{-1} dargestellt.

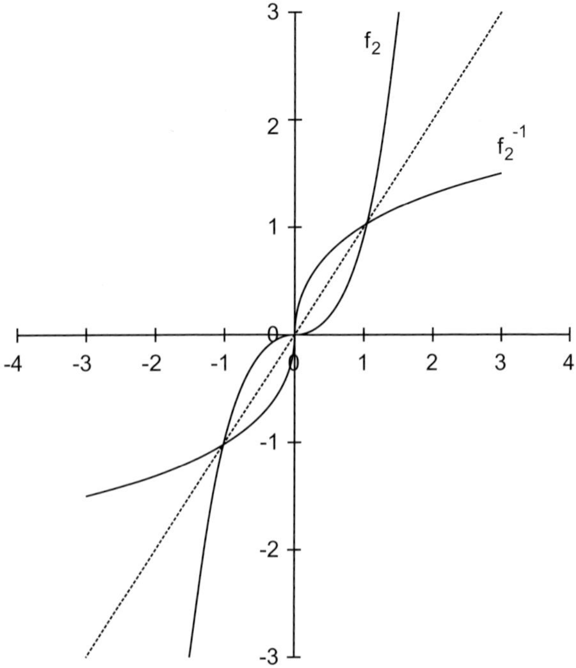

Potenzfunktionen mit negativen ganzzahligen Exponenten
Auch eine Funktion mit der Zuordnung $f\colon \mathbb{R}\setminus\{0\} \to \mathbb{R}\ x \mapsto y = x^{-n}$ ($n \in \mathbb{N}$) heißt Potenzfunktion. Sie ist für $x = 0$ nicht definiert. Der Graph dieser Potenzfunktion heißt Hyperbel n-ter Ordnung.

Auch die Potenzfunktionen mit negativem Exponenten haben alle den Punkt (1, 1) gemeinsam. Sie unterscheiden sich, je nachdem ob n gerade oder ungerade ist.

1. Fall: *n* **gerade**

Die Funktionen *f* und *g* stellen zwei Beispiele für Hyperbeln mit geradem *n* dar und werden zunächst graphisch dargestellt.

$f\colon \mathbb{R}\setminus\{0\} \to \mathbb{R}\ x \mapsto y = x^{-2} = \dfrac{1}{x^2}$

$g\colon \mathbb{R}\setminus\{0\} \to \mathbb{R}\ x \mapsto y = x^{-4} = \dfrac{1}{x^4}$

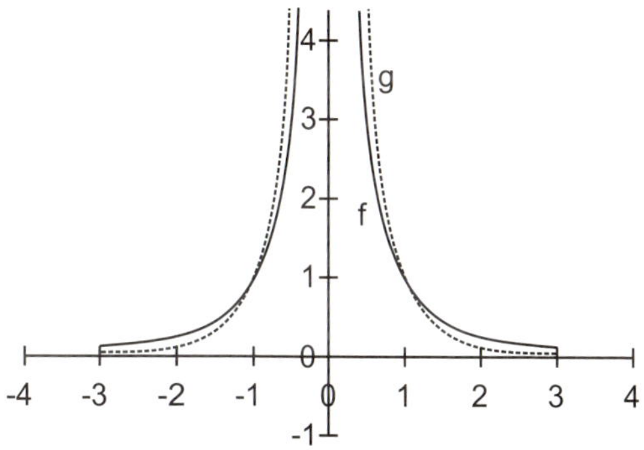

Eigenschaften von Hyperbeln mit geradem *n*:

- Die Wertemenge enthält für gerade *n* nur positive Werte, sie ist $\mathbb{W} = f(\mathbb{D}) = \mathbb{R}^+$.
- Die Hyperbeln *n*-ter Ordnung mit geradem *n* sind symmetrisch zur *y*-Achse. Es gilt: $(-x)^{-n} = x^{-n}$.
- Wie für positive Exponenten errechnet sich die Monotonieeigenschaft der Hyperbeln.

  Für $x > 0$ ist die Funktion streng monoton fallend, denn es gilt: $x_1 < x_2 \Leftrightarrow x_1^{-n} > x_2^{-n}$ und für $x < 0$ ist die Funktion streng monoton steigend, es gilt: $x_1 < x_2 \Leftrightarrow x_1^{-n} < x_2^{-n}$. Die Funktion ist also für $x > 0$ umkehrbar.

Umkehrfunktion

Nach Vertauschen der Variablen erhält man:

$y^{-n} = x \Rightarrow y = x^{-\frac{1}{n}}$. Die Umkehrfunktion ist für $x > 0$ definiert und lautet $f^{-1}\colon \mathbb{R}^+ \to \mathbb{R}\ x \mapsto y = x^{-\frac{1}{n}}$

2. Fall: *n* ungerade

Die einfachsten Beispiele für Hyperbeln mit ungeradem n werden hier graphisch dargestellt.

$$f\colon \mathbb{R}\setminus\{0\} \to \mathbb{R}\ x \mapsto y = x^{-1} = \frac{1}{x}$$

$$g\colon \mathbb{R}\setminus\{0\} \to \mathbb{R}\ x \mapsto y = x^{-3} = \frac{1}{x^3}$$

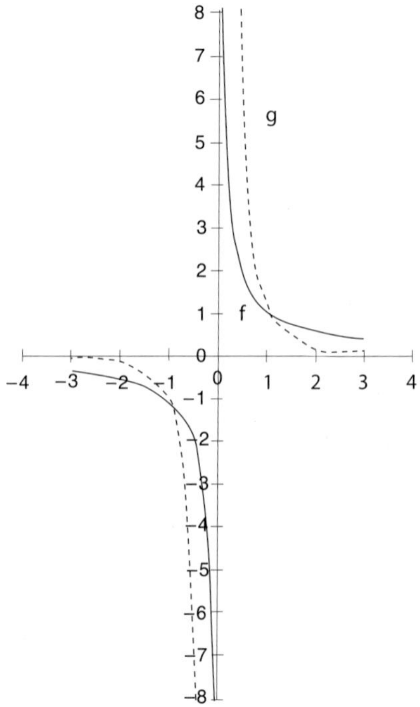

Eigenschaften von Hyperbeln mit ungeradem n:

- Die Wertemenge umfasst alle Zahlen bis auf Null, $\mathbb{W} = \mathbb{R}\setminus\{0\}$
- Die Hyperbeln n-ter Ordnung mit ungeradem n sind punktsymmetrisch zum Schnittpunkt der Koordinatenachsen (0, 0). Es gilt: $(-x)^{-n} = -x^{-n}$.
- Auf Grund der Definitionslücke kann die Monotonieeigenschaft nur gesondert links und rechts von Null betrachtet werden.

Für $x > 0$ ist die Funktion streng monoton fallend, denn es gilt: $x_1 < x_2 \Leftrightarrow x_1^{-n} > x_2^{-n}$. Für $x < 0$ ist die Funktion ebenfalls streng monoton fallend, wieder gilt: $x_1 < x_2 \Leftrightarrow x_1^{-n} > x_2^{-n}$. Die Funktion ist also für $x \neq 0$ umkehrbar.

Umkehrfunktion

Auch hier muss man nach Vertauschen der Variablen eine Fallunterscheidung durchführen, da man nur aus positiven Zahlen Wurzeln ziehen darf.

$$y^{-n} = x \Rightarrow$$
$$y = x^{-\frac{1}{n}} \text{ für } x > 0$$
$$\quad -|x|^{-\frac{1}{n}} \text{ für } x < 0$$

Die Umkehrfunktion ist für $x \in \mathbb{R}\setminus\{0\}$ definiert und lautet

$$f^{-1}: \mathbb{R}\setminus\{0\} \to \mathbb{R}\ x \mapsto y = \begin{cases} x^{-\frac{1}{n}} \text{ für } x > 0 \\ -|x|^{-\frac{1}{n}} \text{ für } x < 0 \end{cases}$$

Alle Hyperbeln n-ter Ordnung nähern sich mit wachsender Entfernung vom Ursprung immer mehr der x-Achse ohne sie jedoch zu berühren. Man sagt, die x-Achse ist eine waagrechte Asymptote der Hyperbeln. Genauso nähert sich der Graph in der Umgebung von Null immer mehr der y-Achse ohne mit ihr zusammenzufallen. Die y-Achse ist eine senkrechte Asymptote der Hyperbeln.

7 Exponentialfunktionen und Logarithmusfunktionen

7.1 Exponentialfunktionen

Für ein festes $a \in \mathbb{R}^+$ und $a \neq 1$ erzeugt die Abbildungsvorschrift $x \mapsto y = a^x$ eine Funktion. Sie ist für jedes $x \in \mathbb{R}$ definiert. Die dazugehörige Funktion $f: \mathbb{R} \to \mathbb{R}\ x \mapsto y = a^x$ heißt Exponentialfunktion. $y = a^x$ ist die Exponentialgleichung. Der Graph einer Exponentialfunktion heißt Exponentialkurve.

Für $a = 1$ wird die Exponentialfunktion zur konstanten Funktion $x \mapsto y = 1^x = 1$. Die nächsten Beispiele stellen Exponentialfunktionen dar, es werden ihre Wertetabellen ermittelt und die dazugehörigen Exponentialkurven dargestellt.

$f_1: \mathbb{R} \to \mathbb{R}\ x \mapsto y = 2^x$

$f_2: \mathbb{R} \to \mathbb{R}\ x \mapsto y = 3^x$

$f_3: \mathbb{R} \to \mathbb{R}\ x \mapsto y = \left(\frac{1}{2}\right)^x$

$f_4: \mathbb{R} \to \mathbb{R}\ x \mapsto y = \left(\frac{1}{3}\right)^x$

x	− 3	− 2	− 1	0	1	2	3
$f_1(x) = 2^x$	$\frac{1}{8}$	$\frac{1}{4}$	$\frac{1}{2}$	1	2	4	8
$f_2(x) = 3^x$	$\frac{1}{27}$	$\frac{1}{9}$	$\frac{1}{3}$	1	3	9	27
$f_3(x) = \left(\frac{1}{2}\right)^x$	8	4	2	1	$\frac{1}{2}$	$\frac{1}{4}$	$\frac{1}{8}$
$f_4(x) = \left(\frac{1}{3}\right)^x$	27	9	3	1	$\frac{1}{3}$	$\frac{1}{9}$	$\frac{1}{27}$

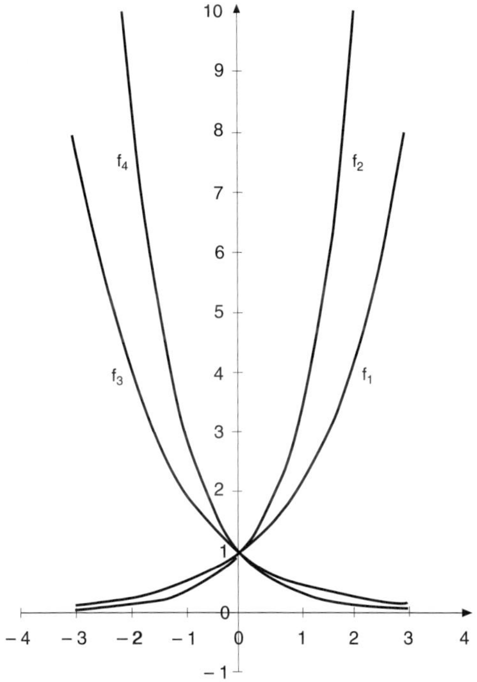

Die Exponentialfunktion hat die folgenden Eigenschaften:
Alle Exponentialkurven verlaufen oberhalb der x-Achse (im I. und II. Quadranten). Die Wertemenge der Exponentialfunktion ist $\mathbb{W} = \mathbb{R}^+$.
Alle Exponentialkurven schneiden die y-Achse im Punkt (0, 1).
Die Exponentialkurven unterscheiden sich danach, ob a zwischen null und eins liegt oder größer als eins ist.

Basis $a > 1$
Für $a > 1$ kommen die Exponentialkurven dem negativen Teil der x-Achse beliebig nahe. Die x-Achse ist waagrechte Asymptote der Exponentialkurve.
Für alle $a > 1$ und $x, z \in \mathbb{R}$ gilt: $x < z \Leftrightarrow a^x < a^z$. Die Graphen der Funktionen sind innerhalb der Definitionsmenge streng monoton steigend. Die Exponentialfunktionen sind darum auch innerhalb der Definitionsmenge umkehrbar.

Basis $0 < a < 1$

Für $0 < a < 1$ kommen die Exponentialkurven dem positiven Teil der x-Achse beliebig nahe. Die x-Achse ist eine waagrechte Asymptote der Exponentialkurve.

Für $0 < a < 1$ gilt bezüglich der Monotonie: $x < z \Leftrightarrow a^x > a^z$. Die Graphen der Funktionen sind innerhalb der Definitionsmenge streng monoton fallend. Sie sind darum innerhalb der Definitionsmenge auch umkehrbar.

Wie man den Graphen von f_1 und f_3 (bzw. f_2 und f_4) entnehmen kann, entsteht der eine jeweils durch Spiegelung an der y-Achse aus dem anderen. Dieser Zusammenhang gilt allgemein. Die Exponentialkurve der Funktion $f\colon \mathbb{R} \to \mathbb{R}\ x \mapsto y = (\frac{1}{a})^x$ geht durch Spiegelung an der y-Achse aus der Exponentialkurve von $g\colon \mathbb{R} \to \mathbb{R}\ x \mapsto y = a^x$ hervor.

Rechnerisch zeigt sich dieser Zusammenhang an der folgenden Gleichung, die die Bedingung für Achsensymmetrie nachweist.

$f(x) = (\frac{1}{a})^x = a^{-x} = g(-x)$

7.2 Logarithmusfunktion

Die Exponentialfunktion ist in ihrem gesamten Definitionsbereich $\mathbb{D} = \mathbb{R}$ umkehrbar. In Mengenschreibweise stellt sich die Funktion $f\colon \mathbb{R} \to \mathbb{R}\ x \mapsto y = a^x$ dar als $f = \{(x, y) \mid x \in \mathbb{R} \text{ und } y = a^x\}$. Ihre Wertemenge ist $\mathbb{W} = \mathbb{R}^+$, die gleichzeitig die Definitionsmenge der Umkehrfunktion f^{-1} ist.

Um die Umkehrfunktion f^{-1} zu erhalten, vertauscht man in der Menge f die Variablen und erhält f^{-1} in Mengenschreibweise:

$f^{-1} = \{(x, y) \mid x \in \mathbb{R}^+ \text{ und } x = a^y\}$. Die Wertemenge von f^{-1} umfasst ganz $\mathbb{R}$.

Die Gleichung $x = a^y$ lässt sich mit den bisher bekannten Rechenoperationen nicht nach y auflösen. Der Existenz- und Eindeutigkeitssatz für Exponenten zeigt aber, dass es für y eine eindeutig bestimmte Lösung gibt.

Existenz- und Eindeutigkeitssatz für Exponenten

Für $a \in \mathbb{R}^+\backslash\{1\}$ gibt es zu jedem $b \in \mathbb{R}^+$ genau ein $x \in \mathbb{R}$, das die folgende Gleichung erfüllt:

$a^x = b.$

Für die Lösung y der Gleichung $x = a^y$ schreibt man
$y = \log_a x$ und es ist

$$x = a^y \Leftrightarrow y = \log_a x$$

y ist der Logarithmus von x zur Basis a.

Die Umkehrfunktion f^{-1} kann man damit schreiben als
$f^{-1} = \{(x, y) \mid x \in \mathbb{R}^+ \text{ und } y = \log_a x\}$ oder
$f^{-1}: \mathbb{R}^+ \to \mathbb{R}\ x \mapsto y = \log_a x$
Ihr Graph geht durch Spiegelung der dazugehörigen Exponentialkurve an der Geraden $y = x$ hervor und heißt Logarithmuskurve.
Die Abbildung zeigt für $a = \frac{1}{2}$ und $a = 2$ die Exponentialkurven und die Graphen der dazugehörigen Umkehrfunktionen.

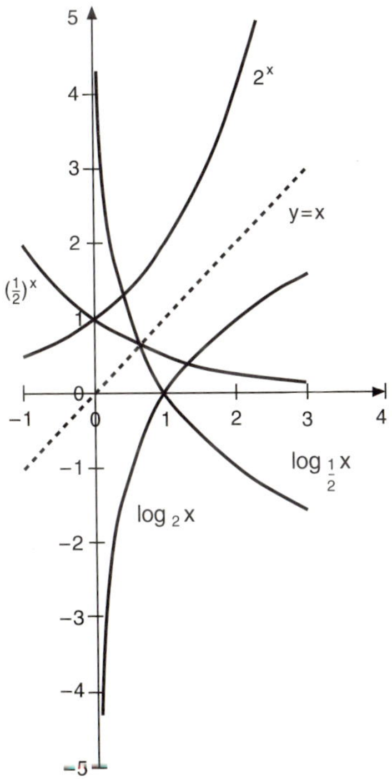

Eigenschaften der Logarithmusfunktion

Da die Exponentialkurven alle oberhalb der x-Achse verlaufen, ergibt sich für die Definitionsmenge aller Logarithmuskurven $\mathbb{D} = \mathbb{R}^+$. Die Logarithmuskurven verlaufen alle rechts von der y-Achse im I. und IV. Quadranten. Sie haben alle den Punkt (1, 0) gemeinsam.

Wie bei den Exponentialkurven unterscheiden sich Logarithmuskurven danach, ob $a > 1$ ist oder $0 < a < 1$.

Für alle $a > 1$ nähert sich die Logarithmuskurve dem negativen Teil der y-Achse an.

Für $0 < a < 1$ kommen die Logarithmuskurven dem positiven Teil der y-Achse beliebig nahe.

In beiden Fällen ist die y-Achse senkrechte Asymptote der Logarithmuskurve.

Für $a > 1$ sind die Logarithmuskurven streng monoton steigend, für $0 < a < 1$ sind sie streng monoton fallend.

Den Zusammenhang zwischen Kurven mit Basis a und Basis $\frac{1}{a}$ findet man auch bei den Logarithmuskurven. Die Logarithmuskurve mit der Gleichung $y = \log_{\frac{1}{a}} x$ geht durch Spiegelung an der x-Achse aus der Logarithmuskurve mit der Gleichung $y = \log_a x$ hervor.

7.3 Rechnen mit Logarithmen

Durch den Zusammenhang $x = a^y \Leftrightarrow y = \log_a x$ sieht man, dass ein Logarithmus ein Exponent ist. Er ist die Lösung der Exponentialgleichung $a^x = b$ mit $a, b \in \mathbb{R}^+$. Nach dem Existenz- und Eindeutigkeitssatz für Exponenten ist die Lösung eindeutig.

Beispielsweise ist $\log_5 3 = y$ die Lösung der Exponentialgleichung $5^y = 3$ und

$$\log_4 0{,}1 = y \Leftrightarrow 4^y = 0{,}1$$

Durch diesen Zusammenhang lassen sich die folgenden Beispiele bereits berechnen.

$$\log_2 512 = y \Leftrightarrow 2^y = 512 \Leftrightarrow 2^y = 2^9 \Leftrightarrow y = 9$$

$$\log_2 \sqrt{2} = y \Leftrightarrow 2^y = \sqrt{2} \Leftrightarrow 2^y = 2^{\frac{1}{2}} \Leftrightarrow y = \frac{1}{2}$$

$$\log_{\sqrt{a}} \sqrt[3]{a} = y \Leftrightarrow \sqrt{a}^y = \sqrt[3]{a} \Leftrightarrow a^{\frac{y}{2}} = a^{\frac{1}{3}} \Leftrightarrow \frac{y}{2} = \frac{1}{3} \Leftrightarrow y = \frac{2}{3}$$

Sonderfälle:

$a^1 = a \Leftrightarrow \log_a a = 1$

$a^x = a^x \Leftrightarrow \log_a a^x = x$

$a^0 = 1 \Leftrightarrow \log_a 1 = 0$

Rechengesetze für Logarithmen

Aus den Potenzgesetzen lassen sich Regeln für das Rechnen mit Logarithmen herleiten.

Dafür wählt man $a \in \mathbb{R}^+ \backslash \{1\}$, $s, t \in \mathbb{R}^+$, $x, y, z \in \mathbb{R}$ und setzt

$s = a^x$, $t = a^y$, also $\log_a s = x$ und $\log_a t = y$

Multiplikation

$s \cdot t = a^x \cdot a^y = a^{x+y}$

$\Rightarrow \log_a (s \cdot t) = \log_a a^{x+y} = x + y = \log_a s + \log_a t$

Division

$\frac{s}{t} = \frac{a^x}{a^y} = a^{x-y}$

$\Rightarrow \log_a \left(\frac{s}{t}\right) = \log_a a^{x-y} = x - y = \log_a s - \log_a t$

Potenzieren

$s^z = (a^x)^z = a^{x \cdot z}$

$\Rightarrow \log_a (s^z) = \log_a (a^{x \cdot z}) = x \cdot z = z \cdot \log_a s$

Damit erhält man die

> Regeln für das Rechnen mit Logarithmen
>
> $\log_a (s \cdot t) = \log_a s + \log_a t$
>
> $\log_a \left(\frac{s}{t}\right) = \log_a s - \log_a t$
>
> $\log_a (s^z) = z \cdot \log_a s$

Durch Anwenden der Regeln lassen sich Logarithmen mit der gleichen Basis wie in den nächsten Beispielen zusammenfassen oder aufteilen.

$$\log_a \frac{x^2 \sqrt{5}}{2y^3} = 2 \cdot \log_a x + \frac{1}{2} \log_a 5 - \log_a 2 - 3 \cdot \log_a y$$

$$\log_a 2 + 5 \log_a x - 3 \log_a y = \log_a \frac{2\,x^5}{y^3}$$

Logarithmische Gleichungen

Logarithmische Gleichungen lassen sich mit den Regeln von oben leicht vereinfachen und zusammenfassen. Stehen dann auf beiden Seiten der Gleichung nur noch Terme der Art $\log_a x$, kann man die Logarithmen auf beiden Seiten weglassen und die Lösung mit bekannten Methoden berechnen.

Beispiel:

$\log_a x = -\log_a x + \log_a 9 \mid + \log_a x$

$2 \log_a x = \log_a 9$

$\log_a x^2 = \log_a 9$

$x^2 = 9 \mid x \in \mathbb{R}^+$

$x = 3$

Exponentialgleichungen

Exponentialgleichungen können sehr unterschiedliche Formen haben, entsprechend gibt es verschiedene Möglichkeiten Exponentialgleichungen zu lösen. Hier werden drei Lösungswege an Hand von Beispielen vorgeführt.

Lösung durch Exponentenvergleich

Bei diesem Weg wandelt man die Gleichung so um, dass sie die Form $a^x = a^y$ annimmt. Die beiden Gleichungsseiten sind genau dann gleich, wenn ihre Exponenten gleich sind. Die Lösung für x ist also $x = y$.

Beispiel:

$2^{2x+3} - \sqrt{2}^{4x-2} = 240$

$2^{2x+3} - 2^{2x-1} = 240$

$2^{2x-1}(2^4 - 1) = 240 \mid : 15$

$2^{2x-1} = 16 = 2^4 \mid$ Exponentenvergleich

$2x - 1 = 4$

$x = \frac{5}{2}$

$3^{4x-12} = 1 \mid 3^0 = 1$ Exponentenvergleich

$4x - 12 = 0$

$x = 3$

Lösung durch Substitution

Einige Gleichungen lassen sich durch Substitution so umformen, dass sie die Gestalt einer quadratischen Gleichung annehmen. Diese lässt sich dann lösen und durch Rückgängigmachen der Substitution kann man die Lösungsmenge ermitteln.

Beispiel: $3^{2x} - 10 \cdot 3^x + 9 = 0$

Substitution: $3^x = u$. Dann lautet die Gleichung

$u^2 - 10u + 9 = 0 \mid$ Lösungsformel

$$u_{1/2} = \frac{10 \pm \sqrt{100 - 36}}{2}$$

$$u_{1/2} = \frac{10 \pm 8}{2}$$

$u_1 = 9$ $\qquad$ $u_2 = 1$ mit $u = 3^x$

$3^x = 9 \Rightarrow x = 2$

$3^x = 1 \Rightarrow x = 0$

Lösung durch Logarithmieren

Die Beispielgleichung $3^x = 81 \Rightarrow x = 4$ lässt sich nur deshalb im Kopf lösen, weil 81 eine ganzzahlige Potenz von 3 ist. Auch die Gleichung $2^x = 5$ ist lösbar. Dazu muss man auf beiden Seiten der Gleichung logarithmieren, das heißt, man nimmt von beiden Seiten der Gleichung den Logarithmus mit der gleichen Basis. Im Beispiel lautet die Gleichung dann $\log_a 2^x = \log_a 5$

$x \log_a 2 = \log_a 5 \mid : \log_a 2$

$$x = \frac{\log_a 5}{\log_a 2}$$

Die Basis des Logarithmus, mit dem man die Gleichung logarithmiert, hat keinen Einfluss auf die Lösung. Aus Einfachheitsgründen verwendet man häufig den Logarithmus zur Basis 10, auch Zehnerlogarithmus oder dekadischer Logarithmus genannt. Man schreibt statt $\log_{10} x$ dann $\lg x$. Der Zehnerlogarithmus hat den Vorteil, dass man ihn mit den meisten Taschenrechnern berechnen kann.

Auf einen Blick: Algebraische Regeln und Sätze

Rechenregeln in $\mathbb{R}$

In $\mathbb{R}$ haben die Gleichungen $x^n = c$ und $a^x = b$ unter bestimmten Bedingungen eine (eindeutige) Lösung. Das besagen die folgenden Sätze:

Eindeutigkeitssatz der n-ten Wurzel

Zu einem $a \in \mathbb{R}^+_0$ und $n \in \mathbb{N}$ gibt es höchstens eine n-te Wurzel, d.h. höchstens ein $x \in \mathbb{R}_0^+$, so dass $x^n = a$ ist. x heißt dann die n-te Wurzel von a und wird geschrieben als $x = \sqrt[n]{a}$.

Existenz- und Eindeutigkeitssatz für Exponenten

Für $a \in \mathbb{R}^+ \setminus \{1\}$ gibt es zu jedem $b \in \mathbb{R}^+$ genau ein $x \in \mathbb{R}$, das die folgende Gleichung erfüllt:

$a^x = b$. Es gilt: $b = a^x \Leftrightarrow x = \log_a b$

Für alle Zahlen aus $\mathbb{R}$ gelten die folgenden Rechenregeln ($a, b, c, d \in \mathbb{R}$):

1. Klammern haben Vorrang
2. Punkt vor Strich
3. Kommutativgesetz
   der Addition $a + b = b + a$
   der Multiplikation $a \cdot b = b \cdot a$
4. Assoziativgesetz
   der Addition $(a + b) + c = a + (b + c) = a + b + c$
   der Multiplikation $(a \cdot b) \cdot c = a \cdot (b \cdot c) = a \cdot b \cdot c$
5. Distributivgesetz
   $a \cdot (b + c) = a \cdot b + a \cdot c$

Daraus leiten sich ab:
Regel zum kreuzweise Ausmultiplizieren von Summen:

$(a + b) \cdot (c + d) = ac + ad + bc + bd$

Binomische Formeln:
1. binomische Formel: $(a + b)^2 = a^2 + 2ab + b^2$
2. binomische Formel: $(a - b)^2 = a^2 - 2ab + b^2$
3. binomische Formel: $(a + b)(a - b) = a^2 - b^2$

Definitionen der Potenzschreibweise, $a \in \mathbb{R}^+$, $m, n \in \mathbb{N}$:

$a^n = a \cdot a \cdot \ldots\ldots \cdot a$ (n Faktoren)

$$a^{-n} = \frac{1}{a^n}$$

$$a^{\frac{1}{n}} = \sqrt[n]{a}$$

$$a^{\frac{n}{m}} = \sqrt[m]{a^n}$$

$$a^{-\frac{n}{m}} = \frac{1}{\sqrt[m]{a^n}}$$

Potenzgesetze

Für $a, b \in \mathbb{R}^+$ und $x, z \in \mathbb{R}$ gilt:

1. $a^x \cdot a^z = a^{x+z}$
2. $a^x : a^z = a^{x-z}$
3. $a^x \cdot b^x = (ab)^x$
4. $a^x : b^x = \left(\frac{a}{b}\right)^x$
5. $(a^x)^z = a^{x \cdot z}$

Regeln für das Rechnen mit Logarithmen, $a, s, t \in \mathbb{R}^+$, $a \neq 1$, $z \in \mathbb{R}$:

$$\log_a (s \cdot t) = \log_a s + \log_a t$$

$$\log_a \left(\frac{s}{t}\right) = \log_a s - \log_a t$$

$$\log_a (s^z) = z \cdot \log_a s$$

Lösungsformel einer allgemeinen quadratischen Gleichung

Die quadratische Gleichung $ax^2 + bx + c = 0$ mit $a, b, c, x \in \mathbb{R}$ und $a \neq 0$ hat die Lösungen

$$x_{1/2} = \frac{-b \pm \sqrt{b^2 - 4ac}}{2a} \text{ falls } b^2 - 4ac > 0$$

die Lösung $x = -\frac{b}{2a}$ falls $b^2 - 4ac = 0$

und keine Lösung, falls $b^2 - 4ac < 0$.

Für quadratische Gleichungen in Normalform gilt der

Satz von Vieta

Sind x_1 und x_2 die Lösungen der quadratischen Gleichung $x^2 + px + q = 0$ mit $x_1, x_2, x, p, q \in \mathbb{R}$, dann gilt

$x_1 + x_2 = -p$ und $x_1 x_2 = q$.

Eigenschaften von Funktionen

Lineare Funktionen

Eine lineare Funktion hat die Form $f: \mathbb{R} \to \mathbb{R}\ x \mapsto y = mx + t$, ihr Graph ist eine Gerade, m ist die Steigung, t der Achsenabschnitt der Geraden. Jede lineare Funktion mit $m \neq 0$ ist umkehrbar. Ihre Umkehrfunktion ist die Funktion $f^{-1}: \mathbb{R} \to \mathbb{R}\ x \mapsto y = \frac{1}{m}x - \frac{t}{m}$

Quadratische Funktionen

Eine Funktion mit der Abbildungsvorschrift
$f: \mathbb{R} \to \mathbb{R}\ x \mapsto y = ax^2 + bx + c\ \ a, b, c \in \mathbb{R}$, $a \neq 0$ ist eine quadratische Funktion, ihr Graph ist eine Parabel. Es gilt:

$a > 0 \Rightarrow$ die Parabel ist nach oben geöffnet
$a < 0 \Rightarrow$ die Parabel ist nach unten geöfnet
und
$a \in]-1, 1[\Rightarrow$ die Parabel ist flacher als die Normalparabel
$a < -1$ oder $a > 1 \Rightarrow$ die Parabel ist steiler als die Normalparabel

Die Scheitelform einer allgemeinen quadratischen Funktion f mit dem Scheitelpunkt S (v, w) ist:
$f: \mathbb{R} \to \mathbb{R}\ x \mapsto y = u(x - v)^2 + w$
Der Scheitelpunkt der allgemeinen quadratischen Funktion hat die Koordinaten

$$S\left(-\frac{b}{2a}, -\frac{b^2}{4a} + c\right)$$

Potenzfunktionen

Funktionen der Art $f: \mathbb{R} \to \mathbb{R}\ x \mapsto y = x^n$ mit $n \in \mathbb{N}$, $n > 1$ heißen Potenzfunktionen. Ihr Graph ist eine Parabel n-ter Ordnung
Auch Funktionen mit der Gleichung $f: \mathbb{R}\backslash\{0\} \to \mathbb{R}\ x \mapsto y = x^{-n}$, $n \in \mathbb{N}$ heißen Potenzfunktionen. Der Graph einer Potenzfunktion mit negativem Exponenten ist eine Hyperbel.

Exponentialfunktionen

$f: \mathbb{R} \to \mathbb{R}\ x \mapsto y = a^x$ mit $a \in \mathbb{R}^+$ und $a \neq 1$ ist eine Exponentialfunktion. Ihre Wertemenge ist $\mathbb{W} = \mathbb{R}^+$. Sie ist in $\mathbb{R}$ umkehrbar. Dazugehörige Umkehrfunktion ist eine Logarithmusfunktion mit der Gleichung
$f^{-1}: \mathbb{R}^+ \to \mathbb{R}\ x \mapsto y = \log_a x$.

3

Stochastik

Experimente wie das Werfen einer Münze, das Ziehen von Losen oder auch die Befragung von vielen Personen zu einer Grundfrage können trotz gleicher Anfangsbedingungen zu verschiedenen Ausgängen führen. Der Zufall kommt ins Spiel.

Stochastik und Wahrscheinlichkeitsrechnung beschäftigen sich mit solchen Zufallsexperimenten. Die möglichen Ausgänge eines Experiments werden beschrieben und – was sowohl für Glücksspiele als auch für Wahlprognosen interessant ist – berechnet, mit welcher Wahrscheinlichkeit man mit bestimmten günstigen Ausgängen rechnen kann.

1 Zufallsexperimente

Ein Zufallsexperiment ist dadurch gekennzeichnet, dass es bei gleichen Anfangsbedingungen verschiedene Ausgänge haben kann. Beim Werfen eines Würfels kann man die Zahlen von 1 bis 6 erhalten, beim Werfen einer Münze sind die Ausgänge »Kopf« und »Zahl« möglich.
Ein erster Schritt, ein Zufallsexperiment zu beschreiben ist, die Menge der möglichen Ausgänge des Experiments zu erfassen.

> Jeder einzelne mögliche Ausgang eines Experiments heißt Ergebnis des Zufallsexperiments.

Ergebnisse werden mit ω bezeichnet.
Die Ergebnisse des Zufallsexperiments »einmaliges Werfen eines Würfels« sind also $\omega_1 = 1$, $\omega_2 = 2$ bis $\omega_6 = 6$.
Die Ergebnisse eines Experiments lassen sich zu einer Menge zusammenfassen:

> Der Ergebnisraum Ω eines Zufallsexperiments ist eine Menge von möglichen Ergebnissen ω_k des Experiments, für die gilt:
> 1. Jedem möglichen Ausgang des Experiments entspricht genau ein Element von Ω.
> 2. Jedes Element von Ω ist ein möglicher Ausgang des Zufallsexperiments.

Beim Werfen eines Würfels kann man als Ergebnisraum angeben:

$\Omega_1 = \{1, 2, 3, 4, 5, 6\}$.

Als möglicher Ausgang des Experiments ist manchmal aber auch nur interessant, ob man eine 6 würfelt oder nicht. Man kann den Ergebnisraum dann schreiben als $\Omega_2 = \{6, \text{keine } 6\}$. Ω_1 und Ω_2 sind beides gültige Ergebnisräume desselben Zufallsexperiments, zu einem Experiment kann es also verschiedene Ergebnisräume geben.

An einer Losbude stehen drei Verkäufer mit jeweils einer Schachtel Lose. Jemand möchte ein Los kaufen. Dazu muss er sich zunächst entschei-

den, bei welchem Verkäufer er ein Los kaufen möchte. Anschließend muss er aus der entsprechenden Schachtel ein Los ziehen.
Hier sind zwei Experimente hintereinander verknüpft. Der erste Schritt ist die Wahl des Verkäufers und damit der entsprechenden Schachtel, der zweite Schritt ist das Ziehen des Loses. Der Ergebnisraum lässt sich wieder auf verschiedene Arten schreiben. Die einfachste Form ist Ω_1 = {Gewinn, Niete}. Will man den ersten und den zweiten Schritt in der Darstellung der Ergebnisse berücksichtigen, bietet sich die Paarschreibweise an. Jedes Ergebnis wird als Paar aus dem ersten und zweiten Schritt geschrieben. Der Ergebnisraum lautet dann: Ω_2 = {(Verkäufer 1, Gewinn), (Verkäufer 1, Niete), (Verkäufer 2, Gewinn), (Verkäufer 2, Niete), (Verkäufer 3, Gewinn), (Verkäufer 3, Niete)}.
Entsprechend lassen sich andere mehrstufige Experimente je nach Anzahl der Stufen als Paare, Tripel oder allgemein als *n*-Tupel $(\omega_1, \omega_2, \dots, \omega_n)$ schreiben. Das viermalige Werfen eines Würfels kann z. B. als 4-Tupel geschrieben werden, ein mögliches Ergebnis ist dabei (1, 4, 3, 6).
Eine andere Möglichkeit, ein mehrstufiges Experiment darzustellen, ist ein Baumdiagramm. Von einem Ergebnis einer Stufe geht dabei für jedes mögliche Ergebnis der nächsten Stufe ein Pfad ab. Jede neue Stufe des Experiments wird in einer neuen Ebene von Pfaden dargestellt.
Eine Münze wird so oft geworfen, bis zum ersten Mal Kopf erscheint, höchstens aber dreimal.

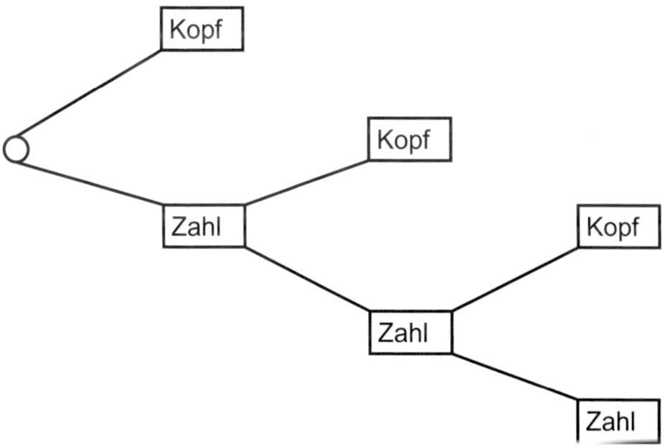

Erscheint im ersten Schritt des Experiments Kopf, so ist das Experiment zu Ende. Entsprechend führen keine weiteren Pfade davon weg. Erscheint Zahl, wird die Münze erneut geworfen. Es kann wieder Kopf oder Zahl fallen. Die beiden Möglichkeiten werden als zwei Pfade dargestellt. Erscheint Kopf, ist das Experiment nach diesem Schritt zu Ende, bei Zahl erfolgt der dritte Schritt analog. Der dazugehörige Ergebnisraum lässt sich schreiben als $\Omega = \{(K), (Z, K), (Z, Z, K), (Z, Z, Z)\}$.
Baumdiagramme eignen sich vor allem zur Darstellung mehrstufiger Experimente, bei denen die Ergebnisse der ersten Stufen den Verlauf des Experiments der folgenden Stufen beeinflussen.
Bei manchen Experimenten gilt das Interesse nicht den einzelnen Ergebnissen von Ω, sondern einer Menge von Ergebnissen, also einer Teilmenge des Ergebnisraums. Zum Beispiel kann man darauf wetten, ob beim Würfeln eine gerade oder ungerade Zahl fällt oder ob die geworfene Zahl größer als 4 ist. Die entsprechenden Teilmengen von $\Omega = \{1, 2, 3, 4, 5, 6\}$ sind dann $E_1 = \{2, 4, 6\}$ bzw. $E_2 = \{1, 3, 5\}$ und $E_3 = \{5, 6\}$.

Jede Teilmenge E des Ergebnisraums Ω, $E \subseteq \Omega$ zu einem Zufallsexperiment heißt Ereignis. Ein Ereignis E ist eingetreten, wenn für das eingetretene Ergebnis ω gilt: $\omega \in E$. Die Menge aller Ereignisse von Ω heißt Ereignisraum von Ω.

Im Beispiel sind E_1, E_2 und E_3 Ereignisse. Wird die Augenzahl 5 gewürfelt, sind E_2 und E_3 eingetreten, E_1 nicht.
Es gibt einige spezielle Teilmengen des Ergebnisraums Ω:

$\Omega \subseteq \Omega$, Ω heißt sicheres Ereignis.
$\{\ \} \subseteq \Omega$, $\{\ \}$ heißt unmögliches Ereignis
$\omega \in \Omega \Rightarrow \{\omega\} \subseteq \Omega$, Teilmengen der Art $\{\omega\}$, die nur ein Element enthalten, heißen Elementarereignis.

Ω heißt sicheres Ereignis, da jeder Ausgang des Experiments in Ω liegt und Ω somit immer eintritt, $\{\ \}$ hat keine Elemente, entsprechend kann das unmögliche Ereignis nicht eintreten. Elementarereignisse treten genau dann ein, wenn ihr Element eintritt.
Vergleicht man E_1 und E_2 von oben, so sieht man, dass E_1 genau dann eintritt, wenn E_2 nicht eintritt und umgekehrt, die geworfene Zahl ist

entweder gerade oder ungerade, niemals beides. E_1 enthält alle Ereignisse aus Ω, die E_2 nicht enthält. Zusammen ergeben die beiden Ereignisse den gesamten Ergebnisraum Ω. Man sagt, E_1 ist das Gegenereignis von E_2. Für Mengen wird dieser Zusammenhang durch das Komplement dargestellt. E_1 ist das Komplement von E_2 bezüglich Ω, man schreibt für das Komplement von E_1: $\overline{E_1} = E_2$. Die formale Definition dazu lautet:

Das Komplement einer Menge E bezüglich einer Grundmenge Ω ist die Menge $\overline{E} = \{x \in \Omega \mid x \notin E\} = \Omega \setminus E$ (»Ω ohne E«).

Das Komplement zu $E_3 = \{5, 6\}$ bezüglich $\Omega = \{1, 2, 3, 4, 5, 6\}$ ist die Menge $\overline{E_3} = \{1, 2, 3, 4\}$. Das Komplement zu Ω ist die leere Menge $\{\ \}$, also ist das unmögliche Ereignis das Gegenereignis zum sicheren Ereignis. Man sieht leicht anhand von Beispielen, dass für ein Ereignis E und sein Gegenereignis gilt: $E \cup \overline{E} = \Omega$, ihre Vereinigung ergibt den Ergebnisraum Ω und $\overline{\overline{E}} = E$.

Für verschiedene Ereignisse E_1 und E_2 in Ω ist es wichtig zu wissen, ob die beiden Ereignisse gleichzeitig eintreten können oder nicht. Betrachtet man wieder das Beispiel des Werfens eines Würfels:

$\Omega = \{1, 2, 3, 4, 5, 6\}$

E_1: Augenzahl gerade	$E_1 = \{2, 4, 6\}$
E_2: Augenzahl durch 3 teilbar	$E_2 = \{3, 6\}$
E_3: Augenzahl kleiner als 3	$E_3 = \{1, 2\}$

E_1 und E_2 haben 6 als gemeinsames Element, sie können also zugleich auftreten. Man sagt E_1 und E_2 sind vereinbare Ereignisse. Ebenso sind E_1 und E_3, die 2 als gemeinsames Element haben, vereinbare Ereignisse. E_2 und E_3 haben keine gemeinsamen Elemente, die Schnittmenge $E_2 \cap E_3 = \{\ \}$ ist leer. Die Ereignisse E_2 und E_3 sind unvereinbar. Formal definiert man:

Zwei Ereignisse E_1 und E_2 in Ω heißen unvereinbar, wenn gilt: $E_1 \cap E_2 = \{\ \}$. Sonst heißen sie vereinbar.

Ein Ereignis E in Ω und sein Komplement $\overline{E}$ sind unvereinbare Ereignisse, $E \cap \overline{E} = \{\}$. Für das unmögliche Ereignis $\{\ \}$ gilt: $E \cap \{\ \} = \{\ \}$, das unmögliche Ereignis ist also mit jedem anderen Ereignis unvereinbar. Analog ist das sichere Ereignis Ω mit jedem Ereignis in Ω vereinbar, weil gilt: $\Omega \cap E = E$. Aus bekannten Ereignissen, die nach Definition Teilmengen von Ω sind, lassen sich durch das Bilden der Komplemente von Schnittmengen und Vereinigungsmengen neue Ereignisse konstruieren. Dabei gelten die folgenden Regeln:

E_1 und E_2 sind Ereignisse in Ω.

logische Verknüpfung	sprachliche Erklärung	Mengenschreibweise
E_1 und E_2	E_1 und E_2 treten gleichzeitig ein	$E_1 \cap E_2$
E_1 oder E_2 (mathematisches, einschließendes »oder«)	es tritt ein Ergebnis aus E_1 oder E_2 oder beiden ein	$E_1 \cup E_2$
nicht E_1, Gegenereignis von E_1	es tritt ein Ergebnis ein, das nicht in E_1 liegt	$\overline{E}_1 = \Omega \backslash E_1$

Betrachtet man wieder das Beispiel vom Werfen eines Würfels mit $\Omega = \{1, 2, 3, 4, 5, 6\}$ und die Ereignisse:

E_1: Augenzahl gerade $E_1 = \{2, 4, 6\}$
E_2: Augenzahl durch 3 teilbar $E_2 = \{3, 6\}$
E_3: Augenzahl kleiner als 3 $E_3 = \{1, 2\}$

Aus den gegebenen Ereignissen lassen sich die folgenden Ereignisse herleiten:

E_4: Augenzahl gerade und durch 3 teilbar
E_5: Augenzahl durch 3 teilbar oder kleiner als 3
E_6: Augenzahl ungerade
E_7: Augenzahl gerade, aber nicht durch 3 teilbar

Damit E_4 eintritt, müssen gleichzeitig E_1 **und** E_2 eintreten, $E_4 = E_1 \cap E_2 = \{6\}$.
Damit E_5 eintritt, muss die Bedingung von E_2 **oder** von E_3 oder von beiden erfüllt sein, $E_5 = E_2 \cup E_3 = \{1, 2, 3, 6\}$.
Die Augenzahl ist genau dann ungerade, wenn sie **nicht** gerade ist. E_6 ist das Gegenereignis von E_1, $E_6 = \overline{E}_1 = \{1, 3, 5\}$.

Bei E_7 sollen zwei Bedingungen gleichzeitig erfüllt sein, nämlich Augenzahl gerade **und** Augenzahl nicht durch 3 teilbar. Es soll also E_1 eintreten **und nicht** E_2. $E_7 = E_1 \cap \overline{E_2} = \{2, 4, 6\} \cap \{1, 2, 4, 5\} = \{2, 4\}$.
Für den Umgang mit Mengen gelten ähnliche Gesetze wie bei den Grundrechenarten, sie lassen sich durch Aufzeichnen anhand von Mengendiagrammen (Venn-Diagrammen) leicht nachvollziehen. Die Gesetze über die Gleichheit von Mengen werden formal bewiesen, indem man zeigt, dass jedes beliebige Element der Menge auf der rechten Gleichungsseite auch Element der Menge auf der linken Gleichungsseite ist und umgekehrt. Hier werden die wichtigsten Gesetze aufgeführt, sie gelten für beliebige Mengen, also insbesondere auch für die Ereignisse $E_1, E_2, E_3 \subseteq \Omega$ als Teilmengen der Grundmenge Ω.
Seien A, B, C Teilmengen einer Grundmenge $\mathbb{G}$.

Kommutativgesetze:
$A \cap B = B \cap A$ $\qquad$ $A \cup B = B \cup A$
Assoziativgesetze:
$(A \cap B) \cap C = A \cap (B \cap C)$ $\qquad$ $(A \cup B) \cup C = A \cup (B \cup C)$
Distributivgesetze:
$A \cap (B \cup C) = (A \cap B) \cup (A \cap C)$ $\qquad$ $A \cup (B \cap C) = (A \cup B) \cap (A \cup C)$
De-Morgan-Gesetze:
$\overline{A \cap B} = \overline{A} \cup \overline{B}$ $\qquad$ $\overline{A \cup B} = \overline{A} \cap \overline{B}$

Mithilfe der Gesetze lassen sich Ausdrücke mit Mengen umformen und vereinfachen. Beispiel:
$\overline{A} \cup (\overline{B} \cap A) =$ | Distributivgesetz
$(\overline{A} \cup \overline{B}) \cap (\overline{A} \cup A) =$
$(\overline{A} \cup \overline{B}) \cap \mathbb{G} =$ | De-Morgan-Gesetz
$\overline{A \cap B}$

2 Häufigkeiten und Wahrscheinlichkeiten

2.1 Absolute und relative Häufigkeiten

Mithilfe der Ergebnisräume und Ereignisse wird der Ausgang eines Zufallsexperiments beschreibbar. Im nächsten Schritt interessiert, wie oft einzelne Ereignisse innerhalb einer Versuchsreihe auftreten und wie sich diese Häufigkeiten zu Aussagen über Wahrscheinlichkeiten verallgemeinern lassen.

Um die Häufigkeit zu bestimmen, mit der ein Ereignis innerhalb einer Versuchsreihe auftritt, wird dasselbe Zufallsexperiment N-mal durchgeführt. N heißt der Umfang der Stichprobe. Dabei wird nach jedem Versuch notiert, welches Ergebnis eingetreten ist.

Beispielsweise wird ein Würfel 50-mal geworfen. Nach jedem Wurf hält man die Augenzahl fest.

4 6 4 5 6 1 3 6 2 1 4 3 2 2 1 6 1 5 5 1 3 4 4 5 4
1 5 1 3 4 6 5 1 1 2 6 2 6 2 4 5 3 6 4 2 6 2 4 3 1

Dann zählt man, wie oft jedes Ergebnis eingetreten ist. Die Ergebnisse sind in den ersten beiden Zeilen der Tabelle festgehalten. Die Zahlen geben an, mit welcher absoluten Häufigkeit bei einem Stichprobenumfang von $N = 50$ die Augenzahlen 1 bis 6 eingetreten sind.

Augenzahl	1	2	3	4	5	6
absolute Häufigkeit k	10	8	6	10	7	9
relative Häufigkeit h	$\frac{10}{50} = 0{,}2$	$\frac{8}{50} = 0{,}16$	$\frac{6}{50} = 0{,}12$	$\frac{10}{50} = 0{,}2$	$\frac{7}{50} = 0{,}14$	$\frac{9}{50} = 0{,}18$

Um Aussagen über Häufigkeiten machen zu können, die unabhängig von der Größe der Stichprobe sind, setzt man die absolute Häufigkeit k eines Ereignisses zum Stichprobenumfang N ins Verhältnis. Aus dem Quotienten erhält man die relative Häufigkeit h. Für das Beispiel sind die relativen Häufigkeiten in der letzten Zeile der Tabelle dargestellt. Allgemein lautet die Definition:

Tritt ein Ereignis E bei einem Stichprobenumfang N genau k-mal ein, so hat das Ereignis die relative Häuigkeit $h(E) = \frac{k}{N}$.

Zählt man die absoluten Häufigkeiten aller Ergebnisse eines Ergebnisraums Ω zusammen, ergibt sich als Summe der Stichprobenumfang N, da bei jeder Wiederholung des Experiments genau eines der möglichen Ergebnisse eintritt. Entsprechend gilt für die Summe der relativen Häufigkeiten der Ergebnisse $\omega_1, \omega_2, \omega_3 \ldots$ eines Ergebnisraums Ω:

$$h(\omega_1) + h(\omega_2) + h(\omega_3) + \ldots$$

$$= \frac{k_1}{N} + \frac{k_2}{N} + \frac{k_3}{N} + \ldots$$

$$= \frac{1}{N} \cdot (k_1 + k_2 + k_3 + \ldots)$$

$$= \frac{1}{N} \cdot N = 1$$

Außerdem gilt offensichtlich:

$0 \leq k \leq N$ und damit $0 \leq h(E) \leq 1$

$$h(\Omega) = \frac{N}{N} = 1,\ h(\{\ \}) = \frac{0}{N} = 0$$

Zwei unvereinbare Ereignisse E_1 und E_2 können nicht gemeinsam eintreten. Tritt $E_1 \cup E_2$ ein, liegt das eingetretene Ergebnis entweder in E_1 oder in E_2, nie in beiden. Entsprechend erhöht sich entweder die absolute Häufigkeit von E_1 oder die von E_2, sie werden nie doppelt gezählt. Die absolute Häufigkeit von $E_1 \cup E_2$ ist demnach $k_1 + k_2$. Für die relative Häufigkeit folgt daraus:

$$h(E_1 \cup E_2) = \frac{k_1 + k_2}{N} = \frac{k_1}{N} + \frac{k_2}{N} = h(E_1) + h(E_2)$$

Für die relative Häufigkeit $h(E) = \frac{k}{N}$ eines Ereignisses E gilt das Gesetz der großen Zahlen von Jakob Bernoulli. Es besagt: Die relative Häufigkeit eines Ereignissses strebt »der Wahrscheinlichkeit nach« für einen großen Stichprobenumfang N gegen die Wahrscheinlichkeit des Ereignisses. Mit anderen Worten: Die Wahrscheinlichkeit dafür, dass mit zunehmendem Stichprobenumfang N die relative Häufigkeit eines Ereignisses stark von der Wahrscheinlichkeit dieses Ereignisses abweicht, wird verschwindend klein.

2.2 Wahrscheinlichkeiten

Durch das Gesetz der großen Zahlen ist also für jedes Ereignis E ein stochastischer Grenzwert p der relativen Häufigkeit gegeben. Mit den Axiomen von Kolmogorow lässt sich ein entsprechendes Wahrscheinlichkeitsmaß definieren.

Ω sei der Ergebnisraum eines Zufallsexperiments. Jedem Ereignis $E \subseteq \Omega$ wird eine reelle Zahl $P(E)$ als Wahrscheinlichkeit zugeordnet. Die Zuordnung heißt Wahrscheinlichkeitsmaß, wenn die folgenden drei Axiome erfüllt sind:

Axiom 1: $P(E) \geq 0$
Axiom 2: $P(\Omega) = 1$
Axiom 3: $E_1 \cap E_2 = \{\ \} \Rightarrow P(E_1 \cup E_2) = P(E_1) + P(E_2)$.

Durch ein Wahrscheinlichkeitsmaß ist für jedes Ereignis eines Zufallsexperiments die zugehörige Wahrscheinlichkeit gegeben oder sie lässt sich aus den gegebenen berechnen.
Beispielsweise ist beim Werfen eines Würfels ein mögliches Wahrscheinlichkeitsmaß, dass alle Augenzahlen mit gleicher Wahrscheinlichkeit vorkommen. P(Augenzahl 1) = P(Augenzahl 2) = P(Augenzahl 3) = P(Augenzahl 4) = P(Augenzahl 5) = P(Augenzahl 6) = $\frac{1}{6}$. Daraus berechnet man mithilfe von Axiom 3:

$$P(\text{Augenzahl gerade}) = P(\{2, 4, 6\}) = P(\{2\}) + P(\{4\}) + P(\{6\}) = \frac{1}{6} + \frac{1}{6} + \frac{1}{6} = \frac{1}{2}$$

Wahrscheinlichkeiten sind immer Zahlen aus dem Intervall [0, 1], sie werden möglichst exakt als Brüche, Dezimalbrüche oder in Prozent angegeben. Gegebenenfalls müssen die Darstellungsformen ineinander umgewandelt werden.
Aus den Axiomen lassen sich weitere Regeln für Wahrscheinlichkeiten herleiten. Sei E ein Ereignis in Ω. $\Omega = E \cup \overline{E}$, E und $\overline{E}$ sind unvereinbar
$\Rightarrow 1 = P(\Omega) = P(E \cup \overline{E}) = P(E) + P(\overline{E}) \Rightarrow P(\overline{E}) = 1 - P(E)$
$P(\{\ \}) = P(\overline{\Omega}) = 1 - P(\Omega) = 1 - 1 = 0$.
Die Wahrscheinlichkeit des Gegenereignisses $\overline{E}$ zu E heißt Gegenwahrscheinlichkeit von E.

Das Axiom 3 gilt nur für unvereinbare Ereignisse. Für eine beliebige Vereinigung von zwei Ereignissen gilt:

$P(E_1 \cup E_2) = P(E_1) + P(E_2) - P(E_1 \cap E_2)$

Anschaulich bedeutet das: Um die Wahrscheinlichkeit von $E_1 \cup E_2$ zu berechnen, zählt man zuerst die beiden Einzelwahrscheinlichkeiten von E_1 und E_2 zusammen. Dabei zählt man dann allerdings die Elemente der Schnittmenge doppelt. Diesen Fehler korrigiert man, indem man anschließend die Wahrscheinlichkeit der Schnittmenge, also aller doppelt gezählter Elemente, wieder abzieht.

Berechnung von Wahrscheinlichkeiten

Lösung durch Baumdiagramme

Eine Münze wird so lange geworfen, bis zum ersten Mal Kopf erscheint, höchstens aber dreimal. Man kann davon ausgehen, dass Kopf und Zahl mit gleicher Wahrscheinlichkeit, nämlich $\frac{1}{2}$ auftreten. An jeder Gabelung des Baums kommt man also mit Wahrscheinlichkeit $\frac{1}{2}$ zu einem der nächsten Knotenpunkte.

> Die Gesamtwahrscheinlichkeit für einen Pfad ist das Produkt der Einzelwahrscheinlichkeiten entlang dieses Pfads.

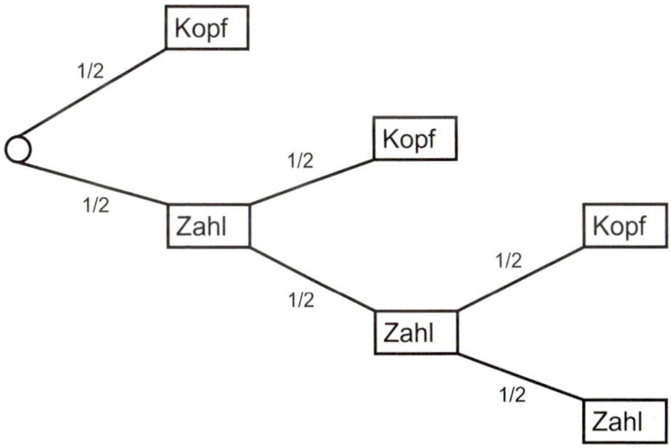

Zum Beispiel ist $P(Z, K) = \frac{1}{2} \cdot \frac{1}{2} = \frac{1}{4}$. Die Wahrscheinlichkeit des Ereignisses »die Münze wird genau dreimal geworfen« ergibt sich als Summe aus den Wahrscheinlichkeiten der Pfade, für die dieses Ereignis eintritt. Im Beispiel sind das die beiden unteren Pfade

$$P(\{(Z,Z,K),(Z,Z,Z)\}) = \frac{1}{2}\cdot\frac{1}{2}\cdot\frac{1}{2}+\frac{1}{2}\cdot\frac{1}{2}\cdot\frac{1}{2}=\frac{1}{4}.$$

Laplace-Experimente

Besonders häufig kommen in der Stochastik Experimente vor, bei denen die möglichen Ergebnisse des Ergebnisraums gleich wahrscheinlich sind. Beispiele hierfür sind das Werfen eines gleichmäßigen Würfels oder einer gleichmäßigen Münze, das zufällige Ziehen einer Kugel aus einer Urne oder einer Karte aus einem gut gemischten Kartenspiel. Solche Experimente nennt man Laplace-Experimente. Der Ausdruck »zufällig« und der Name Laplace werden dabei in Aufgaben oft als sprachlicher Hinweis für die Gleichwahrscheinlichkeit von Ergebnissen verwendet.

Die Zahl der Elementarereignisse ist gleich der Anzahl der Elemente des Ergebnisraums Ω, der Mächtigkeit $|\Omega|$ von Ω, sie wird als **Anzahl der möglichen Fälle** bezeichnet. Die Wahrscheinlichkeit für ein Elementarereignis ist $P(\{\omega\}) = \frac{1}{\text{Anzahl der möglichen Fälle}} = \frac{1}{|\Omega|}$. Bei einem Laplace-Experiment lässt sich die Wahrscheinlichkeit eines Ereignisses leicht ausrechnen.

Da jedes Ereignis E sich aus einer eindeutig bestimmbaren Zahl von unvereinbaren Elementarereignissen zusammensetzt, gilt für die

Wahrscheinlichkeit eines Ereignisses E bei einem LAPLACE-Experiment

$$P(E) = \frac{|E|}{|\Omega|} = \frac{\text{Anzahl der für } E \text{ günstigen Fälle}}{\text{Anzahl der möglichen Fälle}}.$$

Beispiel: Mit welcher Wahrscheinlichkeit zieht man bei einem Skatblatt einen König?

Anzahl der Könige im Skatblatt: 4

Anzahl der Karten: 32

$$P(\text{König}) = \frac{4}{32} = \frac{1}{8}$$

In diesem Fall ist das Abzählen der Fälle noch möglich, bei vielen Beispielen muss die Anzahl der günstigen und der möglichen Fälle erst berechnet werden. Dafür gibt es verschiedene Berechnungsmethoden.

Kombinatorik

Gegeben ist ein Zufallsexperiment, das in mehreren Schritten durchgeführt wird. Zum Beispiel wird zuerst ein Würfel und anschließend zweimal eine Münze geworfen. Für den ersten Schritt ergeben sich sechs Möglichkeiten, für den zweiten und dritten Schritt jeweils zwei. Insgesamt gibt es $6 \cdot 2 \cdot 2 = 24$ mögliche Verläufe des Experiments, die alle gleich wahrscheinlich sind.

Allgemein gilt: Lässt sich ein Zufallsexperiment in k Schritte unterteilen, wobei es für den ersten Schritt n_1, für den zweiten Schritt n_2 usw., den k-ten Schritt n_k mögliche Ausgänge gibt, dann gibt es $n_1 \cdot n_2 \cdot n_3 \cdot \ldots \cdot n_k$ Möglichkeiten für die Durchführung des gesamten Zufallsexperiments.

Daraus lassen sich verschiedene Sonderfälle herleiten:

k-Tupel

Ein Würfel wird dreimal hintereinander geworfen. Wie viele mögliche Ergebnisse gibt es?

Das Experiment findet in drei Schritten statt, die einzelnen Ergebnisse lassen sich als Tripel $(\omega_1, \omega_2, \omega_3)$ der drei Würfe schreiben. Für die Belegung jeder Stelle im Tripel gibt es sechs Möglichkeiten. Insgesamt gibt es also $6 \cdot 6 \cdot 6 = 216$ mögliche Tripel.

Für das Bilden eines allgemeinen k-Tupels $(\omega_1, \ldots, \omega_k)$ aus den Elementen einer Menge Ω mit n Elementen, $|\Omega| = n$, gibt es n^k Möglichkeiten.

Permutationen

Wie viele verschiedene Möglichkeiten gibt es, fünf Kugeln, die mit den Ziffern 1 bis 5 beschriftet sind in eine Reihe zu legen?

Es gibt fünf Plätze, die nacheinander mit den fünf Kugeln belegt werden. Für die erste Kugel gibt es fünf Auswahlmöglichkeiten, für die zweite Kugel gibt es vier, die dritte Kugel hat drei Möglichkeiten, die vierte Kugel noch zwei, der fünften Kugel bleibt nur noch eine Möglichkeit. Insgesamt sind es $5 \cdot 4 \cdot 3 \cdot 2 \cdot 1 = 120$ Möglichkeiten, die Kugeln anzuordnen.

Ein Produkt der Art $1 \cdot 2 \cdot 3 \cdot \ldots \cdot (n-1) \cdot n = n!$ wird für $n \in \mathbb{N}$ als n Fakultät bezeichnet. Es wird angenommen $0! = 1$ und $1! = 1$.

Die verschiedenen Möglichkeiten, Gegenstände in einer Reihe anzuordnen, werden als Permutationen bezeichnet. Für n Kugeln ist die Anzahl der möglichen Permutationen $n!$.

Das folgende Beispiel wird immer wieder abgewandelt (farbige Glühbirnen, Schaufensterarrangements usw.). Die Grundfrage ist, wie viele Möglichkeiten gibt es, eine bestimmte Anzahl von Dingen anzuordnen, wenn einige darunter nicht unterscheidbar sind.

Beispiel: Das Mississippi-Problem

Wie viele verschiedene (unterscheidbare) Möglichkeiten gibt es, die Buchstaben des Wortes Mississippi in einem Wort – egal ob sinnvoll oder nicht – anzuordnen?

Mississippi hat elf Buchstaben, viermal I, einmal *M*, viermal *S* und zweimal *P*. Bei elf Buchstaben gibt es 11! Permutationen. Davon sind allerdings viele nicht unterscheidbar, z.B. immer wenn zwei gleiche Buchstaben Plätze tauschen. Daher muss durch die jeweilige Zahl der Permutationen, die gleiche Buchstaben untereinander ausführen können, geteilt werden. Das Ergebnis ist dann $\frac{11!}{4! \cdot 1! \cdot 4! \cdot 2!} = 34\,650$.

Auswahl aus einer Grundgesamtheit

Auf einem Wühltisch liegen 50 unterschiedliche T-Shirts. Jemand kauft für seine drei Söhne jeweils eines. Wie viele Möglichkeiten gibt es?
Bei der Auswahl gibt es für das T-Shirt für den ältesten Sohn 50 Möglichkeiten, für den mittleren 49 und den jüngsten 48, insgesamt gibt es $50 \cdot 49 \cdot 48 = 117\,600$ Möglichkeiten.
Wählt man allgemein aus n verschiedenen Elementen einer Menge nacheinander k Elemente aus, wobei auf die Reihenfolge der ausgewählten Elemente geachtet wird, so gibt es dafür

$n \cdot (n-1) \cdot (n-2) \cdot \ldots \cdot (n-k+1)$ Möglichkeiten (k, Anzahl der Faktoren). Man kann dafür auch schreiben

$$\frac{n \cdot (n-1) \cdot (n-2) \cdot \ldots \cdot (n-k+1) \cdot (n-k) \cdot (n-k-1) \cdot \ldots \cdot 2 \cdot 1}{(n-k) \cdot (n-k-1) \cdot \ldots \cdot 2 \cdot 1} =$$

$$= \frac{n!}{(n-k)!}.$$

Wandelt man obiges Beispiel etwas ab, sodass jemand aus 50 T-Shirts drei für sich selbst auswählt, dann spielt die Reihenfolge in dem Experiment keine Rolle mehr. Die Frage lautet dann, wie viele Möglichkeiten gibt es, aus 50 verschiedenen T-Shirts drei auszuwählen. Man muss das

Ergebnis von oben also noch durch die Anzahl der Permutationen der drei T-Shirts teilen. Die Lösung ist also $\frac{50!}{(50-3)! \cdot 3!} = 19600$.

Allgemein ist die Anzahl der möglichen Teilmengen mit k Elementen aus einer n-elementigen Menge $\frac{n!}{(n-k)! \cdot k!} = \binom{n}{k} \cdot \binom{n}{k}$, sprich »$n$ über k«, heißt Binomialkoeffizient. Der Binomialkoeffizient ist für gängige Werte tabelliert.

Das Urnenmodell

Laplace-Experimente lassen sich mit dem Urnenmodell häufig gut beschreiben und berechnen. Dazu stellt man sich eine Urne vor, in der n unterscheidbare Kugeln liegen. Aus der Urne werden zufällig Kugeln gezogen. Dabei werden zwei Fallunterscheidungen gemacht.

1. Ziehen mit und ohne Zurücklegen
Beim Ziehen mit Zurücklegen wird die gezogene Kugel, nachdem das Ergebnis notiert wurde, wieder in die Urne gelegt. Dadurch bleibt die Ausgangsbedingung für jedes erneute Ziehen dieselbe. Beim Ziehen ohne Zurücklegen bleibt die Kugel außerhalb der Urne, die Zahl der Kugeln, aus denen gezogen wird, reduziert sich nach jedem Schritt um 1.

2. Ziehen mit und ohne Berücksichtigung der Reihenfolge
Beim Ziehen mit Berücksichtigung der Reihenfolge werden die Kugeln nacheinander gezogen und die Ergebnisse in der entsprechenden Reihenfolge festgehalten. Beim Ziehen ohne Reihenfolge spielt die Reihenfolge keine Rolle.

Im Fall des Ziehens mit Zurücklegen ohne Berücksichtigung der Reihenfolge ist es häufig einfacher, bei der Berechnung von Wahrscheinlichkeiten die Reihenfolge sowohl bei der Anzahl der günstigen Fälle als auch bei der Anzahl der möglichen Fälle »künstlich« mit zu berücksichtigen. Das Ergebnis bleibt dabei gleich.
Beispiel: Drei nicht unterscheidbare Würfel werden gemeinsam geworfen. Die Würfel werden gedanklich (künstlich) unterscheidbar gemacht, die Ergebnisse sind Zahlentripel, wobei Würfel 1 das Ergebnis der ersten Stelle des Tripels, Würfel 2 das Ergebnis der zweiten und Würfel 3 das Ergebnis der dritten Stelle bestimmt. Das Beispiel wird also auf »Ziehen mit Reihenfolge mit Zurücklegen« zurückgeführt. Für die anderen Fälle berechnet sich die Anzahl der Möglichkeiten für k-maliges Ziehen aus n Kugeln einer Urne:

	Anzahl der Möglichkeiten	Beispiel
mit Zurücklegen mit Reihenfolge	n^k	dreimaliges Werfen eines Würfels
ohne Zurücklegen mit Reihenfolge	$\frac{n!}{(n-k)!}$	Anordnung der Besucher in einem Wartezimmer
ohne Zurücklegen ohne Reihenfolge	$\binom{n}{k} = \frac{n!}{(n-k)! \cdot k!}$	Ankreuzen von sechs Zahlen von 49 auf einem Lotterieschein

Beispiele für das Rechnen mit Wahrscheinlichkeiten:

1. In einer Keksmischung sind 20 Kekse ohne und fünf Kekse mit Schokolade. Es werden drei Kekse zufällig herausgegriffen. Wie groß ist die Wahrscheinlichkeit, dass genau ein Keks mit Schokolade dabei ist?
Es handelt sich um ein Experiment der Art »Ziehen ohne Reihenfolge ohne Zurücklegen« mit $n = 25$ und $k = 3$. Die Anzahl der möglichen Fälle beträgt $\binom{25}{3}$. Ein günstiger Fall tritt genau dann ein, wenn ein Schokoladenkeks **und** zwei Kekse ohne Schokolade gezogen werden.

$$P(\text{genau 1 Schokoladenkeks}) = \frac{\binom{5}{1} \cdot \binom{20}{2}}{\binom{25}{3}} = \frac{19}{46} \approx 0{,}41$$

2. Man betrachtet eine beliebige Familie mit drei Kindern. Wie groß ist die Wahrscheinlichkeit, dass von den drei Kindern

a) höchstens eines ein Mädchen ist
b) mindestens eines ein Mädchen ist?

Es handelt sich um ein Experiment »Ziehen mit Reihenfolge mit Zurücklegen« mit $n = 2$ und $k = 3$. (Z.B. stellt man sich eine Urne vor, in der zwei Kugeln liegen, jeweils mit »Junge« und »Mädchen« beschriftet, in der Reihenfolge des Alters der Geschwister wird das Geschlecht gezogen.) Die Zahl der möglichen Fälle ist $2^3 = 8$.

a) $P(\text{»höchstens 1 Mädchen«}) = P(\text{»kein Mädchen«}) + P(\text{»genau ein Mädchen«}) = \frac{1}{8} + \frac{\binom{3}{1}}{8} = \frac{1}{2}$

b) Hier ist es sinnvoll, mit der Gegenwahrscheinlichkeit zu rechnen.

$P(\text{»mind. 1 Mädchen«}) = 1 - P(\text{»kein Mädchen«}) = 1 - \frac{1}{8} = \frac{7}{8}$

In einer Perlenkette von insgesamt 20 Perlen sind drei falsch. Mit welcher Wahrscheinlichkeit sind die drei falschen Perlen in der Kette nebeneinander?

Hier handelt es sich um ein Experiment »Ziehen mit Reihenfolge ohne Zurücklegen« (für jede falsche Perle wird ein Platz ausgewählt) mit $n = 20$ und $k = 3$. Die Anzahl der möglichen Fälle ist $\frac{20!}{(20-3)!} = 6840$.

Anzahl der günstigen Fälle: Zunächst wird die erste falsche Perle platziert, und zwar so, dass die anderen beiden die beiden Plätze rechts davon einnehmen. Dafür gibt es 18 Möglichkeiten. Nun könnten die falschen Perlen in jeder dieser Anordnungen beliebig Plätze tauschen, insgesamt jedes Mal 3!-mal. Insgesamt ergibt das $18 \cdot 3! = 108$ günstige Fälle.

$P(\text{»falsche Perlen liegen nebeneinander«}) = \frac{108}{6840} = \frac{3}{190} \approx 0{,}0158$

> Bei Laplace-Experimenten übersetzt sich bei der Berechnung der günstigen Fälle im Normalfall ein »und« in ein »Mal« und ein »oder« in ein »Plus«.

Beispiel:

Ein Würfel wird dreimal geworfen. Mit welcher Wahrscheinlichkeit erscheint höchstens einmal eine Augenzahl kleiner als 3?

Es liegt ein Experiment »mit Reihenfolge mit Zurücklegen« mit $n = 6$ und $k = 3$ vor. Die Anzahl der möglichen Fälle ist $6^3 = 216$.

Anzahl der günstigen Fälle: Es erscheint keinmal eine Augenzahl kleiner als 3 **oder** genau einmal.

Keine Augenzahl kleiner als 3 bedeutet, die erste Augenzahl ist größer oder gleich 3 **und** die zweite Augenzahl ist größer oder gleich 3 **und** die dritte Augenzahl ist größer oder gleich 3; es gibt jeweils vier Möglichkeiten, insgesamt also $4 \cdot 4 \cdot 4 = 64$.

Genau eine Augenzahl kleiner als drei bedeutet: Die erste **oder** die zweite **oder** die dritte Augenzahl ist kleiner als 3, insgesamt $2 + 2 + 2$ Möglichkeiten. Die anderen beiden Augenzahlen sind größer oder gleich 3, $(2 + 2 + 2) \cdot 4 \cdot 4 = 96$ Fälle. Die Anzahl der günstigen Fälle ist damit $64 + 96 = 160$.

$P(\text{»höchstens einmal Augenzahl kleiner als 3«}) = \frac{160}{216} = \frac{20}{27} \approx 0{,}74$

3 Bedingte Wahrscheinlichkeiten

Beim Hintereinanderschalten von Zufallsexperimenten kann der Ausgang eines Experiments Einfluss auf die nächsten Experimente haben. Ein Beispiel ist das Ziehen ohne Zurücklegen. Nach jedem Ziehen ändert sich die Grundgesamtheit der Kugeln in der Urne.
Ein anderes Beispiel sind die Merkmale, die in bestimmten Kombinationen häufiger auftreten als in anderen. Betrachtet man die Merkmale Augenfarbe und Haarfarbe bei einer Person, bei einer Gruppe von Personen, in der nur blonde und brünette und nur blau- und braunäugige Personen sind. Die folgende Tabelle zeigt eine Wahrscheinlichkeitsverteilung; dabei geben die Ränder (rechts und unten) die Wahrscheinlichkeit für ein Merkmal an, die Felder in der Mitte die Wahrscheinlichkeit für das gleichzeitige Auftreten zweier Merkmale.

Haarfarbe/Augenfarbe	blau	braun	
blond	0,4	0,1	0,5
brünett	0,2	0,3	0,5
	0,6	0,4	1

Offensichtlich gibt es einen starken Zusammenhang zwischen Augenfarbe und Haarfarbe. Während in der Gesamtgruppe mehr Personen blaue Augen als braune Augen haben, ist das unter den brünetten Personen genau umgekehrt. Das führt zur folgenden Definition:

> Zwei Ereignisse E_1 und E_2 heißen unabhängig, wenn gilt:
> $P(E_1 \cap E_2) = P(E_1) \cdot P(E_2)$, andernfalls heißen sie abhängig.

Formal berechnet sich für die Ereignisse E_1: Augenfarbe blau und E_2: blonde Haare

$P(E_1 \cap E_2) = 0{,}4$ und $P(E_1) \cdot P(E_2) = 0{,}5 \cdot 0{,}6 = 0{,}3$

Die Ereignisse sind also abhängig.
Beispiele für unabhängige Ereignisse sind das mehrmalige Werfen eines LAPLACE-Würfels, Ziehen aus einer Urne mit Zurücklegen, der Ausfall voneinander unabhängiger Maschinenteile, Gewinnwahrscheinlichkeit von zwei verschiedenen Personen bei der gleichen Lotterie etc.

Beispiel:
Ein Würfel wird zweimal geworfen. Sind die Ereignisse E_1 »Summe der Augenzahl größer als 10« und E_2 »Augensumme ungerade« unabhängig? Dabei ist zu unterscheiden: Die Augenzahl beim ersten und beim zweiten Wurf sind unabhängige Ereignisse. Hier soll die Unabhängigkeit zweier zusammengesetzter Ereignisse überprüft werden.

$P(E_1) = P(\{(5, 6), (6, 5), (6, 6)\}) = \frac{3}{6^2} = \frac{1}{12}$

$P(E_2) = P($»erste Augenzahl gerade, zweite ungerade«$) + P($»erste Augenzahl ungerade, zweite gerade«$) = \frac{3 \cdot 3}{6^2} + \frac{3 \cdot 3}{6^2} = \frac{1}{2}$

$P(E_1) \cdot P(E_2) = \frac{1}{12} \cdot \frac{1}{2} = \frac{1}{24}$

$P(E_1 \cap E_2) = P(\{(5, 6), (6, 5)\}) = \frac{2}{6^2} = \frac{1}{18} \neq P(E_1) \cdot P(E_2).$

Die Ereignisse sind abhängig.

Im Beispiel der Merkmale Augenfarbe und Haarfarbe ist die Wahrscheinlichkeit für das Merkmal Augenfarbe blau $P($»Augenfarbe blau«$) = 0{,}6$. Weiß man von einer ausgewählten Person bereits, dass sie blond ist, so ist die Wahrscheinlichkeit, bei ihr das Merkmal Augenfarbe blau anzutreffen, höher. Allgemein definiert man für die Wahrscheinlichkeit eines Ereignisses E unter dem Vorwissen, dass ein Ereignis B bereits eingetreten ist:

$P_B(E) = P(E|B) = \frac{P(E \cap B)}{P(B)}$ heißt für $P(B) \neq 0$ die bedingte Wahrscheinlichkeit von E unter der Bedingung B.

Im Beispiel ist

$P($»Augenfarbe blau«$|$»blond«$) = \frac{P(\text{»blaue Augen und blond«})}{P(\text{»blond«})} =$

$= \frac{0{,}4}{0{,}5} = \frac{4}{5} \approx 0{,}8.$

Für unabhängige Ereignisse E_1 und E_2 mit $P(E_2) \neq 0$ gilt nach der Definition: $P(E_1 | E_2) = \frac{P(E_1 \cap E_2)}{P(E_2)} = \frac{P(E_1) \cdot P(E_2)}{P(E_2)} = P(E_1)$

Für das Rechnen mit bedingten Wahrscheinlichkeiten gilt die

Formel von BAYES:

$$P(E|B) = \frac{P(B|E) \cdot P(E)}{P(B|E) \cdot P(E) + P(B|\overline{E}) \cdot P(\overline{E})}$$

Beispiel:
Ein Bauteil einer Maschine geht mit 20-prozentiger Wahrscheinlichkeit kaputt. Ein zweites Bauteil funktioniert abhängig vom ersten unterschiedlich gut. Ist das erste Bauteil funktionstüchtig, funktioniert das zweite zu 90 Prozent, ist das erste defekt, funktioniert das zweite nur zu 60 Prozent.
Bei einer Kontrolle wird festgestellt, dass das zweite Bauteil defekt ist. Mit welcher Wahrscheinlichkeit ist in diesem Fall auch das erste defekt?

Man setzt E: Bauteil 1 kaputt, B: Bauteil 2 kaputt

$$P(E|B) = \frac{P(B|E) \cdot P(E)}{P(B|E) \cdot P(E) + P(B|\overline{E}) \cdot P(\overline{E})} = \frac{0{,}4 \cdot 0{,}2}{0{,}4 \cdot 0{,}2 + 0{,}1 \cdot 0{,}8} = \frac{1}{2}$$

Bedingte Wahrscheinlichkeiten lassen sich häufig auch gut mithilfe von Baumdiagrammen darstellen.

4 Bernoulli-Ketten

4.1 Bernoulli-Experimente

Zahlreiche Zufallsexperimente liefern nur zwei Ergebnisse, zum Beispiel das Werfen einer Münze, Jungen/Mädchen-Geburt oder Treffer und Niete beim Ziehen von Losen. Viele weitere Experimente lassen sich auf einen zweiwertigen Ergebnisraum zurückführen, zum Beispiel interessiert beim Werfen eines Würfels häufig nur 6 oder keine 6 oder allgemein bei Glücksspielen, ob das Ergebnis ein Treffer ist oder nicht.

Ein Zufallsexperiment, dessen Ergebnisraum die Form $\Omega = \{T, N\}$ hat, mit $P(\{T\}) = p$ und $P(\{N\}) = q$ und $p + q = 1$, heißt Bernoulli-Experiment.

4.2 Bernoulli-Ketten

Führt man n unabhängige Bernoulli-Experimente hintereinander aus, wobei die Reihenfolge beachtet wird, erhält man eine Kette von Ergebnissen. Das Experiment entspricht dann dem Ziehen mit Zurücklegen aus einer Urne mit schwarzen und weißen Kugeln, wobei die Wahrscheinlichkeit, eine schwarze Kugel zu ziehen, gleich der Trefferwahrscheinlichkeit p ist, die Wahrscheinlichkeit, eine weiße Kugel zu ziehen, gleich q. Der Ergebnisraum ist eine Menge von n-Tupeln und hat die Mächtigkeit 2^n. Er lässt sich als n-faches Kreuzprodukt des Ergebnisraums Ω des einfachen Bernoulli-Experiments schreiben
$\Omega \times \Omega \times .... \times \Omega = \Omega^n$.

Eine Kette von n unabhängigen, gleichen Bernoulli-Experimenten mit Trefferwahrscheinlichkeit p heißt Bernoulli-Kette der Länge n mit Parameter p.

Bei einer Bernoulli-Kette interessiert die Wahrscheinlichkeit für das Eintreten einer bestimmten Anzahl k von Treffern in der Kette.

Beispiel: Man betrachtet eine Bernoulli-Kette der Länge $n = 6$ mit $p = \frac{1}{3}$ und $q = \frac{2}{3}$.

Gesucht ist die Wahrscheinlichkeit für genau zwei Treffer.
Ein Treffer tritt mit Wahrscheinlichkeit $p = \frac{1}{3}$ ein, eine Niete mit $q = \frac{2}{3}$, die Abfolge (T, T, N, N, N, N) hat also die Wahrscheinlichkeit $p^2 \cdot q^4 = (\frac{1}{3})^2 \cdot (\frac{2}{3})^4$. Jedes Ergebnis mit genau zwei Treffern hat diese Wahrscheinlichkeit. Wie viele Möglichkeiten gibt es also, genau zwei Treffer zu haben? Es gibt $\binom{6}{2}$ Möglichkeiten, zwei Treffer in einer Kette mit sechs Plätzen zu platzieren.

$$P(\text{»genau zwei Treffer«}) = \binom{6}{2} \cdot \left(\frac{1}{3}\right)^2 \cdot \left(\frac{2}{3}\right)^4 = \frac{80}{243} \approx 0{,}329$$

Allgemein erhält man für eine Bernoulli-Kette der Länge n mit Parameter p:

$$P(\text{»genau } k \text{ Treffer«}) = \binom{n}{k} \cdot p^k \cdot q^{n-k}$$

Die dazugehörige Funktion B: $B(x|n; p) = \binom{n}{x} \cdot p^x \cdot q^{n-x}$, die jeder Trefferzahl $x \in \{0, 1, \dots, n\}$ mit $n \in \mathbb{N}$ eine reelle Zahl $B(x|n; p)$ zuordnet, heißt Binomialverteilung mit den Parametern n und p.

Die Binomialverteilung ist ein Wahrscheinlichkeitsmaß.

Beispiel:
Bei einem Badmintonspiel stehen sich zwei ungleiche Gegner A und B gegenüber. A gewinnt ein Spiel mit 75-prozentiger Wahrscheinlichkeit.
a) Mit welcher Wahrscheinlichkeit gewinnt A von fünf Spielen genau vier? Es liegt eine Bernoulli-Kette der Länge $n = 5$ mit Parameter $p = 0{,}75$ vor.
$P(\text{»A gewinnt genau vier von fünf Spielen«}) = B(4|5; 0{,}75)$
$= \binom{5}{4} \cdot 0{,}75^4 \cdot 0{,}25^1 \approx 0{,}3955.$

b) Mit welcher Wahrscheinlichkeit gewinnt A von fünf Spielen mindestens vier? (»Mindestens 4« bedeutet »genau 4« oder »genau 5«.)
$P(\text{»A gewinnt mindestens vier Spiele«}) =$
$P(\text{»A gewinnt genau vier Spiele«}) + P(\text{»A gewinnt genau fünf Spiele«}) =$
$B(4|5; 0{,}75) + B(5|5; 0{,}75) = 0{,}3955 + 0{,}75^5 \approx 0{,}6328.$

Im zweiten Fall handelt es sich um eine Summe von Wahrscheinlichkeiten.

Für geeignete Parameter p und n ist die Binomialverteilung tabelliert. Man kann also die Werte für $B(k|n;\,p)$ einfach in einer Tabelle nachschlagen und muss sie nicht alle selbst ausrechnen. Meistens sind auch (manchmal auch nur) die kumulierten Werte angegeben, dann ist $\sum_{i=0}^{k} B(i|n;\,p) = B(0|n;\,p) + B(1|n;\,p) + \ldots + B(k|n;\,p)$ $= P(»\text{höchstens } k \text{ Treffer}«)$ in der Tabelle aufgeführt. Aus ihnen lassen sich dann mithilfe der Gegenwahrscheinlichkeiten, und, da nur ganzzahlige Trefferergebnisse auftreten können, weitere Wahrscheinlichkeiten berechnen. Dabei muss man besonders darauf achten, ob die angegebenen Grenzen k zur Ereignismenge dazugehören sollen oder nicht.

Hilfen für den Umgang mit **kumuliert** tabellierten Binomialverteilungen: x sei die Zahl der Treffer.
Der Wert in der Tabelle bei k ist $P(x \leq k)$ und bezeichnet die Wahrscheinlichkeit, dass höchstens k Treffer eintreten.
$P(x < k) = P(x \leq k-1)$, $\quad P(x > k) = 1 - P(x \leq k)$
$P(x \geq k) = 1 - P(x < k) = 1 - P(x \leq k-1)$
$P(k_1 \leq x \leq k_2) = P(x \leq k_2) - P(x < k_1) = P(x \leq k_2) - P(x \leq k_1 - 1)$

Beispiel:
In einer Lieferung von Schrauben sind im Durchschnitt 10 Prozent defekt. Es werden zufällig 100 Schrauben ausgewählt.
a) Mit welcher Wahrscheinlichkeit sind genau zehn Schrauben defekt?
Gegeben ist eine Bernoulli-Kette der Länge $n = 100$ mit Parameter $p = 0{,}1$. Es ist $P(k = 10) = B(10|100;\,0{,}1) = 0{,}13187$ (abgelesen aus der Tabelle für einfache Wahrscheinlichkeiten). Sind nur die kumulierten Wahrscheinlichkeiten tabelliert, rechnet man:

$$P(k = 10) = P(k \leq 10) - P(k \leq 9) = 0{,}58316 - 0{,}45129 = 0{,}13187$$

b) Mit welcher Wahrscheinlichkeit ist die Zahl der defekten Schrauben zwischen 5 und 15 (Grenzen eingeschlossen)?

$$P(5 \leq k \leq 15) = P(k \leq 15) - P(k < 5) = P(k \leq 15) - P(k \leq 4) = 0{,}96011 - 0{,}02371 = 0{,}9364$$

c) Mit welcher Wahrscheinlichkeit ist die Zahl der defekten Schrauben größer als 14? Hier errechnet man das Ergebnis durch die Gegenwahrscheinlichkeit.

$P(k > 14) = 1 - P(k \leq 14) = 1 - 0{,}92743 = 0{,}07257.$

Die »Dreimal-mindestens-Aufgabe«

Ein häufig vorkommender Aufgabentyp ist der folgende: Wie oft muss man ein Bernoulli-Experiment **mindestens** wiederholen, damit man mit einer Wahrscheinlichkeit von **mindestens** x Prozent **mindestens** einen Treffer erzielt? Gesucht ist also der Stichprobenumfang n einer Bernoulli-Kette mit gegebenem Parameter p, sodass $P(k \geq 1) \geq x\%$ wird.
Der Lösungsweg zeigt ein konkretes Beispiel:
Wie oft muss man einen Laplace-Würfel mindestens werfen, damit man mit einer Wahrscheinlichkeit von mindestens 90 Prozent mindestens eine Sechs erhält?

Es ist die Trefferwahrscheinlichkeit $p = \frac{1}{6}$, $q = \frac{5}{6}$, gesucht ist n.

Es soll gelten: $P(k \geq 1) \geq 90\%$
Bilden der Gegenwahrscheinlichkeit: $P(k \geq 1) = 1 - P(k < 1) = 1 - P(k = 0)$
$1 - P(k = 0) \geq 0{,}9$
$1 - 0{,}9 \geq P(k = 0)$
$P(k = 0) \leq 0{,}1 \mid P(k = 0) = B\left(0 \mid n, \frac{1}{6}\right) = \binom{5}{0} \cdot \left(\frac{1}{6}\right)^0 \cdot \left(\frac{5}{6}\right)^n = \left(\frac{5}{6}\right)^n$

$\left(\frac{5}{6}\right)^n \leq 0{,}1 \mid$ Logarithmieren

$n \lg\left(\frac{5}{6}\right) \leq \lg 0{,}1 \mid : \lg\left(\frac{5}{6}\right)$ Vorsicht! $\lg\left(\frac{5}{6}\right) < 0$, Richtung der Ungleichung ändert sich.

$n \geq \frac{\lg 0{,}1}{\lg\left(\frac{5}{6}\right)}$

$n \geq 12{,}6$
$n \geq 13$

Auf einen Blick: Regeln und Sätze in der Stochastik

Definition eines Wahrscheinlichkeitsmaßes nach den Axiomen von Kolmogorow:
Ω sei der Ergebnisraum eines Zufallsexperiments. Jedem Ereignis $E \subseteq \Omega$ wird eine reelle Zahl $P(E)$ als Wahrscheinlichkeit zugeordnet. Die Zuordnung heißt Wahrscheinlichkeitsmaß, wenn die folgenden drei Axiome erfüllt sind:
Axiom 1: $P(E) \geq 0$
Axiom 2: $P(\Omega) = 1$
Axiom 3: $E_1 \cap E_2 = \{\ \} \Rightarrow P(E_1 \cup E_2) = P(E_1) + P(E_2)$

Ein Experiment heißt Laplace-Experiment, wenn alle Ergebnisse des Ergebnisraums gleich wahrscheinlich sind. Die Wahrscheinlichkeit eines Ereignisses E berechnet sich als:

$$P(E) = \frac{|E|}{|\Omega|} = \frac{\text{Anzahl der für } E \text{ günstigen Fälle}}{\text{Anzahl der möglichen Fälle}}$$

Definition der Unabhängigkeit von Ereignissen:
Zwei Ereignisse A_1 und B_2 heißen unabhängig, wenn gilt:
$P(A_1 \cap B_2) = P(A_1) \cdot P(B_2)$, andernfalls heißen sie abhängig.

Dabei heißt $P_B(A) = P(A|B) = \dfrac{P(A \cap B)}{P(B)}$ für $P(B) \neq 0$
die bedingte Wahrscheinlichkeit von A unter der Bedingung B.

Bernoulli-Ketten
Ein Zufallsexperiment, dessen Ergebnisraum die Form $\Omega = \{T, N\}$ hat, mit $P(\{T\}) = p$ und $P(\{N\}) = q$ und $p + q = 1$, heißt Bernoulli-Experiment.
Für eine Bernoulli-Kette der Länge n mit Parameter p ist
$P(\text{»genau } k \text{ Treffer«}) = \binom{n}{k} \cdot p^k \cdot q^{n-k}$
Die dazugehörige Funktion B: $B(x|n; p) = \binom{n}{x} \cdot p^x \cdot q^{n-x}$ heißt Binomialverteilung mit den Parametern n und p.

4

Geometrie

Das Wort »Geometrie« stammt aus dem Griechischen und bedeutet so viel wie »Feldmesskunst«. Diese Kunst, Flächen und Räume zu berechnen, wurde bereits im antiken Griechenland zur Blüte gebracht.

Die Geometrie wird nach unterschiedlichen Gesichtspunkten gegliedert. Die folgenden Abschnitte befassen sich mit der Elementargeometrie, bei der unterschieden wird zwischen ebener Geometrie (Planimetrie), die sich mit der Berechnung von Flächen beschäftigt, räumlicher Geometrie (Stereometrie) zur Berechnung dreidimensionaler Körper und der Trigonometrie, die sich mit den Besonderheiten des ebenen, vor allem rechtwinkligen Dreiecks auseinander setzt.

1 Geometrische Grundformen und Grundbegriffe

1.1 Grundbegriffe

Die Geometrie hilft, die Objekte oder Gegenstände in unserer Welt zu erfassen, indem sie diese Objekte in einer berechenbaren Form darstellt, z.B. die Entfernung zweier Städte ⇒ Strecke in einer Ebene, ein Zimmer ⇒ Quader, einen Tunnel durch einen Berg ⇒ Kreiszylinder. So können wir sie untersuchen, vermessen, berechnen, zeichnen und in ihrer Lage zu anderen Objekten beschreiben. Für die Geometrie ist dabei nur die Form dieser Objekte ausschlaggebend, unwichtig sind dagegen ihre Eigenschaften wie Farbe, Gewicht, Geruch, Material. Die Geometrie hat ihre eigene Sprache. Zu den Grundbegriffen gehören Punkt, Gerade, Ebene.

Der Mathematiker Euklid legte einst fest: »Ein Punkt ist, was keine Teile hat.«
Damit ist der Punkt eine kleinste Einheit, also nicht mehr teilbar.

Geometrische Gebilde versteht man heute als Menge von Punkten, als so genannte Punktmengen, die man mithilfe von Lineal und Zirkel zeichnen kann.

Axiome legen die Beziehungen zwischen den Grundbegriffen (Punkt, Gerade, Ebene) fest. Alle weiteren geometrischen Aussagen wie Definitionen und Sätze benutzen nur diese Grundbegriffe und Axiome.
Beispiel zu einem Axiom:
Zu zwei verschiedenen Punkten A und B gibt es genau eine Gerade g.
Bezeichnung: $g = (AB)$

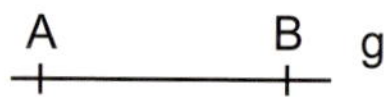

Zum Erreichen einer einheitlichen Darstellungsform wurden in der Geometrie folgende Schreibungen vereinbart:

Punkte mit Großbuchstaben	(A, B, C)
Geraden/Strecken mit Kleinbuchstaben	(g, h, k)
Ebenen mit	(E, E_1, E_2, E_3)
Winkel mit griechischen Buchstaben	$(\alpha, \beta, \gamma, \delta)$

Punkt, Gerade, Halbgerade, Strecke, Ebene

Die Ebene wird als eine Menge festgelegt, deren Elemente Punkte genannt werden.
In der Ebene ist ein System von Teilmengen ausgezeichnet, dessen Elemente Geraden genannt werden.

Eine gerade Linie mit einem Anfangs- und Endpunkt wird als Strecke bezeichnet. Da nicht immer klar ist, welcher Punkt der Anfang und welcher das Ende der Strecke sein soll, werden beide Punkte Endpunkte genannt.

Jede Strecke hat zwei Endpunkte.

Die Strecke $\overline{AB}$ ist die Menge aller Punkte auf der kürzesten Verbindung von A nach B, einschließlich der beiden Randpunkte.

Eine gerade Linie, die in einem Punkt beginnt und auf der anderen Seite unbegrenzt weiterläuft, kann man auf einem Blatt nicht zeichnen, da das Papier ein Ende hat. Das Problem wird gelöst, indem eine Strecke mit einem Startpunkt versehen und auf der anderen Seite der Endpunkt nicht eingezeichnet wird. Diese Punktmenge wird als Halbgerade oder Strahl bezeichnet.

Eine Halbgerade oder ein Strahl ist eine Strecke, die zwar einen Anfangspunkt A hat, aber keinen Endpunkt.

Wenn sowohl End- als auch Anfangspunkt weggelassen werden, ist diese Linie nach beiden Seiten unbegrenzt und wird Gerade genannt.

> Die unbegrenzte Verlängerung einer Strecke $\overline{AB}$ in beide Richtungen heißt Gerade *AB* (oder *g*), sie hat weder Anfangs- noch Endpunkt.

Analog zum Zeichnen von Geraden und Halbgeraden auf einem Blatt Papier ist dieses Blatt als Zeichenebene ein Ausschnitt aus der idealen Ebene:

> Eine Ebene ist eine zweidimensionale Punktmenge mit unendlicher Länge und Breite. Jede Teilmenge davon, die endlich oder unendlich sein kann, nennt man ebene Figur.

Lage von Punkten und Geraden in einer Ebene

a) Der Punkt *A* liegt auf der Geraden *g*; $A \in g$.

b) Der Punkt *B* liegt nicht auf der Geraden *g*; $B \notin g$.

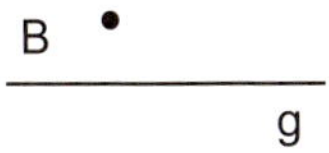

c) Die Punkte *A* und *B* liegen beide auf der Geraden *g*; $g = (AB)$.
Diese Gerade wird auch **Verbindungsgerade** genannt.
Alle auf derselben Geraden liegenden Punkte heißen **kollinear**.
Demnach sind zwei verschiedene Punkte immer kollinear, drei Punkte dagegen nicht immer.

d) Der Punkt *P* liegt auf der Geraden *g* und gleichzeitig auf der Geraden *h*. $P \in g \cap h$.
Der Punkt *P* ist der Schnittpunkt der beiden Geraden.

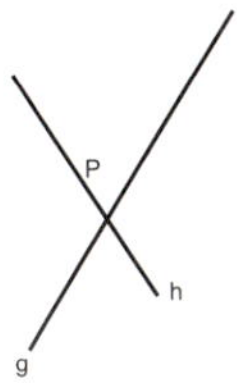

e) Eine Gerade wird durch jeden ihrer Punkte in zwei Halbgeraden zerlegt.

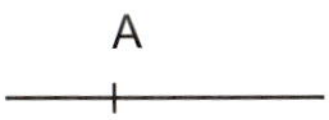

f) Mithilfe von drei nicht kollinearen Punkten lassen sich drei sich schneidende Geraden bestimmen. Damit kann man eine Ebene eindeutig festlegen. In derselben Ebene liegende Punkte heißen komplanar.

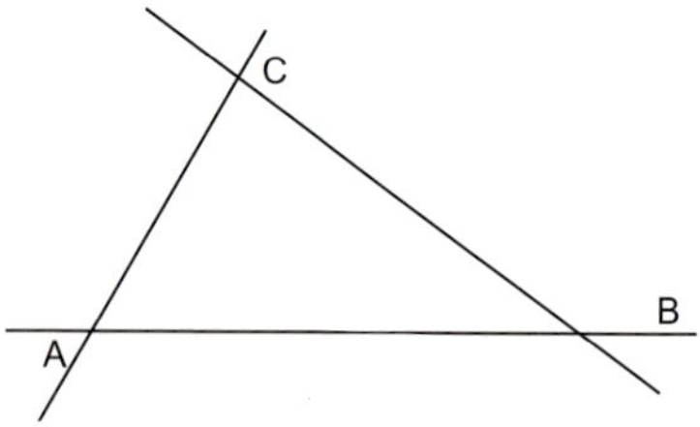

g) Eine Ebene wird durch jede ihrer Geraden in zwei Halbebenen zerlegt.
h) Durch einen einzelnen Punkt verlaufen beliebig viele Geraden.
Diese Menge an Geraden nennt man Geradenbüschel.

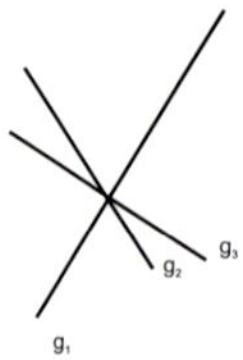

i) Ein Sonderfall der Geradenkreuzung: Zwei senkrecht aufeinander stehende Geraden bilden einen rechten Winkel, sie schneiden sich unter einem Winkel von 90 Grad.

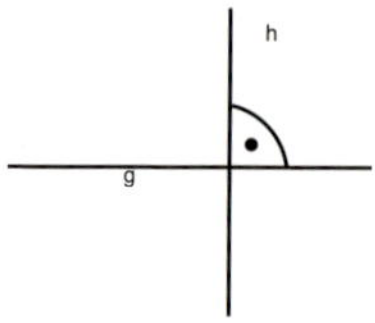

j) Wenn zwei Geraden g und h in einer Ebene liegen und sich nicht schneiden, nennt man sie **parallel**. $g \cap h = \{\ \}$.

Zueinander parallele Geraden schneiden sich nicht, auch nicht in großer Entfernung.

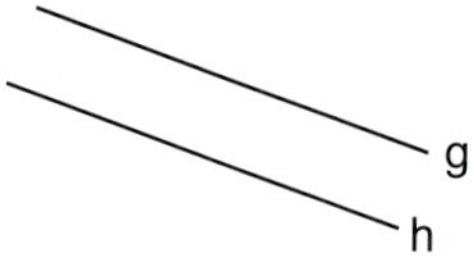

k) Die Menge aller Geraden einer Ebene, die parallel zueinander sind, bilden ein **Parallelenbüschel**.
l) Wenn zwei Geraden im Raum verlaufen, kann es sein, dass sie sich nicht schneiden und auch nicht parallel sind.

Zwei Geraden, die sich nicht schneiden und nicht parallel liegen, sind stets **windschief**.
Zusammenfassend kann man zu den Beziehungen von Geraden untereinander sagen:
Zwei Geraden *g* und *h* schneiden sich in einem einzigen Punkt, oder sie sind zueinander parallel, oder sie sind windschief zueinander.

Die Strecke und ihre Länge

Die Strecke $\overline{AB}$ wird von zwei verschiedenen Punkten *A* und *B* sowie der Menge aller Punkte gebildet, die zwischen *A* und *B* auf der Geraden *g* = (*AB*) liegen. Demnach ist die Strecke $\overline{AB}$ eine Teilmenge der Geraden *g*. A und *B* sind die Endpunkte der Strecke $\overline{AB}$.
Die Länge *s* der Strecke $\overline{AB}$ ist die Entfernung der Endpunkte *A* und B. Sie ist eine auch in der Physik verwendete Größe, sie besteht aus einer positiven Maßzahl und der Maßeinheit. In der Geometrie legt man dazu eine Einheitsstrecke fest und misst ihre Länge.

1 Längeneinheit = 1 cm (meistens)

Längenmessung bedeutet nun das Vergleichen der Länge *s* der Strecke $\overline{AB}$ mit der Einheitsstrecke.
Die Strecke $\overline{AB}$ ist viermal so lang wie die Einheitsstrecke $\overline{EF}$, also 4 cm.

Längeneinheiten:

1 mm	Millimeter	1 mm = 0,1 cm = 0,01 dm = 0,001 m
1 cm	Zentimeter	1 cm = 10 mm = 0,1 dm = 0,01 m
1 dm	Dezimeter	1 dm = 10 cm = 100 mm = 0,1 m = 0,0001 km
1 m	Meter	1 m = 10 dm = 100 cm = 1000 mm = 0,001 km
1 km	Kilometer	1 km = 1000 m = 10 000 dm = 100 000 cm

1.2 Ebene Grundformen

Vierecke

Definition des Vierecks:

Verbindet man vier Punkte, von denen keine drei Punkte auf einer Geraden liegen, miteinander durch einen geschlossenen Streckenzug ohne Überschneidungen, so entsteht ein Viereck.

In diesem Buch werden nur **konvexe** Vierecke behandelt, also keine mit einspringenden Ecken.

Begriffe und Bezeichnungen beim allgemeinen Viereck

Das Hauptmerkmal dieser geometrischen Form sind die vier Ecken und vier Seiten.

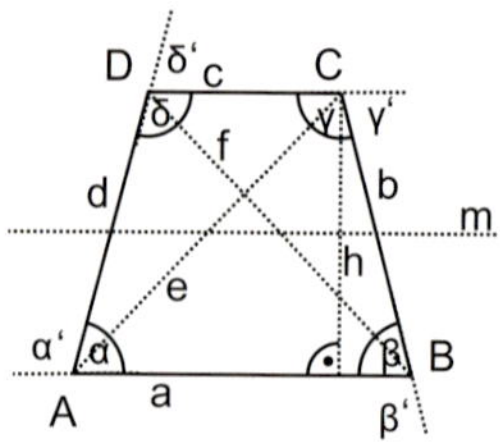

Die **Eckpunkte** sind *A, B, C, D* im mathematisch positiven Umlaufsinn, gegen den Uhrzeiger.
Die **Seiten** sind *a* mit (*AB*), *b* mit (*BC*), *c* mit (*CD*), *d* mit (*DA*).
Die **Diagonalen** sind *e* mit (*AC*) und *f* mit (*BD*).
Die **Winkel** sind α, β, γ, δ.
Zur **Fläche** im Viereck gehören alle Punkte auf den vier Seiten sowie innerhalb dieser Abgrenzung.
Die Winkelsumme der Innenwinkel im Viereck beträgt 360 Grad.
Die Winkelsumme der Außenwinkel beträgt auch 360 Grad.
Die Außenwinkel sind die Nebenwinkel der Innenwinkel.

Besondere Formen des allgemeinen Vierecks

Parallelogramm

Jedes Viereck, bei dem die gegenüberliegenden Seiten parallel zueinander stehen, heißt **Parallelogramm**.

Jeweils gegenüberliegende Seiten sind gleich lang ($a = c$, $b = d$).
Jeweils gegenüberliegende Winkel sind gleich groß ($\alpha = \gamma$, $\beta = \delta$).
Die Diagonalen halbieren sich im Zentrum Z.
Z ist das Symmetriezentrum der Figur (Punktsymmetrie).

Umfang: $U = 2 \cdot a + 2 \cdot b$
Fläche: $F = a \cdot h(a) = b \cdot h(b)$

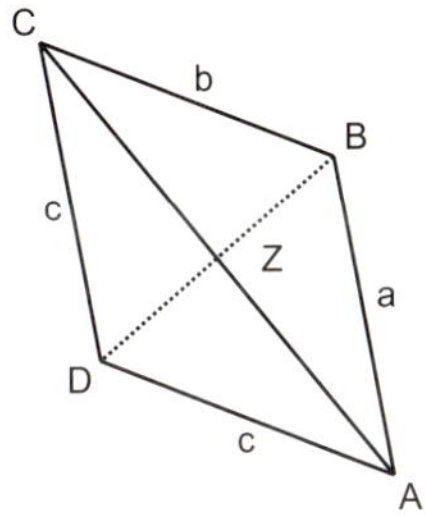

Raute

Als Spezialfall des Parallelogramms bezeichnet man die Raute:

Jedes Viereck mit vier gleich langen Seiten heißt **Raute.**

Alle Seiten sind gleich lang ($a = b = c = d$).
Ihre Diagonalen stehen aufeinander senkrecht und halbieren sich.

Umfang: $U = 4 \cdot a$
Fläche: $F = \dfrac{e \cdot f}{2}$

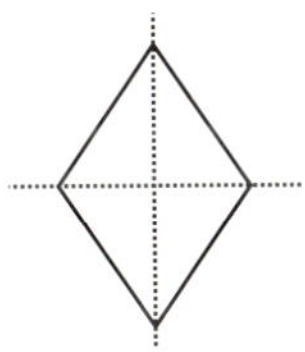

Rechteck

Jedes Viereck mit vier rechten Winkeln heißt **Rechteck.**

Jeweils die Gegenseiten sind gleich lang und parallel.
Alle Winkel (α, β, γ, δ) betragen 90 Grad.
Die Diagonalen sind gleich lang und halbieren sich.
Jedes Rechteck hat einen Umkreis und zwei Symmetrieachsen.

Umfang: $U = 2 \cdot a + 2 \cdot b$
Fläche: $F = a \cdot b$

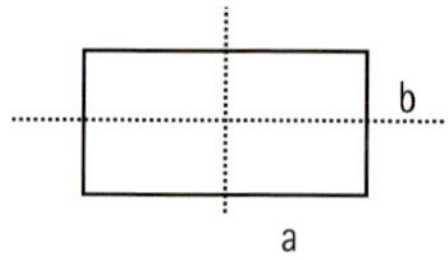

Quadrat

Jedes Viereck mit vier gleich langen Seiten und vier rechten Winkeln heißt **Quadrat.**

Die Seiten a, b, c, d sind gleich lang.
Die Winkel $\alpha, \beta, \gamma, \delta$ betragen 90 Grad.
Die Diagonalen sind gleich lang, halbieren sich und stehen aufeinander senkrecht.
Jedes Quadrat hat vier Symmetrieachsen.

Umfang: $U = 4 \cdot a$
Fläche: $F = a \cdot a$

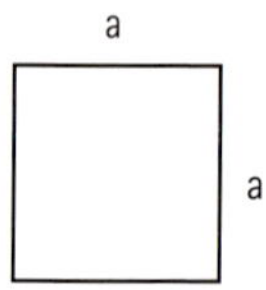

Drachen

Jedes Viereck mit zwei Paaren gleich langer Nachbarseiten heißt **Drachen.**

Für die Seiten gilt: $a = d$, $b = c$.
Jedes Drachenviereck hat eine Symmetrieachse (eine der Diagonalen). Diese steht senkrecht auf der zweiten Diagonalen, halbiert diese, deren beide Gegenwinkel ebenso.
Die Gegenwinkel zur Achse sind gleich groß.

Umfang: $2 \cdot a + 2 \cdot b$
Fläche: $F = \frac{e \cdot f}{2}$

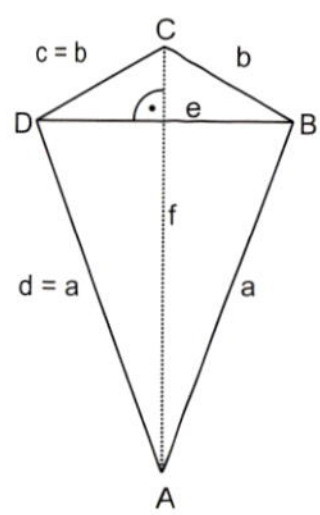

Trapez

Jedes Viereck mit zwei Paaren gleicher Nachbarwinkel heißt **gleichschenkeliges Trapez.**

Die benachbarten Winkel an den beiden Grundseiten sind gleich groß. Jedes gleichschenkelige Trapez hat eine Symmetrieachse. Diese steht senkrecht auf der Grundseite und halbiert sie.
Die beiden Schenkel sind gleich lang.
Die beiden Diagonalen sind gleich lang und schneiden sich auf der Symmetrieachse.

Umfang: $U = a + 2 \cdot b + c$
Fläche: $F = m \cdot h$

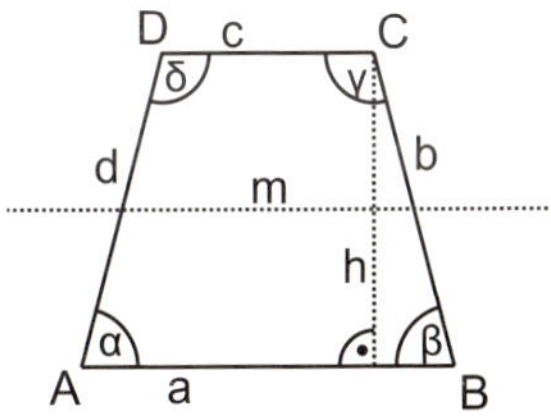

Jedes Viereck mit wenigstens einem Paar paralleler Gegenseiten heißt **Trapez.**

Die Verbindungsstrecke der Schenkelmitten ist parallel zu den Grundseiten, sie heißt Mittelparallele *m*.

Länge der Mittelparallelen *m*: $m = \dfrac{a + c}{2}$

Die Winkel an den beiden Schenkeln ergänzen sich auf 180 Grad.

Umfang: $U = a + b + c + d$
Fläche: $F = m \cdot h$

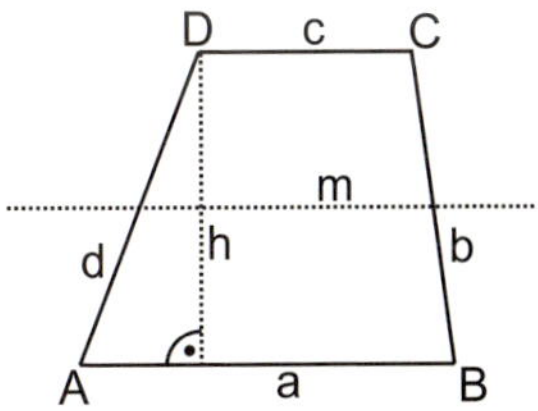

Weitere geometrische Figuren in der Ebene

Dreieck

Wenn sich drei nicht parallele Geraden in der Ebene in drei verschiedenen Punkten schneiden, entsteht ein **Dreieck**.

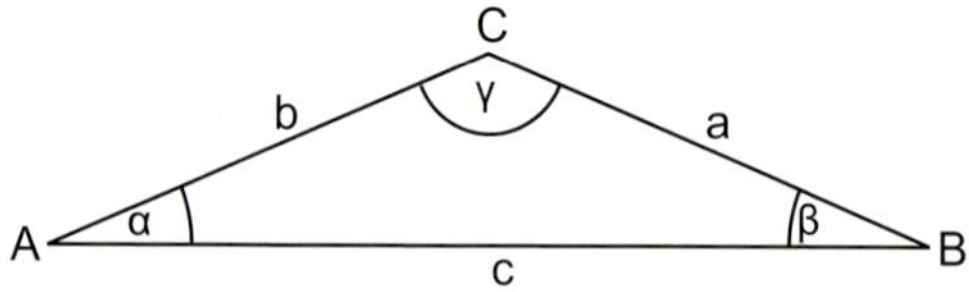

Beim spitzwinkeligen Dreieck sind alle Winkel kleiner als 90 Grad.
Beim stumpfwinkeligen Dreieck ist ein Winkel größer als 90 Grad.

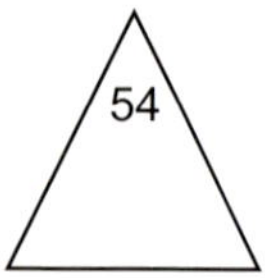

spitzwinkelig

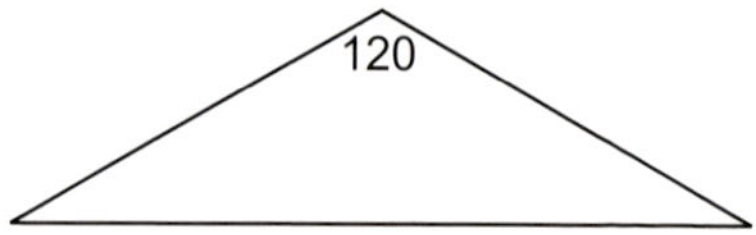

stumpfwinkelig

Begriffe und Benennungen im Dreieck:

Die Eckpunkte sind *A*, *B*, *C* im mathematisch positiven Umlaufsinn (gegen den Uhrzeiger).
Die Dreiecksungleichung lautet: In jedem Dreieck ist die Summe der Längen zweier Seiten immer größer als die Länge der dritten Seite.
Für je zwei Seiten im Dreieck gilt:
Der größeren der beiden Seiten liegt der größere Winkel gegenüber und umgekehrt.
Die Innenwinkel heißen α, β, γ und addieren sich zu 180 Grad.
Die Summe der Außenwinkel beträgt 360 Grad.
Zur Dreiecksfläche gehören alle Punkte auf den Dreiecksseiten und innerhalb dieser Abgrenzung.

Spezielle Dreiecke

Dreiecke mit gleich langen Seiten heißen **gleichseitige Dreiecke.**

Jedes gleichseitige Dreieck hat drei gleich lange Seiten, $a = b = c$.
Alle Winkel sind gleich groß, $\alpha = \beta = \gamma = 60$ Grad.
Es gibt drei Symmetrieachsen, die sich im Punkt S schneiden.
S ist auch Schnittpunkt von den Seitenhalbierenden und damit Schwerpunkt des Dreiecks.
Die Seitenhalbierenden sind gleichzeitig Mittelsenkrechte, Winkelhalbierende und Höhen.

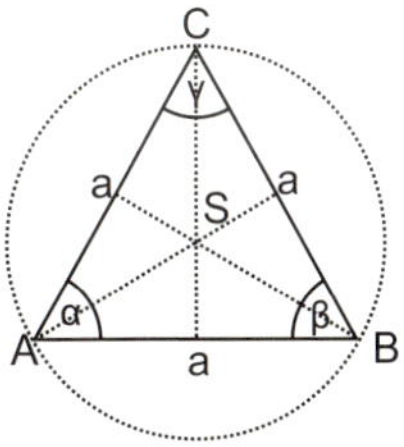

Dreiecke mit zwei gleich langen Schenkeln heißen **gleichschenkelige Dreiecke.**

Jedes gleichschenkelige Dreieck hat zwei gleich lange Seiten, die Schenkel. Ihr Schnittpunkt ist die Spitze.
Die dritte Seite heißt Basis. An der Basis liegen zwei gleich große Winkel, die Basiswinkel.
Die Symmetrieachse verläuft von der halbierten Basis zur Spitze. Sie ist gleichzeitig Mittelsenkrechte, Höhe und Seitenhalbierende über der Basis und auch Winkelhalbierende des Winkels an der Spitze.

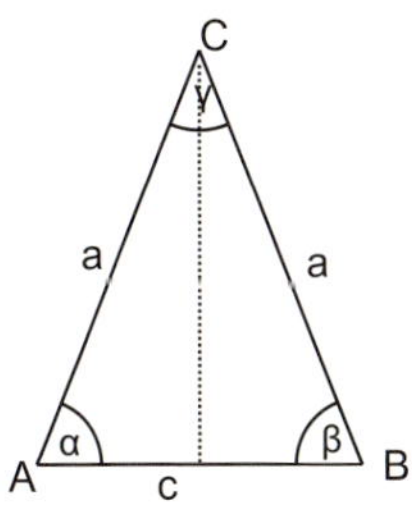

Jedes Dreieck mit einem rechten Winkel heißt **rechtwinkeliges Dreieck.**

Ein rechtwinkeliges Dreieck hat genau einen rechten Winkel (90 Grad). Die Schenkel des rechten Winkels heißen Katheten, die Gegenseite Hypotenuse.

Die Winkel an der Hypotenuse ergänzen sich zu 90 Grad.

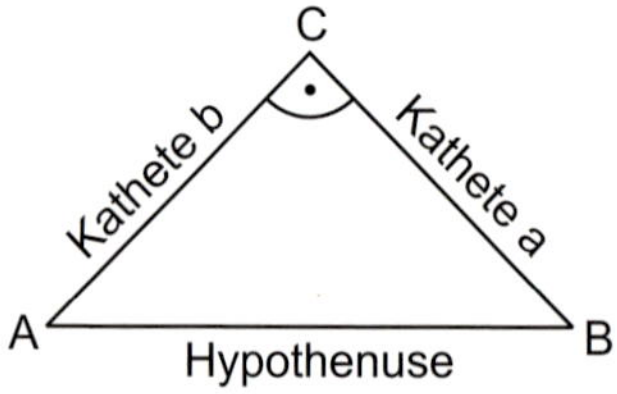

Zeichnet man über der Hypotenuse *AB* alle möglichen rechtwinkeligen Dreiecke, so liegen die Scheitel *C* ihrer rechten Winkel auf einem Kreis über der Strecke $\overline{AB}$, genannt **Thales-Kreis.**

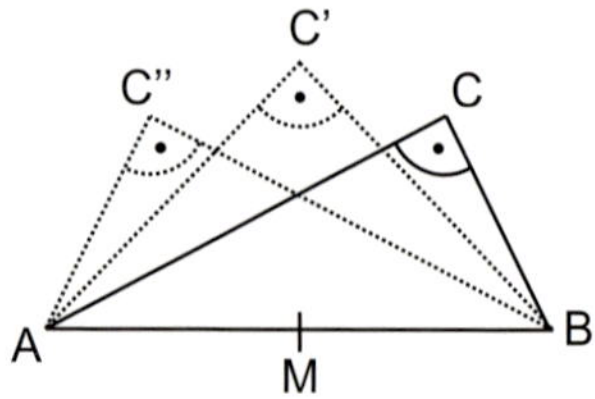

Beim gleichschenkelig rechtwinkeligen Dreieck sind die Basiswinkel 45 Grad, der Winkel an der Spitze 90 Grad.

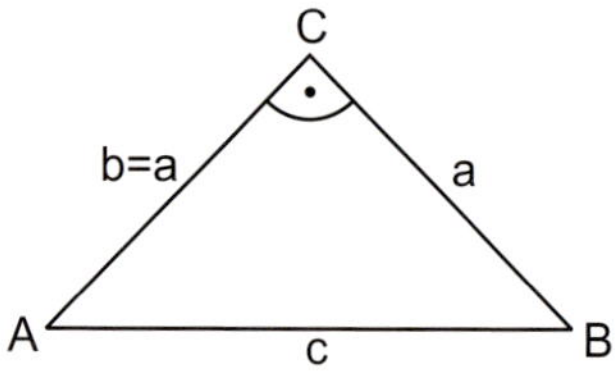

Besondere Punkte und Strecken im Dreieck

Mittelsenkrechte und Umkreismittelpunkt

Bei jedem Dreieck schneiden sich die Mittelsenkrechten im Punkt *M*, der von seinen Ecken die gleiche Entfernung hat.
M ist Mittelpunkt des Kreises.
Der Kreis um *M* mit dem Radius $r = (MA)$ heißt Umkreis des Dreiecks. *M* liegt innerhalb des Dreiecks (beim spitzwinkeligen), außerhalb (beim stumpfwinkeligen), auf dem Mittelpunkt der Hypotenuse (beim rechtwinkeligen Dreieck).

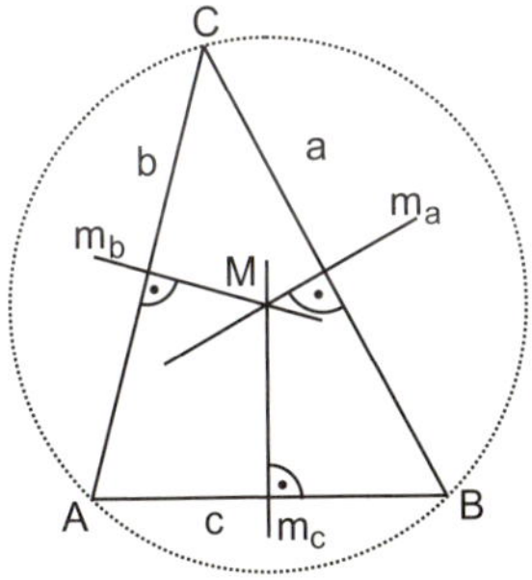

Winkelhalbierende und Inkreismittelpunkt

Die drei Winkelhalbierenden in einem Dreieck schneiden sich in einem Punkt *M*, der von allen Seiten den gleichen Abstand hat. Dieser Punkt *M* ist der Mittelpunkt des Inkreises, der die Dreieckseiten von innen berührt.

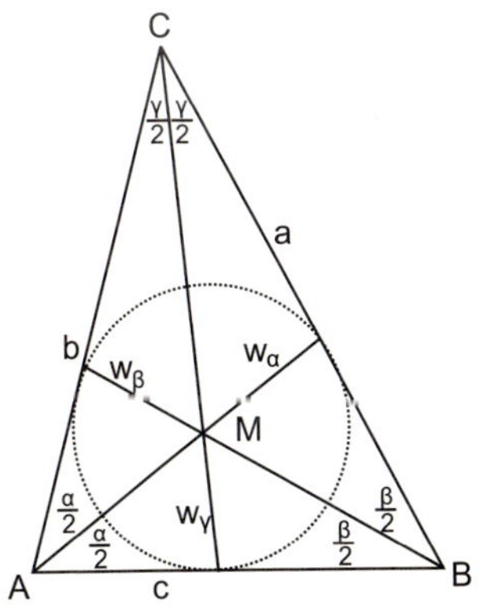

Seitenhalbierende und Schwerpunkt
Die drei Seitenhalbierenden eines Dreiecks schneiden sich im Schwerpunkt *S*. *S* teilt die Seitenhalbierenden im Verhältnis 2 : 1. *S* entspricht dem physikalischen Schwerpunkt des Dreiecks.

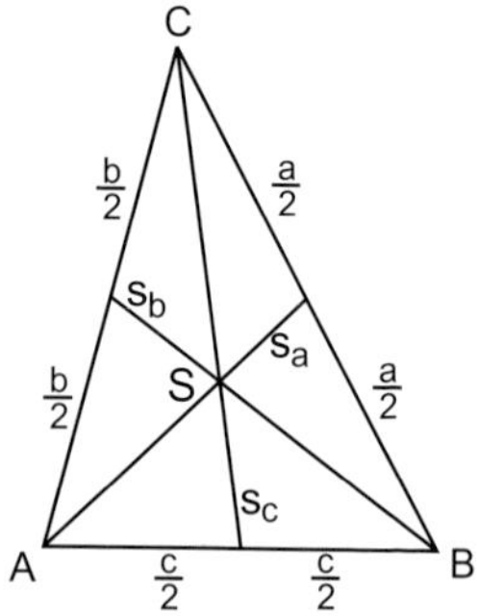

Höhen und Höhenschnittpunkte
Bei jedem Dreieck schneiden sich die Höhen in einem Punkt *H*. *H* liegt beim spitzwinkeligen Dreieck innerhalb des Dreiecks, beim stumpfwinkeligen außerhalb, beim rechtwinkeligen fällt er auf den Scheitel des rechten Winkels.

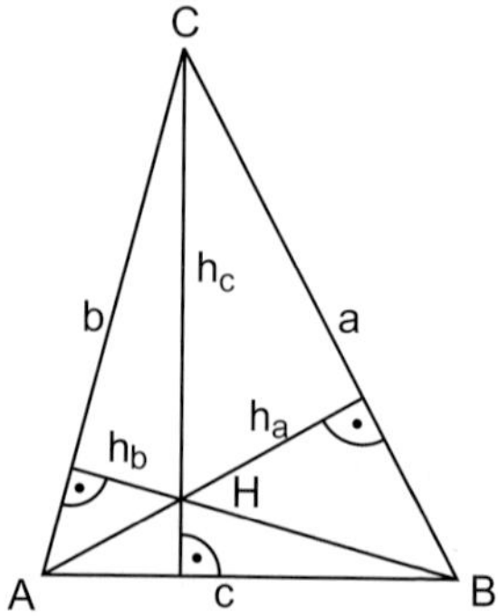

Der Kreis
Der Kreis nimmt unter den geometrischen Figuren eine Sonderrolle ein, da er keine Ecken hat und somit nicht als Vieleck dargestellt werden kann.
Er ist die Menge aller Punkte, die vom Mittelpunkt *M* einen festen Abstand haben. Die Verbindungslinie von *M* zum Kreis hat immer dieselbe Länge *r* und wird Radius genannt.
Der Durchmesser *d* ist die Strecke zwischen zwei Kreispunkten, die durch den Mittelpunkt *M* verläuft (also doppelter Radius). Er ist auch eine Symmetrieachse.
Der Kreis hat beliebig viele Symmetrieachsen.

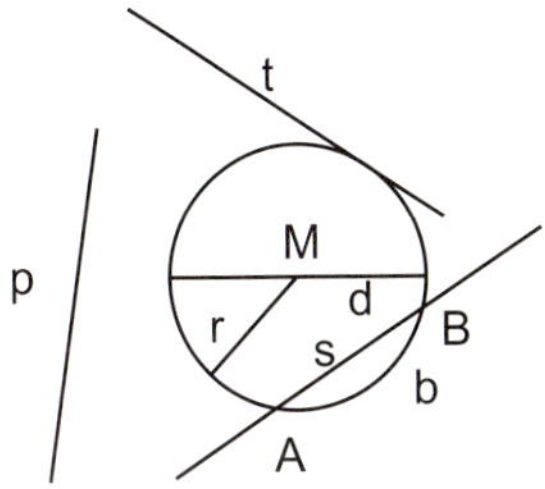

Besondere Geraden, die eine bestimmte Lage zum Kreis haben:
Die **Passante** *p* berührt den Kreis in keinem Punkt.
Die **Sekante** schneidet den Kreis in zwei Punkten (A und B). Die **Sehne** ist die Strecke zwischen den Schnittpunkten A und B.
Die **Tangente** *t* berührt den Kreis in einem Punkt.
Die Verbindungsstrecke zwischen dem Tangentenberührungspunkt und dem Kreismittelpunkt (ein Radius) steht immer senkrecht zur berührenden Tangente.

Konzentrische Kreise sind zwei Kreise mit demselben Mittelpunkt, aber verschiedenen Radien.
Exzentrische Kreise haben verschiedene Mittelpunkte und verschiedene Radien. Sie können ineinander (Berührung von innen oder ganz im Innern), sich berührend (ein gemeinsamer Punkt), sich schneidend (Schnittmenge, zwei gemeinsame Kreispunkte) oder auseinander (keine gemeinsamen Punkte) liegen.
Die Fläche, die vom Kreis eingeschlossen wird, heißt Kreisscheibe.
Schneidet eine Gerade den Kreis in zwei Punkten *P* und *Q*, wird die Kreisscheibe in zwei Segmente (oder Kreisabschnitte) geteilt.
Wird aus dem Kreis entlang zweier Radien ein Teil ausgeschnitten, der auch den Mittelpunkt enthält, so wird dieser Kreissektor (oder Kreisausschnitt) genannt.

Zur Berechnung des Kreises:

Ein Kreis mit dem Radius r hat den Umfang $U = 2 \cdot r \cdot \pi$ mit $\pi \approx 3{,}14$.
Ein Kreis mit dem Radius r hat die Fläche $F = r \cdot r \cdot \pi = r^2 \cdot \pi$ mit $\pi \approx 3{,}14$.

1.3 Räumliche Grundformen

Was für ebene Figuren Umfang und Fläche sind, kann bei den räumlichen Körpern als Oberfläche und Volumen interpretiert werden.
Die Oberfläche F des Körpers K ist die Gesamtheit seiner äußeren Flächen.
Das Volumen oder der Rauminhalt eines Körpers wird durch seine Längen-, Breiten- und Höhenmaße bestimmt.

Quader

Der Quader ist ein von sechs Rechtecken begrenzter Körper.
Ein Quader mit den Kantenlängen a, b und c hat eine Oberfläche und ein Volumen von:

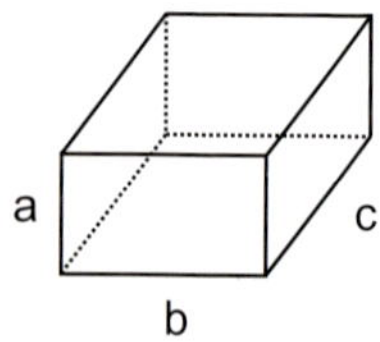

Fläche $F = 2 \cdot a \cdot b + 2 \cdot a \cdot c + 2 \cdot b \cdot c$
Volumen $V = a \cdot b \cdot c$

Würfel

Der Würfel ist ein besonderer Quader mit zwölf gleich langen Kanten.
Ein Würfel mit den Kantenlängen a hat Oberfläche und Volumen von:

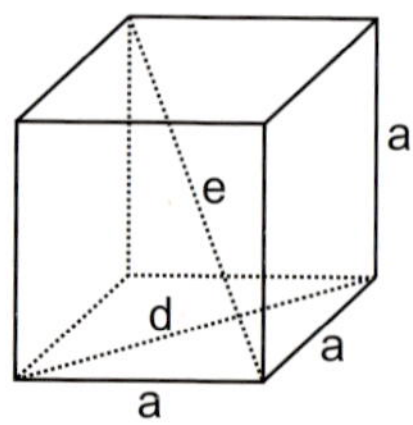

Fläche $F = 6 \cdot a \cdot a = 6a^2$
Volumen $V = a \cdot a \cdot a = a^3$

Prisma

Ein dreiseitiges Prisma hat als Grundflächen zwei Dreiecke; die drei Seitenflächen werden zusammen auch Mantelfläche genannt.
Es gibt auch mehrseitige Prismen.

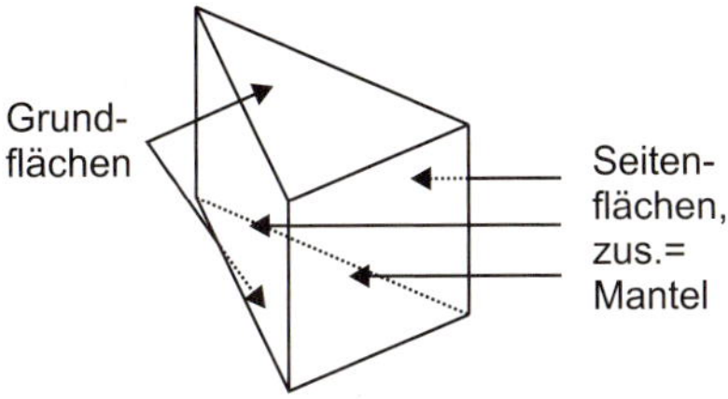

Oberfläche $F = 2 \cdot$ Grundfläche + Mantelfläche
Volumen $V =$ Grundfläche · Höhe

Zylinder

Beim Zylinder sind die Grundflächen (zum Unterschied von den Prismen) keine Vielecke, sondern zwei Kreise.
Bei einem Zylinder mit der Höhe h und dem Radius r betragen Volumen und Oberfläche:

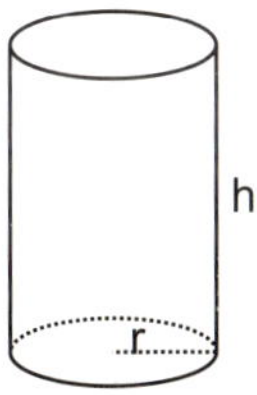

Volumen $V =$ Grundfläche $\cdot h = r \cdot r \cdot \pi \cdot h = \pi r^2 \cdot h$
Oberfläche $F = 2 \cdot$ Grundfläche + Mantelfläche $= 2 \cdot \pi \cdot r \cdot (r + h)$

Kugel

Eine Kugel ist die Menge aller Punkte im Raum, deren Abstand zu einem gegebenen Mittelpunkt M gleich dem Radius r ist.
Bei einer Kugel mit dem Radius r betragen Volumen und Oberfläche:

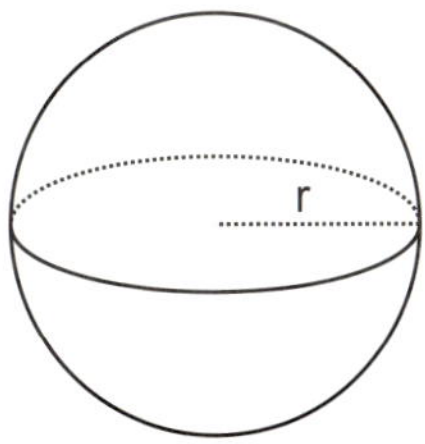

Volumen $V = \frac{4}{3} \cdot \pi \cdot r \cdot r \cdot r = \frac{4}{3} \pi r^3$
Oberfläche $F = 4 \cdot \pi \cdot r \cdot r = 4\pi r^2$

Kegel

Ein Kegel hat als Grundfläche einen Kreis; darüber wird in einer Höhe *h* ein Punkt *S* festgelegt und von allen Punkten der Kreislinie je eine Verbindungslinie dazu gezogen.

Bei einem Kegel mit Radius *r* des Grundkreises, der Mantellinie *s* und der Höhe *h* betragen Volumen und Oberfläche:

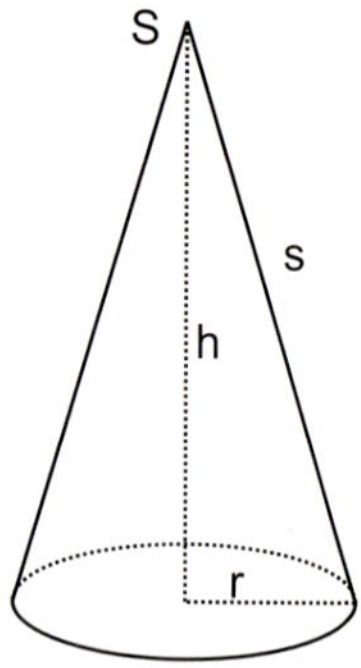

Volumen $V = \frac{1}{3} \pi r^2 h$

Oberfläche $F = \pi \cdot r \cdot r + \pi \cdot r \cdot s = \pi r(r + s)$

Pyramide

Eine Pyramide hat als Grundfläche meist ein Dreieck oder Quadrat, darüber wird in einer Höhe *h* ein Punkt *S* festgelegt und von allen Ecken aus eine Verbindung dazu gezogen.

Bei einer Pyramide mit der Grundfläche *G* und der Höhe *h* betragen:

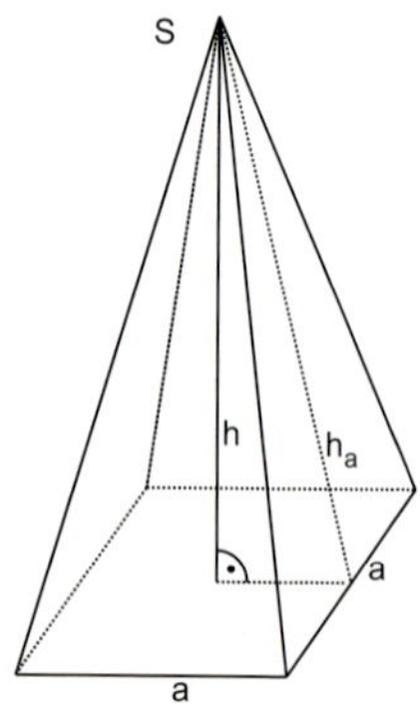

Volumen $V = \frac{1}{3} G h$

Oberfläche F = Grundfläche + Mantelfläche

2 Grundbegriffe der ebenen Geometrie

2.1 Flächeninhalt

Die Fläche eines Rechtecks ist der Teil einer Fläche, der von den Seiten umschlossen wird. Ihr Inhalt steht also in einem Bezug zur Länge der verschieden langen Seiten *a* und *b*. Um den in Formeln üblicherweise als *F* bezeichneten Flächeninhalt eines Rechtecks zu errechnen, müssen die Längen der Seiten multipliziert werden:

$$F = a \cdot b$$

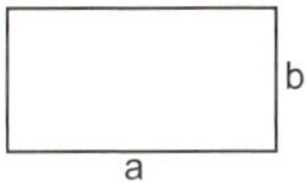

Die in Europa heute übliche Maßeinheit zur Bestimmung von Längen ist der Meter. Aus ihm leiten sich die anderen Längenmaße wie Millimeter als Tausendstel eines Meters oder der Kilometer als das Tausendfache eines Meters ab.

Da der Flächeninhalt das Produkt aus zwei Längen ist, ist auch die Maßeinheit, in der er angegeben wird, ein Produkt aus den Längenmaßen. Ein Meter mal ein Meter ergibt einen Quadratmeter.

$$1\text{ m} \cdot 1\text{ m} = 1\text{ m}^2$$

Entsprechend der Längenmaße ergeben sich daraus die folgenden Flächenmaße:

Flächenmaße:
1 Quadratmeter (m^2) = 10 000 cm^2 = 100 dm^2
1 Quadratmillimeter (mm^2)
1 Quadratdezimeter (dm^2) = 100 cm^2 = 10 000 mm^2
1 Ar (a) = 100 m^2
1 Hektar (ha) = 100 a = 10 000 m^2
1 Quadratkilometer (km^2) = 1 000 000 m^2

Die Ermittlung von Flächeninhalten ist im Alltag wichtig, um beispielsweise den Wert von Grundstücken oder Wohnungen, der von der Größe der Grundfläche abhängig ist, zu ermitteln. Ein Garten, der sich hinter dem Haus bis zur Straße acht Meter erstreckt und so breit wie das zwölf Meter lange Haus ist, hat also eine Fläche von 96 Quadratmetern.

Einen Spezialfall des Rechtecks stellt das Quadrat dar: Alle Seiten sind gleich lang. Um also den Flächeninhalt eines Quadrats zu ermitteln, muss nur eine Seite gemessen und dieser Wert mit sich selbst multipliziert beziehungsweise zum Quadrat erhoben werden.

$F = a \cdot a$
oder
$F = a^2$

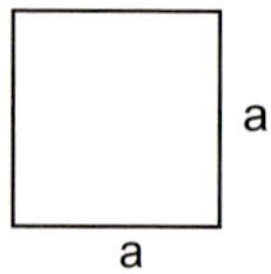

2.2 Winkel

Winkelbegriff

Ein Winkel entsteht, wenn zwei Halbgeraden beziehungsweise Strahlen von einem gemeinsamen Punkt ausgehen. Der Ausgangspunkt wird Scheitelpunkt genannt und mit S bezeichnet. Die beiden Strahlen heißen Schenkel. Diese Schenkel werden mit a und b bezeichnet. Sie begrenzen einen Winkel. Es gibt verschiedene Möglichkeiten, einen Winkel zu benennen. Meist benutzt man einen kleinen griechischen Buchstaben, beginnend bei α. Für eine andere Schreibweise benutzt man das Winkelzeichen $\sphericalangle$ und die Bezeichnungen der Schenkel: $\sphericalangle(a, b)$. Auf den Schenkeln können auch Punkte ausgezeichnet sein: Punkt A auf Schenkel a und Punkt B auf Schenkel b. Ein Winkel, der den Punkt A auf einem Schenkel, einen Scheitelpunkt S und einen Punkt B auf dem anderen Schenkel enthält, lässt sich als $\sphericalangle ASB$ beschreiben.

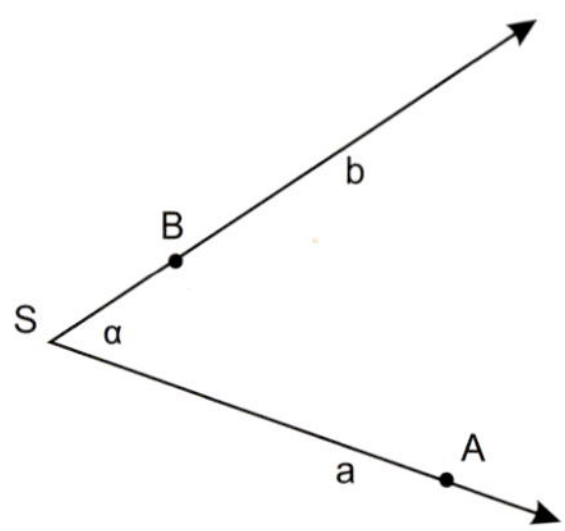

Winkel an zwei sich schneidenden Geraden

In der Geometrie gibt es verschiedene Möglichkeiten, wie Winkel entstehen können. So bilden sich z. B. dann Winkel, wenn zwei Geraden sich schneiden. Beim Schnitt zweier Geraden g_1 und g_2 einer Ebene treten vier Winkel auf. Wie bereits im vorigen Abschnitt geschildert werden Winkel mit kleinen griechischen Buchstaben bezeichnet: α, β, γ, δ. Die Benennung erfolgt entgegen dem Uhrzeigersinn.

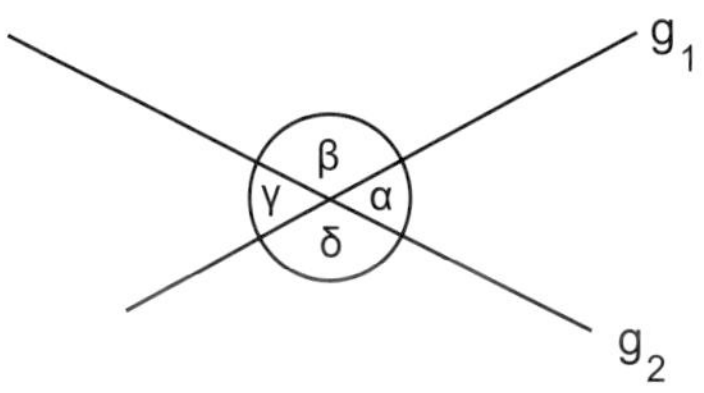

Beim Schnitt zweier Geraden treten folgende Winkelpaare auf.

Nebenwinkel: Benachbarte Winkel an zwei sich schneidenden Geraden mit einem gemeinsamen Scheitel *S* und einem gemeinsamen Schenkel. Die beiden nicht gemeinsamen Schenkel liegen auf einer Geraden, jedoch auf zwei verschiedenen von *S* ausgehenden Strahlen. In der Abbildung bilden die Winkelpaare (α, β), (β, γ), (γ, δ) und (α, δ) Nebenwinkel.

Scheitelwinkel: Sich an zwei schneidenden Geraden gegenüber liegende und gleich große Winkel mit einem gemeinsamen Scheitelpunkt S, aber ohne gemeinsame Schenkel. In der Abbildung sind die Winkelpaare (α, γ) und (β, δ) Scheitelwinkel.

Komplementwinkel: Zwei Winkel, die sich zu einem rechten Winkel (90 Grad) ergänzen. Dabei ist jeder Winkel jeweils der Komplementwinkel des anderen.

Supplementwinkel: Zwei Winkel, deren Winkelmaße sich zu 180 Grad ergänzen. In der Abbildung sind die Winkelpaare (α, β), (β, γ), (γ, δ) und (α, δ) Supplementwinkel. Man nennt sie auch Ergänzungswinkel. Damit sind wie oben dargestellt alle Nebenwinkel auch Supplement- beziehungsweise Ergänzungswinkel.

Winkelpaare an geschnittenen Parallelen

Weitere charakteristische Winkelbeziehungen entstehen, wenn eine Gerade zwei Parallelen schneidet. Neben den oben getroffenen Unterscheidungen zwischen Scheitelwinkeln und Nebenwinkeln mit einem gemeinsamen Scheitelpunkt *S* entstehen beim Schnitt einer Geraden *k* durch zwei Parallelen *g* und *h* zwei verschiedene Scheitelpunkte, an denen nun zusätzlich zwischen Wechselwinkeln, Stufenwinkeln und entgegengesetzten Winkeln unterschieden wird. Insgesamt treten acht Winkel auf.

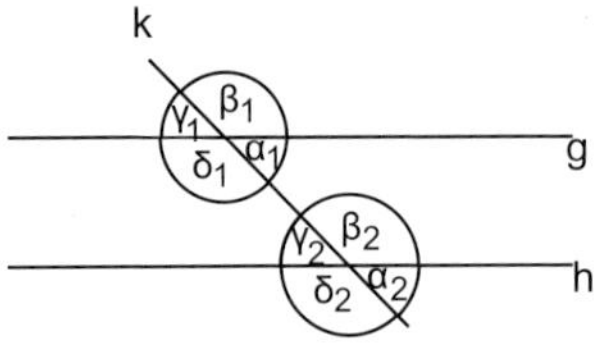

Wechselwinkel: Gleich große, aber auf verschiedenen Seiten der Geraden und der Parallelen liegende Winkel. Die Schenkel von Wechselwinkeln sind paarweise entgegengesetzt gerichtet. In der Abbildung sind die Winkelpaare (α_1, γ_2), (β_1, δ_2), (γ_1, α_2) und (δ_1, β_2) Wechselwinkel.

Stufenwinkel: Diese Winkel liegen auf der gleichen Seite der Geraden und den gleichen Seiten der Parallelen. Die Schenkel sind paarweise gleich gerichtet. In der Abbildung sind die Winkelpaare (α_1, α_2), (β_1, β_2), (γ_1, γ_2) und (δ_1, δ_2) Stufenwinkel.

Entgegengesetzte Winkel: Die Lage ist zu gleichen Seiten der Geraden, aber auf verschiedenen Seiten der Parallelen oder umgekehrt. Je zwei der entgegengesetzten Winkel ergänzen sich aber stets zu insgesamt 180 Grad. In der Abbildung sind (α_1, β_2), (β_1, α_2), (γ_1, δ_2), (δ_1, γ_2) entgegengesetzte Winkel.

Winkelmaß

Wie im Abschnitt »Winkelbegriff« bereits dargestellt ist der Winkel die Fläche zwischen zwei Strahlen. Es ist nicht möglich, das Winkelmaß dadurch zu ermitteln, dass man die Länge zwischen den beiden Endpunkten der Schenkel misst. Wird der Winkel so groß, dass er größer ist als bei vollständig gestreckten Schenkeln – also wenn *a* und *b* vom gemeinsamen Punkt *S* aus in genau entgegengesetzte Richtungen weisen –, dann wird der Abstand zwischen den Endpunkten wieder kleiner.

Zeichnet man die Endpunkte der Schenkel mit *A* und *B* aus und betrachtet Strahl *a* als beweglich, so beschreibt Punkt *A* einen Kreisbogen um den Punkt *S* herum. Da der Kreisbogen zwischen *A* und *B* im Gegensatz zu der Geraden zwischen *A* und *B* bis zur Deckung beider Schenkel mitwächst, steht er in einem Bezug zur Größe des Winkels, den die beiden

Schenkel umschließen. Es hat sich in der langen Geschichte der Mathematik eingebürgert, einen Kreis in 360 gleich große Stücke zu zerlegen. Damit ergibt sich als Maßeinheit der 360. Teil eines Kreisbogens. Dieser Teil wird ein Grad genannt, geschrieben: 1°. Wie auch der Meter wird das Gradmaß in kleinere Einheiten unterteilt, allerdings nicht wie dieser nach dem Dezimalprinzip, sondern wie die Zeit nach der so genannten Sexagesimaleinteilung:

1 Grad = 60 Minuten (1° = 60')
1 Minute = 60 Sekunden (1' = 60")

Hat man es beispielsweise mit einem Winkel von 42 Grad, 17 Minuten und 30 Sekunden zu tun, so wäre die korrekte Schreibweise: 42° 17' 30".

Winkelbezeichnungen

Je nachdem, wie die Schenkel eines Winkels zueinander stehen, gibt es sechs unterschiedliche Arten von Winkeln. Sonderfälle sind der Nullwinkel und der Vollwinkel, bei dem beide Schenkel zur Deckung kommen, der gestreckte Winkel, bei dem beide Schenkel vom gemeinsamen Scheitelpunkt *S* aus in genau entgegengesetzte Richtung weisen, und der rechte Winkel, der in Zeichnungen durch einen kleinen Kreisbogen mit einem Punkt in der Mitte gekennzeichnet wird. Darüber hinaus gibt es spitze, stumpfe und überstumpfe Winkel.

Nullwinkel: $\alpha = 0°$

Nullwinkel

spitzer Winkel: $0° < \alpha < 90°$

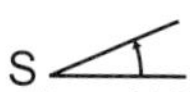

spitzer Winkel

rechter Winkel: $\alpha = 90°$

rechter Winkel

stumpfer Winkel: 90° < α < 180°

stumpfer Winkel

gestreckter Winkel: α = 180°

gestreckter Winkel

überstumpfer Winkel: 180° < α < 360°

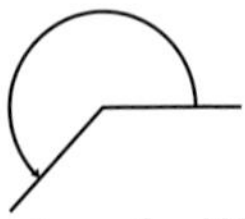

überstumpfer Winkel

Vollwinkel: α = 360°

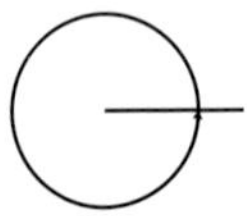

Vollwinkel

2.3 Grundkonstruktionen

Die geometrischen Grundkonstruktionen sind eine Reihe von Aufgaben, die in dieser, abgewandelter oder auch kombinierter Form immer wieder für die Darstellung von Figuren, die Lösung von Problemen oder die Beweisführung erforderlich sind. Für das Zeichnen der Grundkonstruktionen sind ausschließlich der Zirkel und das Lineal notwendig. Letzteres wird in der Praxis häufig ersetzt durch das Geodreieck, das sowohl Zeichenhilfe für die Darstellung einer Geraden als auch Messinstrument für Länge und Gradmaß ist. Die auf dem Geodreieck abgetragenen Hilfslinien ermöglichen es ebenso, ohne Konstruktion Parallelen und Senkrechte zu zeichnen.

Abtragen einer Strecke

Vorgegeben ist eine Halbgerade *p*. Um auf ihr eine Strecke einer bestimmten Länge *a* abzutragen, muss mit dem Zirkel an einem Punkt *P* eingestochen und ein Kreis mit dem Radius *a* gezogen werden. Dieser Kreis wird *p* an einem Punkt *Q* schneiden. Die so entstandene Strecke $\overline{PQ}$ hat dann die Länge *a* und wird mit dem Lineal eingezeichnet.

Antragen eines Winkels

Die Aufgabe besteht darin, einen gegebenen Winkel der Größe α an die Halbgerade *p* anzutragen. Man zeichnet mit dem Zirkel einen Kreis mit beliebigem Radius, dessen Mittelpunkt der Scheitelpunkt *S* des Winkels ist und die Schenkel *a* und *b* in den Punkten *A* und *B* schneidet. Dann wird ein Kreis mit gleichem Radius um den Anfangspunkt *P* der Halbgeraden gezogen. Dieser schneidet die Halbgerade *p* in einem Punkt *Q*, der wiederum Mittelpunkt eines weiteren Kreises ist. Der Radius dieses Kreises entspricht der Länge der Strecke $\overline{AB}$ und schneidet den Kreis, der zuvor um *P* gezogen wurde, an einem Punkt R. Der aus $\sphericalangle$ ASB hergeleitete $\sphericalangle$ RPQ hat jetzt ebenfalls die Größe α.

Halbieren einer Strecke/Errichten einer Mittelsenkrechten

Es geht hier darum, den Mittelpunkt *M* einer Strecke $\overline{AB}$ zu konstruieren. Mit dem Zirkel sind zwei Bögen zu schlagen: Einer mit dem Endpunkt *A*, der zweite mit dem Endpunkt *B* als Mittelpunkt. Dabei ist darauf zu achten, den Radius so groß zu wählen, dass beide Bögen sich schneiden. Es entstehen auf diese Weise zwei Schnittpunkte *C* und *D*. Verbindet man diese Schnittpunkte mit dem Lineal, so ist die Strecke $\overline{CD}$ die Mittelsenkrechte. Sie halbiert die Strecke $\overline{AB}$. Der Schnittpunkt von $\overline{AB}$ und $\overline{CD}$ ist der gesuchte Mittelpunkt *M*.

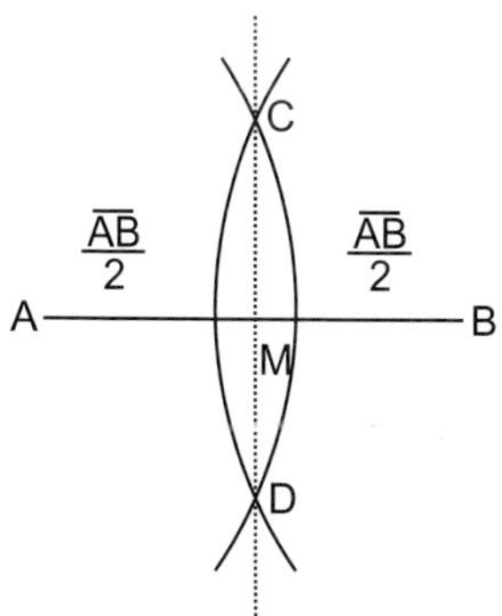

Errichten einer Senkrechten im Endpunkt

Soll die Senkrechte auf einem Endpunkt der Strecke errichtet werden, so ist um diesen – beispielsweise Punkt *B* – zunächst mit dem Zirkel ein Bogen mit beliebigem Radius zu schlagen. Dadurch entsteht auf der Strecke $\overline{AB}$ ein Schnittpunkt *C* von Bogen und Halbgerade. Schnittpunkt *C* wird zum Mittelpunkt eines neuen Bogens, der sich außerhalb der Strecke $\overline{AB}$ am Punkt *D* mit dem Bogen um *B* schneidet. Um diesen Punkt *D* ist ein weiterer Bogen zu schlagen (alle Bogen haben den gleichen Radius). Mit dem Lineal konstruiert man nun eine Gerade durch die Punkte *C* und *D*, die den Kreis um *D* an einem Punkt *E* schneidet. Die gesuchte Senkrechte im Endpunkt *B* lässt sich nun als Gerade, die durch *B* und *E* verläuft, antragen.

Errichten einer Senkrechten an einer Geraden in einem Geradenpunkt

Die Senkrechte soll im Punkt *P* der Geraden *g* errichtet werden. Anders ausgedrückt: Es soll eine senkrechte Gerade zu *g* durch *P* konstruiert werden. Als Erstes zeichnet man mit dem Zirkel einen Kreis um den Punkt *P*, der die Gerade *g* in den Punkten *A* und *B* schneidet. Um Punkt *A* und Punkt *B* schlägt man jeweils einen gleich großen Bogen. Im Schnittpunkt dieser beiden Kreise entsteht ein Punkt *C*. Die mit dem Lineal zu ziehende Gerade durch *C* und *P* ist die gesuchte Senkrechte.

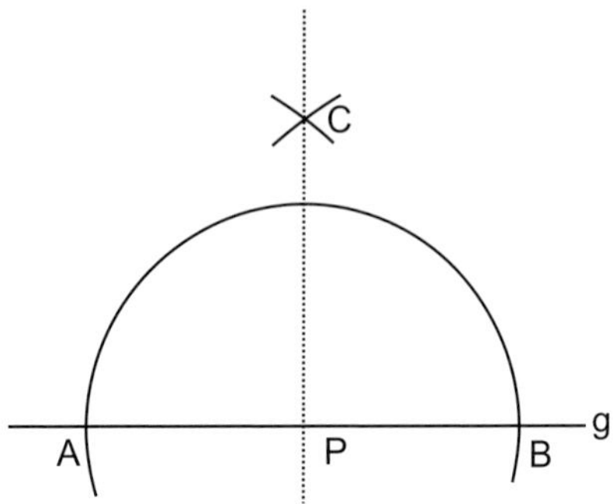

Fällen eines Lotes auf eine Gerade durch einen Punkt außerhalb der Geraden

Wenn der Punkt *P*, der nicht auf der Geraden *g* liegt, festgelegt ist, wird mit dem Zirkel ein Bogen um ihn geschlagen. Der Radius des Kreises muss so groß sein, dass die Gerade *g* in zwei Punkten *A* und *B* geschnitten wird. Sowohl um *A* als auch um *B* sind dann Bögen mit gleichem Radius zu schlagen. Der Schnittpunkt beider Kreisbögen ist der Punkt *P'*. Mit dem Lineal wird eine Gerade gezogen, die durch *P'* und *P* verläuft. Sie ist das gesuchte Lot.

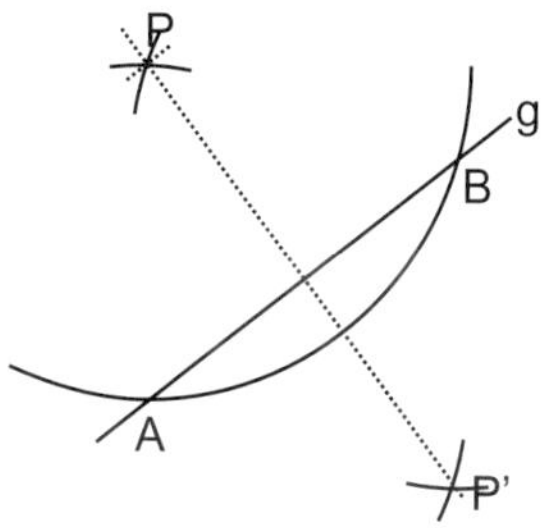

Halbieren eines Winkels

Um einen gegebenen Winkel α zu halbieren, wird mit dem Zirkel um den Scheitelpunkt *S* ein Kreis gezogen. Der Radius ist beliebig. Der Kreis schneidet die beiden Schenkel *a* und *b* jeweils in den Punkten *A* und *B*. Sowohl um *A* als auch *B* sind dann Bögen mit gleichem Radius zu schlagen. Der Schnittpunkt beider Kreisbögen ist der Punkt *C*. Mit dem Lineal wird eine Gerade gezogen, die durch *C* und *S* verläuft. Sie ist die Winkelhalbierende. Neu entstanden sind die gleich großen ∢ *ASC* und *CSB* mit der halben Winkelgröße von ∢ *ASB*.

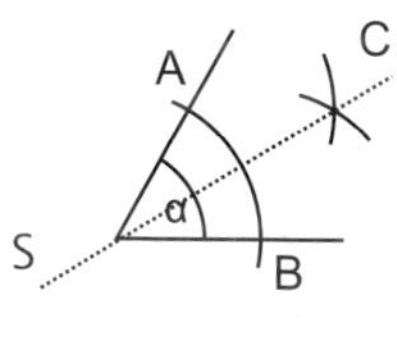

Zeichnen einer Parallelen durch einen gegebenen Punkt

Um eine Parallele durch einen gegebenen Punkt *P*, der nicht auf der Geraden *g* liegt, zu konstruieren, muss zunächst mit dem Zirkel ein Kreisbogen um den Punkt *P* gezogen werden. Der Radius ist beliebig, muss aber größer sein als der Abstand von Punkt *P* zur Geraden *g*. Auf *g* entsteht so der Schnittpunkt *C*. Der nächste Kreis wird um diesen Punkt *C* gezogen, der sich im Punkt *B* mit der Geraden *g* schneidet. Ein dritter Bogen wird um Punkt *B* geschlagen, der sich mit dem ersten um Punkt *P* gezogenen Kreis im Punkt *A* schneidet. Mit dem Lineal wird jetzt eine Gerade durch die Punkte *P* und *A* gezogen. Sie ist die gesuchte Parallele.

Verbindet man zusätzlich die Punkte *P*, *C*, *B* und *A*, so hat man die Raute mit den Eckpunkten *PCBA* konstruiert.

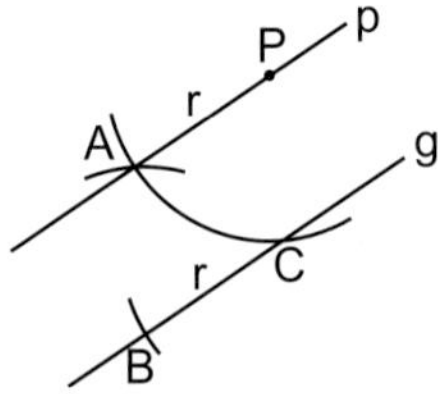

Bei einer anderen Variante der Konstruktion einer Parallelen durch einen gegebenen Punkt lassen sich bereits die Grundkonstruktionen »Errichten einer Senkrechten an einer Geraden in einem Geradenpunkt« und »Fällen eines Lots auf eine Gerade durch einen Punkt außerhalb der Geraden« praktisch anwenden: Zunächst fällt man das Lot zur Geraden *g* durch den Punkt *P*. Auf dieser wiederum ist eine Senkrechte durch den Punkt *P* zu errichten. Diese ist die gesuchte Parallele.

Zeichnen einer Parallelen in gegebenem Abstand

Bei der Konstruktion einer Parallelen *p* zur Geraden *g* in einem vorgegebenen Abstand *a* kommen die Grundkonstruktionen »Errichten einer Senkrechten an einer Geraden in einem Geradenpunkt« und »Abtragen einer Strecke« zum Einsatz: Zunächst legt man auf der Geraden *g* zwei beliebige Punkte *A* und *B* fest (die allerdings nicht zusammenfallen dürfen). Auf diesen wird jeweils eine Senkrechte errichtet. Dann wird der

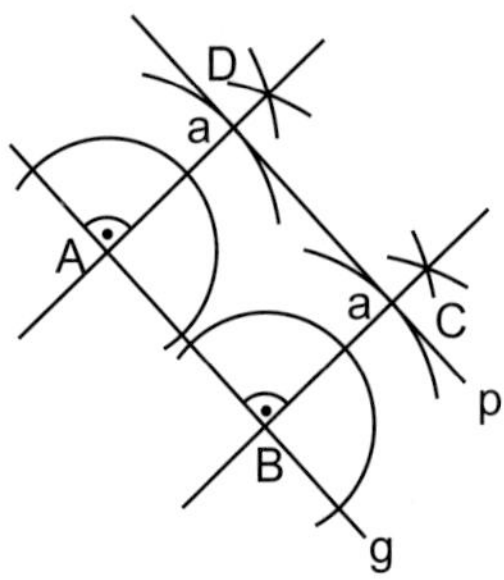

gegebene Abstand *a* auf beiden Senkrechten abgetragen. Es entstehen die Punkte *C* und *D*, die im Abstand *a* von der Geraden *g* entfernt sind. Die Gerade durch die Punkte *C* und *D* ist die gesuchte Parallele *p*. Zugleich hat man auf diese Weise das Rechteck mit den Eckpunkten *ABCD* konstruiert.

Unterteilen einer Strecke in gleiche Teile
Bei dieser Grundkonstruktion finden die bereits oben dargestellten Grundkonstruktionen »Abtragen einer Strecke«, »Antragen eines Winkels« und »Zeichnen einer Parallelen in gegebenem Abstand« Anwendung. Gegeben ist die in gleiche Teile zu teilende Strecke zwischen *A* und B. Von einem der beiden Punkte *A* oder *B* aus ist ein beliebiger Winkel α zur Strecke $\overline{AB}$ anzutragen. Der auf diese Weise entstandene Schenkel wird als Hilfsstrahl dienen. Auf den Hilfsstrahl wird nun eine beliebige (aber entsprechend gewählte) Strecke sooft abgetragen, wie viel die Anzahl der gleichen Teile auf der Strecke *AB* betragen soll, zum Beispiel 5. Die Endpunkte der abgetragenen Strecken liegen in C_1, C_2, C_3, C_4, C_5. C_5 wird mit *B* verbunden und durch C_1, C_2, C_3, C_4 jeweils eine Parallele zu C_5B gelegt. Diese Parallelen teilen $\overline{AB}$ in gewünschter Weise.

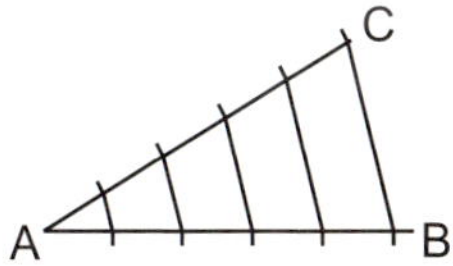

2.4 Ähnlichkeitsdarstellungen

Will man zwei geometrische Figuren in der Ebene miteinander vergleichen, so gibt es zwei Möglichkeiten. Zum einen kann man die Kongruenz – dies ist die Deckungsgleichheit – überprüfen. Dieses Thema wird später ausführlich erläutert. Die zweite Vergleichsmöglichkeit für geometrische Figuren ist die Ähnlichkeit. Dies ist der Fall, wenn zwei Figuren nicht genau gleich groß sind, denn nur gleich große Figuren können auch deckungsgleich sein. Um die Ähnlichkeit festzustellen, werden die Geradentreue, die Parallelentreue, die Winkeltreue und die Streckenverhältnistreue untersucht. Ähnlich sind Figuren dann, wenn die Geraden wieder in Geraden abgebildet werden und die Längenverhältnisse bei der Abbildung unverändert bleiben. Ebenso werden Parallelen wieder als Parallelen dargestellt und Winkel verändern ihre Größe bei der Abbildung nicht. Ein Beispiel aus dem praktischen Leben ist das Kino: Ein Bild auf dem Filmstreifen hat Seitenlängen von nur wenigen Zentimetern. Bei der Projektion durch den langen Vorführsaal entsteht ein viel größeres Bild von mehreren Metern Seitenlänge, das aber die gleichen Eigenschaften aufweist und damit ähnlich ist.

An einer einfachen geometrischen Figur wie dem Dreieck – das später ausführlicher behandelt wird – lässt sich das Prinzip der Ähnlichkeit anschaulich darstellen:

Ähnlichkeitssätze für Dreiecke

Zwei Dreiecke sind ähnlich, wenn sie übereinstimmen
1. ... im Verhältnis ihrer drei Seiten a_1, a_2, b_1, b_2, c_1, c_z.
$a_1 : b_1 = a_2 : b_2$; $b_1 : c_1 = b_2 : c_2$; $c_1 : a_1 = c_2 : a_2$
2. ... im Verhältnis von zwei Seiten sowie der Größe des eingeschlossenen Winkels:
$a_1 : b_1 = a_2 : b_2$; $\gamma_1 = \gamma_2$
3. ... in der Größe zweier Winkel.

Zwei Methoden werden zur Ähnlichkeitsabbildung beziehungsweise für Verhältnisgleichungen angewendet: die Strahlensätze und die zentrische Streckung.

Strahlensätze

Die Strahlensätze gehören zu den zentralen Lehrsätzen der Geometrie. Ausgangspunkt für die Herleitung ist die Grundkonstruktion »Unterteilen einer Strecke in gleiche Teile«. Nachdem die Aufgabe gelöst ist, gleich große Teilstrecken abzutragen oder – anders formuliert – eine Reihe von Punkten genau gleichen Abstands zu konstruieren, ist die Frage zu klären, ob auch die Entfernungen auf dem anderen Schenkel gleich groß sind. Der besseren Übersichtlichkeit wegen soll aber kein Winkel mit zehn Parallelen verwendet werden, sondern zwei Strahlen mit einem gemeinsamen Scheitelpunkt *S*, die von zwei Parallelen geschnitten werden.

Die Untersuchung der Figur ergibt für die beiden Strahlen s_1 und s_2 folgende Streckenverhältnisse (da es in den folgenden Formeln nicht mehr

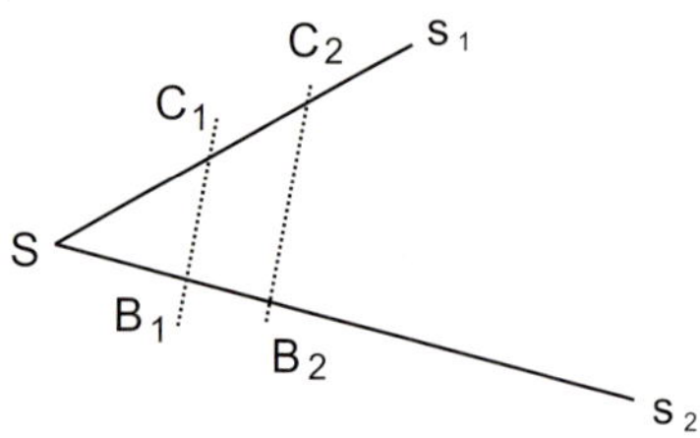

um die Strecke geht, sondern um den Betrag beziehungsweise die Länge der Strecke, werden die Streckenbezeichnungen in Betragszeichen (vertikale Linien) gesetzt, also beispielsweise $|AB|$ statt $\overline{AB}$:

Erster Strahlensatz

$|SB_1| : |SB_2| = |SC_1| : |SC_2|$; $|SB_1| : |B_1B_2| = |SC_1| : |C_1C_2|$; $|SB_2| : |B_1B_2| = |SC_2| : |C_1C_2|$

Werden zwei Strahlen s_1 und s_2 mit einem gemeinsamen Scheitelpunkt S von zwei zueinander parallelen Geraden geschnitten, so verhalten sich die Längen der Abschnitte auf dem einen Strahl wie die entsprechenden Längen der Abschnitte auf dem anderen Strahl.

Die Verhältnisgleichungen des ersten Strahlensatzes lassen sich auch auf die zwischen Strecken und Parallelen herrschenden Proportionen übertragen. Es ergeben sich dann folgende Streckenverhältnisse:

Zweiter Strahlensatz

$|B_1C_1| : |B_2C_2| = |SB_1| : |SB_2|$; $|B_1C_1| : |B_2C_2| = |SC_1| : |SC_2|$

Werden zwei Strahlen s_1 und s_2 mit einem gemeinsamen Scheitelpunkt S von zwei zueinander parallelen Geraden geschnitten, so verhalten sich die Längen der Abschnitte auf einem Strahl wie die entsprechenden Längen der Abschnitte auf den Parallelen.

Zentrische Streckung

Neben den Strahlensätzen ist die zentrische Streckung eine grundlegende Methode der Ähnlichkeitsabbildung. Dieses einfache Prinzip, geometrische Figuren zu vergleichen, lässt sich leicht aus den Strahlensätzen herleiten, wenn den beiden Strahlen aus dem vorigen Abschnitt ein dritter hinzugefügt wird.

Verbindet man die Punkte A_1, B_1 und C_1 sowie A_2, B_2 und C_2, so entstehen $\triangle A_1B_1C_1$ und $\triangle A_2B_2C_2$. Beide sind unterschiedlich groß, aber sie sind einander ähnlich, denn alle Strecken und alle Winkel haben das gleiche Verhältnis zueinander. Das größere Dreieck $A_2B_2C_2$ ist das Ergebnis einer zentrischen Streckung. Anschaulich wird das ebenso an der Figur des Kreises (mehr dazu im Kapitel »Kreis- und Raummessung«), dessen Radius *r* die Senkrechte zu einem der Strahlen bildet und $|r|$ damit im Verhältnis steht zur Länge der Strecke $|SM|$,

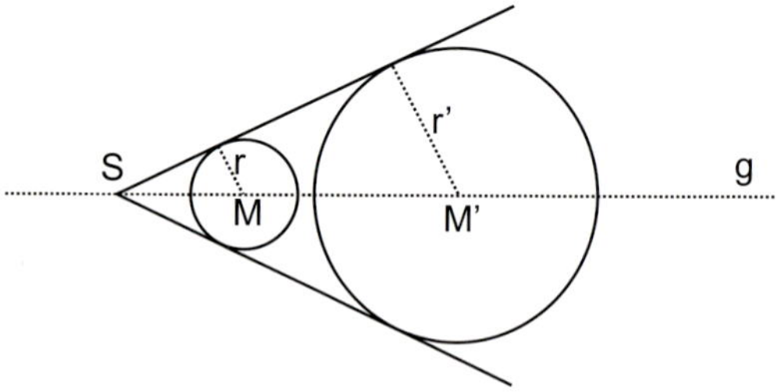

Zentrische Streckung

$|A_1B_1| : |A_2B_2| = |SB_1| : |SB_2|$; $|SC_1| : |SC_2| = |SB_1| : |SB_2|$;
$|SA_1| : |SA_2| = |SB_1| : |SB_2|$; $|SC_1| : |SC_2| = |SA_1| : |SA_2|$;
$|A_1C_1| : |A_2C_2| = |SA_1| : |SA_2|$

Eine zentrische Streckung von einem Scheitelpunkt *S* aus ist die ähnliche Abbildung einer Figur *F* auf *F'*. Jeder Punkt *P* der Figur *F* wird in einem Punkt *P'* der Figur *F'* abgebildet. Dabei muss Punkt *P'* auf derselben Geraden *g* liegen, die durch *S* und *P* verläuft. Allen Punkten auf den Längen der Strecken $|SP|$ und $|SP'|$ ist dasselbe Verhältnis *k* gemeinsam: $|SP'| = k \cdot |SP|$. *k* ist der Streckfaktor der Abbildung. Für ihn gilt $k \neq 0$.

k-Wert	Wirkung
$k = 1$	Identische Abbildung: Alle Seiten haben das Verhältnis $|SP'| = |SP|$ (siehe auch Punktspiegelung).
$k > 1$	Vergrößerung: Es gilt $|SP'| > |SP|$, womit die Figur *F'* größer ist als die Figur *F*.
$0 < k < 1$	Verkleinerung: Es gilt $|SP'| < |SP|$, womit die Figur *F'* kleiner ist als die Figur *F*.
$k < 0$	Gegenläufige Streckung: *F'* und *F* liegen auf verschiedenen Seiten von *S*.

2.5 Koordinatensystem

Bisher wurden alle Zeichnungen und Konstruktionen gewissermaßen ohne eindeutige Orientierung auf das Papier gebracht. Für viele Zwecke ist es aber notwendig, ein eindeutiges und leicht reproduzierbares System zur Verfügung zu haben. Dazu ist das Strahlenpaar, das einen gemeinsamen Scheitelpunkt *S* hat und bei vielen Darstellungen eine Rolle spielt, ein idealer Ausgangspunkt. Die Schenkel beschreiben dabei den Spezialfall des rechten Winkels von 90°. So ergibt sich eine horizontale und eine vertikale Gerade mit einem Schnittpunkt. Die beiden Geraden haben Namen: Die erste wird x-Achse oder Abszissenachse, die zweite y-Achse oder Ordinatenachse genannt. Die Bezeichnungen »x« und »y« für die beiden Achsen des Koordinatensystems sind allerdings nicht zwingend. Sie sind lediglich sehr gebräuchlich und können jederzeit durch eine andere Buchstabenkombination ersetzt werden. Zuletzt erhalten die Geraden eine »Richtung«, die durch einen Pfeil angezeigt ist: Der Pfeil bedeutet, dass die Achsen ohne Begrenzung ins Unendliche laufen, obwohl in der Praxis natürlich nur ein endlich großer Ausschnitt der Ebene dargestellt werden kann. Die beiden Achsen schneiden einander in einem Punkt, den man Ursprung nennt.

Diese Konstruktion ermöglicht es, die Position von Punkten in Form von Zahlen angeben zu können. Angenommen, *P* sei ein Punkt auf der Zeichenebene. Die beiden Abstände seien beispielsweise 3 und 2. Die erste Zahl ist die x-Koordinate, die zweite Zahl die y-Koordinate des Punktes *P*. Diese beiden Zahlen bestimmen die Position des Punktes (in Bezug auf die Achsen) eindeutig.

Grundsätzlich funktioniert diese Methode der Positionsbestimmung nur, wenn der Punkt rechts von der y-Achse und oberhalb der x-Achse, also bei einem Wert größer 0 liegt. Allgemein müssen aber auch negative Koordinatenwerte eingezeichnet werden können: Liegt ein Punkt links von der y-Achse, so ist seine x-Koordinate das Negative des Abstands von der y-Achse. Liegt ein Punkt unterhalb der x-Achse, so ist seine y-Koordinate das Negative des Abstands von der x-Achse.

3 Symmetrie und Kongruenz von Figuren

3.1 Achsensymmetrie/Achsenspiegelung

Definition: Symmetrie ist das spiegelbildliche Gleichmaß, die Spiegelgleichheit.

Eine Figur in der Ebene nennt man achsensymmetrisch, wenn sie durch eine Gerade in zwei spiegelbildlich gleiche Hälften zerlegt werden kann. Die Gerade, welche die beiden Hälften teilt, heißt Symmetrieachse oder Spiegelachse.

Die Symmetrieachse halbiert jede Verbindungsstrecke zwischen einem Punkt und seinem Spiegelpunkt und steht auf ihr senkrecht.

Beispiel der Bezeichnungen der Symmetriepunkte:
A zu *A'*, wobei *A'* der Spiegelpunkt von *A* ist.

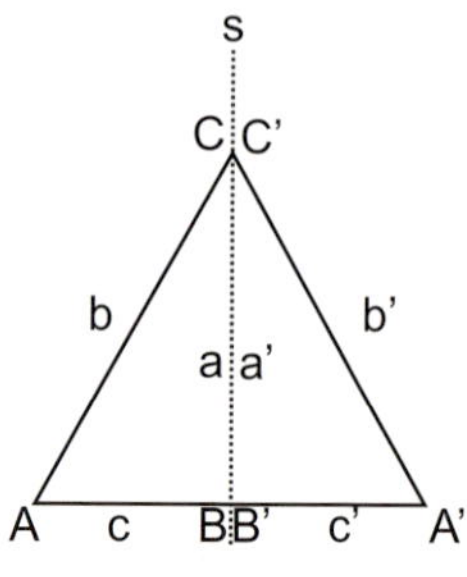

Dieses gleichschenklige Dreieck veranschaulicht die Deckungsgleichheit aller Bildpunkte der Figur und die Tatsache, dass durch die Symmetrieachse auch symmetrisch gleich liegende Winkel entstehen.

Ein gleichseitiges Dreieck hat dementsprechend drei mögliche Symmetrieachsen, da alle Seiten gleich lang sind.
Alle anderen Arten von Dreiecken haben keine Symmetrieachse.

Durch eine Achsenspiegelung wird jede Strecke auf eine Strecke der gleichen Länge abgebildet.

Ein Kreis ist bezüglich jeder seiner Zentralen = Durchmesser = Spiegelachsen achsensymmetrisch.

Jeder Kreispunkt wird bei der angegebenen Spiegelung wieder auf einen Kreispunkt abgebildet.

Neben Dreieck und Kreis sind auch das Quadrat, die Raute und das Rechteck mit zwei seitenhalbierenden Achsen symmetrisch.
Bei der Raute sind beide Diagonalen Symmetrieachsen.
Bei einem Quadrat kommen folgende Symmetrieachsen infrage:

a) Diagonalen – wonach diese Achsen diagonalsymmetrisch genannt werden.

b) Verbindungsgerade der Mittelpunkte von je zwei Gegenseiten; diese werden lotsymmetrisch genannt.

Getrennte Figuren, die durch Umklappen um eine dazwischen liegende Achse zur Deckung gebracht werden können, nennt man achsensymmetrisch.

Für Geraden gilt der Satz:
Jede Senkrechte zu einer Geraden ist für diese Gerade eine Symmetrieachse.
Allgemein gilt:
Bei der Achsenspiegelung wird jeder Punkt der Achse und kein anderer Punkt der Ebene auf sich selbst abgebildet.

3.2 Punktsymmetrie/Punktspiegelung

Bei einer Punktspiegelung sind alle Geraden durch den Punkt *S* »Fixgeraden«. Jede Figur, die durch eine Punktspiegelung auf sich selbst abgebildet werden kann, nennt man punktsymmetrisch.
Den Punkt, an dem die Figur gespiegelt wird, nennt man Symmetriepunkt oder Symmetriezentrum.
Vereinfacht kann man sagen:

Figuren, die man durch Drehung um einen Punkt *S* um 180° zur Deckung bringen kann, nennt man punktsymmetrisch.

Die Punktspiegelung kann an einem einfachen Beispiel veranschaulicht werden:

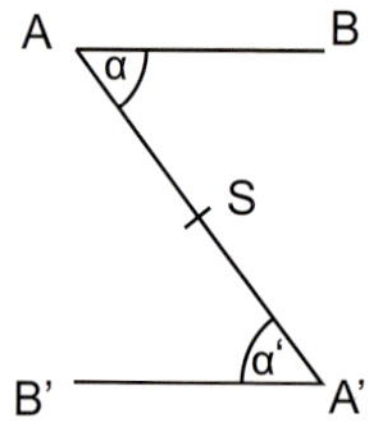

Die Eigenschaften der Punktspiegelung lassen sich folgendermaßen zusammenfassen:

Bei einer Punktspiegelung wird jede Gerade durch einen Punkt *S* auf sich selbst, jede andere Gerade auf eine zu ihr parallele Gerade abgebildet. Strecke und Bildstrecke sind gleich lang. Winkel und Bildwinkel sind gleich groß.

Die Punktspiegelung von Strecken lässt sich folgendermaßen darstellen:

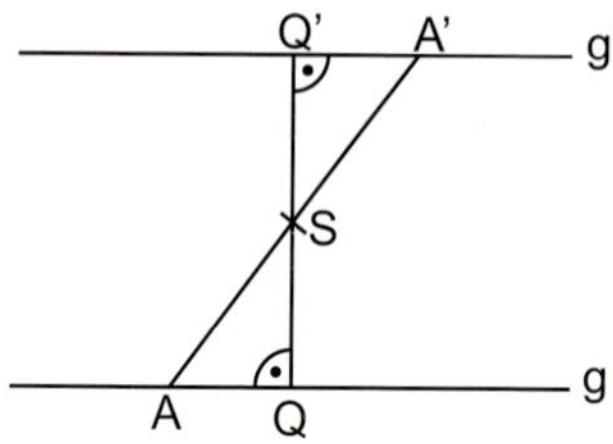

Das Ergebnis der Punktspiegelung einer Strecke ist eine Strecke gleicher Länge.

Auch das Parallelogramm ist ein punktsymmetrisches Viereck, bei dem der Diagonalenschnittpunkt im Symmetriezentrum liegt:

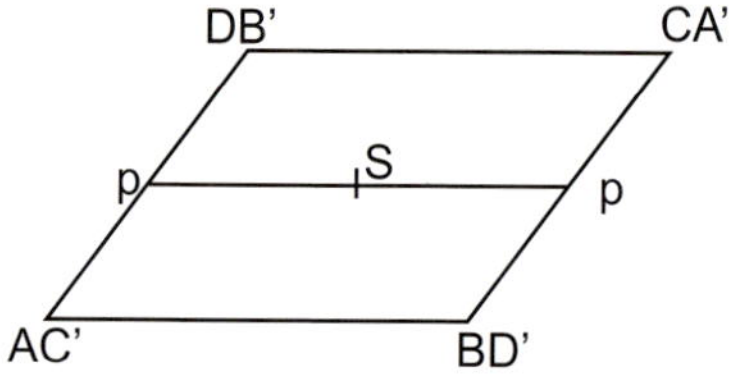

Bei der Punktspiegelung des Parallelogramms am Diagonalenschnittpunkt S werden die Strecken $\overline{AB}$ auf $\overline{CD}$ und $\overline{AD}$ auf $\overline{CB}$ abgebildet.

Jede Mittelparallele des Parallelogramms halbiert zwei Seiten und ist ebenso lang wie die beiden anderen Seiten.

Die Punktspiegelung eines Rechtecks an einem Mittelpunkt S erzeugt ein dem Ausgangsbild deckungsgleiches Rechteck.
Die gleiche Aussage gilt für den Kreis.

Dreiecke sind nicht punktsymmetrisch.

Die Aussage wird durch diese Abbildung verdeutlicht:

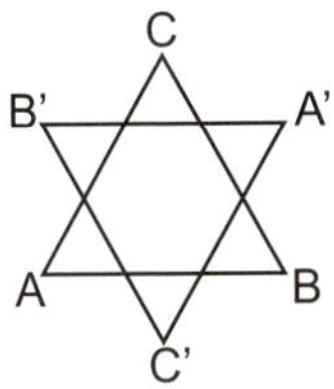

Drehungen um 0° und um 360° gelten nicht als Symmetrien.

3.3 Drehungen/Verschiebungen

Bei einer Drehung beschreiben alle Punkte einer Figur Kreisbögen um den Symmetriepunkt S im Zentrum der Figur.
Jeder Punkt der Figur wird um denselben Winkel gedreht, sodass die Figur nach der Drehung die gleiche Form und Größe hat wie vorher.

Eine Figur heißt drehsymmetrisch in Bezug auf den Symmetriepunkt im Zentrum, wenn sie durch eine Drehung auf sich selbst abgebildet werden kann.

Die einfachste drehsymmetrische Figur ist der Kreis. Der Drehwinkel ist beim Kreis nicht von Bedeutung, er behält bei beliebiger Drehung um seinen Mittelpunkt Form und Größe.

Auch alle regelmäßigen Vielecke sind drehsymmetrisch zu ihrem Symmetriepunkt S, allerdings immer nur für Drehwinkel ganz bestimmter Größen.
Für das Dreieck gilt:

Ein gleichseitiges Dreieck ist drehsymmetrisch bei Drehwinkeln von 120° und 240°.

Ein Quadrat ist drehsymmetrisch, wenn es um 90° oder ein Mehrfaches von 90° gedreht wird.

3.4 Verschiebungen

Neben der Achsenspiegelung und Punktspiegelung sind die Verschiebungen eine weitere Art von Abbildungen.
Eine andere Bezeichnung für Verschiebung ist »Parallelverschiebung« oder »Translation«.

Folgende Lehrsätze gelten für die Verschiebung:
Verschiebungen sind kongruente Abbildungen.
Bei einer Verschiebung sind jede Gerade und ihre Bildgerade gleich gerichtet.

Verschiebungen werden mithilfe von Pfeilen beschrieben. Dabei bildet die Menge aller gleich langen, gleich gerichteten und parallelen Pfeile den »Verschiebungsvektor«.
Schreibweise für den Verschiebungsvektor: $V\vec{a}$
$\vec{a}$
Alle Parallelen zu a sind Fixgeraden, d.h., ein Punkt auf einer solchen Geraden wird auf einen anderen Punkt derselben Geraden abgebildet. Dabei kennzeichnet der Pfeil die Strecke der Verschiebung.
Die Verschiebung ist also durch die Angabe der Vektorlänge und der Vektorrichtung eindeutig bestimmt.

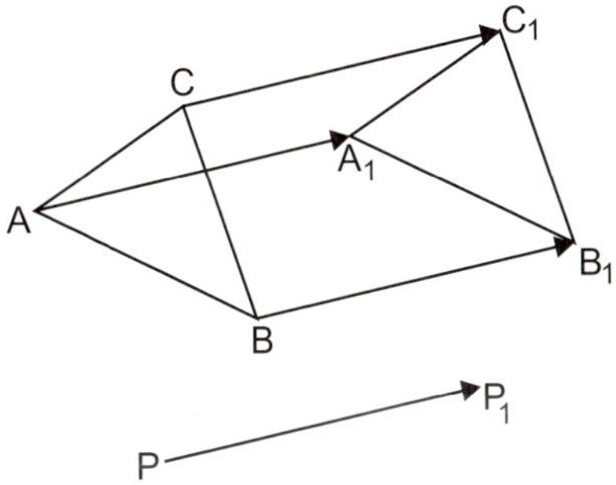

3.5 Kongruenz/Kongruenzabbildungen

Der Name »Kongruenz« leitet sich von dem lateinischen Wort für Übereinstimmung ab: »congruentia«.
Soll für zwei Figuren eine Aussage darüber gemacht werden, ob sie gleich sind, ist es zunächst erforderlich festzulegen, ob damit gemeint ist, dass die Figuren an Form, an Umfang oder an Fläche gleich sind und ob sie sich durch Verschiebungen, Drehungen und Spiegelungen wieder auf eine Figur mit denselben Maßen abbilden lassen. Die Eigenschaften dieser Bewegungen dürfen die Längen und die Winkel von Figuren nicht verändern.
Der Begriff »Kongruenz« präzisiert ganz generell die Aussage über die Gleichheit von Figuren:

> Zwei geometrische Figuren *A* und *B*, die in ihren Winkeln und Längen übereinstimmen, sind kongruent zueinander.

Für die Kongruenz ist folgende Schreibweise vereinbart: ≡

Darüber hinaus sind für je zwei einzelne geometrische Figuren folgende Aussagen zur Kongruenz zu treffen:

Strecken	sind nur dann kongruent, wenn sie gleich lang sind.
Winkel	sind nur dann kongruent, wenn sie gleich groß sind.
Dreiecke	sind schon dann zueinander kongruent, wenn man nur nachgewiesen hat, dass sie in den drei Seitenlängen jeweils paarweise übereinstimmen = Kongruenzsatz »sss«.

Dreiecke sind schon dann kongruent, wenn nachgewiesen ist, dass sie in zwei Seitenlängen und der Größe des Winkels, der von den beiden Seiten eingeschlossen wird, übereinstimmen = Kongruenzsatz = »sws«.

Dreiecke sind schon dann kongruent, wenn feststeht, dass sie in der Größe von zwei entsprechenden Winkeln und in der Länge einer entsprechenden Seite übereinstimmen = Kongruenzsätze »wsw« und »sww«.

Dreiecke sind schon dann zueinander kongruent, wenn man nur weiß, dass sie in den Maßen zweier Seiten und des Gegenwinkels der größeren dieser Seiten übereinstimmen.

Kreise sind dann kongruent, wenn sie gleich große Radien haben.

Daraus folgt: Zu Kongruenzabbildungen zählt man alle
Achsenspiegelungen,
Punktspiegelungen,
Drehungen,
Verschiebungen sowie
alle Abbildungen, die durch Verkettung von Achsenspiegelungen, Punktspiegelungen, Drehungen und Verschiebungen entstehen.

Gleichsinnig kongruent nennt man diese Kongruenzabbildungen, wenn sogar der Umlaufsinn unverändert bleibt – gegensinnig kongruent nennt man Kongruenzabbildungen, wenn sich der Umlaufsinn umkehrt.

Festlegung der Kongruenzabbildungen und deren unverändert bleibende Eigenschaften (Treueeigenschaften):
Achsen- und Geradenspiegelung werden um die Achse a = Spiegelachse gespiegelt.
Punktspiegelungen werden um das Zentrum, den Spiegelpunkt gespiegelt.
Drehungen werden um das Drehzentrum und den Drehwinkel gespiegelt.
Verschiebungen werden durch den Verschiebungspfeil ausgezeichnet.

4 Dreiecke und der Satz des Pythagoras

Alle Vielecke (Polygone) können in Dreiecke zerlegt werden. Dadurch werden die Eigenschaften der Vielecke auf jene der Dreiecke zurückgeführt.
Das Studium der Eigenschaften von Dreiecken und das der Zusammenhänge zwischen diesen ist eine Denkschule der Geometrie. Das Stellen und Lösen entsprechender Aufgaben fördert das logische Denken.
Außer geraden Linien, von denen je drei auch die Dreiecke bilden, kommen hier auch Kreise vor. In der Sprache der Hilfsmittel heißt das: Lineal und Zirkel. Das gilt aber nur im Prinzip, denn das geometrische Denken braucht keine Hilfsmittel.

4.1 Das allgemeine Dreieck

Drei Geraden können sich paarweise in drei Punkten *A*, *B*, *C* schneiden. Die drei Schnittpunkte bestimmen auf den entsprechenden Geraden drei Strecken $\overline{BC}$, $\overline{CA}$, $\overline{AB}$, deren Längen *a*, *b*, *c* oder *BC*, *CA*, *AB* Seitenlängen des Dreiecks oder kürzer »Seiten« genannt werden. Oft werden mit *a*, *b*, *c* die Seiten selbst, mit *BC*, *CA*, *AB* die Geraden durch diese Punkte bezeichnet.
Die drei Punkte *A*, *B*, *C* sind die »Ecken« oder »Eckpunkte« des Dreiecks *ABC*. Bei der Angabe eines Dreiecks werden seine Eckpunkte in der Reihenfolge aufgezählt, die dem »Gegenuhrzeigersinn« entspricht.

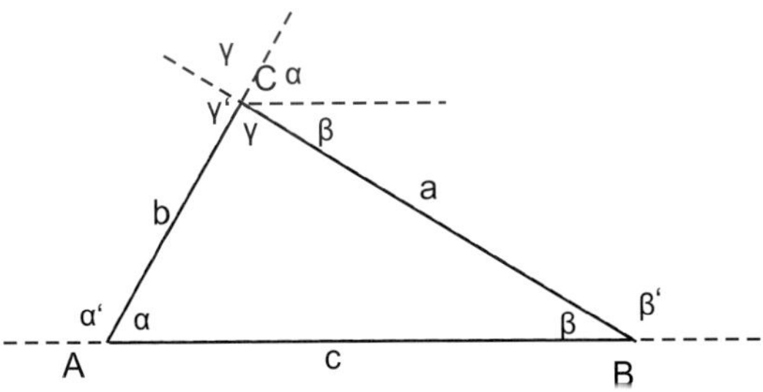

In den Eckpunkten bildet sich je ein »innerer Winkel« α, β, γ. Durch einen der Eckpunkte, z. B. durch *C*, wird eine Parallele zur gegenüberliegenden Seite, im Beispiel zu $\overline{AB}$, gelegt. Nach den Gesetzmäßigkeiten bezüglich der »Winkel an Doppelkreuzungen von Geraden« ist zu bemerken, dass mit der Spitze im ausgewählten Eckpunkt (C) auf einer Seite der Geraden AC die drei Winkel α, β, γ nebeneinander erscheinen, sodass ihre Summe offensichtlich der »gestreckte Winkel« ist.

$$\alpha + \beta + \gamma = 180° = 2R$$

Ebenfalls zwei rechte Winkel $2R = 180°$ beträgt die Summe eines jeden inneren Winkels mit einem seiner beiden »Außenwinkel«:

$$\alpha + \alpha' = \beta + \beta' = \gamma + \gamma' = 180°$$

Aus den beiden letzten Beziehungen folgt eine wichtige Regel: Jeder Außenwinkel ist gleich mit der Summe der beiden ihm nicht anliegenden Innenwinkel.

Somit: $\alpha' = \beta + \gamma$; $\beta' = \gamma + \alpha$; $\gamma' = \alpha + \beta$.

4.2 Transversalen im Dreieck

Die Geometrie des Dreiecks wird mit «Transversalen« ergänzt. Das sind gerade Linien, welche die das Dreieck bildenden Geraden schneiden. Besonders wichtig sind vier Tripel von Transversalen mit der gemeinsamen Eigenschaft, dass sich die drei Geraden in je einem Punkt treffen.

Die Mittelsenkrechten

In den Mittelpunkten der drei Seiten wird je eine Senkrechte auf die jeweilige Seite gefällt. Das sind Symmetrieachsen, denen gegenüber je zwei Eckpunkte miteinander symmetrisch sind. Man kann sie also auch als »geometrische Örter« definieren.

Eine Mittelsenkrechte ist der geometrische Ort aller Punkte P, die von zwei Eckpunkten gleich weit entfernt sind.

m_a: $P_aB = P_aC$; m_b: $P_bC = P_bA$; m_c: $P_cA = P_cB$

Zwei Mittelsenkrechte, zum Beispiel m_a und m_b, treffen sich in einem Punkt M. Dieser Punkt M liegt also sowohl auf m_a als auch auf m_b.

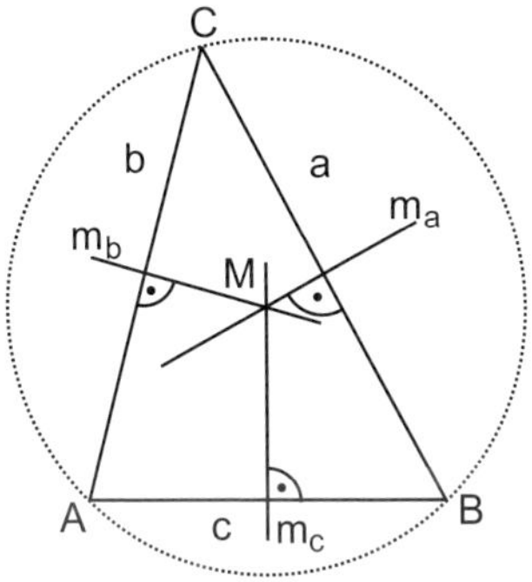

Für ihn sind danach zwei Gleichungen gültig:

MB = *MC* und *MA* = *MC*

Aus diesen beiden folgt aber, dass für *M* auch die dritte Gleichung *MB* = *MC* gilt. Also liegt *M* auch auf der dritten Mittelsenkrechten. Die drei Mittelsenkrechten schneiden sich in einem Punkt. Dieser Punkt hat die gleiche Distanz *R* von allen drei Eckpunkten.
Man kann einen Kreis mit dem Radius *r* und mit dem Mittelpunkt *M* so zeichnen, dass er durch alle drei Eckpunkte geht. Dieser Kreis ist dem Dreieck »umschrieben«. Der gemeinsame Schnittpunkt aller drei Mittelsenkrechten ist der Mittelpunkt des Umkreises.

Höhenlinien

Aus jedem Eckpunkt des Dreiecks wird je eine Senkrechte auf die gegenüberliegende Seite (parallel zur entsprechenden Mittelsenkrechten) gefällt. Die Längen h_a, h_b, h_c dieser Linien, also die Distanzen der Eck-

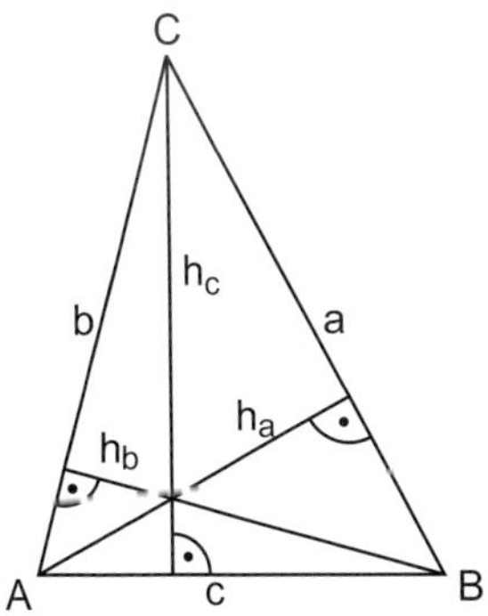

punkte von den gegenüberliegenden Seiten, sind die Höhen des Dreiecks. Auch die Höhenlinien schneiden sich in einem einzigen Punkt. Am leichtesten kann man sich mittels eines kleinen Kunstgriffs davon überzeugen.

Durch jeden Eckpunkt wird je eine Parallele zur gegenüberliegenden Seite gezogen. Diese drei Parallelen bilden ein Dreieck mit den doppelten Seitenlängen im Vergleich mit dem ursprünglichen Dreieck. Die Höhenlinien des Dreiecks *ABC* sind Mittelsenkrechten im Dreieck *A'B'C'*, und als solche treffen sie sich im Zentrum des Umkreises des großen Dreiecks.

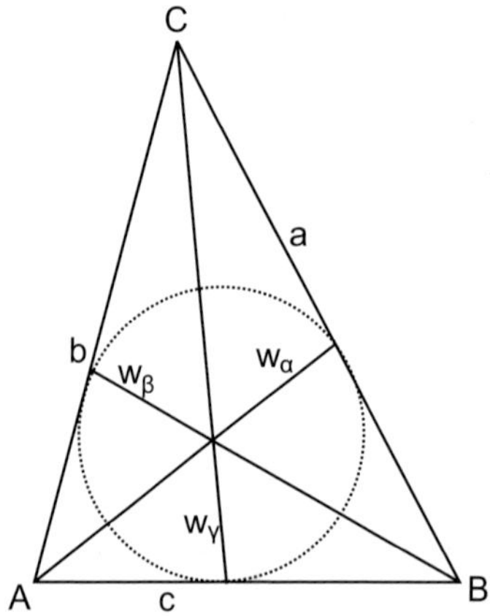

Die Winkelhalbierenden

Die Halbierenden w_α, w_β, w_γ sind die geometrischen Örter von Punkten, die von den beiden Schenkeln der betreffenden Winkel gleich weit entfernt sind.

Der Schnittpunkt *W* zweier Winkelhalbierenden w_α und w_β ist einerseits gleich weit entfernt von *b* und *c*, andererseits von *a* und *c*. Dann ist er aber gleich weit entfernt auch von *b* und *c*, liegt also auf w_γ.

Der gemeinsame Schnittpunkt sämtlicher drei Winkelhalbierenden liegt also auf der gemeinsamen Distanz *r* von allen drei Seiten. Um diesen Punkt als Mittelpunkt mit dem Radius *r* kann der »Inkreis« gezeichnet werden, der in je einem Punkt alle drei Seiten berührt und dessen restliche Punkte alle im Innern des Dreiecks liegen.

Die Seitenhalbierenden (Schwerlinien)

Die drei Seitenhalbierenden des Dreiecks verbinden die Ecken *A, B, C* mit den Mittelpunkten *D, E, F* der gegenüberliegenden Seiten. Die Seitenhalbierenden *AD* und *BE* schneiden sich in *S*. Die Gerade *ED* ist parallel mit der Geraden *AB*. (Die Zeichnung kann leicht angefertigt werden.) Folglich bilden sich hier manche Paare von gleichen Winkeln:

$$\sphericalangle SED = \sphericalangle SBA; \sphericalangle SDE = \sphericalangle SAB$$

Daraus folgt, dass die beiden Dreiecke *ABS* und *DES* miteinander ähnlich und danach die Verhältnisse der entsprechenden Seitenlängen gleich sind. Das Verhältnis der Längen von *AB* und *DE* ist aber gleich mit 2. Es folgt:

$$\frac{AS}{SD} = \frac{BS}{SE} = \frac{AB}{DE} = 2$$

Der Schnittpunkt *S* von zwei Seitenhalbierenden teilt diese beiden im Verhältnis *2 : 1* (Distanz vom Eckpunkt/Distanz vom Mittelpunkt der Seite = 2). Der Schnittpunkt einer der beiden Seitenhalbierenden mit der dritten muss auch diese beiden im Verhältnis *2 : 1* teilen, er muss also derselbe Punkt sein. Alle drei Seitenhalbierenden schneiden sich in einem Punkt. Dieser Punkt heißt »Schwerpunkt« des Dreiecks. Danach werden die Seitenhalbierenden auch Schwerlinien genannt.

4.3 Besondere Dreiecke

Dreiecke spezieller Formen können zusätzliche Eigenschaften haben.

Das gleichseitige Dreieck

Wenn alle drei Seiten des Dreiecks miteinander gleich sind, dann sind auch alle drei Winkel miteinander gleich, und zwar gleich mit je 60°. Die Mittelsenkrechten sind gleichzeitig auch Höhenlinien, Seitenhalbierende und Winkelhalbierende, alle mit einem einzigen Schnittpunkt, der gleichzeitig Mittelpunkt des Umkreises, des Inkreises sowie auch Schwerpunkt ist.

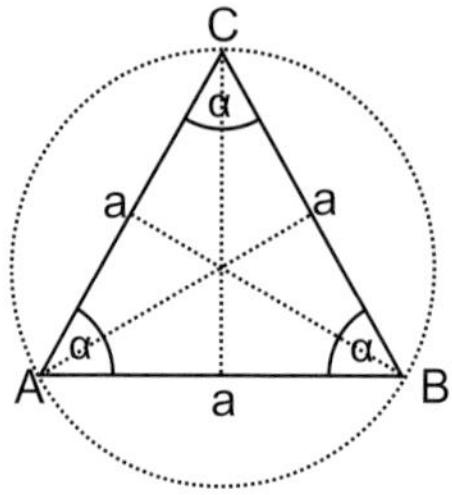

Das gleichschenkelige Dreieck

Wenn zwei Seiten eines Dreiecks gleich sind, heißen diese »Schenkel« des Dreiecks und das Dreieck selbst ist »gleichschenkelig«. Die dritte Seite heißt »Basis«, der Eckpunkt gegenüber der Basis heißt »Spitze«. Höhenlinie, Mittelsenkrechte, Seitenhalbierende, Winkelhalbierende aus der Spitze fallen zusammen und bilden die Symmetrieachse des Dreiecks.

Wegen dieser Symmetrie sind alle Elemente wie Winkel, Höhen usw., die zu den beiden zueinander symmetrischen Ecken oder Seiten gehören, paarweise miteinander gleich.

Ein gleichschenkeliges Dreieck kann spitzwinkelig oder stumpfwinkelig sein, je nach der Art des Winkels an der Spitze.

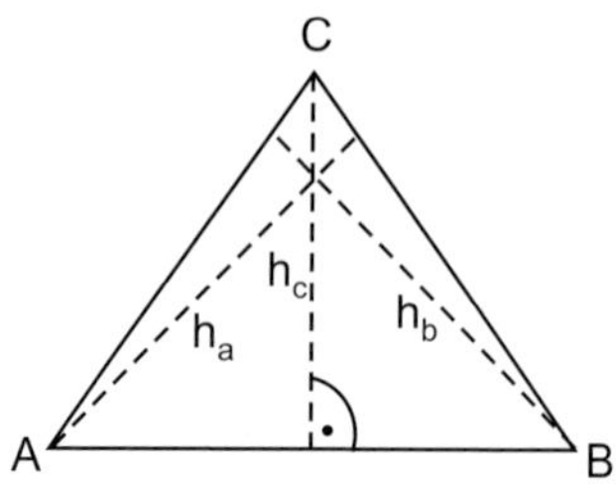

Das rechtwinklige Dreieck

Wenn ein Winkel des Dreiecks ein rechter Winkel ist (also gleich 90° = R), ist das Dreieck rechtwinklig. Die Summe der beiden anderen (spitzen) Winkel muss 90° ausmachen. Sie sind zueinander »komplementär«. Die Seite gegenüber dem rechten Winkel heißt »Hypotenuse«. Entlang der beiden Schenkel des rechten Winkels liegen die beiden »Katheten«. Die zu einer Kathete gehörende Höhe ist die andere Kathete.

Rechtwinklige Dreiecke spielen in der Mathematik eine ganz besondere Rolle. Manche von diesen sollen später näher betrachtet werden.

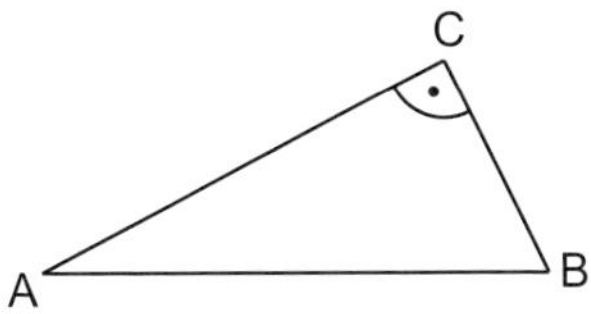

4.4 Dreieckskonstruktionen

Die Aufgabe lautet: Man konstruiere (mithilfe von Lineal und Zirkel) Dreiecke mit vorgegebenen Elementen.

Konstruktionsaufgabe 1:
Gegeben sind die drei Seiten *(a, b, c)*. Gesucht wird das Dreieck *ABC* (die Eckpunkte wurden im Gegenuhrzeigersinn aufgezählt).

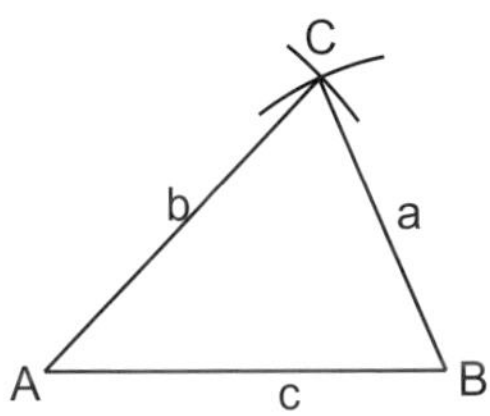

Lösung:
Auf einer Halbgeraden wird aus *A* die Strecke $AB = c$ abgetragen (mithilfe des Zirkels). Mit dem Mittelpunkt in *A* wird ein Kreisbogen mit dem Radius *b* gezogen und mit dem Mittelpunkt in *B* ein Bogen mit dem Radius *a*. Der Schnittpunkt der beiden Bogen, wenn es ihn gibt, ist der dritte Eckpunkt des Dreiecks.
Es ist leicht ersichtlich, dass die beiden Bogen einander nur dann schneiden, wenn *B* von *A* nicht zu weit entfernt ist. Die Bedingung ist:

$c < a + b$ und ähnlicher Weise $a < b + c$, $b < c + a$

Damit die Aufgabe lösbar ist, also ein Dreieck wie das verlangte existiert, muss jede Seite kleiner sein als die Summe der beiden anderen. Die erste Aufgabe ist also bedingt lösbar.

Wäre die Reihenfolge der Ecken A, B, C nicht im Gegenuhrzeigersinn festgelegt worden, wäre diese Aufgabe zweideutig. Der Eckpunkt C könnte dann auch unterhalb der Geraden AB liegen. Das Dreieck ACB wäre eine zweite Lösung der Aufgabe.

Konstruktionsaufgabe 2:
Gegeben sind zwei Winkel und ihr gemeinsamer Schenkel, z. B. α, β, c.

Lösung:
Aus den beiden Endpunkten der Strecke $\overline{AB}$ werden die beiden anderen Schenkel in den von den gegebenen Winkeln bestimmten Richtungen gezogen.
Damit sich die Schenkel oberhalb der Geraden AB treffen, muss

$$\alpha + \beta < 180°$$

gelten. Mit dieser Bedingung ist die Aufgabe lösbar.

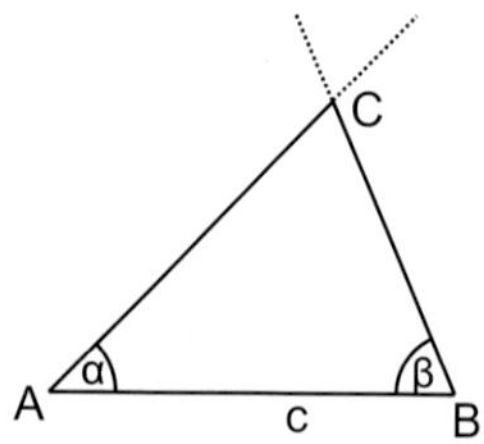

Konstruktionsaufgabe 3:
Gegeben sind eine Seite und zwei Winkel, deren einer der Seite nicht anliegt, z. B. c, α, γ. Wieder gilt die Bedingung $\alpha + \gamma < 180°$.

Lösung:
Der gesuchte dritte Eckpunkt C liegt auf dem zweiten Schenkel des in A konstruierten Winkels α. In einem beliebigen Punkt C' dieses Schenkels

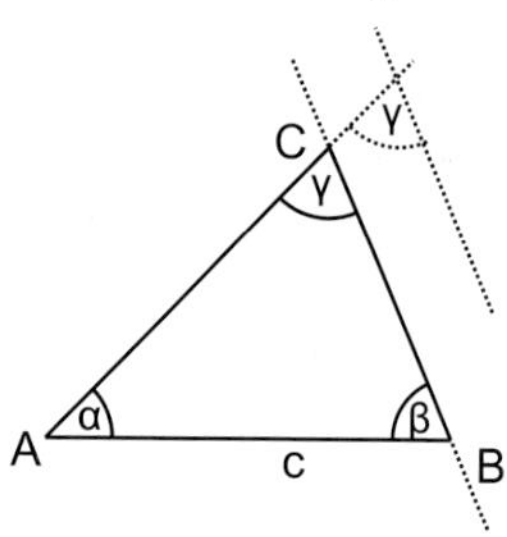

wird der Winkel γ konstruiert. Dadurch ist die Richtung der dritten Seite bekannt. Eine Parallele durch *B* zu dieser Richtung stellt die dritte Seite dar.

Konstruktionsaufgabe 4:
Gegeben sind zwei Seiten und der von ihnen eingeschlossene Winkel, z. B. b, c, α.

Lösung:
Die beiden Seiten werden auf die Scheitel des Winkels α abgetragen. Die beiden Endpunkte sind *B* und *C* (banale Bedingung: $\alpha < 180°$).

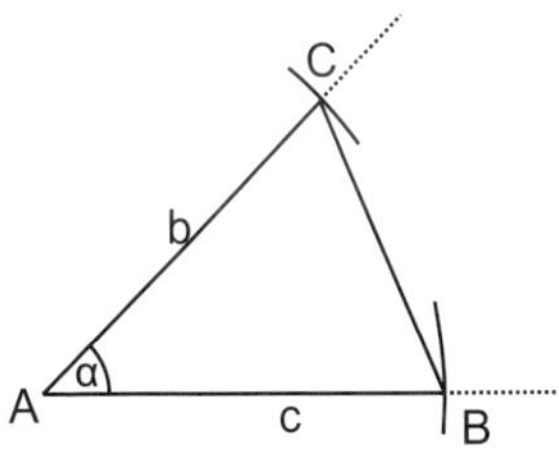

Konstruktionsaufgabe 5:
Gegeben sind zwei Seiten und ein von ihnen nicht eingeschlossener Winkel, z. B. c, a, α.

Lösung:
Die eine bekannte Seite ($c = AB$) liegt auf einem Schenkel des bekannten Winkels (zum Beispiel α). Mit dem Mittelpunkt in *B* und mit dem Radius a (die zweite bekannte Seite) wird ein Bogen gezeichnet. Jetzt gibt es zwei Möglichkeiten:

1) $a < c$ (der bekannte Winkel liegt der kleineren gegebenen Seite gegenüber). In diesem Fall gibt es eine Grenzsituation, in der die Halbgerade aus *A* den Kreis berührt. Dieser Berührungspunkt ist der dritte Eckpunkt *C* des gesuchten und gefundenen, in *C* rechtwinkligen Dreiecks. Die Halbgerade aus *A* kann den Kreis in zwei Punkten schneiden, das bedeutet zwei Lösungen, oder kann ihn nicht schneiden, das bedeutet, dass es keine Lösung gibt
2) $a \geq c$ (der bekannte Winkel liegt der größeren gegebenen Seite gegenüber). In diesem Fall gibt es genau eine Lösung.

Konstruktionsaufgabe 6:
Gegeben sind sämtliche drei Winkel.
Diese Aufgabe ist »unterdeterminiert«. Wegen $\alpha + \beta + \gamma = 180°$ sind das jetzt nur zwei unabhängige Daten. Ungenügend, um die Aufgabe zu lösen.
Als allgemeine Regel gilt: Um das Dreieck konstruieren zu können, wenn es überhaupt konstruierbar ist, also existiert, sind drei Daten nötig, davon aber mindestens eines linear (also nicht Winkel, sondern z.B. Seite). Außer Winkeln und Seiten können auch andere Daten gegeben sein; die am häufigsten vorkommenden sind: Höhen, Seitenhalbierende, Winkelhalbierende, Radien von Umkreis und Inkreis.
Achtung! Nicht alle formulierbaren Aufgaben sind lösbar. Fast alle Aufgaben, in denen eine Winkelhalbierende gegeben ist, sind unlösbar, aber auch das ist keine allgemeine Regel, weil zum Beispiel die Aufgaben $(\alpha, \beta, w_\gamma)$; (α, h_a, w_α); (a, b, w_γ) usw. lösbar sind.
Lösbar bedeutet aber keineswegs, dass die in diesem Buch angebotenen Kenntnisse ausreichen.
Einige weitere Aufgaben, die auch mit den angebotenen Kenntnissen lösbar sind, sollen hier folgen.

Konstruktionsaufgabe 7:
Gegeben sind zwei Seiten und der Radius des Umkreises a, b, r.

Lösung:
Aus einem beliebigen Punkt C des Kreises werden zwei Sehnen mit den gegebenen Längen konstruiert. Sie sind zwei Seiten des Dreiecks, die dritte Seite ist die Sehne, die die beiden Endpunkte verbindet.

Konstruktionsaufgabe 8:
Gegeben sind c, h_c, α.

Lösung:
Auf eine Gerade wird die Strecke $c = \overline{AB}$ abgetragen. Der dritte Eckpunkt C muss sich auf einer Parallelen zu $\overline{AB}$ auf der Distanz h_c von die-

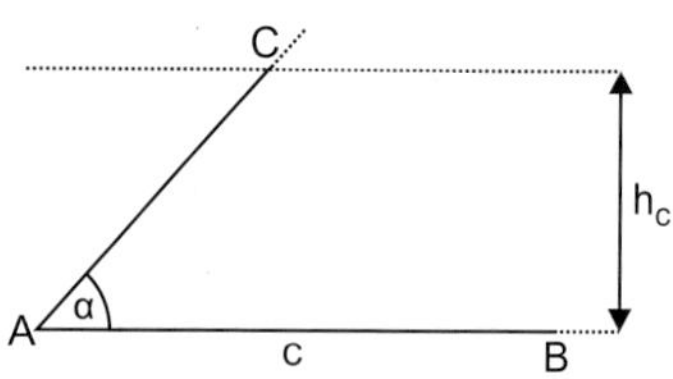

ser befinden. Er muss auch auf dem zweiten Schenkel des in *A* konstruierten Winkels α liegen, also im Schnittpunkt dieser beiden Geraden.

Konstruktionsaufgabe 9:
Gegeben sind b, c, h_c.

Lösung:
Ähnlich wie bei der vorigen Aufgabe, aber die Parallele zu $\overline{AB}$ wird jetzt mit einem Kreisbogen geschnitten, dessen Radius b und dessen Mittelpunkt A ist.

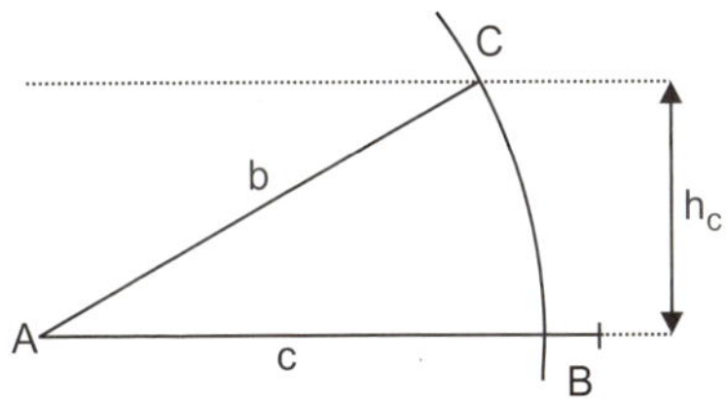

Um Konstruktionsaufgaben lösen zu können, muss man entsprechende Eigenschaften kennen und verwenden.
Wenn es sich z. B. um Seitenhalbierende handelt, muss man wissen, dass diese sich im Verhältnis 2 : 1 teilen. Beispiel:

Konstruktionsaufgabe 10:
Gegeben sind c, s_a, s_b.

Lösung:
Auf eine Gerade wird die Strecke $\overline{AB}$ abgetragen. Der Schnittpunkt S der beiden gegebenen Seitenhalbierenden liegt auf der Distanz $\frac{2}{3}\,s_a$ von A und auf der Distanz $\frac{2}{3}\,s_b$ von B, also im Schnittpunkt der beiden entsprechenden Kreisbogen. Auf den Verlängerungen von AS und BS, in der Entfernung $\frac{1}{3}\,s_a$ bzw. $\frac{1}{3}\,s_b$ von S, befinden sich die Mittelpunkte der beiden gegenüberliegenden Seiten usw.

4.5 Der Thales-Satz und seine Anwendungen

Durch den Mittelpunkt M der Hypotenuse eines rechtwinkligen Dreiecks wird je eine Parallele zu den beiden Katheten gelegt. Die zu einer der Katheten parallele Gerade ist senkrecht auf die andere Kathete, und da sie durch den Mittelpunkt der Hypotenuse geht, wird sie auch die von ihr geschnittene Kathete halbieren. Die beiden betrachteten Geraden sind also eben die Mittelsenkrechten der Katheten und als solche müssen sie sich im Mittelpunkt des Umkreises treffen. Folglich ist der Mittelpunkt der Hypotenuse eben der Mittelpunkt des Umkreises. Die Hypotenuse ist der Durchmesser des Umkreises.

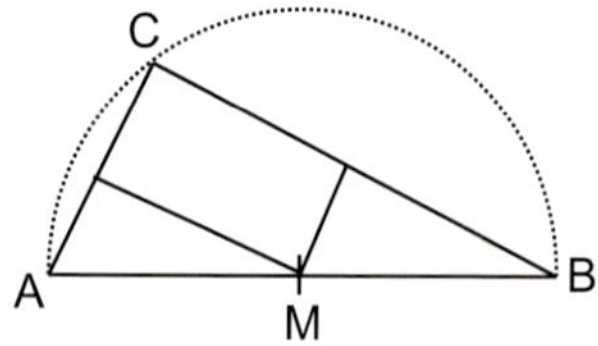

Weitere äquivalente Aussagen sind:

Aus jedem Punkt des Umkreises (des Thales-Kreises) «sieht man» alle Durchmesser unter einem rechten Winkel.
Der geometrische Ort aller Punkte, aus denen man eine gegebene Strecke unter einem rechten Winkel sieht, ist ein Kreis (der Thales-Kreis), dessen Durchmesser die Strecke ist (der Thales-Satz).

Da die Höhen auf die entsprechenden Seiten senkrecht sind, bilden Konstruktionsaufgaben, in denen auch Höhen vorkommen, typische Anwendungen des Thales-Satzes.

Konstruktionsaufgabe 11:
Gegeben sind a, c, h_b.

Lösung:
Auf eine Gerade wird die Strecke $c = AB$ abgetragen. Aus dem Fußpunkt der Höhe h_b sieht man die Seite AB unter einem rechten Winkel, also

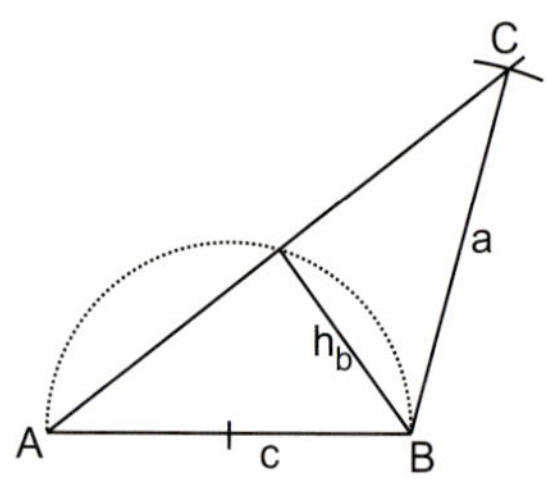

befindet sich dieser Fußpunkt auf dem Thales-(Halb-)Kreis über der Seite *AB*, und zwar in dem Punkt des Kreises, der sich von *B* in der Entfernung h_b befindet. Nach diesem Punkt kann die Gerade der Seite *AC* konstruiert werden. Der Eckpunkt *C* befindet sich auf dieser Geraden in der Entfernung *a* von *B*.

Konstruktionsaufgabe 12:
Gegeben sind c, h_b, α.

Lösung:
In der vorigen Aufgabe war ersichtlich, dass c und h_b die Richtung der Seite *AC*, also den Winkel bestimmen, dieser also keine von den beiden anderen unabhängige Angabe ist. Die Aufgabe ist unlösbar.

Konstruktionsaufgabe 13:
Gegeben sind c, h_a, h_b.

Lösung:
Die Fußpunkte der beiden Höhenlinien befinden sich auf dem Thales-Kreis der Strecke $\overline{AB}$. Mithilfe der Distanzen von *A* bzw. *B* können die beiden Fußpunkte, anschließend die beiden Seiten konstruiert werden.

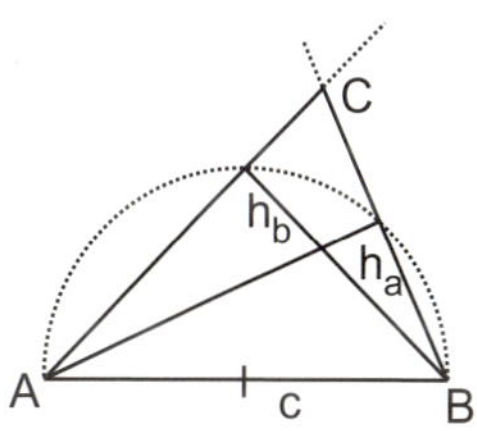

4.6 Metrische Beziehungen in rechtwinkligen Dreiecken

In einem rechtwinkligen Dreieck *ABC* mit dem rechten Winkel in *C* wird die Höhenlinie aus *C* gelegt. Ihr Fußpunkt ist *D*. Für die Ähnlichkeit rechtwinkliger Dreiecke genügt die Gleichheit von zwei spitzen Winkeln. Der Winkel α ist gemeinsam für die Dreiecke *ABC* und *ACD*. Der Winkel β ist gemeinsam für die Dreiecke *ABC* und *CBD*. Alle drei Dreiecke sind miteinander ähnlich. Das heißt:

$$ABC \sim ACD \sim CBD$$

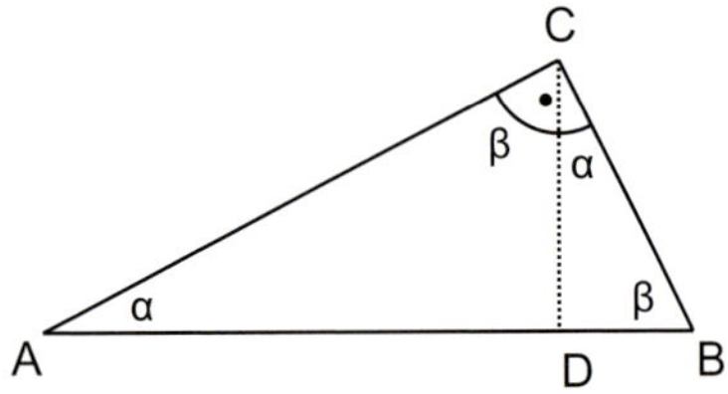

Folglich sind die Verhältnisse homologer Paare von Seiten miteinander gleich:

$$\frac{BC}{AC} = \frac{CD}{AD} = \frac{DB}{CD} \Rightarrow CD^2 = AD \cdot DB$$

$$\frac{BC}{AB} = \frac{CD}{AC} = \frac{DB}{BC} \Rightarrow BC^2 = AB \cdot DB$$

$$\frac{AC}{AB} = \frac{AD}{AC} = \frac{CD}{BC} \Rightarrow AC^2 = AB \cdot AD$$

Von Interesse sind die Folgerungen. Sie stellen wichtige Lehrsätze dar:

Höhensatz: Im rechtwinkligen Dreieck ist das Quadrat der Höhe auf die Hypotenuse gleich mit dem Produkt der beiden durch den Fußpunkt der Höhe auf der Hypotenuse bestimmten Abschnitte.
Kathetensatz (auf beide Katheten angewendet): Im rechtwinkligen Dreieck ist das Quadrat jeder Kathete gleich mit dem Produkt aus der Hypotenuse und der Strecke, die von der betreffenden Kathete auf der Hypotenuse bestimmt wird.
Die Addition der beiden Anwendungen des Kathetensatzes ergibt den vielleicht «berühmtesten» Lehrsatz der Mathematik, den Pythagoras-Satz:

$$AC^2 + BC^2 = AB \cdot (AD + DB) = AB^2$$

Wörtlich: Im rechtwinkligen Dreieck ist die Summe aus den Quadraten der Katheten gleich mit dem Quadrat der Hypotenuse.

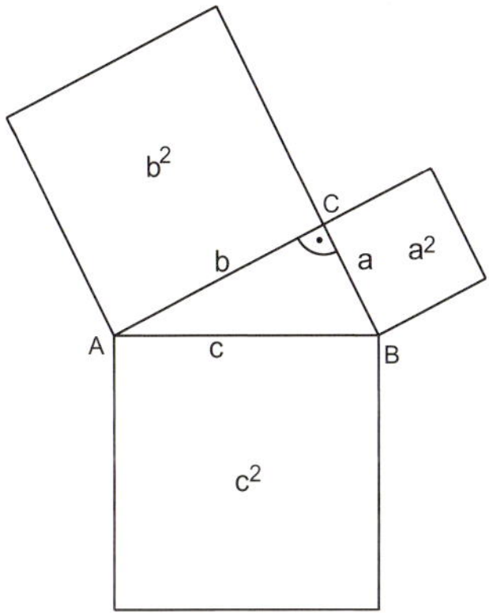

Pythagoras hat vor etwa zweieinhalb Jahrtausenden gelebt, aber der von ihm verwendete und gelehrte Lehrsatz ist viel älter.
Den Satz des Pythagoras kann man in Einzelfällen auch mit natürlichen Zahlen »darstellen«. Die bekannteste solche Darstellung ist »das pythagoreische Zahlentripel«: $a = 3$, $b = 4$, $c = 5$ mit $3^2 + 4^2 = 5^2$. Aber es gibt unendlich viele solcher Zahlentripel. Mithilfe der algebraischen Gleichung

$$(m^2 + n^2)^2 = (m^2 - n^2)^2 + 4m^2n^2$$

also mit $a = m^2 - n^2$, $b = 2\,mn$ und $c = m^2 + n^2$ kann man sie »herstellen«. Z.B. $m = 2$ und $n = 1$ liefern $a, b, c = 3, 4, 5$; $m = 3$ und $n = 2$ ergeben $a, b, c = 5, 12, 13$ usw.
Ein Dreieck mit diesen Maßzahlen seiner Seiten ist rechtwinklig mit dem rechten Winkel gegenüber der größten Seite.

Jahrtausendelang verwendeten Baumeister und Erdvermesser sehr verschiedener Völker, um rechte Winkel zu konstruieren, Seile, auf denen voneinander gleich entfernte Knoten angebracht waren. Die Distanz zwischen zwei aufeinander folgenden Knoten soll die Maßeinheit der Länge sein. Wenn man das Seil zwischen drei Punkten so aufspannt, dass die Längen der Seiten des Dreiecks drei, vier und fünf Einheiten betragen, dann entsteht gegenüber der längsten Seite ein rechter Winkel.

5 Trigonometrie

In der ebenen Geometrie waren zunächst nur Berechnungen zwischen Seiten oder zwischen Winkeln möglich. Durch Anwendung der Winkelfunktionen gelingt die Verknüpfung von Seitenlängen und Winkeln und ermöglicht so die Berechnung der jeweils fehlenden Teile. Dieses Teilgebiet der Mathematik wird Trigonometrie genannt.

Der Begriff Trigonometrie stammt aus der griechischen Sprache und bedeutet Dreiecksmessung.

Die Trigonometrie ist die Lehre von der Dreiecksberechnung mithilfe von Winkelfunktionen (trigonometrische Funktionen).

Zahlreiche geometrische Figuren können in Dreiecke und durch eingezeichnete Höhen in rechtwinklige Dreiecke zerlegt werden, sodass auch in diesen Figuren Streckenlängen und Winkelweiten in Zusammenhang gestellt werden können. Das rechtwinklige Dreieck ist die Ausgangsfigur der Trigonometrie.

Die Ausweitung der Berechnungen auf beliebige und sogar sphärische Dreiecke gibt der Trigonometrie ihre Bedeutung in Landvermessung, Kartografie, Bauwesen, Seefahrt und Astronomie.

Durch Ausweitungen und Loslösung von der Dreiecksberechnung bietet sich schließlich die Möglichkeit zur Berechnung von periodischen – sich in regelmäßigen Zeitabständen wiederholenden – Vorgängen in Technik, Physik und Biologie.

5.1 Winkelfunktionen im rechtwinkligen Dreieck

In einem rechtwinkligen Dreieck gilt der Satz des Pythagoras:

$a^2 + b^2 = c^2$

Das heißt, sind zwei Seiten bekannt, lässt sich die dritte berechnen.

Aufgrund des Winkelsummensatzes (Die Summe der Innenwinkel im Dreieck ist 180°) gilt im rechtwinkligen Dreieck

$\alpha + \beta = 90°$ (da $\gamma = 90°$).

Die beiden spitzen Winkel sind so genannte Komplementwinkel, also $\beta = 90° - \alpha$.

Im rechtwinkligen Dreieck heißt die längste Seite Hypotenuse. Sie liegt dem rechten Winkel gegenüber. Die beiden anderen Seiten (Schenkel des rechten Winkels) werden Katheten genannt. Bezüglich eines der spitzen Winkel werden Ankathete und Gegenkathete unterschieden.

Beispiel: Gegeben sei das folgende Dreieck:

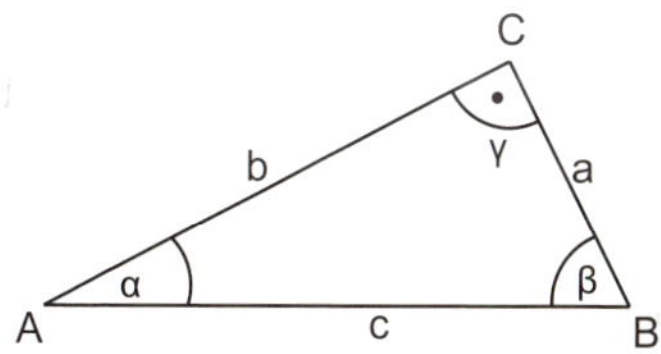

Dann ist die Seite *c* die Hypotenuse, weil sie dem rechten Winkel gegenüberliegt, und die Seiten *a* und *b* die Katheten. Bezüglich des Winkels α ist *b* die Ankathete, da sie dem Winkel α anliegt, und *a* die Gegenkathete, da sie dem Winkel α gegenüberliegt. Die Seite *a* liegt aber auch am Winkel β an und ist deshalb gleichzeitig die Ankathete von β.

Stimmen zwei Dreiecke in einem Winkel überein, so stimmen sie auch im dritten Winkel überein (Winkelsummensatz) und sind somit einander ähnlich. Ähnliche Dreiecke haben gleiche Seitenverhältnisse (**Ähnlichkeitssätze für Dreiecke**).

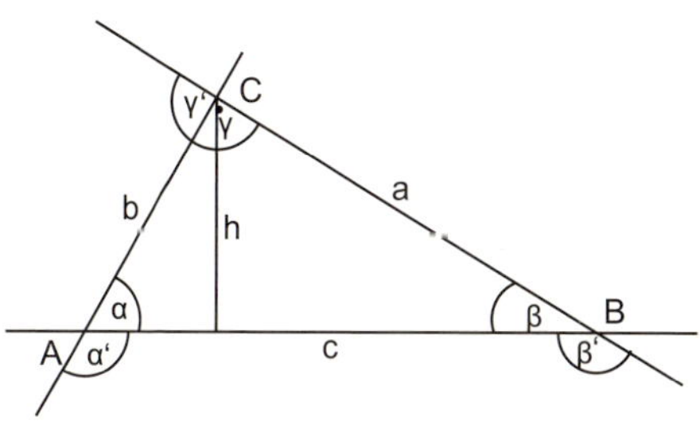

Das Verhältnis zweier Seiten im rechtwinkligen Dreieck ist somit eine Funktion der Winkel (bzw. des Winkels α). Diese konstanten Quotienten werden als Winkelfunktionen oder trigonometrische Funktionen bezeichnet.

Die trigonometrischen Funktionen sind definiert als das Verhältnis zweier Seiten im rechtwinkligen Dreieck.

Im Einzelnen heißen diese winkelabhängigen Seitenverhältnisse:

- Gegenkathete zu Hypotenuse = Sinus des Winkels $\alpha = \sin\alpha$
- Ankathete zu Hypotenuse = Kosinus des Winkels $\alpha = \cos\alpha$
- Gegenkathete zu Ankathete = Tangens des Winkels $\alpha = \tan\alpha$

Selbstverständlich können die beiden Katheten auch umgekehrt zueinander ins Verhältnis gesetzt werden. Dann heißt es:

- Ankathete zu Gegenkathete = Kotangens des Winkels $\alpha = \cot\alpha$

Mit dieser Winkelfunktion wollen wir uns hier nicht beschäftigen.

Bezogen auf unser Dreieck gilt dann für den Winkel α:

Sinus, Kosinus und Tangens für den Winkel α:

Sinusfunktion: $$\sin\alpha = \frac{\text{Gegenkathete}}{\text{Hypotenuse}} = \frac{a}{c}$$

Kosinusfunktion: $$\cos\alpha = \frac{\text{Ankathete}}{\text{Hypotenuse}} = \frac{b}{c}$$

Tangensfunktion: $$\tan\alpha = \frac{\text{Gegenkathete}}{\text{Ankathete}} = \frac{a}{b}$$

Für den Winkel β gilt entsprechend:

Sinus, Kosinus und Tangens für den Winkel β:

Sinusfunktion: $$\sin\beta = \frac{\text{Gegenkathete}}{\text{Hypotenuse}} = \frac{b}{c}$$

Kosinusfunktion: $\cos\beta = \dfrac{\text{Ankathete}}{\text{Hypotenuse}} = \dfrac{a}{c}$

Tangensfunktion: $\tan\beta = \dfrac{\text{Gegenkathete}}{\text{Ankathete}} = \dfrac{b}{a}$

Dabei wird für die beiden Grenzfälle von α bzw. $\beta = 0°$ oder $90°$ Folgendes festgelegt:

- $\sin 0° = 0$ und $\sin 90° = 1$
- $\cos 0° = 1$ und $\cos 90° = 0$

Bei Anwendung der Winkelfunktionen auf das gleichschenklig-rechtwinklige Dreieck bzw. auf die Hälfte des gleichseitigen Dreiecks ergeben sich folgende besondere Funktionswerte:

Gradmaß α	0	30	45	60	90
Bogenmaß b	0	$\frac{\pi}{6}$	$\frac{\pi}{4}$	$\frac{\pi}{3}$	$\frac{\pi}{2}$
sin	0	$\frac{1}{2}$	$\frac{\sqrt{2}}{2}$	$\frac{\sqrt{2}}{2}$	1
cos	1	$\frac{\sqrt{3}}{2}$	$\frac{\sqrt{3}}{2}$	$\frac{1}{2}$	0
tan	0	$\frac{\sqrt{3}}{3}$	1	$\sqrt{3}$	–

5.2 Wechselbeziehungen von Sinus, Kosinus und Tangens

Die beiden spitzen Winkel im rechtwinkligen Dreieck sind Komplementwinkel. Daher gilt: $\beta = 90° - \alpha$. Aus der Definition der trigonometrischen Funktionen folgt dann:

$$\sin\alpha = \frac{a}{c} \qquad \cos\beta = \frac{a}{c} \qquad \Rightarrow \sin\alpha = \cos\beta$$

$$\cos\alpha = \frac{b}{c} \qquad \sin\beta = \frac{b}{c} \qquad \Rightarrow \cos\alpha = \sin\beta$$

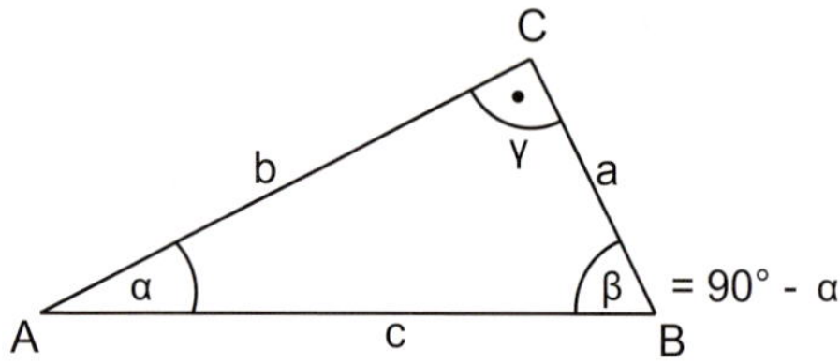

Komplementwinkel: $\sin\alpha = \cos(90° - \alpha)$
$\cos\alpha = \sin(90° - \alpha)$

Aus $\sin\alpha = \frac{a}{c}$ folgt $a = c \cdot \sin\alpha$

Aus $\cos\alpha = \frac{b}{c}$ folgt $b = c \cdot \cos\alpha$

Aus $\tan\alpha = \frac{a}{b}$ folgt:

Grundregel: $\tan\alpha = \frac{\sin\alpha}{\cos\alpha}$

5.3 Trigonometrische Funktionen für beliebige Winkel

Die trigonometrischen Funktionen eines Winkels können im rechtwinkligen Dreieck nur für spitze Winkel (also $0° < \alpha < 90°$) definiert werden. Über ein rechtwinkliges Dreieck im Einheitskreis gelingt jedoch die Ausweitung auf beliebige Winkel.

Der Einheitskreis ist ein Kreis mit dem Radius von einer Längeneinheit ($r = 1$). Das bedeutet nicht, dass der Kreis 1 cm oder 1 m misst, sondern heißt vorläufig nur, dass die Länge der Komponenten im Einheitskreis in der Einheit »*Radius r*« gemessen wird. Der Kreismittelpunkt befindet sich im Ursprung O eines rechtwinkligen Koordinatensystems. In jedem Quadranten befindet sich ein Viertel des Einheitskreises. Ein beliebiger Punkt $P = P(x \mid y)$ auf dem Einheitskreis legt einen Winkel zwischen der x-Achse und der Geraden durch O und P fest, den Winkel α. Der Winkel

α wird dabei in mathematisch positiver Richtung, also gegen den Uhrzeigersinn gemessen.

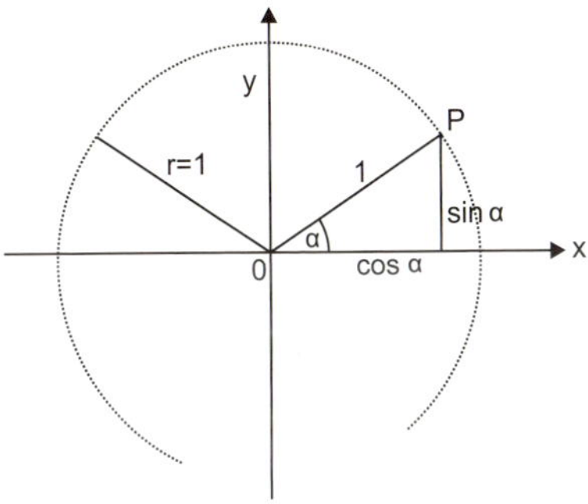

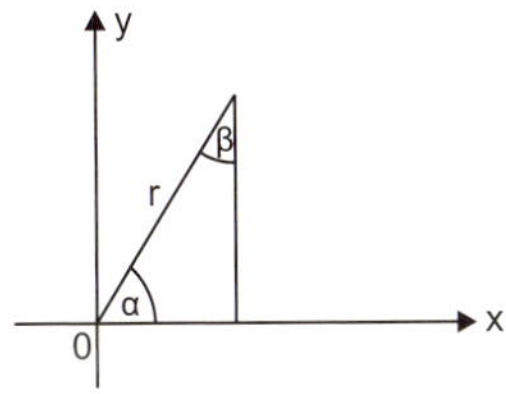

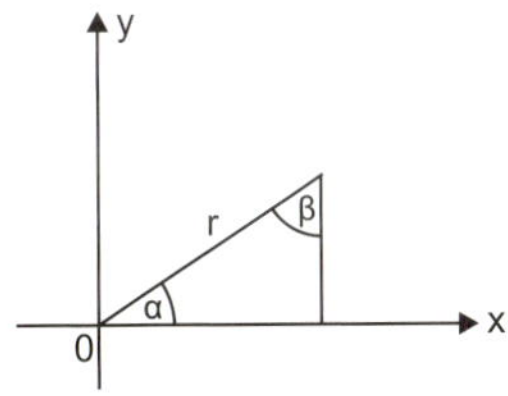

Wandert der Punkt *P* auf der Kreislinie, so erhält man rechtwinklige Dreiecke, denen Winkel zwischen 0° und 360° zugeordnet werden können. Im ersten Quadranten nimmt α Werte von 0° bis 90° an, im zweiten Werte von 90° bis 180°, im dritten von 180° bis 270° und im vierten von 270° bis 360°. Die Hypotenuse entspricht dabei jeweils dem Radius und ist demnach immer 1. Die Katheten entsprechen einer *x*- und einer *y*-Komponente. Ihre Länge hängt von der Größe des Winkels α ab.

Entsprechend der Sinusdefinition gilt: $\sin\alpha = \frac{y}{r} = \frac{y}{1} = y$

Entsprechend der Kosinusdefinition gilt: $\cos\alpha = \frac{x}{r} = \frac{x}{1} = x$

Der Tangens hat seinen Namen aus dem Erscheinungsbild im Einheitskreis erhalten. Er ergibt sich aus einer Tangente an den Einheitskreis, die durch den Punkt $x = 1$ geht und parallel zur *y*-Achse verläuft. Der Tangens ist die Strecke, die sich zwischen dem Schnittpunkt mit der *x*-Achse und dem Schnittpunkt mit der Verlängerung des Radius *r* ergibt. Man erhält zwei ähnliche Dreiecke.

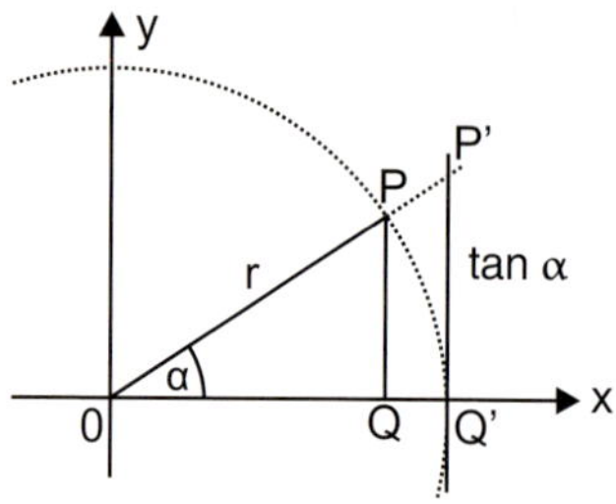

Die trigonometrischen Funktionen können demnach im Einheitskreis definiert werden durch:

Sinusfunktion:	$\sin\alpha = y$
Kosinusfunktion:	$\cos\alpha = x$
Tangensfunktion:	$\tan\alpha = \frac{y}{x} = \frac{\sin\alpha}{\cos\alpha}$
Kotangensfunktion:	$\cot\alpha = \frac{x}{y} = \frac{\cos\alpha}{\sin\alpha}$

Die Winkelfunktionen wurden für rechtwinklige Dreiecke hergeleitet, für die der Satz des Pythagoras $c^2 = a^2 + b^2$ gilt. Aus Hypotenuse $r = 1$ und den Katheten $x = \cos\alpha$ und $y = \sin\alpha$ ergibt sich dann:

$$r^2 = \sin^2(\alpha) + \cos^2(\alpha)$$
$$1^2 = \sin^2(\alpha) + \cos^2(\alpha)$$
$$1 = \sin^2(\alpha) + \cos^2(\alpha)$$

Für alle Winkelmaße α gilt: $\sin^2(\alpha) + \cos^2(\alpha) = 1$

Bogenmaß des Winkels:

Oft ist es üblich, den Winkel nicht in Grad anzugeben, sondern durch den entsprechenden Bogen im Einheitskreis. Da dieser Bogen eine Länge ist, also z. B. die Längeneinheit cm besitzt, hat dies den Vorteil einer dezimalen Unterteilung. Außerdem sind die Zahlenbeträge kleiner als beim Gradmaß.

Definition: Das Bogenmaß ist der Quotient $\frac{b}{r} = \frac{2\pi}{360°} \cdot \alpha = x$.

Im Einheitskreis entspricht:

360°	dem Bogen	2π	45°	dem Bogen	$\frac{\pi}{4}$
180°	dem Bogen	π	30°	dem Bogen	$\frac{\pi}{6}$
90°	dem Bogen	$\frac{\pi}{2}$	1°	dem Bogen	$\frac{\pi}{180}$
60°	dem Bogen	$\frac{\pi}{3}$			

Der Abschnitt des Einheitskreises zwischen x-Achse und Punkt P ist das Bogenmaß x des Winkels α. Durchläuft P den Einheitskreis im mathematisch positiven Drehsinn, sind der Winkel α und das Bogenmaß x ebenfalls positiv. Durchläuft P den Einheitskreis jedoch im mathematisch negativen Drehsinn, dann sind auch α und x negativ.

Allerdings kann man einen Winkel im Einheitskreis statt beispielsweise um *– 45°* zu drehen, auch um *+ 315°* drehen, um das gleiche Dreieck zu erhalten. Deshalb gilt:

> Der Sinus (Kosinus) eines negativen Winkels $-\alpha$ ist gleich dem Sinus (Kosinus) des Winkels $360° - \alpha$.

Damit sind im Einheitskreis die trigonometrischen Funktionen für beliebige Winkel α im Gradmaß oder für beliebige reelle Zahlen x (Bogenmaß von α), für die die entsprechenden Nenner nicht verschwinden, definiert.

Durch die Aufteilung in Quadranten ergeben sich sowohl für die x- als auch für die y-Achse positive und negative Koordinaten:

- Im ersten Quadranten sind x und y positiv.
- Im zweiten Quadranten ist x negativ und y positiv.
- Im dritten Quadranten sind x und y negativ.
- Im vierten Quadranten ist x positiv und y negativ.

Für die trigonometrischen Funktionen ergeben sich daraus in den einzelnen Quadranten folgende Vorzeichen:

Quadrant	sin	cos	tan	cot
I	+	+	+	+
II	+	–	–	–
III	–	–	+	+
IV	–	+	–	–

Fragestellung: Jedem Winkel α kann eindeutig ein Wert $\sin\alpha$ zugeordnet werden. Gilt diese Definition auch umgekehrt, d.h., kann jedem Wert von $\sin\alpha$ auch eindeutig ein Wert α zugeordnet werden?

Antwort: Ein positiver Sinuswert kann dem Quadranten I und dem Quadranten II zugeordnet werden, d.h., ein positiver Sinuswert tritt im Einheitskreis bei zwei Winkeln auf.

Beispiel: Dem Sinus 0,5 kann der Winkel α_1 von 30° im ersten und der Winkel α_2 von 150° im zweiten Quadranten zugeordnet werden.

5.4 Die Graphen der trigonometrischen Funktionen

Ein anschauliches Bild der trigonometrischen Funktionen erhält man, wenn man neben dem Einheitskreis ein rechtwinkliges Koordinatensystem abbildet, auf der Abszisse (x-Werte) die Gradzahlen einträgt und auf den Ordinaten (y-Werte; Werte von – 1 bis + 1) die Werte der betreffenden trigonometrischen Funktionen.

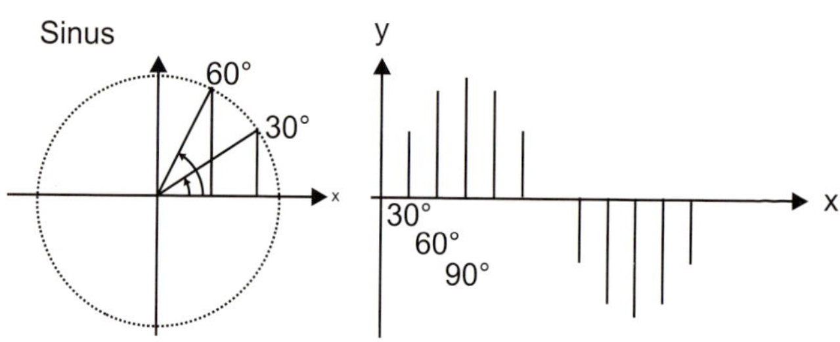

Wandert nun der Punkt P auf der Kreislinie von $\alpha = 30°$, über $\alpha = 60°$ usw. bis $\alpha = 360°$, so kann ich jedem Sinus (im Einheitskreis) einen Punkt im Koordinatensystem zuordnen. Die dadurch entstehende Kurve wird als Graph der Sinusfunktion bezeichnet oder auch als Sinuskurve.

Da die Funktion nicht nur für diese einzelnen Winkel definiert ist, sondern für jeden beliebigen Winkel α einen zugehörigen Sinus ergibt, kann die Darstellung als eine durchgehende Kurve mit folgenden Eigenschaften erweitert werden:

Eigenschaften der Sinusfunktion:

- Die Sinusfunktion hat eine Periode von 360°.
  Das heißt, dass sich die Sinusfunktion ab 360° wiederholt. Es gilt also für alle Winkel über 360°:

  > Der Sinus eines Winkels von $n \cdot 360° + \alpha$ ist gleich dem Sinus des Winkels α.

- Die Sinusfunktion ist eine ungerade Funktion.
  Das bedeutet, ihr Graph liegt punktsymmetrisch zum Ursprung des Koordinatensystems. Man erhält beispielsweise den Punkt P_2, indem man einen Punkt P_1 am Ursprung (0/0) spiegelt.
- Werden die Winkel der Sinuskurve im Bogenmaß x angegeben, so hat die Sinusfunktion die Periode 2π.

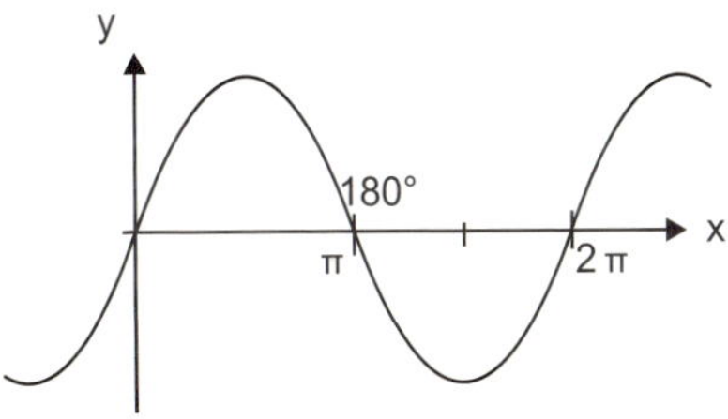

Die Sinuskurve hat die Form einer Welle. Sinuswellen spielen in verschiedenen Bereichen eine Rolle und in ihrem Zusammenhang werden verschiedene Begriffe gebraucht.

Phase: Dieser Begriff wird vor allem in Zusammenhang mit einer Phasenverschiebung verwendet, d.h. statt mit dem Funktionswert 0 zu beginnen, wird mit einem anderen Winkel/Funktionswert begonnen und die Kurve bildlich gesprochen nach links oder rechts verschoben.

Frequenz: Dieser Begriff ist in Bezug auf die Zeit definiert. Er gibt die Anzahl der vollständigen Phasendurchläufe einer Kurve innerhalb einer bestimmten Zeitspanne an. Eine hohe Frequenz bedeutet demnach viele Phasendurchläufe innerhalb einer Zeiteinheit. Bildlich gesprochen heißt das, die Wellen sind eng zusammengedrängt.

Wellenlänge: Dieser Begriff findet sich beispielsweise bei Rundfunkwellen, als Langwellen, Mittelwellen, Kurzwellen und Ultrakurzwellen (UKW) mit entsprechend unterschiedlicher Frequenz.

Der Graph der Kosinusfunktion hat die gleiche Form wie eine nach links verschobene Sinusfunktion.

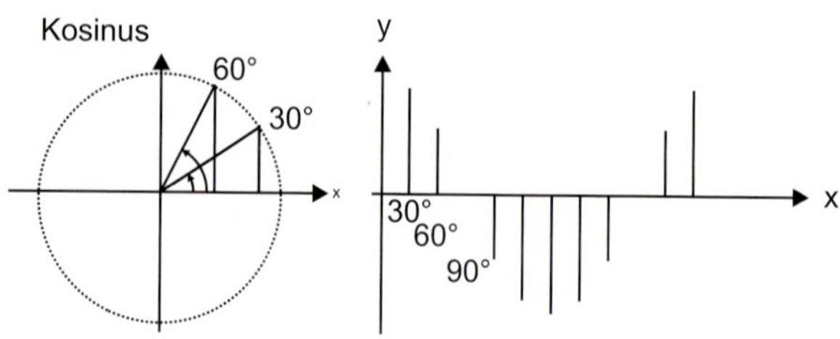

Eigenschaften der Kosinusfunktion:

- Die Kosinusfunktion hat eine Periodizität von 360°.
- Die Kosinusfunktion ist eine gerade Funktion, das heißt, der Graph der Kosinusfunktion liegt symmetrisch zur *y*-Achse.
- Im Bogenmaß dargestellt hat die Kosinusfunktion eine Periodizität von 2π.

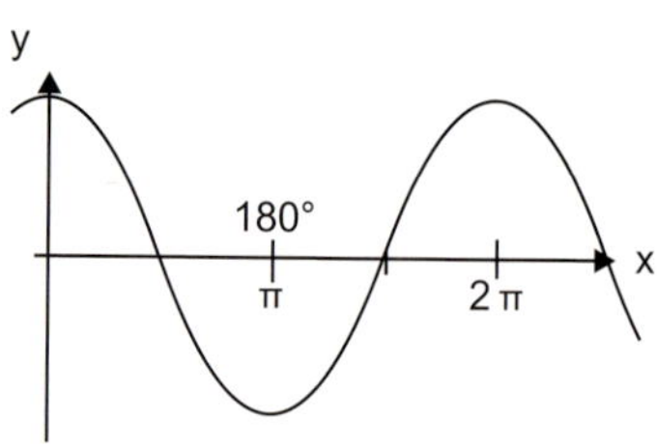

Eigenschaften der Tangensfunktion:

- Die Tangensfunktion hat eine Periodizität von 180° oder π.
- Die Tangensfunktion ist eine ungerade Funktion. Sie ist also symmetrisch zum Koordinatenursprung.

- Mit wachsenden x-Werten strebt der Tangens gegen ∞ (unendlich).
- Der Graph der Tangensfunktion verläuft durch den Koordinatenursprung 0/0 »asymptotisch« nach oben.

Eigenschaften der Kotangensfunktion:

- Die Kotangensfunktion hat eine Periodizität von 180° oder π.
- Die Kotangensfunktion ist eine ungerade Funktion. Sie ist also symmetrisch zum Koordinatenursprung.
- Mit wachsenden x-Werten strebt der Kotangens gegen ∞.
- Der Graph der Kotangensfunktion verläuft »asymptotisch« nach unten, ohne den Koordinatenursprung zu durchlaufen.

5.5 Winkelfunktionen im allgemeinen Dreieck

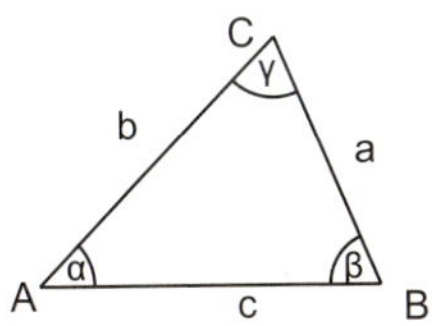

Zusammenhänge zwischen Seitenlängen und Winkelweiten lassen sich bei schiefwinkligen Dreiecken auch ohne die Zerlegung in rechtwinklige Dreiecke berechnen. Dazu werden folgende Sätze benötigt:

Der Sinussatz

In einem beliebigen Dreieck verhalten sich die Längen der Seiten wie die Sinuswerte der gegenüberliegenden Winkel.

Sinussatz: $$\frac{\sin\alpha}{a} = \frac{\sin\beta}{b} = \frac{\sin\gamma}{c}$$

$$\sin\alpha : \sin\beta : \sin\gamma = a : b : c$$

Der Sinussatz wird benötigt, wenn zwei Winkel und eine Seite gegeben sind (z.B. Winkel α und β und Seite b) und das fehlende Objekt (bei diesem Beispiel Seite a) berechnet werden soll.

Der Kosinussatz

Der Kosinussatz wird auch der auf allgemeine Dreiecke erweiterte Satz des Pythagoras genannt: In einem beliebigen Dreieck ist das Quadrat einer Seitenlänge gleich der Summe der Quadrate der beiden anderen Seitenlängen vermindert um das doppelte Produkt aus den Längen dieser beiden anderen Seiten und dem Kosinus des von ihnen eingeschlossenen Winkels.

Kosinussatz: $a^2 = b^2 + c^2 - 2bc \cdot \cos\alpha$
$b^2 = a^2 + c^2 - 2ac \cdot \cos\beta$
$c^2 = a^2 + b^2 - 2ab \cdot \cos\gamma$

Den Kosinussatz kann man einsetzen, wenn die zwei Seiten und der von ihnen eingeschlossene Winkel bekannt sind (z.B. Seiten b und c und Winkel α).

Weitere Berechnungen können mithilfe des Flächensatzes und des Projektionssatzes durchgeführt werden:

Flächensatz: Die Fläche eines Dreiecks ist das halbe Produkt aus zwei Seiten und dem Sinus des von ihnen eingeschlossenen Winkels.

$$F = \frac{1}{2} ab \sin\gamma = \frac{1}{2} ac \sin\beta = \frac{1}{2} bc \sin\alpha$$

Projektionssatz: Eine Seite eines Dreiecks besteht aus zwei Abschnitten, und zwar den senkrechten Projektionen der anderen Seiten auf diese Seite:

$$a = b \cdot \cos\gamma + c \cdot \cos\beta$$
$$b = c \cdot \cos\alpha + a \cdot \cos\gamma$$
$$c = a \cdot \cos\beta + b \cdot \cos\alpha$$

5.6 Additionstheoreme

Additionstheoreme sind Formeln für die trigonometrischen Funktionen von Winkelsummen und Winkeldifferenzen. Sie geben an, wie sich der Funktionswert bei einer Summe oder Differenz von zwei Winkeln aus den Einzelfunktionswerten zusammensetzt. Mit ihrer Hilfe können die

Winkelfunktionen von Summen und Differenzen in Funktionen einfacher Winkel umgeformt werden. Sie werden beim Auflösen trigonometrischer Gleichungen gebraucht.

Additionstheoreme erster Art:
(trigonometrische Funktionen der Summe und der Differenz zweier Winkel)

Summe:

$$\sin(\alpha + \beta) = \sin\alpha\cos\beta + \cos\alpha\sin\beta$$

$$\cos(\alpha + \beta) = \cos\alpha\cos\beta - \sin\alpha\sin\beta$$

$$\tan(\alpha + \beta) = \frac{\tan\alpha + \tan\beta}{1 - \tan\alpha\tan\beta}$$

Differenz:

$$\sin(\alpha - \beta) = \sin\alpha\cos\beta - \cos\alpha\sin\beta$$

$$\cos(\alpha - \beta) = \cos\alpha\cos\beta + \sin\alpha\sin\beta$$

$$\tan(\alpha - \beta) = \frac{\tan\alpha - \tan\beta}{1 + \tan\alpha\tan\beta}$$

Die Additionstheoreme eignen sich auch dazu, so genannte Doppelwinkelformen herzuleiten:

Additionstheoreme zweiter Art:
(Summen und Differenzen zweier trigonometrischer Funktionen)

Summe:

$$\sin\alpha + \sin\beta = 2 \cdot \sin\left(\frac{1}{2}(\alpha + \beta)\right) \cdot \cos\left(\frac{1}{2}(\alpha - \beta)\right)$$

$$\cos\alpha + \cos\beta = 2\cos\left(\frac{1}{2}(\alpha + \beta)\right) \cdot \cos\left(\frac{1}{2}(\alpha - \beta)\right)$$

$$\tan\alpha + \tan\beta = \frac{\sin(\alpha + \beta)}{\cos\alpha\cos\beta}$$

Differenz:

$$\sin\alpha - \sin\beta = 2\cos\left(\frac{1}{2}(\alpha + \beta)\right) \cdot \sin\frac{1}{2}(\alpha - \beta)$$

$$\cos\alpha - \cos\beta = -2\sin\left(\frac{1}{2}(\alpha + \beta)\right) \cdot \sin\frac{1}{2}(\alpha - \beta)$$

$$\tan\alpha - \tan\beta = \frac{\sin(\alpha - \beta)}{\cos\alpha\cos\beta}$$

5.7 Zusammengesetzte und modifizierte trigonometrische Funktionen

Leider reichen die trigonometrischen Funktionen häufig nicht aus, um reale periodische Vorgänge zu beschreiben. Das liegt erstens daran, dass Sinus und Kosinus nur Werte von – 1 bis + 1 liefern und zweitens auch daran, dass die in der Realität betrachteten Vorgänge normalerweise nicht winkel-, sondern zeitabhängig sind mit einer Periode, die nicht ein Vielfaches von 2π ist. Aus diesem Grunde ist es notwendig, entweder das Argument der trigonometrischen Funktion (α oder x) zu ändern, oder die gesamte Winkelfunktion mit anderen Funktionen zu kombinieren oder sogar beides.

Eine »gedämpfte Schwingung« wird durch die Gleichung der Form $y(t) = y(0) \cdot e^{-k \cdot t} \cos(\omega\, t)$ beschrieben, wobei mit »t« die bereits verstrichene Zeit angegeben wird und mit »$\omega = \frac{2\pi}{T}$« die so genannte Winkelgeschwindigkeit zur Schwingungsdauer »T«, und »k« die Dämpfung der Schwingung beschreibt, wie sie z. B. durch Reibung entsteht.

Von dieser Gleichung gibt es eine Reihe von Variationen:

- $y = \sin(x + c)$
  Beschreibung einer Phasenverschiebung (z. B. Strom- und Spannungsverläufe im Wechselstromkreis)
- $y = a \sin x$
  Multiplikation mit einer reellen Zahl, die eine Änderung der Amplitude bewirkt (z. B. bei Pendelschwingungen)
- $y = \sin(b \cdot x)$
  Eine Multiplikation im Argument, die die Periode – die Dauer der einzelnen Schwingung – verändert:
  $b > 1$ (die Periode wird kleiner)
  $0 > b > 1$ (die Periode wird größer)
- $y = a \sin(bx + c)$
  Ein komplexer periodischer Vorgang wird durch die Kombination dieser Veränderungen beschrieben.
- $y = \sin x + k$
  Verschiebung in y-Richtung durch die Addition einer Konstanten (z. B. Überlagerungen von Gleich- und Wechselspannungen).

6 Kreis- und Raummessung

6.1 Umfang und Flächeninhalt eines Kreises

Der Kreis ist eine ebene, geschlossene Linie. Alle Punkte eines Kreises sind von seinem Mittelpunkt gleich weit entfernt. Folgende Bezeichnungen sind geltende Vereinbarung:

AB = Sehne, die Strecke, die entsteht, wenn eine Gerade den Kreis an den Punkten *A* und *B* schneidet.
b = Kreisbogen *AB*.
d = Durchmesser, d. h. die Sehne durch den Mittelpunkt des Kreises.
M = Mittelpunkt des Kreises.
p = Passante, eine Gerade außerhalb des Kreises.
r = Radius, der Abstand der Kreislinie vom Mittelpunkt.
s = Sekante (*AB*), eine Gerade, die den Kreis in zwei Punkten schneidet.
t = Tangente, eine Gerade, die den Kreis in einem Punkt berührt.
π = Pi, die mathematische Konstante 3,141592653589793 … . π wurde im Jahr 1596 durch van Ceulen auf 32 Stellen, inzwischen mithilfe von Computern auf mehr als 51 Milliarden Stellen genau bestimmt. Mit der Zahl Pi werden der Umfang und der Flächeninhalt eines Kreises errechnet. Für Berechnungen genügt der Wert 3,14.

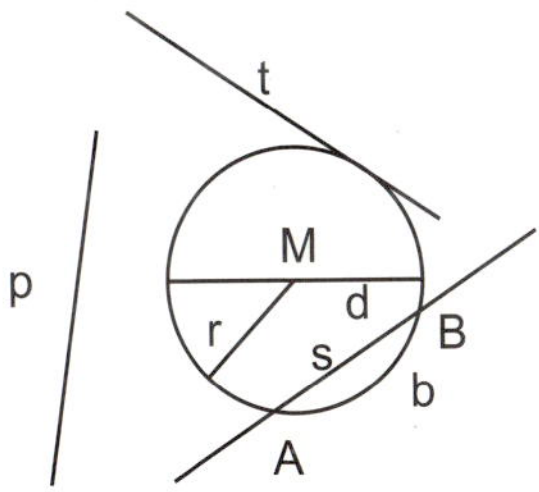

Die Fläche eines Kreises wird berechnet mit der Formel: $A = r^2\pi$.

Beispiel: Ein Radius von 3 cm ergibt die Kreisfläche von 28,26 cm^2.

Der Umfang eines Kreises wird berechnet mit der Formel: $U = d \cdot \pi$.

Beispiel: Ein Radius von 3 cm ergibt den Kreisumfang von 18,84 cm.

6.2 Länge eines Kreisbogens

Ein Kreisbogen ist ein durch zwei Punkte eines Kreises begrenztes Stück eines Kreises. Der Kreisbogen wird als *b* bezeichnet.
Einen Winkel, dessen Scheitel im Mittelpunkt des Kreises liegt, nennt man Zentriwinkel. Jedem Zentriwinkel ist ein Kreisbogen zugeordnet, der innerhalb des Winkels liegt. Daraus ergibt sich, dass der einem gestreckten Zentriwinkel zugeordnete Kreisbogen ein »Halbkreis« ist.

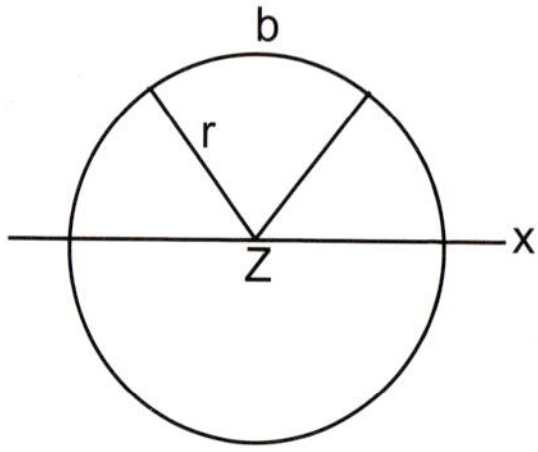

Berechnung eines Kreisbogens *b*, der zu einem Mittelpunktswinkel gehört:

$$b = d \cdot \pi \cdot \frac{\alpha}{360°}$$

6.3 Flächeninhalt eines Kreissektors

Dem Kreisflächeninhalt liegt ein Winkel von 360° zugrunde. Daraus folgt, dass der Flächeninhalt F_α eines Kreissektors in dem Verhältnis kleiner wird, wie der Winkel α kleiner wird.

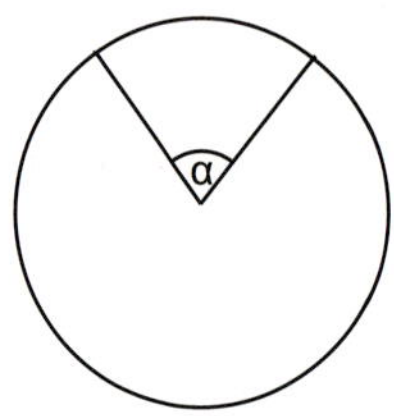

Formel zur Berechnung des Flächeninhalts eines Kreissektors F_α:

$$F_\alpha = \frac{\alpha}{360°} \cdot F = \frac{\pi r^2 \alpha}{360°}$$

6.4 Maßeinheiten für den Raum

Das Volumen (der Rauminhalt) eines Körpers wird mit V bezeichnet.
Ein Würfel mit einem Rauminhalt von 1 m^3,

$1\ m^3 = a\,(= 1\ m) \cdot b\,(= 1\ m) \cdot c\,(= 1\ m)$,

gilt als die Grundeinheit der Raummaße.

Nachfolgend eine Zusammenstellung der Maßeinheiten für den Raum:

mm^3 = Kubikmillimeter
cm^3 = Kubikzentimeter
dm^3 = Kubikdezimeter
km^3 = Kubikkilometer
hl = Hektoliter
l = Liter
dl = Deziliter
cl = Zentiliter

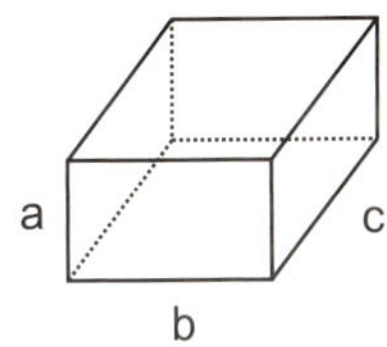

Gegenüberstellung der Raummaße:

$$
\begin{aligned}
1\ cm^3 &= 1000\ mm^3 \\
1\ dm^3 &= 1000\ cm^3 = 1\,000\,000\ mm^3 \\
&= 100\ cl \\
&= 10\ dl \\
&= 1\ l \\
1\ m^3 &= 1000\ dm^3 = 1\,000\,000\ cm^3 = 1\,000\,000\,000\ mm^3 \\
&= 1000\ l \\
&= 10\ hl \\
1\ km^3 &= 10^9\ m^3 = 10^{12}\ l
\end{aligned}
$$

6.5 Rauminhalt von Quadern und Würfeln

Für die Berechnung des Volumens gilt:

Alle Kantenlängen sind vor dem Einsetzen in die Formel auf die gleiche Maßeinheit umzurechnen.

Das Volumen V eines Quaders ergibt sich aus

$V(\text{Quader}) = a \cdot b \cdot c$

Für den Würfel gelten alle Aussagen für die Volumenberechnung des Quaders, da sich der Würfel vom Quader nur dadurch unterscheidet, dass seine Kantenlängen gleich sind.

Eine andere Schreibweise für die Volumenberechnung ist

$$V(\text{Quader}) = G \cdot h,$$

wobei hier *G* für die bereits berechnete Grundfläche steht, die mit der Höhe des Quaders multipliziert wird. Auch hier müssen die Maßeinheiten entsprechend sein.

6.6 Rauminhalt von Pyramiden

Als Pyramiden werden Körper bezeichnet, deren dreieckige Seitenflächen sich in einem Punkt *S* in der Höhe *h* über einer Grundfläche treffen.
In Gizeh/Ägypten wurden ca. 3000 v. Chr. riesige Pyramiden errichtet, die den Pharaonen als Grabmäler dienten. Die Cheops-Pyramide hat eine quadratische Grundfläche von 230 m Kantenlänge und eine Höhe von 147 m.

Beispiel einer Pyramide:
Vereinbarte Bezeichnungen sind:

V = Volumen
S = Pyramidenspitze
h = Höhe, d.h. Abstand der Pyramidenspitze von der Grundfläche
G = Grundfläche der Pyramide

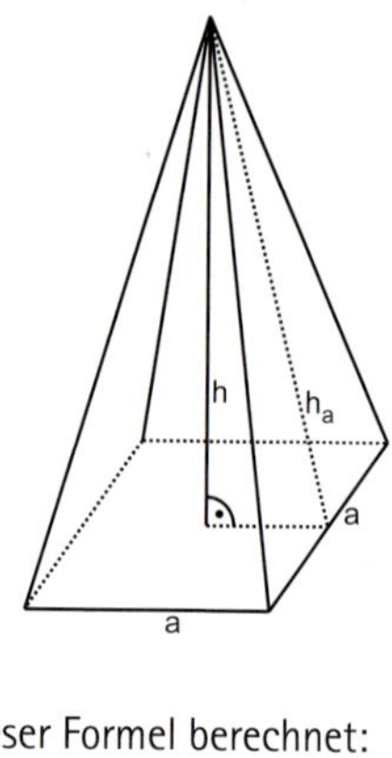

Das Volumen einer Pyramide wird mit dieser Formel berechnet:

$$V = \frac{1}{3} \cdot G \cdot h$$

Das Volumen der Pyramide entspricht also dem dritten Teil des Produkts von Grundfläche mal Höhe.
Berechnung des Volumens der oben abgebildeten Pyramide mit $a = 4$ cm, $h = 6$ cm:

$G = 4 \text{ cm} \cdot 4 \text{ cm} = 16 \text{ cm}^2$
$h = 6 \text{ cm}$
$V = 32 \text{ cm}^3$

Vom italienischen Mathematiker Cavalieri (1591–1647) stammt folgender Lehrsatz für die Volumenberechnung:

> Haben zwei Körper den gleichen Grundflächeninhalt, gleiche Höhe und in gleicher Höhe flächeninhaltsgleiche Parallelquerschnitte zur Grundfläche, so sind ihre Rauminhalte gleich.

6.7 Oberfläche von Zylinder und Kegel

Die Oberfläche eines Zylinders setzt sich zusammen aus
a) der Mantelfläche, das ist die Seitenfläche, und
b) zweimal der Grundfläche (Boden und Decke).

Stellt man sich die Mantelfläche senkrecht zur Grundlinie aufgeschnitten und aufgeklappt vor, so erkennt man ein Rechteck mit der Länge U = Umfang des Zylinders und der Breite h = Höhe des Zylinders.
Daraus leitet sich die Formel für die Oberfläche des Zylinders ab:

$$O = 2 \cdot \pi \cdot r^2 + 2 \cdot \pi \cdot r \cdot h$$
$$= 2\pi r \cdot (r + h)$$

Wird bei einem geraden Kegel der Mantel entlang der Mantellinie s aufgeschnitten, so ergibt sich eine Fläche, die dem Sektor eines Kreises mit dem Radius s entspricht. Hinzugerechnet wird die Grundfläche des Kegels, also eine Kreisfläche.

Die Oberflächenberechnung für einen Kegel $F(K)$ ergibt sich analog zu der des Zylinders. Sie wird mit folgender Formel berechnet:

$$F(K) = \pi \cdot r^2 + \pi \cdot r \cdot s$$
$$= \pi r(r + s)$$

6.8 Rauminhalt von Zylinder und Kegel

Der Rauminhalt V (das Volumen) eines geraden Kreiszylinders mit dem Grundflächenradius r und der Höhe h berechnet sich mit folgender Formel:

$$V = \pi \cdot r^2 \cdot h$$

Der Rauminhalt V eines geraden Kreiskegels mit dem Grundflächenradius r und der Kegelhöhe h berechnet sich mit folgender Formel:

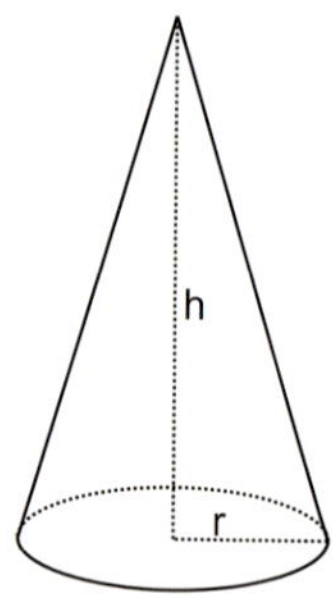

$$V = \frac{1}{3} \cdot \pi \cdot r^2 \cdot h$$

6.9 Rauminhalt und Oberfläche der Kugel

Die Definition der Kugel ist ähnlich der des Kreises:
Die Kugel ist die Menge aller Punkte, deren Abstand zu einem gegebenen Mittelpunkt M gleich dem Radius ist, oder anders ausgedrückt:
Eine Kugel entsteht durch Drehung eines Kreises um seinen Durchmesser. Sie ist eine geschlossene Fläche mit konstanter Krümmung.
Beachte: Der Schatten einer Kugel (auf eine senkrecht zum Strahleneinfall liegende Ebene) ist ein Kreis.

Die Oberfläche F einer Kugel mit einem Radius r wird mit folgender Formel berechnet:

$$F = 4\pi \cdot r^2$$

Die Oberfläche der Erdkugel hat man durch Längenkreise (Meridiane) unterteilt, damit man Orte besser lokalisieren kann.
Der mittlere Erdradius beträgt ca. 6367 km.
Das Volumen V einer Kugel wird mit folgender Formel berechnet:

$$V = \frac{4\pi}{3} \cdot r^3$$

Die Rauminhalte von Zylinder, Kugel und Kegel mit jeweils gleichem Durchmesser und gleicher Höhe verhalten sich wie 3 : 2 : 1.

6.10 Einfache Rotationskörper

Ein Rotationskörper entsteht bei der Drehung einer ebenen Fläche um eine Achse, welche Rotationsachse genannt wird.

Ein einfacher Rotationskörper ist beispielsweise der Kreiszylinder. Man kann sich den Kreiszylinder vorstellen als Rotation (= Drehung) eines Rechtecks um eine seiner Seiten.

Ein weiterer einfacher Rotationskörper ist ein gerader Kreiskegel. Er entsteht bei Drehung eines rechtwinkligen Dreiecks um eine Kathete. Die andere Kathete wird zum Radius der Grundfläche.

Auch eine Kugelfläche ist eine Rotationsfläche. Sie entsteht bei der Drehung einer Kreislinie um einen Kreisdurchmesser.

Auf einen Blick: Geometrische Regeln und Sätze

Winkel

Ein Winkel α besteht aus zwei Strahlen a und b, die einen gemeinsamen Scheitelpunkt S haben. Die Strahlen heißen Schenkel.

Winkelmaß

1 Grad (°) = 60 Minuten (')
1' = 60 Sekunden (")

Winkelbezeichnungen

Nullwinkel: $\alpha = 0°$
spitzer Winkel: $0° < \alpha < 90°$
rechter Winkel: $\alpha = 90°$
stumpfer Winkel: $90° < \alpha < 180°$
gestreckter Winkel: $\alpha = 180°$
überstumpfer Winkel: $180° < \alpha < 360°$
Vollwinkel: $\alpha = 360°$

Ähnlichkeitssätze für Dreiecke

Zwei Dreiecke sind ähnlich, wenn sie übereinstimmen
... im Verhältnis ihrer drei Seiten a_1, a_2, b_1, b_2, c_1, c_2.
$a_1 : b_1 = a_2 : b_2;\ \ b_1 : c_1 = b_2 : c_2;\ \ c_1 : a_1 = c_2 : a_2$
... im Verhältnis von zwei Seiten sowie der Größe des eingeschlossenen Winkels.
Beispiel:
$a_1 : b_1 = a_2 : b_2;\ \gamma_1 = \gamma_2$
... in der Größe zweier Winkel.

Strahlensätze

Werden zwei Strahlen s_1 und s_2 mit einem gemeinsamen Scheitelpunkt S von zwei zueinander parallelen Geraden geschnitten, so verhalten sich die Längen der Abschnitte auf dem einen Strahl wie die entsprechenden Längen der Abschnitte auf dem anderen Strahl.

Werden zwei Strahlen s_1 und s_2 mit einem gemeinsamen Scheitelpunkt S von zwei zueinander parallelen Geraden geschnitten, so verhalten sich die Längen der Abschnitte auf einem Strahl wie die entsprechenden Längen der Abschnitte auf den Parallelen.

Zentrische Streckung

Eine zentrische Streckung von einem Scheitelpunkt S aus ist die ähnliche Abbildung einer Figur F auf F'. Jeder Punkt P der Figur F wird in einem Punkt P' der Figur F' abgebildet. Dabei muss Punkt P' auf derselben Geraden g liegen, die durch S und P verläuft. Allen Punkten auf den Längen der Strecken $\overline{SP}$ und $\overline{SP'}$ ist dasselbe Verhältnis k gemeinsam: $|SP'| = k \cdot |SP|$. k ist der Streckfaktor der Abbildung. Für ihn gilt $k \neq 0$.

Achsensymmetrie

Durch eine Achsenspiegelung wird jede Strecke auf eine Strecke der gleichen Länge abgebildet.

Drehsymmetrie

Wird eine Figur durch eine Drehung um einen Winkel an einem Punkt auf sich selbst abgebildet, so nennt man die Figur drehsymmetrisch.

Punktsymmetrie

Figuren, die man durch Drehung um einen Punkt S um 180° zur Deckung bringen kann, nennt man punktsymmetrisch.

Verschiebungen

Bei einer Verschiebung ist jede Gerade zu ihrer Bildgeraden parallel und durch einen Vektor beschrieben.

Kongruenz

Lässt sich eine Figur durch eine oder mehrere hintereinander ausgeführte Achsenspiegelungen auf eine andere Figur abbilden, so ist sie zu dieser kongruent.

Thales-Satz

Der geometrische Ort aller Punkte, aus denen man eine gegebene Strecke unter einem rechten Winkel sieht, ist ein Kreis (der Thales-Kreis), dessen Durchmesser die Strecke ist.

Satz des Pythagoras

Höhensatz: Im rechtwinkligen Dreieck ist das Quadrat der Höhe auf die Hypotenuse gleich mit dem Produkt der beiden durch den Fußpunkt der Höhe auf der Hypotenuse bestimmten Abschnitte.

Kathetensatz (auf beide Katheten angewendet): Im rechtwinkligen Dreieck ist das Quadrat jeder Kathete gleich mit dem Produkt aus der Hypotenuse und der Strecke, die von der betreffenden Kathete auf der Hypotenuse bestimmt wird.

Die Addition der beiden Anwendungen des Kathetensatzes ergibt den vielleicht »berühmtesten« Lehrsatz der Mathematik, den Pythagoras-Satz:

$$AC^2 + BC^2 = AB \cdot (AD + DB) = AB^2$$

Goldener Schnitt

Die Teilung in zwei Teile soll so geschehen, dass das Verhältnis der ganzen Länge zum größeren Teil gleich sein soll mit dem Verhältnis des längeren Teils zu dem kürzeren.

Trigonometrie

Die trigonometrischen Funktionen sind definiert als das Verhältnis zweier Seiten im rechtwinkligen Dreieck:

Gegenkathete zu Hypotenuse = Sinus des Winkels $\alpha = \sin\alpha = \frac{a}{c}$

Ankathete zu Hypotenuse = Kosinus des Winkels $\alpha = \cos\alpha = \frac{b}{c}$

Gegenkathete zu Ankathete = Tangens des Winkels $\alpha = \tan\alpha = \frac{a}{b}$

Aus dieser Definition folgt: $\sin\alpha = \cos\beta$

$$\cos\alpha = \sin\beta$$

$$\tan\alpha = \frac{\sin\alpha}{\cos\alpha}$$

Im Einheitskreis gilt: $\sin\alpha = y$

$\cos\alpha = x$

$\tan\alpha = \frac{y}{x} = \frac{\sin\alpha}{\cos\alpha}$

$\sin^2(\alpha) + \cos^2(\alpha) = 1$

Sinussatz

In einem beliebigen Dreieck verhalten sich die Längen der Seiten wie die Sinuswerte der gegenüberliegenden Winkel:

$$\frac{\sin\alpha}{a} = \frac{\sin\beta}{b} = \frac{\sin\gamma}{c}$$

Kosinussatz = erweiterter Satz des Pythagoras:

$a^2 = b^2 + c^2 - 2bc \cdot \cos\alpha$

$b^2 = a^2 + c^2 - 2ac \cdot \cos\beta$

$c^2 = a^2 + b^2 - 2ab \cdot \cos\gamma$

Kreis- und Raummessung

Fläche Kreissektor:	$F_\alpha = \frac{\alpha}{360°} \cdot F = \frac{\pi r^2 \alpha}{360°}$
Kreisbogen:	$b = \frac{d \cdot \pi \cdot \alpha}{360°}$
Kreisfläche:	$A = r^2\pi$
Kreisumfang:	$U = d \cdot \pi$
Oberfläche Kegel:	$F = \pi \cdot r^2 + \pi \cdot r \cdot s = \pi r(r + s)$
Oberfläche Kugel:	$F = 4\pi \cdot r^2$
Oberfläche Zylinder:	$F = 2 \cdot \pi \cdot r^2 + 2 \cdot \pi \cdot r \cdot h = 2\pi r \cdot (r + h)$
Volumen Kreiskegel:	$V = \frac{1}{3} \pi \cdot r^2 \cdot h$
Volumen Kreiszylinder:	$V = \pi \cdot r^2 \cdot h$
Volumen Kugel:	$V = \frac{4\pi}{3} \cdot r^3$
Volumen Pyramide:	$V = \frac{1}{3} \cdot G \cdot h$
Volumen Quader:	$V = a \cdot b \cdot c$

Register

H

I

K

L

M

N

O

P

Q

R